Factories of Death

In Manchuria, before and during World War II, the Japanese army conducted numerous, and quite horrific, biological warfare experiments upon live human beings. After the war, the Japanese scientists who had been engaged in these activities were granted immunity, by the US army, from investigation for war crimes, in return for the results of their experiments.

Sheldon Harris's book is a controversial investigation of the activities of the Japanese scientists involved in these experiments and the subsequent US cover-up. The author covers the sensitive areas concerning which scientists were involved and who in the upper echelons of the army and the political establishment knew of the activities going on inside Manchuria. Harris also investigates the claims that allied POWs were subject to experimentation. In the second part of the book the questions concerning why the scientists were not prosecuted as war criminals and the nature of the deal that was struck with the US occupation authorities are examined.

Sheldon Harris has produced a work that is backed up by rigorous fieldwork and research in China. He has also obtained access to US and KGB archives containing material previously unavailable to other academics. This book should appeal to those interested in Japanese history, the ethics of scientists and the conduct of armies in war.

Sheldon H. Harris is Emeritus Professor of History, California State University, Northridge. In 1984 he became involved in research on Japanese biological warfare experimentation in Manchuria. His research led him to deliver several papers to international conferences on science and ethics and to the publication of a number of scholarly articles that have aroused considerable interest in the United States, Europe, Japan and China.

Factories of Death

Japanese biological warfare 1932–45
and the American cover-up

Sheldon H. Harris

London and New York

First published 1994
by Routledge
11 New Fetter Lane, London EC4P 4EE

Simultaneously published in the USA and Canada
by Routledge
29 West 35th Street, New York, NY 10001

First published in paperback 1995
Reprinted 1997, 1999

Routledge is an imprint of the Taylor & Francis Group

© 1994 Sheldon H. Harris

Typeset in Times by Megaron, Cardiff, Wales

Printed and bound in Great Britain by
Clays Ltd, St Ives plc

British Library Cataloguing in Publication Data
A catalogue record for this book is available from the British Library

Library of Congress Cataloguing in Publication Data
A catalogue record for this book is available from the Library of Congress

ISBN 0–415–09105–5 (hbk)
ISBN 0–415–13206–1 (pbk)

To my wife Sheila
and
to the thousands of Chinese martyred in the struggle
for freedom, 18 September 1931 to 4 June 1989

Contents

Preface to the paperback edition

I

Japan's unconditional surrender to the United Nations in mid-August 1945 marked the end of active fighting in World War II. One half-century later reverberations from the most horrific war of the twentieth century still shock generations born in the post-war era. Former war criminals, now elderly men living in the United States, Canada, Great Britain and elsewhere are still being discovered and charged with executing heinous crimes against humanity. In Germany, the nation is constantly reminded of the unspeakable horrors committed by the Nazis during their twelve-year reign over a nation that once produced a Beethoven, a Schiller and a Goethe.

Curiously, the Japanese, unlike the Germans, do not confront the reality of the actions perpetrated by their militaristic leaders before and during World War II. The horrors of the 1937 rape of Nanking, the exploitation of hundreds of thousands of Korean and Filipino young women as "comfort women" (sex slaves) for Japanese troops, and the use of humans by scientists in experiments designed to develop viable chemical and biological warfare weapons are not discussed in most Japanese circles.

Over the past half-century, Japan witnessed changes in government leadership many times. Not one of the various prime ministers or their spokesmen repudiated the actions of the past. Until recently, no one in power even apologized for their country's wartime misdeeds. The powerful and reactionary bureaucrats who run Japan's Ministry of Education turned these actions into non-events. This ministry's minions excise any mention of Nanking, comfort women or biological warfare from texts before they are approved for use in Japanese schools. Consequently, the average Japanese citizen today is ignorant of his country's past brutality.

Here and there an isolated voice attempts to rouse the nation. In the 1980s Sei-ichi Morimura shocked the nation with his novel, *The Devil's Gluttony*, which described in realistic detail Japan's biological warfare research on humans. Professor Kei-ichi Tsuneishi is devoting his professional career to outlining the history of Japanese biological warfare activities. In the early 1990s the Citizens' Committee for the Exhibit of Unit 731 Crimes mounted an exhibition detailing Japan's biological warfare research.

The exhibition toured many cities in Japan; more than 250,000 people viewed the exhibit. And, more recently, Dr Shingo Shibata, Professor Emeritus of Philosophy and Sociology at Hiroshima University, began to expose the questionable research activities on humans of Japan's National Institute of Health. Unfortunately, their activities thus far have made little permanent impact on the nation.[1]

II

Secret research conducted upon humans in Manchuria and China by Japanese scientists in their quest for viable biological warfare weapons is a major theme of this book. Of equal importance is the discussion of the United States' cover-up, and the motives for the cover-up, of these inhuman practices in the post-war period. The time-frame for this study is roughly 1930–48 when the Tokyo War Crime Trials were concluded with none of those responsible for human experiments brought to the bar of justice.

It must be emphasized that it was scientists who initiated the movement to create biological, chemical and nuclear weapons. Neither the military nor the politicians in those countries who supported research in these areas considered sponsoring such projects until they were approached by their nation's leading scientists. It was the German chemist Fritz Haber in his 1919 Nobel Prize speech who declared that poison gas is "a higher form of killing." Albert Einstein and other eminent scientists urged President Franklin D. Roosevelt to sponsor research that would lead ultimately to the development of the atomic bomb. In Japan, Ishii Shiro and his fellow researchers promoted development of biological warfare weapons, not the fanatical militarists who dominated government in the decades before World War II.

Most distressing is the fact that the ultimate disclosures in the mid- to late-1940s of Japanese biological warfare human experimentation did not appall those individuals who were apprised of these criminal acts. Instead, the disclosures whetted the appetites of scientists and military planners among both the victors and the vanquished. Rather than being motivated to abandon such actions, research using involuntary or uninformed subjects has proliferated over the past fifty years. Scientists in the United States alone conducted at least several hundred tests with human subjects who were not informed of the nature of the experiments, or of the danger to their health. Other subjects were misinformed or deceived concerning the objectives of the experiments for which they were recruited to volunteer.

The results of these massive studies are being revealed today reluctantly and in piecemeal fashion. The United States, the former Soviet Union, Japan, South Africa and, possibly, the People's Republic of China, continued to work with human subjects in frantic attempts to develop even more hideous weapons of mass destruction than those which devastated so much of Europe and Asia in the first half of the 1940s. Equally alarming is the growing knowledge that so-called Third World countries such as Iraq, Iran and Libya are actively engaged in attempts to produce biological warfare weapons with which they can threaten their neighbors.

In 1993 and 1994 the Clinton administration began to lift the veil of secrecy concerning United States' experiments with human subjects in hundreds of studies during and since the end of World War II. We now know that American scientists tested humans with mustard gas, other chemical agents, exposed others to radiation tests, and still others to a variety of pathogens without the subjects' knowledge or consent. In many instances, the most distinguished scientists from the most prestigious American universities participated both in deceiving their patients and in conducting the experiments. Even today, those scientists still active in the field, and their host universities, deny involvement.

Recently opened former Soviet archives disclose that the Soviet Union inaugurated a large-scale biological warfare program beginning in the mid-1920s. Humans were used often in experiments that covered a variety of diseases potentially useful in biological warfare. Research facilities were established throughout that vast nation, and, according to Russia's President Boris Yeltsin, such research continues covertly today.[2]

The Soviet cover was partially blown in 1979 when a massive outbreak of anthrax affected a large area around the Urals city of Sverdlovsk. The most conservative estimates are that at least ninety-six people were infected, and that some sixty-six people died as a result of the outbreak. The true figures, no doubt, are higher. The most terrifying aspect of the outbreak was the disclosure that the Sverdlovsk biological warfare plant accidentally released less than one gram of anthrax spores, possibly as little as several milligrams. It does not take much imagination to calculate how much death and destruction the release of a few grams of anthrax spores into a heavily populated community could cause.[3]

In Japan, scientists who participated in involuntary human experiments during World War II, and earlier, dominated the administration and controlled the areas of research of the country's National Institute of Health for one half-century after the war ended. Although the role of these men is discussed in the text, it should be noted here that at least seven of the NIH's Directors and five of the Institute's Vice Directors, during the 1930s and 1940s, engaged in biological warfare experiments which employed human test subjects.

The National Institute of Health is a government-supported agency. Yet these known war criminals were employed by this institution, were given great powers within the organization and continued to use humans without their consent, and often without their knowledge, in investigations that were carried on during the course of more than forty years. It is known that experiments were authorized on prisoners, babies and patients in psychiatric hospitals in 1947, and from 1952 until 1955 by the NIH's Vice Director Masami Kitaoka. Another researcher conducted bacteriological experiments on infants hospitalized in Tokyo's National First Hospital in 1952. Later, this same researcher, from 1967 until 1971, used shigella in experiments on soldiers in Japan's Self-Defence Forces. In May 1985, an NIH researcher experimentally injected an unapproved vaccine against a Japanese encephalitis virus into nearly 200 hospitalized children without their parents' consent. At different times over a three-year period, 1987, 1988, 1989, Kuniaki Nerome experimentally tested two types of genetically modified vaccine against influenza on approximately forty hospitalized children. Their parents were unaware of the tests and did not give their informed consent for the vaccines to be used on their children.[4]

There are a number of international treaties being drawn up that seek to outlaw biological warfare, and, by implication, involuntary human experimentation. The United States, Russia (the former Soviet Union) and Japan are signatories to the various international agreements outlawing human experimentation, and the production of biological warfare agents. Nevertheless, both these activities appear to be flourishing today in all three countries, as well as elsewhere in various parts of the world. It appears that human testing, biological and chemical weapons will be part of former President George Bush's so-called new world order for some time to come.

NOTES

1 See also the *Los Angeles Times*, 11 February 1995, p. A10.
2 *New York Times*, 15 September 1992, p. A7; *Los Angeles Times*, 15 September 1992, p. A1, 6.
3 See *Science*, 18 November 1994, and the *New York Times*, 18 November 1994, p. A4.
4 Professor Shingo Shibata to the writer, Tokyo, 25 January 1995; Tokyo *Shimbun*, 11 November 1990; weekly *Sunday Mainichi*, 8 July 1990; Dr Benjamin Garrett, a distinguished biological and chemical warfare disarmament specialist to the writer, Moscow, 25 March 1995.

Acknowledgements

Although one name appears on the title page, this book was written with the collaboration of countless scholars, researchers, and interested and informed persons. These people shared with me their great knowledge, and generously took time from their own work to assist me in a multitude of ways with this project. In truth, the book could not have been written without their help, and I regard them as my co-authors. They provided me with the information that is the basis for the book, but I alone am responsible for any errors of fact or interpretation. If some names are omitted below, it is due to an unfortunate mistake on my part. I apologize for the oversight.

Professor Ding Zemin[1] of Northeast Normal University, Changchun, People's Republic of China, first suggested the topic to me in 1985, and has been a continuous source of encouragement over the years. His colleagues, Professors Tien Zi Hei and Zhu Yuan, and graduate student An-Yu Feng, patiently helped me to learn the history of Changchun and the activities of Unit 100. Mr Li Mao Jie, Director of the Emperor Pu Yi Museum in Changchun, kindly provided me with photographs of the Unit 100 camp as well as other useful information. Mr Han Xiao, Deputy Director of the Unit 731 Museum in Ping Fan, was an invaluable resource. He is China's leading expert on Unit 731's activities, and unselfishly shared with me the fruits of his many years' research in this treacherous field. In Harbin, I was helped by Harbin Teachers University Professors Xu Wei, Li Hongan, and Sheng Zhan Jie, and by Mr Li Changshan, Head of the University's Foreign Affairs Office. Donald and Clair Egge, two American teachers residing in Harbin, were of tremendous assistance during a difficult time in June 1989. Mr Zhou Ru Yi, Director of Harbin's Museum of the Martyrs, provided useful information. My friends Professors He Zhongyi and Yen Peiren of Beijing Institute of Technology assisted me in many ways during my frequent research trips to China. I am greatly indebted to them.

In Hailar, Inner Mongolia, I was extended every courtesy by Mr Wu Li Ji, Chief of Alliance (Governor of Hulunbeiere Province), of the Inner Mongolia Autonomous Region Hulunbeiere Alliance. Mr Wu's associates, Mr Feng Tian Min, Foreign Affairs Section Chief, Mr Zhou Chun-Mei, Secretary General of the Hailar City People's Government Foreign Affairs Office, Mr

Zhao Hua, Director of the Hailar City People's Government Foreign Affairs Office, Mr Ge Zhan-xue, Assistant to Mr Wu, Mr E Er-dun, one of Inner Mongolia's leading local historians, Ms Qi Xinjun, and Ms Zhu Xiao Yang devoted countless hours to showing me the site of Hailar's biological warfare camp, the city's mass grave of martyred Chinese victims of biological warfare experiments, and the remains of a major Japanese encampment, during an extraordinary three-day visit to the area in June 1991.

In the United States, I was aided immensely in my research by Mr John Taylor and Mr Richard Boylan of the National Archives. These gentlemen, and their associates, are truly dedicated public servants. My gratitude to Richard and John cannot be expressed in a few simple words. Mr Norman Covert, Public Information Officer at Fort Detrick, Maryland, is one of those rare individuals occasionally found in government service. He is knowledgeable and personable, knows where many of the bodies are buried, and is willing to help researchers to the best of his ability. He is another of the hard-working public servants who rarely receive acknowledgement and appreciation for their service to scholars. Mrs Hazel Solomon, Major Robert Horelik, Mr Ron Stricklett, and Mr Fred Baker showed me every courtesy during my visit to Dugway Proving Grounds, Dugway, Utah. Congressman Wayne Owens (Dem., Utah) and his assistant, Mr Mike Yeager, were an essential element in helping me receive permission to do research at Dugway. Congressman Howard Berman (Dem., Calif.) and Senator Allen Cranston Dem., Calif.) also facilitated my securing access to material that several government agencies sought to withhold from public view.

Dr Mark Ryan, Professor Milton Leitenberg, Dr Eric Arnett of the American Association for the Advancement of Science, Mr John Fosholt of television station KUSA, Denver, Colorado, Mr Edward A. Boone, Jr, Archivist at the General Douglas A. MacArthur Memorial Library, Ms Judith Schiff, Archivist at Yale University, Mr Jim Seino, former Public Information Officer at Fort Meade, Maryland, Mr Kal Wang, Jr, Mr Albert Yo, Mrs Carole Levitt, Professor Benno Muller-Hill of Cologne University, Dr Friedrich Hansen of Hamburg, Germany, Professor Michael Kator, Dr James Poupard, Archivist of the American Society for Microbiology, Professor Ray Zilinskas of the Center for Public Issues in Biotechnology, University of Maryland, Baltimore County, Professor John Ellis van Courtland Moon, Professor Shuichi Kato of the University of California, Davis, School of Medicine, Mr Eddie Shuji Noguchi of Japan's NHK Television, Colonel (Ret.) Donald R. Reinhard of General Atomics Co., each in their own way, helped me in my work.

Mr Gregory Rodriguez, Jr, Ms Peggy Tadej, Mr John W. Powell, Jr, and the late Lt. Colonel (Res.) Sig Schreiner deserve special acknowledgement. Greg and Peggy have conducted extensive research on the question of possible Japanese biological warfare (BW) experiments with American prisoners of war. They unselfishly shared with me all of their findings. They also extended to me many other courtesies during my frequent visits to Washington, DC. Bill

Powell was the first American to write extensively about Japanese BW experiments. His pioneering study published in 1981 in the *Bulletin of Atomic Scientists*, paved the way for others to follow. He graciously submitted to several interviews in 1988 and 1989 which were most useful to me. Sig Schreiner kept a diary throughout his long and painful incarceration as a prisoner of war in Mukden, Manchuria. He granted me complete access to this invaluable document, and shared with me in several interviews his reminiscences of that terrible moment in his life.

Peter Williams and David Wallace, two British television journalists, produced a study of Unit 731 in 1989. Although I have a different approach to the subject, I found their book of use in preparing my own work. Their associate, Dr R. John Pritchard, read a fairly complete version of my manuscript, and I want to thank him for catching my errors in the proper use of Japanese terms and for some worthwhile suggestions for improving the study. I am also indebted to Japan's foremost historian of biological warfare, Professor Tsuneishi Kei'ichi, for his most interesting publications. They enabled me to gain a unique insight into Japanese efforts in this area.

Three friends were especially generous with their time and with their willingness to share their research with me. Professor Charles G. Roland of McMaster University and Professors Peter Duus and Barton J. Bernstein of Stanford University helped me avoid committing many errors while writing this study. In addition, Chuck Roland read an early version of the manuscript, and confirmed once more his outstanding talent as an editor.

At California State University, Northridge, I was most fortunate to have colleagues who were delighted (so they said) to assist me either by reading my various drafts, or by providing me with reassigned time, or by helping me secure research funds from the CSUN Foundation or from the School of Social and Behavioral Sciences. Professor Albert Baca translated portions of an important German article on biological warfare that helped me understand the state of Nazi biological warfare research during World War II. Professor Alex Muller translated a series of Russian documents that shed new light on postwar efforts to expose Japanese biological warfare atrocities. Professor Ron Davis read more than one third of the manuscript. I profited from his incisive as well as insightful comments. He is both a friend and an excellent scholarly critic. Professors Paul Koistinen, Ronald Schaffer, John Broesamle, Deans James O'Donnell, and Donald Bianchi read portions of the manuscript at one stage or another during its genesis. Professors Paul Chow, I-shou Wang, Joseph Chen, and Angela Lew helped me greatly by contacting their friends and families in China on my behalf. My former Department Chairman, Michael Meyer, encouraged my research in many ways. Dean Ralph Vicero and his financial assistant, Ms Lyndia Wurthman, came to my rescue several times during what appeared to be continuing fiscal crises involving needed travel funds to conduct my research. They were always there when I needed them as benefactors. Grateful appreciation as well to my colleagues who served on the California State University, Northridge, Research and

Grants Committee, who awarded me several grants to continue with my research.

I must add a separate acknowledgement for the great help Professor Charles Spotts of our Biology Department gave me. Professor Spotts is a distinguished microbiologist. He generously read the entire manuscript, and enabled me to avoid making countless errors that otherwise would have been unknown to a historian struggling to understand the complexities of the world of micro-biology.

I was blessed, also, with excellent student assistants. Mr Adam Lid energetically pursued my inter-library loan requests, poured through micro-film files of key newspapers, and diligently searched for books that were missing from library shelves. Reiko Rose (Japanese translator) and Ching Ling Wang, Lu Cheng, and Wang Gang, exchange students from China, shared their native language skills with me and are responsible for the Chinese and Japanese translations quoted in the text. My secretary, Ms Marcia Dunicliffe, helped me maintain a perspective on life throughout the creative process.

My greatest debt is to my wife Sheila and to my two children, Robin and David. Sheila has been my best friend and an excellent, constructive critic for more than thirty-five years. Robin and David read portions of the manuscript with the expertise they gained in the legal profession. They were merciless in their probing questions, and the manuscript was improved considerably as a result. I have been most fortunate in the assistance my family, friends, and associates gave me during the long journey the creative process required.

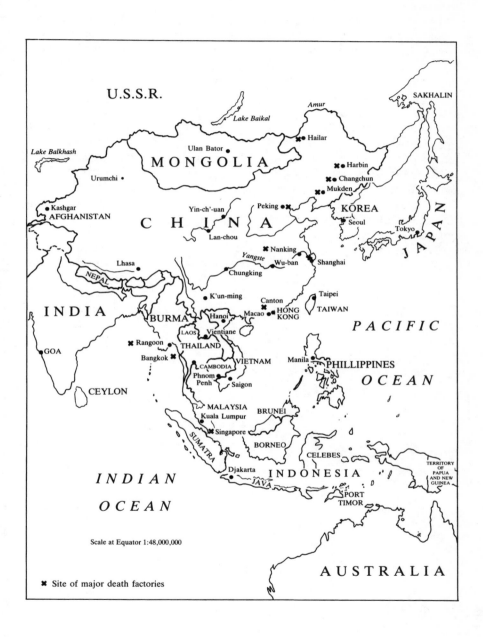

U.S.S.R.

SAKHALIN

Lake Baikal

Amur

Lake Balkhash

Ulan Bator •

✖• Hailar

MONGOLIA

✖• Harbin

Urumchi •

✖• Changchun
✖• Mukden

Kashgar •
AFGHANISTAN

Yin-ch'uan •

Peking •✖

KOREA

C H I N A

• Seoul

Lan-chou •

Tokyo

JAPAN

Lhasa •

✖ Nanking

Yangtse

Wu-ban •

NEPAL

Chungking •

• Shanghai

INDIA

K'un-ming •

Canton

• Taipei

BURMA

Hanoi •

Macao • ✖ HONG
KONG

TAIWAN

PACIFIC

LAOS

Vientiane •

GOA •

✖ Rangoon •

THAILAND

VIETNAM

Manila •

PHILLIPPINES

Bangkok ✖

CAMBODIA

Phnom
Penh •

• Saigon

OCEAN

CEYLON

MALAYSIA

BRUNEI

Kuala Lumpur •

✖ Singapore

BORNEO

CELEBES

SUMATRA

• Djakarta

INDONESIA

TERRITORY
OF
PAPUA
AND NEW
GUINEA

INDIAN

JAVA

PORT
TIMOR

OCEAN

Scale at Equator 1:48,000,000

✖ Site of major death factories

AUSTRALIA

Part I
Death factories

I heard about preparations for bacteriological warfare in Japanese Army for the first time after assuming my post on December in 1939 as a member of the Quarantine Unit of the Kwantung Army . . . namely the Ishii Unit, by the War Ministry and assumed my post, I engaged in the culture of bacteria. . . . I was reluctantly a witness for the preparation activities for bacteriological warfare. I definitely believed that Lieutenant General Ishii had done a great scientific experiment there regarding preparation for bacteriological warfare. . . . On the basis of the facts and the work carried on in the corps under the leadership of . . . Ishii, with which I was well acquainted, I hereby certify on my responsibility that experiments were conducted in the Ishii Corps in which living human bodies were sacrificed in testing.

(Statement of Major Karasawa Tomio, September 1946, Doc. 9306, Record Group 153, Records of the Office of the Judge Advocate General (Army), 107-0, National Archives)

Biological warfare is inhumane and advocating such a method of warfare would defile the virtue and benevolence of the Emperor.

(Interrogation of Lt. General Ishii Shiro in Tokyo, 8 February 1946)

Q: What does the Japanese General Staff think of biological warfare as a weapon?
A: We had no idea of its potentialities because we did so little work in that field.

(Interrogation of Lt. Colonel Seiichi Niizuma, Head of the Japanese Army Technical Research Department, Tokyo, 1 October 1945)

Introduction

It was unusually warm and humid throughout much of northern Manchuria on 8 August 1945. There was little breeze anywhere to relieve the blistering heat that seared the land. Anxious, frightened Japanese and Soviet soldiers who confronted each other along the tense Manchurian–Siberian border later recalled how sweat dripped constantly down the sides of their summer uniforms. Both sides were heavily armed because bloody skirmishes had punctured the peace of the region periodically from the late 1930s to the present. In anticipation of an inevitable future Japanese–Soviet war, fortifications were extensive along much of the flat terrain of the frontier. Japan, hemorrhaging from the constant fire bombing by the Allied forces, who were preparing to move in on the Home Islands, expected Manchuria to be one of the sites for a last stand in an Asian version of *Götterdämmerung*.

The world had been stunned two days earlier, when the Enola Gay, an American B-29 bomber, dropped an atomic bomb on the city of Hiroshima, heralding the Atomic Age. Neither the Soviet soldiers, nor those of Japan, who glared at each other behind their fortifications, were even dimly aware of the momentous event that took place on the 6th, but they knew that war between their two countries would begin momentarily. In fact, the Soviet Union informed Japan on the 8th that the two countries were at war, and Soviet troops were ordered that day to cross the border and liberate Manchuria.

The Japanese leaders, if not the ordinary foot soldier, were aware that these were the closing days of World War II, and that their country's defeat was impending. Nevertheless, they exhorted their depleted army to continue to fight ferociously and bravely in defense of their occupied colony. Emperor Hirohito officially announced Japan's capitulation and surrender on 15 August, but fighting continued for some weeks. Casualties on both sides during the brief struggle were high. Later, virtually every city and town in Manchuria erected memorials, in the heroic Stalinesque style of architecture, commemorating the sacrifice of many thousands of dead Soviet soldiers who helped to free China's northeastern provinces.

Civilian and military facilities were destroyed during the fierce firestorm of war in Manchuria. This was to be expected, and was considered by both sides

to be a routine wartime consequence. The Soviets soon learned, however, that
some of the destruction carried out by retreating Japanese was neither normal
nor routine. In towns near the Soviet border, such as Hailin, Linkow, Sunyu,
and Hailar, the invading soldiers discovered that certain curious and highly
secret installations were leveled by the retreating forces shortly after Japanese
intelligence reported that the Soviets were nearby.[1] On the outskirts of Hailar,
soldiers made a grim discovery: a vast shallow grave that contained at least
10,000 bodies. The grave was filled with Chinese and Mongolian men, women
and children. Some of the dead were still warm, clear evidence that they had
been killed in the course of the hasty Japanese retreat from the city.[2]

The liberators discovered the same phenomenon was repeated as they
moved into the heart of Manchuria. All buildings at the Anda airfield were
destroyed. In Harbin, certain structures were obliterated while others nearby
remained untouched. A super-secret military complex in Harbin's suburb of
Ping Fan was a shattered wasteland, except for one massive building that was
so huge that hasty efforts to destroy it were futile.

Further south, the Soviets encountered similar experiences. Changchun, the
showcase capital city for Japan's puppet state of Manchukuo, was virtually
untouched by war, but its suburb of Mokotan, which housed a secret base, lay
in ruins. The industrial city of Mukden was captured practically intact, but
several isolated locations were nearly obliterated during the chaotic Japanese
retreat. In the lovely port city of Dairen, Soviet officials were told of similar
last-minute destruction of mysterious bases that previously had been off limits
to local Chinese. The same story was repeated in the towns of Rako, Kokuzan,
Toan, Keinei, and Tonei.

What was most puzzling to the Soviet and Chinese officials was the fact that
the area surrounding the ruins was a veritable Noah's Ark. Tens of thousands
of rodents roamed in and around the devastation of the formerly secret bases.
Other small animals, such as rabbits and guinea pigs, were found there in huge
numbers. Herds of sick cattle, sheep, goats, and other livestock, as well as
mules and donkeys, were discovered untended nearby. Even more puzzling
was the fact that hundreds of monkeys wandered in the vicinity, while several
unattended camels meandered about.[3] New and shocking discoveries soon
took place. Buried beneath the rubble were untold thousands of animal and
human bones, pieces of clothing, and artifacts that suggested they once
belonged to humans.

Local inhabitants could tell their liberators little about what had occurred
in the past at these facilities. They knew that wide areas surrounding these
bases were forbidden territory under the occupation. A few speculated that
terrible things took place behind the high barricades that typically surrounded
each of the camps. Some knew the names of Japanese units in charge of the
posts, and listed Unit 731, Unit 100, Unit Ei 1644, Unit 565, and Unit 2646[4] as
major components in a network of special army teams. Several were aware of
the names of some of the leaders, and noted a Lt. General Ishii Shiro, a Lt.

General Wakamatsu Yujiro, and a Major General Kitano Masaji as principals.

Gradually, and with many deliberate omissions, captured Japanese officers added pieces to the intriguing puzzle. The former Commander-in-Chief of the Kwantung Army, General Yamada Otozoo, former Chief of Medical Administration for the Kwantung Army, Lt. General Kajitsuka Ryuji, former Chief of the Kwantung Army Veterinary Service, Lt. General Takashi Takaatsu, and several dozen other high-ranking officers were interrogated by Soviet intelligence in late 1945 and 1946. The officers revealed an appalling story of Japanese atrocities in Manchuria that rivaled some of the worst excesses of Nazi Germany.

Japanese scientists had engaged in research on biological (BW) and chemical warfare (CW) throughout the region from the moment Japan occupied all of Manchuria in 1931–1932 until its surrender in August 1945. The scientists, with the enthusiastic support of the highest government leaders, erected secret bases throughout the territory. Here scientists could experiment freely on animals and human subjects without interference from any authority. Japan, during its occupation, in effect, turned Manchuria into one gigantic biological and chemical warfare laboratory.[5]

1 Manchuria

> While China proper suffered constantly from extreme unrest, not only during the confusion of the [1911] revolution, but also even after the establishment of the Republic, Manchuria was recognized as a paradise of peace and comfort. This was absolutely the blessing brought about by the Japanese influence.
>
> (*The Manchukuo Year Book, 1934*, Tokyo, 1934)

I

To the Western ear, the term Manchuria conjures romantic images of a remote isolated land inhabited by fierce nomadic warriors. Since early times, it is believed, these simple people living north of the Great Wall, and operating under the Manchu Banner system of government, roamed the vast plains of the region in search of food and plunder. But life for the nomads was more than loot and pillage.

The Manchus were organized into tribes, and one of them, the Jurched, produced the Ch'ing dynasty of leaders who in the seventeenth century ultimately deposed the decaying Ming dynasty in China.[1] For the next several hundred years, it was these outsiders who reigned as Emperors of all China until they were unseated in the 1911 Revolution that ushered in China's modern era. Nevertheless, the last of the Manchu Ch'ing Emperors, Henry Pu Yi, as he preferred to be known, was destined to play a significant role in Manchuria a generation after the upheaval that ended his family's reign in China.

The Manchus came from a region of enormous size, but one which was limited in population. The three provinces comprising modern Manchuria[2] – Liaoning, in the south, Jilin, in the middle, and Heilongjiang, in the north – embrace a geographic unit which exceeds the combined land mass of France and Germany. Yet in 1908, the population was a little more than 17 million people. By 1930, the Manchurians barely reached 30 million,[3] whereas France's and Germany's inhabitants exceeded 80 million.

Manchuria is a land that endures extreme weather conditions. Although it is designated as a region with a "continental climate," winters are fiercely cold, while summers are uncomfortably warm and humid. In winter, temperatures can drop to 40 degrees below zero Farenheit, with gale force winds, and summer temperatures reach a sizzling 95–100 degrees Farenheit.

The area may not enjoy the most salubrious climate, but its soils are some of the most fertile in all China. In addition, Manchuria is rich in mineral deposits, and thanks to its vast river systems, it possesses sources for massive hydroelectric power. It was, and remains today, one of China's principal bread baskets, despite a short growing season. Each year large quantities of soy beans, sorghum, wheat, rice, and barley are harvested on the plains of Manchuria. And each year, huge quantities of iron and coal are extracted from the earth under extremely difficult working conditions. The three northeastern provinces hold 9 percent of China's coal deposits as well as 95 percent of the country's iron ore.[4]

During the nearly three centuries of their rule over the Middle Kingdom, the Ch'ing Emperors expected to keep Manchuria pure Manchu in character, but their hopes were doomed. Despite various Imperial decrees ordering Han Chinese to remain south of the Great Wall, the Hans gradually infiltrated the territory. The pace of migration increased rapidly after 1860, until by 1900 the Manchus were a tiny minority in their own country. Poverty-stricken peasants, principally from Shandong province, as well as lesser numbers from Hopei province, fled famine-ridden communities for the promised land of the northeast. Manchuria became for the desperate peasants of northern China what the United States' Great Plains region provided for the European immigrants of the late nineteenth century: a last frontier.

The Han Chinese immigrants found Manchuria an inhospitable place to settle. Arable land was owned principally by Manchu Banner knights, Chinese merchants, government bureaucrats and military officers. The newcomers became tenant farmers of the ruling oligarchy, who exploited them and treated them cruelly. But despite the abuse they suffered, life was better for the immigrants than in their former homeland.

II

It was in this setting that Russia, in the late nineteenth century, set its sights on developing an economic and political stranglehold over this naturally wealthy region. In the closing decades of the nineteenth century, Russians poured across the Amur River into Manchuria. What had been formerly small Chinese towns and villages, under Russian stimulus, became major cities. The hamlet of Harbin, in northern Heilongjiang province, took on the appearance of a Russian metropolis, complete with Russian Orthodox churches and onion-shaped towers, European-style villas and mansions, and a cuisine emphasizing Russian delicacies such as caviar and vodka.

Russian ingenuity, bolstered with capital raised from French banks, built a network of railroads that spanned the three provinces. Russians set up factories throughout the region to process grain and sugar beets and other agricultural products. Russian Jews migrated to Harbin and other northern cities. Some were adventurous entrepreneurs seeking their fortune; others were refugees from the periodic pogroms that were a feature of Russian life. In Manchuria, the Jews operated department stores, lumber mills, textile factories, cigarette and cigar manufacturing plants, and other light industry enterprises. Many worked for the railroad as bookkeepers and clerks.[5]

Russian political influence on the region became a significant factor after their economic advance. In 1898, the Russians forced the Chinese to grant them a lease covering Port Arthur, Dairen, and much of the Kwantung peninsula in southern Liaotung province. This strategic area, with the most moderate climate in Manchuria, and with its fabulous and beautiful ice-free ports, was to be under Russian control for twenty-five years, with renewal options. In the early years of the twentieth century, Russia increased its control over most of Manchuria, stationing troops at key points throughout the country. To retain the fiction that Manchuria was still nominally under Chinese control, Russian soldiers were disguised as "railway guards."

Russian dominance did not last. Their defeat in the 1905 Russo-Japanese War led to Japan replacing Russia as the principal foreign power in Manchuria. Humiliated by the military might of the Land of the Rising Sun, Russia was forced to surrender its Kwantung leasehold to the Japanese. Much of the southern railway system now came under Japanese control. Russia still exercised great influence in the northern region of the country, but Czarist Russia's days were numbered even in this territory.

The decaying Ch'ing dynasty pretended that it maintained nominal control over Manchuria, but in reality foreign overlords and local warlords exercised effective rule. Han Chinese, encouraged by the new economic and political developments in the northeast, accelerated their migration north, fleeing Shandong, Hopei, and other famine-ridden provinces. Hundreds of thousands of Chinese peasants abandoned their ancestral villages to come north to work on the railroads, in the new factories, and on the land.

III

Emulating their Russian predecessors, the new Japanese masters of southern Manchuria employed a variety of devices to enhance both their economic and their political domination of the territory. A crazy quilt series of bureaus and agencies emerged during the first decade of Nippon's dominance. But in 1919, the military created an organization that would play a decisive role in Japanese affairs in Manchuria for the next twenty-five years. The War Ministry in Tokyo established a Kwantung Army to protect its investment in the territory.

The Kwantung Army was never much of an army. For many years, it consisted of little more than one division, supplemented by "railway guards" who ostensibly were civilian employees of the Japanese-controlled South Manchurian Railway. The Kwantung Army commander was always either a lieutenant general or a full general. The Tokyo High Command had absolute control over the appointment of the Kwantung Army commander, and he was subject solely to its instructions. The commander, therefore, enjoyed complete independence from civilian authority either in Japan or in Manchuria. He could act as he pleased without fearing possible interference by meddling Japanese politicians. Over the years, the Kwantung Army leaders took full advantage of their operational freedom.[6]

IV

Japan faced great difficulties during the 1920s. At the beginning of the era, Japanese soldiers botched the famous expedition to Siberia sent to help crush the Bolshevik Revolution. The country, although one of the victors in World War I, was humiliated by its allies at Versailles. Domestically, Nippon experienced liberal reforms that were disconcerting for the military. In addition, throughout the 1920s, there were major financial scandals, a series of bank failures, the devastating 1923 Tokyo earthquake, industrial over-production, and, capping the decade, the tidal-wave effect of Wall Street's 1929 crash.

As one destructive blow after another was hammered home, Japan's junior and middle-level officers began to lose faith in the basic institutions (except for the Emperor) that buttressed the nation's emergence as a modern power. Liberal bourgeois democracy seemed incapable of dealing with the social and political problems of the day. Western-style capitalism was a failure, because it did not provide for economic needs. Coming largely from the rural agrarian class, these officers grew increasingly frustrated when they saw peasant families forced to sell their daughters into the slavery of prostitution and their sons resigned to accept defeat and poverty as their heritage. The country seemingly suffered from overpopulation, and there appeared to be no hope for the ever increasing masses.

Nationalistic in outlook when they entered the military, many of these junior and middle-level officers became even more ultra-nationalist in response to the serious problems afflicting the motherland. Increasingly in the 1920s, and more so in the 1930s, the officers at this level turned to the solutions of National Socialism in their search for answers to Japan's massive difficulties. Benito Mussolini's Italy seemed to be advancing into a new era of economic prosperity and social stability under the banner of Fascism. Adolf Hitler's Nazi creed appeared to offer a welcome liberation from the defeatism and degradation of the corrupt democratic Weimar Republic. Hitler's avowed racism did not disturb the young militarists since they were nurtured in a racist society. They hoped to try a Japanese variation of the European formulas.

The militarists and like-minded politicians formed many secret societies to promote their objectives in the two decades before World War II. A new right-wing organization seemingly appeared each week. It is estimated that, by 1941, Japan nurtured between 800 and 900 fanatical, emperor-worshipping, expansionist, proto-Fascist secret groupings. Some of these organizations were more powerful than others. The Cherry Society, founded in 1927, was perhaps the most influential body within the right-wing militarist network. But each group, no matter how small or insubstantial, made its contribution to Japan's increasing militarization.[7]

The new ideas that spewed from the secret, lunatic fringe associations were especially attractive to the junior officer corps in the Kwantung Army. Most believed that Japan must expand in order to survive as a great nation. In their view, the Home Islands were simply too limited in resources to meet the needs of the country. For them, Manchuria was the logical place to overcome Japan's limitations. The country was wealthy, while its population was relatively small. The Manchurian people were a mixture of races and, therefore, they believed, racially inferior to the ethnocentric Japanese. Those who currently ruled the territory were senile and divided.

The militarists, fired with this new ultra-nationalism, believed that the appropriation of Manchuria would be nothing more than a logical and inevitable extension of Japanese influence on the Asian mainland. First came the annexed Korea in 1895. Then moving northward a decade later, the Japanese acquired the Russian holdings in the lower half of the Manchuria region. Now, Japan's manifest destiny demanded that all of Manchuria become part of the nation's empire. With Manchuria as the core of the overseas empire, perhaps in time, the remaining parts of China could be absorbed into the Land of the Rising Sun.

Lower-level officers engaged in several plots to achieve their goal, but either bad planning, lack of coordination, or strong opposition from senior officers foiled their attempts. Then, on the evening of 18 September 1931, all the parts of the scheme came together. Led by Colonel Itagaki Seishiro, Lt Colonel Ishiwara Kanji, and Captain Imada Shintaro, the junior officers staged an "incident" outside Mukden. The "incident" led quickly to a Japanese takeover of the entire country. Although the Chinese Army outnumbered the Japanese forces fifteen or twenty to one, in combat they proved to be little more than a minor inconvenience to the aggressors' advance. By the end of 1932, the Kwantung Army controlled all of Manchuria. "Reluctantly," the central government in Tokyo accepted the independent actions of its insubordinate military officers on the Asian mainland.[8]

From 1932 to 1934, the new Japanese rulers attempted to create a facade of legitimacy concerning their new possession. They established several different forms of "independent governments" for their Manchurian subjects. All the "governments" centered around the person of the hapless and docile Henry Pu Yi, "the Last Emperor," who formerly lived in splendor in a fantasy world in the Japanese-controlled section of Tianjin, China. The independent state of Manchukuo emerged in early 1932 with Pu Yi as Regent. In 1934, he was enthroned as puppet Emperor in his new capital city, Changchun. After much thought, and with unintended irony, Pu Yi elected to name his reign "K'ang-te," Prosperity and Virtue.[9]

Pu Yi was given a palace in Changchun as well as working quarters. He presided over a governmental system that was administered by Chinese officials. But just as Hitler later would enjoy the support of local Quislings in his occupied territories, the Japanese ruled through the cooperation of Manchurian collaborators. Every Chinese official had a Japanese advisor who made the decisions for him. No serious issue was decided independently from his Japanese "advisor."

Manchuria-Manchukuo for all intents and purposes became a colony of Japan, despite its Potemkin Village facade of independence. Flaunting world public opinion, the Japanese proceeded to exploit fully their new territory, regardless of League of Nations resolutions, investigations, or non-recognition proclamations of world powers such as the United States. The young officer group in the Kwantung Army, eager to introduce their National Socialist, anti-capitalist notions unhampered by outside control, now felt free to "utilize Manchuria as an experimental laboratory for the application of these ideas."[10] In addition, tens of thousands of poor Japanese citizens deserted the Home Islands for Manchuria in the hope of bettering their lot in life. Many of these newcomers joined earlier settlers as diligent farmers and small shopkeepers. Many others were little more than fast-yen artists, eager to make a quick killing and to return home to enjoy their gains.[11]

Some Japanese scientists, with specific agendas, were delighted with the opportunities for research that were now opened to them with the acquisition of Manchuria.[12] Many rushed to settle in the colony because they believed they could engage in research that would be impossible in the homeland. According to Professor Hiroshige Toru:

> Manchuria was used as a test site for national command planning by the bureaucrats . . . and as a test site for the Continental Institute of Science which was established in 1935 at Harbin . . . as an experimental model of a science mobilization system that would never have been permitted in Japan proper.[13]

Another authority, Professor Tsuneishi Kei-ichi, notes that "The scientists and technologists were better accommodated in Manchuria than in Japan with respect to availability of research funds and freedom to select research themes. Manchuria was probably like a newly found paradise for these people."[14] Professor Tsuneishi concludes that, in Manchuria,

> scientists and technologists were able to immerse themselves in research without frustration from shortage of funds and harassment from non-specialist bureaucrats and others. There are those who believe that this was indeed the ideal environment for a scientific research system.[15]

The scientists and the body of their research that forms the basis for this study did find Manchuria a "paradise" for their work.

V

Japanese nationals in Manchuria had nothing to fear from the local citizenry. The natives were kept under strict control by the Kwantung Army and the local Manchukuo police who were largely of Korean descent, and who seemingly enjoyed brutalizing the Han Chinese. Then there were the railway police who were thinly disguised Japanese soldiers. And, finally, there were the Kwantung Army Military Police (the Kempei or Kempeitai) who specialized in dealing with political cases. Few people caught in the clutches of the Kwantung Kempei ever forgot the experience. These policemen were experts in sadistic torture, and were the Japanese equivalent to the Soviet NKVD and to the German Gestapo.[16]

Under the circumstances, the junior and middle-level Kwantung Army officers, along with the newly appointed Japanese "advisors," saw in their new status a golden opportunity to enrich themselves at the expense of the unfortunate natives. They controlled the Army and all local law enforcement authorities. Poorly paid by a niggardly government mired in the quicksands of the worldwide Depression, they quickly became corrupted as they exploited the possibilities for personal enrichment that seemed to present themselves everywhere. They utilized any resource available to become wealthy, including monopolizing the distribution and sale of opium to local addicts and potential abusers.[17] Most officials, and virtually the entire officer corps, returned to Japan, at the completion of their tours of duty, far wealthier than when they took up their assignments in Manchuria. Embezzlement, extortion, graft, sales of narcotics, and expropriation were their favorite devices.

2 Major Ishii Shiro comes to Manchuria

Were it not for the war and his chosen career, his genius might have flourished in a field other than medical science, possibly politics. My father might have made a unique statesman. What he did, or was alleged to have committed in the line of duty as a medical officer and soldier in the Imperial Japanese Army, shall be denounced by any moral standard. Even so, one must not forget that it all happened under extremely abnormal circumstances. It was war.
(Ishii Harumi, Ishii Shiro's eldest daughter, the *Japan Times*, 29 August 1982, p. 12)

The Manchurian village of Beiyinhe in 1933 was a nondescript community of perhaps twenty to thirty families. It was one of several tiny villages that collectively the locals called "Zhong Ma City." The inhabitants were simple illiterate peasants trying to produce sufficient food for themselves and to earn a few coins to purchase a necessity.

There was nothing special about Beiyinhe. Manchuria was dotted with thousands of tiny hamlets similar in composition to Beiyinhe. However, it did have one thing in its favor. Beiyinhe was located on the Beiyin River and adjacent to the Northeastern Lafa–Harbin Railroad line. It was only 2 *li* (less than one kilometer) from the railroad station. Harbin, Heilongjiang province's principal city, was little more than 100 kilometers north of the town. By train, Harbin could be reached in less than one and one half hours.[1]

One day in either July or August 1932,[2] several Japanese officers, along with supporting troops, roared into Beiyinhe, and ordered everyone to pack their belongings and to be prepared to leave the village within three days. Those who did not obey the orders would be killed on evacuation day, and their homes and belongings would be burned. The villagers, aware of the brutality of the Japanese occupation, complied reluctantly with the order.

The officer in charge of the Beiyinhe operation was a young Army major whom the Chinese called Zhijiang Silang, but who is better known as Ishii Shiro. Major Ishii had recently been posted to Manchuria. He was anxious to put into practice some novel ideas he had developed on modern warfare, and, he believed, what better place could there be to experiment with these concepts than in Manchuria, Japan's newest colony? Consequently, he is reported to have written to his superiors in Tokyo in late 1931 that "due to your great help we have already achieved a great deal in our bacteria research. It is time we start to experiment. We appeal to be sent to Manchukuo to develop new weapons."[3]

There were many miscreants who share responsibility for Japan's chemical and biological warfare programs. In fact, so many members of Japan's scientific establishment, along with virtually every military leader of note, either participated in chemical or biological warfare research, or supported these projects with men, money, and material, that it is difficult today to apportion exact blame or responsibility. But there is no doubt that the person most responsible for converting Manchuria into one huge biological warfare laboratory during the Japanese occupation was the young Army doctor, Major Ishii Shiro.

Ishii was born on 25 June 1892 in the village of Chiyoda Mura, Kamo district, Chiba prefecture. His birthplace lies southeast of Tokyo, not too far today from Narita airport. Fortunately for him, his family was quite wealthy by the standards of the area, and as the community's largest landholder, Ishii's relatives exercised a kind of feudal dominance over the home village as well as surrounding hamlets. The Ishii family expected feudal obeisance from the local peasants, and they received it. This peasant fealty continued long after feudalism was abolished in Japan during the Meiji Restoration. Local peasant fidelity to the Ishii family would prove to be useful to Ishii Shiro later on during his Manchurian sojourn.

There is much confusion and some mystery concerning Ishii's childhood and early teens. Even his height is controversial. One authority describes him as being "A small, thin, bespectacled man" whose "outwardly scholarly appearance belied a powerful personality."[4] Another source notes that "For a Japanese he was a giant, measuring a full 1 metre 80 cm (nearly 6 feet) in height. He bore himself well and had a booming voice."[5] In 1938 a Chinese intellectual met Ishii at the Kwantung Army headquarters in Manchukuo's capital city, Changchun. The intellectual describes him as "medium sized, very prudent, with a sharp voice and a hypnotic appearance."[6] It can be said with certainty that Ishii was taller than most Japanese of his generation, and that he did wear spectacles on occasion. In later years he bore a striking resemblance to one of his heros, Tojo Hideki, Japan's wartime leader.

Ishii, as the fourth son of this establishment family, presumably received a traditional primary and secondary school education. The young Ishii apparently attended local schools in the Kamo district. He was an extremely apt pupil, and several of his teachers marked him as one with genius potential. Ishii enjoyed an extraordinary memory, and it was said that he could memorize a difficult text from cover to cover in one reading. No doubt, he was "teacher's favorite," but some of his classmates regarded him as being brash, abrasive, and arrogant.[7]

By adolescence, he certainly accepted the values held by the turn-of-the-century Japanese elite. He was fanatically loyal to country and Emperor. An ultra-nationalist, Ishii at an early age set his sights upon serving his country by becoming a member of the military. His natural bent was toward medicine, and he decided to follow a career as a medical doctor in Imperial Japan's Army.

Extremely intelligent, one might even classify him as being brilliant, and with extraordinary, almost superhuman physical energy, the multi-talented young man was admitted to the Medical Department of Kyoto Imperial University in April 1916. Here he quickly came to the attention of the better professors, and was given research assignments that were advanced for his age and training. Unfortunately, his quick mind was not exposed to one course dealing with medical ethics.

Western medicine came to Japan not long before Ishii's birth.[8] The relatively new Japanese medical schools did not offer courses in ethics; instead, emphasis was placed upon practical instruction and clinical experience. Medical educators training young men of Ishii's generation, and later, assumed that doctors would behave ethically, that medical students would understand that their calling was to heal people, and not view their patients as involuntary candidates for experiments that were potentially harmful. Occasionally a senior professor would discuss informally with select students the issue of medical ethics. Medical school graduating seniors were not administered the Hippocratic Oath, however, or a Japanese adaptation.[9] Ishii, as will be seen, never concerned himself with medical or other forms of ethics.

A clever student, Ishii did not find his medical studies too challenging. He was graduated from the Medical Department of Kyoto Imperial University in December 1920. Dr. Ishii Shiro was twenty-eight years old, and burning with ambition to make a name for himself within the medical profession. He also was prepared to serve his country in the post-World War I era of disarmament mania as a medical doctor in the Imperial Army.

Less than one month after graduating from Kyoto University, Ishii began his military training as a probational officer in the Third Regiment of the Imperial Guard Division. Some five months later, on 9 April 1921, he received his commission as a Surgeon–First Lieutenant. The young officer was assigned to duties with the Imperial Guards Division.

Interested more in research than in general practice, Ishii managed to be transferred to the First Army Hospital in Tokyo on 1 August 1922.[10] His skill at manipulating superior officers no doubt came into play this early in his career. Ishii at the beginning of his professional work exhibited an adroit talent for sycophancy with superiors and bluster and harassment with subordinates. The First Lieutenant's brilliance was evident to even the dimmest career officer. The raw physical energy Ishii displayed astonished his few friends among his peer group.

In Tokyo, Ishii soon acquired a reputation for being a womanizer, a night owl, and a heavy drinker. He was known for his ability to carouse most of the night away in bars and geisha houses after a hard day at the hospital. Ishii was seen frequently in Tokyo's red light district where he apparently displayed an interest in securing the services of only young girls. Rarely could they be over the age of fifteen or sixteen. These were the young apprentice geisha women who flocked around him like buzzing bees surrounding a honey pot. Although paid a pittance as a First Lieutenant, Ishii was known as a big spender. He was never short of cash, and appeared to have an unlimited supply of money. Fellow officers envied him.[11]

Later, in the early 1930s, he increased his visits to the Tokyo geisha houses. His spending sprees became legendary there. Ishii's drinking bouts also were famous. When drunk, and that was frequently, he would complain loudly that military physicians were limited in promotion opportunities, and that the highest military rank they could achieve was that of major general. This was blatantly unfair, he would bellow in his loud booming voice.[12]

In spite of his growing notoriety, or, perhaps, because of it, Ishii increasingly came to his superiors attention. They believed that he was one of their most promising young officers. Several monitored his progress closely, and decided that he should be sent back to university for advanced training. In 1924 Ishii returned to Kyoto Imperial University.

At Kyoto, he studied and did research in bacteriology, serology, pathology, and preventive medicine. While at Kyoto, he was sent to Japan's Shikoku Island to study a new disease that had developed in the Kagawa district on the island. Eventually this disease reached epidemic proportion, claiming many thousand lives. The outbreak was ultimately recognized as a new strain of encephalitis, and was called the "Japanese B" variety because of its initial location.

Ishii's task was to attempt to locate and isolate the virus believed responsible for the malady. He worked on filtration systems as well as other techniques in this difficult assignment. His introduction into the world of epidemic prevention and water filtration systems would have a far reaching impact on Ishii's later career.[13]

During his post-graduate studies at Kyoto Imperial University, Ishii continued to exploit his ability to ingratiate himself with people who could further his ambitions. Many of his professors admired him greatly. The University President, Araki Torasaburo, became one of his supporters. The graduate student frequently dropped by to visit President Araki at his home, which was located near the laboratory in which Ishii worked and studied. One of his mentors, Professor Kimura, thought this was "really cheeky, pushing his way into a place like that." However, Ishii's aggressive behavior paid him handsomely. He married Araki's daughter and advanced his career significantly by acquiring a father-in-law who occupied such a powerful and prestigious position in medical science.[14]

Once again, however, Ishii failed to ingratiate himself with his fellow graduate students. His pushy behavior and his indifference, if not contempt, for his colleagues were resented by many. He could infuriate them with his conduct. Professor Kimura, one of the few authorities who was not one of Ishii's supporters, recalled:

Ishii was something else. He would use test tubes and apparatus that other students had washed clean at night. He came at night because he was lodging in the village of Kawahara. At that time there were thirty or forty research students, and they had to be careful to share the laboratory equipment because there wasn't enough to go around. He would come at night to do his work after everyone else left.

That would have been all right if he hadn't used the equipment that the other students had spent so much time cleaning. The others would really be mad when they came in and found them dirty the next morning."[15]

In 1946 or 1947 a scientist who knew Ishii offered an assessment of him that summarized his multi-personality. The unidentified microbiologist noted:

2. He is very clever and a hard worker. However, he is not a scholarly minded person. He is very ambitious and likes to do big things (in a way he is a boaster). He is very eager about promoting himself to a higher position by achieving meritorious deeds. 3. His attitude is rather rough (t.n. arrogant). He takes [a] haughty attitude toward his senior fellows. . . . 5. In so far as his bad rumors [that Ishii engaged in human experimentation] were concerned, it can be said that he, himself, was responsible for them. The reasons are that he showed cold-blooded films (of actual scenes where American and Japanese soldiers were dead side by side) and he had a habit of telling people all kinds of things concerning support from a secret source.[16]

Ishii remained at the university for two years. In either late 1926 or early 1927, he received his doctorate in microbiology. His senior thesis supervisor, ironically, was Professor Kimura Ren. The thesis topic was "Research on Gram Positive Twin Bacteria." Dr. Ishii received his degree while wearing the insignia of a captain in the Army Medical Corps, having been promoted in August 1924.

The young military scholar did not leave Kyoto after graduation, the Army posting him to Kyoto Army Medical Hospital. Here, he settled, superficially, into the routine expected from a rising professional soldier officer. Ishii worked diligently at all tasks assigned him. He tried constantly to curry favor with senior officers. He began to raise a large family, although his spousal responsibilities did not interfere with his after-hours tours of the local bars and geisha houses. And, increasingly, he identified with the goals and aspirations of his fellow junior and middle-level officers. Ishii openly supported the ultra-nationalists, espousing their anti-capitalist, anti-bourgeois, anti-liberal, and pro-National Socialist views.

Ishii did not turn his back upon Kyoto Imperial University after receiving his degree. He maintained close ties with his alma mater, and was a loyal alumnus. Faithfully, Ishii tried to return to the university at least once each year to renew his friendship with senior professors and administrators, and to entice promising medical students for his projects. Almost every year, "Ishii would speak before the assembled medical students about 'How Physicians Could Help the Military.' He was even allowed to show a movie to them" concerning his research. According to one observer, "This was probably permitted because the institution felt inferior as one of the later blooming imperial universities[17] and because of the rivalry with Tokyo University and desire to establish their presence firmly in China and Manchuria."[18] However, he did not focus all his energies on Kyoto Imperial University. In the coming decade, Ishii Shiro would not ignore Tokyo Imperial University or other leading Japanese research facilities as recruiting centers for talented scientists willing to serve his needs.

Gradually, Ishii began to acquire a reputation as a medical scholar. He published a series of papers in scientific journals that won him respect in his profession. Ishii collaborated with a close friend and fellow Chiyoda villager, Masuda Tomosada, on a paper dealing with the treatment of gonorrhea through fever inducement. Entitled "Sedimentation Rate of Artificially Transplanted Malaria Blood Cells and Their Effects," the paper caused a small stir at the time.[19]

In keeping abreast of scientific literature, Ishii stumbled upon a report on biological warfare by Second Class (First Lieutenant) Physician Harada that would change the course of his life. Harada was a member of the War Ministry's Bureau, and attended the 1925 Geneva Disarmament Convention which outlawed, at least on paper, both chemical and biological warfare. His report on the Geneva deliberations was circulated throughout the medical community, where it did not arouse much interest. Ishii, however, was deeply impressed with the potential for biological warfare and sought to begin investigating its possibilities for the Japanese military.

Employing his connections with ultra-nationalists in the War Ministry, he flitted back and forth between Kyoto and Tokyo in 1927 in an attempt to make a case for biological warfare (BW).[20] The military leadership at the time was not impressed with the idea. Endo Saburo, later to rise to be a Lt. General, recalled in his diary that "At the time, Ishii's face was well known around staff headquarters, he always emphasized the role of bacteriological warfare in our tactical planning."[21]

Frustrated at the lack of military receptivity to the concept of BW, Ishii began a two-year tour of inspection and study overseas in April 1928. His study tour is shrouded in some mystery, however, in terms of who sponsored and paid for Ishii's expenses. It is traditional in most military establishments to send their best and brightest young officers abroad to meet their opposite numbers in other countries. At the same time, they are expected to inspect military and other installations, and to gather as much intelligence as opportunities may provide.

In Ishii's case, there is uncertainty as to his patron. It was later claimed that "The pushy Ishii decided he would take off on his own to Europe." Kitano Masaji, one of Ishii's rivals, wrote many years later that "Ishii paid out of his own pocket for the study abroad at first, and only received official expenses later."[22]

It is doubtful, however, that Ishii would have been permitted to go off on his own for two years. The Japanese military system was highly structured and rigid in its discipline. For Ishii to receive a casual leave of absence for two years so that he could study BW research overseas, in the face of supposed high level indifference to BW, sounds a little far fetched.

In any event, Ishii traveled around the world on his inspection tour. His itinerary reads as if it was the fulfillment of a travel agent's fantasy brochure. He visited Singapore, Ceylon, Egypt, Greece, Turkey, Italy, France, Switzerland, Germany, Austria, Hungary, Czechoslovakia, Belgium, Holland, Denmark, Sweden, Norway, Finland, Poland, the Soviet Union, Estonia, Latvia, East Prussia, Hawaii, Canada, and the mainland of the United States.[23] How much he could have learned by following such an exhausting itinerary is difficult to tell. In retrospect, it would appear to be very little. Some of the countries he visited were engaged in secret BW research. Others were not. In the United States, Kitano noted later, the Japanese Embassy in Washington, DC, "had forgotten his name," but the Military Attaché "said that he had heard that Ishii had studied bacteriological warfare at the Massachusetts Institute of Technology in Boston [Cambridge]."[24]

Ishii returned from his odyssey in 1930 to find that the Japanese High Command leadership was radically different in mood and attitude from that of the 1928 group. The jingoists now were in control. Younger officers prodded their seniors constantly on the need for Japanese expansion in order to survive as a great nation. And their aggressiveness usually met with a positive response.

Four months after returning to Tokyo, Ishii was appointed as a Professor of Immunology at the Tokyo Army Medical School. He was promoted also to Major in the Army. Ishii's world tour evidently yielded great personal rewards.

As a Professor of Immunology at Japan's most prestigious military medical school, Ishii now was in a position to carry on a constant lobbying effort for inaugurating serious BW research. And he did. He bombarded the High Command, as well as his scientific colleagues, with propaganda advocating BW as the weapon of the future, one that was essential to Japan's ability to safeguard its interests. He offered many plausible reasons for Japan to initiate such research, including BW's paltry cost factor compared to conventional weapons. His most telling argument, though, was "that biological warfare must possess distinct possibilities, otherwise, it would not have been outlawed by the League of Nations."[25]

Ishii lobbied also for the Army Medical College to establish a new department, the Department of Immunology, with Major/Professor Ishii as its Chairman. He intended that the proposed new department be the center for BW research in Japan. His intensive efforts ultimately were successful.

Somehow, Ishii came to the attention of perhaps Japan's most important military scientist, Koizumi Chikahiko. Koizumi was a pioneer in medical-military science, and rose rapidly in rank and prestige. For a time he became the Army's Surgeon General, and, later, he served as Japan's Minister of Health. Koizumi was a fierce nationalist, one who supported Japan's expansionist program. This physician was something of a philosopher, too, and he delighted in quoting frequently the Chinese proverb that "Great doctors tend their country, good doctors tend people, and lesser doctors heal illnesses." Koizumi also preached the doctrine that one should "Do the work you're given before breakfast, then for the rest of the day, find your own work and do it."[26] He fancied himself to be a humanitarian as well, and dedicated his life to the improvement of mankind. At the same time, he believed in developing weapons that would make Japan the dominant power in East Asia. At first, he supported research efforts in CW, but eventually abandoned this path as offering little potential value for Japan. Nevertheless, he rightfully can be called The Father of Japan's CW program.[27]

Intrigued by Ishii's BW initiative, and his commitment to the Koizumi doctrine of hard work, Koizumi soon became convinced that Japan should become pre-eminent in the field. He supported Ishii's struggle to establish a Department of Immunology, and, due in large part to his patronage, the department was created. By 1936 Ishii and Koizumi's brainchild gained sufficient prestige with the dominant faction then in control of the military to receive excessive praise for their achievement. In the official Fifty Year History of the Army Medical School, published in Tokyo in 1936, it was noted:

> The Epidemic Prevention Laboratory is newly established in the Army Military Surgeon School as a research facility associated with the national military epidemic prevention tactical warfare mission operations. . . . Army Surgeon Colonel Ishii Shiro . . . noting there were no corresponding facilities in our country, felt keenly a severe defect in our national defense; and upon completing his European tour in 1930, and returning to Japan, pointed out the aforementioned defect . . . and proposed to his superiors that this was an issue that required top priority research implementation. Since that time (Ishii) has continued to build up on his test research day and night, on the side, while teaching students as an instructor at the Army Surgeon School. In 1932, the issue met with the approval of the superiors because of the tremendous support from Instructor Koizumi.[28]

In many respects, the humanitarian minded Koizumi was the father of both Japan's BW and CW programs.[29]

Within one year after Ishii formed his new department, Koizumi returned to the Army Medical College as its Dean. Koizumi apparently knew little about Ishii, except that he was a strong advocate for BW research. As such, he could become an important instrument for Koizumi to employ in achieving his goal of making Japan the leading BW nation. He took Ishii under his wing, even though he periodically was shocked by his protégé's erratic if not bizarre conduct both at the college and in the geisha houses. Koizumi is reputed to have remarked to a member of his family, "Ishii is a strange one, but I think he is good at his work."[30]

Ishii continued to antagonize his colleagues with his arrogance and boorishness. But, no matter. He enjoyed the support of Dean Koizumi and several key military leaders. Among them were the then War Minister Araki Sadao, the extremely powerful General Nagata Tetsuzan, and leading jingoists Lt. Colonel Suzuki Yorimichi and Colone Kajitsuka Ryuji. General

Nagata was Ishii's principal patron and his hero. Nagata helped Ishii extricate himself from several escapades that otherwise would have led to the termination of his military career, and possible imprisonment. As a sign of his respect for Nagata and for what he did for him, Ishii kept a bust of the General in his laboratory. An associate testified later that "Ishii was so grateful to him, that he always kept his [Nagata's] bust about him."[31]

These powerful connections enabled Ishii to move ahead on BW research. Initially he worked in the school's immunology laboratory. But in late 1932 Dean Koizumi set aside some land behind his own office for Ishii's use. An existing two-story reinforced-concrete building was already in place on the land. Another building, measuring 1795 square meters, was built adjacent to the original structure in August 1933. This complex became Ishii's Tokyo center until Japan's 1945 defeat. It also was a signal that BW research was a respectable and routine form of study in the Army Medical College.

Ishii achieved some success with his BW experiments in Tokyo. But he was troubled. Would BW work in the field? How could one be certain that experimental developments which appeared promising in the laboratory would be successful in warfare? The solution appeared to Ishii to be that he must employ humans as experimental subjects. But even he knew that he could not dare attempt to try something so rash and dangerous in the capital. His colleagues would certainly learn about such unconventional and illegal activities, and expose him to the authorities. In fact, given their scarcely concealed hostility toward him, he feared that his enemies would welcome the opportunity to destroy his career. Ishii often remarked that "There are two types of bacteriological warfare research, A and B. A is assault (Angriff) research, and B is defense research. Vaccine research is of the B type, and this can be done in Japan. However, A type research can only be done abroad."[32]

Once more Professor Ishii turned for help to his admirers in the military hierarchy. Utilizing his connections, Ishii managed to wangle an assignment to Japan's recently acquired Manchurian colony. On 31 August 1932 Ishii and his childhood friend Masuda Tomosada were posted to the prized territory. The two friends began their tour of duty by traveling throughout Manchuria for approximately one month, but it is unclear as to their objective. Quite possibly they were in search of a site to construct Ishii's human experiment laboratory. However, the trip could have been nothing more than an innocent desire to see the sights in Japan's latest acquisition.

This uncertainty about what Ishii and Masuda were seeking during their tour is compounded by the observation found in the Fifty Year History of the Army Medical School that the medical school loaned the services of Ishii and four other scientists for unspecified purposes to private industry. The scientists were accompanied by five assistants in order to complete the assignment. But the assignment was not identified.[33] Nevertheless, Ishii remained in Manchuria upon completion of his private-industry assignment. He was about to commence his venture into human experimentation.

3 Beiyinhe bacteria factory

> No matter what was done, anything was permissible so long as it was "for the country" or for the "good of society." . . . In everyday society, there is no such distinction on reasons for killing. In the field of science, however, killing can result in new findings or a revolutionary breakthrough which would benefit all of mankind. The sc¹ ntist who brought about the same would naturally make quite a name for himself.
>
> (Tsuneishi and Asano, *Suicide of Two Physicians*, p. 4)

Japanese troops occupied Harbin, capital of Heilongjiang province, in northern Manchuria, on 5 February 1932. Ishii and his confederates arrived in the fear-ridden city a few months later. Once settled in Harbin, Dr Ishii did not find it difficult to launch his BW project. The Kwantung Army now was more completely dominated by the ultra-nationalists than ever before. And after the recent triumph of Japanese arms in the northeast, the junior and middle-level officers were so powerful that the High Command was in no position to defy their wishes. Moreover, Ishii retained the confidence and support of his influential friends in Tokyo and in the upper echelons of the Kwantung Army.

In reality, the Kwantung Army leaders were delighted with their new colleague. His plans for BW research met with an enthusiastic response from almost every key player in Manchuria, since the principals were convinced that war with the Soviet Union was inevitable, and BW theoretically could play an important role in defeating enemy armies. Japanese troops were now stationed along the long border between Manchuria and the Soviet Union, and Kwantung Army fireaters expected a clash between the two sides would come in the near future. They belonged to the faction in the Japanese military that subscribed to the "Strike North" theory, a notion that future conquests for Japan lay in Northern China and in Siberia, rather than in a southern move to overpower European-controlled colonies in Southeast Asia.

The militarist hierarchy, calculating that the Bolsheviks greatly outnumbered the Japanese, concluded that BW would be an important weapon as a counterweight in such a future conflict. Vigorously anti-communist, and certain that conflicting Japanese and Soviet ambitions in that part of the world must lead to armed struggle, the Kwantung leaders sought to increase the Army's ability to defeat anticipated Soviet moves with any feasible weapon. It did not matter to them whether the weapon was high-speed planes, new, heavier, and more accurate artillery, CW, or BW. Their concern was that the weapon be effective in the coming war.

Moreover, the Japanese believed that the Soviets were already engaged in extensive BW research. And as with military strategists in other countries, the Japanese military both in the Home Islands and in Manchuria believed in mutual deterrence. If the Bolsheviks were working on BW, then the anti-communist Japanese must do as well for self-protection. General Umezu Yoshijiro, Chief of Staff of the Japanese General Staff from 1944 until the surrender, neatly summarized these views when he commented in 1945:

under the supposition that BW could be employed in modern warfare, the Japanese military made a considerable study and research in BW in order that it might be able to cope with it in the event that it were used. I may say that in this connection, I have received no report on the use of BW by the US, Britain, or China. But neither did I receive reports that this weapon would NOT be used. Therefore the Japanese Army had to extend itself to study BW and to obtain knowledge in this field. As to the Soviets . . . reports were received concerning their intentions to use BW in the eventuality of war . . . . This was considered one of the principal motives of the Japanese study in BW.[1]

The Army gave Ishii virtually carte blanche to begin his work. In spite of Japan's Depression-ridden economy, he was provided initially with an annual budget of 200,000 yen from a secret account,[2] a very large sum for the time. His research budget was increased each fiscal year after 1932 even though other Army units endured penurious allotments.

Throughout his thirteen-year campaign in Manchuria, Ishii, despite periodic grumbling about insufficient funds to conduct his work, never lacked for ample resources. He always enjoyed a large and ready treasury, the best equipment, both of domestic and of foreign manufacture, that money could buy, and, until the waning days of World War II, all the personnel he required.[3] Initially, Major Ishii was given command over a unit of 300 men to carry out his plans. He was promised additional help as it would be needed.

Since his work would be in secret, Ishii was required to adopt a false name for his persona and his unit. For his command, he adopted the code name "Togo Unit," after his great hero Admiral Togo Heihachiro of Russo-Japanese War fame; and, among other disguises that he employed throughout his career, Ishii frequently used the name Captain Togo Hajime. Ishii and his men began operations immediately after the secret funding became assured.

Harbin possessed both advantages and disadvantages as a base for secret BW research. On the one hand, it was a new city with a diverse, polyglot population, although traces of ancient man are present in the city that go back at least 25,000 years. In the modern era, a Manchu village was located on a site adjacent to the Samur River for at least 800 years. It was known in the old Manchu dialect as the hamlet "where the fishing nets are dried." New Harbin emerged only in 1897 when the Russians decided to make it a major railway hub and a commercial-industrial center.

Thousands of Han Chinese, Koreans, Mongols, Russians and other European nationalities flocked to this northern El Dorado. Harbin at its peak housed thirty different ethnic groups, including such exotics as Gypsies, Poles, English expatriates, French pseudo-aristocrats, stateless White and Red Russians, Dutch and Belgian confidence men. A few Americans also found a congenial life in the city. It was an ideal gathering place for spies of various countries, and Harbin soon acquired a reputation for being a center for international intrigue. The city was home to Buddhists, Taoists, Shintoists, Muslims, Jews, Russian Orthodox, Catholic and Protestant Christians. A magnificent wooden Russian Orthodox cathedral dominated Harbin's city center. Within a few years of its Russian resurrection, a modern metropolis emerged from the din of belching factories and roaring freight and passenger trains.

The 1920s saw the cultural apex of Harbin. Many newspapers and magazines were published there. Theaters presenting dramas, operas, symphonies, and musicals flourished in the sophisticated, urbane, multinational community. The city was able to support a circus as well as other popular entertainments. Because of the railroad, many renowned European artists came to Harbin for guest appearances. The European community established several institutions of higher learning, such as the University of Oriental and Commerce Sciences, a Law School, and a School of Engineering. Many future communist "martyrs of the Revolution" attended these universities.

Harbin, as with most "Concession" cities, was divided into three parts. One section of the city was reserved for industry and the desperately poor. Later, it would be called "Old Harbin." Housing in this part of town was little more than rabbit warrens. Life was so grim for many of the inhabitants that Sherlock Holmes's Limehouse would be considered fashionable by comparison.[4] Another area was for the moderate to well-to-do Chinese. And the third section, the so-called Russian Concession, was restricted to foreigners, the few Japanese who arrived with the occupation, and a handful of wealthy, influential Chinese, who paid dearly for the privilege of living there. This part of town would be called "New Harbin."

It was in this part of the city that Russian Orthodox churches with their onion-shaped domes and magnificent Russian villas predominated. The streets in the Russian Concession were paved with cobble stones, and well-dressed Europeans bustled up and down, hurrying from one European high-fashion boutique to another, or to one of the great department stores that lined its principal avenues. The Europeans were usually accompanied by at least a few Chinese servants whenever they traveled about the city, since local labor was so inexpensive. Europeans of even truly humble means could afford servants. Life was very good in Harbin for Europeans, even under Japanese occupation. All that was required was that they stay out of trouble, and not fall under the clutches of the dreaded Kwantung police.

Although Imperial Japan would formally ally itself with anti-semitic Germany, the Harbin Jewish community managed to enjoy Japanese protection and tolerance, so long as it demonstrated outward loyalty to the new order. Thus, the organ of this thriving sub-community of 6000 persons noted in August 1940 in a characteristic article:

> The attitude of the Japanese government pertaining to the China Emergency was at the beginning that of non-aggravation. When this position became untenable, due to the Chinese refusal to effect a local settlement, the Nippon policy was transformed to one seeking the speedy termination of the Sino-Nippon conflict and the early realization of the ideal of Sino-Nippon cooperation, mutual prosperity, and co-existence.

Moreover, only after repeated efforts toward resolving differences between China and Japan failed, only then did "the Japanese government for the first time decide and embark upon the policy of thorough destruction of the Kuomintang government."[5]

The principal problem with locating a BW research center in the heart of such a large[6] and cosmopolitan city was the danger of discovery. Ishii's famous metaphor of research A and B applied to Harbin as well as to Tokyo. Initially, he assumed, however, that with a Manchurian puppet government as a front, and the Kwantung Army gendarmerie at his call, he could exercise immediate damage control should an unforeseen problem develop.

Ishii established his original research laboratory in the industrial sector of the city known as the Nan Gang District. He chose an entire block where Xuan Hua and Wu Miao Streets intersect. It was a seedy, run-down street which housed many different small enterprises and an abandoned sake factory. The shopkeepers and craftsmen were told one day in 1932 peremptorily to leave, and on the following day, the Togo Unit occupied the abandoned buildings.[7]

It was apparent to Ishii as well as to his superiors that the Harbin installation was adequate for B, or innocuous research. Exercising special precautions, occasionally they could experiment safely there with a few humans. But it soon became evident that another site would be necessary for conducting A, or large-scale human experiments. Harbin was too dangerous and open a site to implement Ishii's grand scheme. A new plan, therefore, was drafted. Ishii and his associates would continue to work on BW vaccines in Harbin. Once vaccine research appeared promising, human testing would begin, but outside the city. In summer 1932, Ishii found his ideal place for an A camp, isolated, but accessible, Beiyinhe.

Ishii and his cohorts, as described earlier, roared into the village, forcefully evacuated all the inhabitants and burned most of the buildings. They retained only one large multi-purpose structure which they employed as their temporary administrative offices. This building previously supported nearly 100 Chinese vendors who sold either clothing or food to local villagers.

An area of one Chinese *li* (approximately one half-kilometer) square was cordoned off in Beiyinhe by the Japanese. Here they planned to build a combination prison/experimental laboratory. Local Chinese peasants were drafted to construct buildings on the site. This was done under Togo Unit supervision. With the traditional arrogance the Japanese militarists displayed toward colonials, they brutalized the Chinese laborers during the process of constructing the new facility. Draft peasants were forced to work long hours and endure harsh living conditions, and were paid a pittance for their work, even by the standards of the time.

The Zhong Ma Prison Camp, as the BW experimental base was known locally, was surrounded by a brick wall three meters tall, and topped with several strands of barbed wire and a separate strand of high-voltage wire. Enormous watchtowers with powerful searchlights were located at the four corners of the wall. An area 250 square meters around Zhong Ma Prison Camp was declared off limits to local residents; anyone caught within this perimeter without permission was severely punished by the camp authorities. Members of the Togo Unit mounted patrols twenty-four hours each day.

Within the compound itself, which was extensive in area, Chinese laborers constructed some one hundred brick buildings within less than one year. Workers were required to wear eye-shields that prevented them from securing a clear impression of what they were really erecting. Most of the buildings were designed to house the members of the Togo Unit. In addition, a fairly large building was constructed within the camp's center. This structure was a combination prison and human experiment laboratory. Because of its size, the area residents referred to the building as "Zhong Ma Castle." Other buildings housed experimental animals. The Togo Unit personnel were known to Beiyinhe citizens as the Zhong Ma Troop.

The Zhong Ma Castle compound was divided into two wings. The first wing consisted of the prison, the laboratories, a crematorium to dispose of human and animal carcasses, and a munitions dump. The other wing contained offices, barracks, warehouses, a canteen, and a parking lot for military vehicles. Chinese workers were prohibited from entering the first wing, but they became aware that it housed Chinese prisoners. Rumors soon spread throughout the area that many of the prisoners were being killed in secret.

Normally, the Castle held 500–600 prisoners, but it was built for a capacity of 1000 persons. The inmates were a mixed lot. Some were innocents who happened to be caught in a roundup of "suspicious persons." Some were underground anti-Japanese workers. Others were so-called bandits. These, generally, were members of guerrilla bands who continued to harass the Japanese long after formal Chinese resistance terminated in Manchuria. A few of the "bandits" followed Chiang Kai Shek and his Kuomintang. Many were communist rebels. Still others ran foul of the law, and the police sent them to Ishii for use in the laboratory or to serve their prison sentences in the Castle. These common criminals could be pressed into service as laboratory experimental fodder in the event that a shortage of political prisoners developed.

Ishii's prisoners were confined to tiny cells, and were handcuffed and shackled most of the time. By Japanese colonial standards, they were treated humanely. They were well fed. Future victims were given a diet far superior to what the ordinary Chinese peasant enjoyed. The inmates were permitted to exercise frequently, but always under strict supervision of the guards. Their health was checked constantly by a staff of doctors.

On average, Ishii or one of his subordinates would draw 500 cc of blood from each prisoner every three to five days. The blood-taking routine was never interrupted. As a result, most "patients" grew progressively weaker. They were eliminated with an injection of poison when they no longer were of research value. The bodies were dissected, and then disposed of in the Zhong Ma crematorium.[8] A few prisoners who Ishii or one of his subordinates determined were no longer useful experimental subjects were simply shot to death by a member of the Togo Unit. Pathologists then conducted autopsies, and, as with the other victims, disposed of the remains in the crematorium.

Ishii's initial experiments were crude and limited in scope in comparison to the refinements he devised later. Although he engaged in research relating to many different diseases, Ishii apparently concentrated his efforts in the direction of three principal contagions: anthrax, glanders, and plague. The Beiyinhe records were evidently destroyed in 1945, but an account of several of Ishii's experiments is still available.

One was an early test performed on three communist guerrillas. Ishii prepared for the test by commandeering forty mice that were captured in a natural plague area along the Manchurian–Soviet border. Some fleas were lured from the mice, and a bacterium produced from the plague-infected fleas was injected into the prisoners. All three victims were soon delirious with fever. On the twelfth day, one guerrilla was observed with a temperature of 40 degrees Celsius. Another's fever was recorded as 39 degrees Celsius on the nineteenth day of his ordeal. There is no record for the third patient. However, all three were dissected while unconscious.[9]

In 1939 Ishii, in a nostalgic moment, recalled to a subordinate some of his earlier exploits at Beiyinhe. One story involved human experiments with plague and cholera. Major Karasawa Tomio, during intensive Soviet interrogation in 1946, remembered that "In the winter of 1939 . . . Ishii told me that he had experimented on cholera and plague on the mounted bandits of Manchuria during 1933–1934 and discovered that plague was effective" as a BW weapon.[10]

Still another series of experiments was observed by a close friend and sometime rival of Ishii. Endo Saburo, a military officer who rose to Lt. General's rank, recorded in his diary that on "Thursday, November 16 [1933], A bright day. 8:30 a.m. With Colonel Ando and Lieutenant Tachihara I visited the Transportation Company Experimental Station [still another Ishii-invented pseudonym] and observed experiments." Endo and his fellow visitors inspected

The Second Squad [which] was responsible for poison gas, liquid poison; [and] the First Squad [which was responsible for] electrical experiments. Two bandits were used [by each squad for the experiments]. 1. Phosgene gas – 5 minute injection of gas into a brick-lined room; the subject was still alive one day after inhalation of gas; critically ill with pneumonia. 2. Potassium

cyanide – the subject was injected with 15 mg. of it; [subject] lost cons-
ciousness approximately 20 minutes later. 3. 20,000 volts – several jolts of
that voltage not enough to kill the subject; injection [of poison] required to
kill the subject. 4. 5000 volts – several jolts not enough; after several minutes
of continuous currents, [subject] was burned to death. Left at 1:30 p.m.

Later, "At night, talked with Colonel Tsukada till 1:30 a.m., but could not fall
asleep, nor did I sleep soundly."[11]

Endo returned to Beiyinhe on 8 December 1933. It was a sunny day, but
snow began to fall shortly after Ishii and an aide greeted him. Endo "inspected
the germ warfare research facility" in depth, and was most impressed. He
noted that laboratory space was "600 meters square. A huge compound, a
superb facility. Operating cost of 200,000 yen may not be unreasonable."[12]

General Okamura Yasutsugu, Deputy Commander-in-Chief of the
Kwantung Army from August 1932 until November 1934, visited Ishii's unit
sometime during that period. He left Beiyinhe most persuaded with the
Major's achievements. The General was especially influenced by Ishii's
pioneer work with the problem of frostbite. This was a predicament that
threatened the Kwantung Army's efficiency during the extremely cold
Manchurian winters. Now, thanks to the research conducted at Beiyinhe,
there appeared to be a reasonable approach to its treatment. Okamura noted
in a report to his superior that "The best treatment for frozen limbs is soaking
in water 37 degrees celsius." This finding was "the result based on invaluable
data from in vivo experiments with humans who repeatedly were frozen and
then defrosted."[13]

Usually, Ishii did not keep a patient longer than one month before
eliminating him. There was always available a ready supply of "bandits" who
could be employed as experimental subject replacements. These replacements,
too, would be killed when they were no longer useful for research. Later,
the operative word used by Ishii and his associates would be "sacrificed," a
more clinical or neutral term than the pejorative "kill," "eliminate," or
"terminate."

The Togo Unit employed gruesome tactics to secure specimens of select
body organs. If Ishii or one of his co-workers wished to do research on the
human brain, then they would order the guards to find them a useful sample. A
prisoner would be taken from his cell. Guards would hold him while another
guard would smash the victim's head open with an ax. His brain would be
extracted and rushed immediately to the laboratory. The body would then be
whisked off to the pathologist, and then to the crematorium for the usual
disposal.[14] It was such dedicated research, and the results that allegedly were
forthcoming, that led Ishii's longtime friend General Okamura Yasutsugu to
note with pride in his memoirs that "I did not know the details of the medical
advances he made, but after the war Ishii told me that his work produced more
than 200 patents."[15]

The number of victims "sacrificed" at Beiyinhe is unknown. The Zhong Ma
Camp began operations sometime in late 1932, even before the complex was

complete. Beiyinhe continued to kill prisoners until at least fall 1934 (possibly as late as 1936),[16] when a prisoner rebellion interrupted the camp routine and endangered the security as well as the secrecy of the Togo operation.

It was the "Mid-Autumn Festival," a time for joyous celebration for the Togo Unit. Sake and other spirits flowed in an endless stream into the gullets of the guards. Security became lax as by mid-day most of the Japanese were extremely drunk. Many were in stupor; others had passed out. Just as security was at its most vulnerable, a prisoner whose last name was Li urged his fellow prisoners to rebel. Their days were numbered, he reportedly shouted. If they stayed, they surely would be killed by cruel and painful means. Better to die as free men than to become sacrificial beasts to the Japanese doctors.

Seizing a wine bottle from a drunken guard, Li smashed the bottle over the guard's head, knocked him unconscious, and snatched the keys to the prisoners' cells. All the prisoners fled, except ten persons who were too weak from the blood-taking experiments to run away. Burdened by the shackles that hobbled their legs, many of the prisoners were soon recaptured and were subjected to sadistic treatment as reprisal. However, some sixteen prisoners made good their escape.

Four of these men soon died from exposure, hunger, cold, and the debilitating effects of their earlier treatment in the Zhong Ma Camp. The remaining dozen met an old man on the third day of their flight, who guided them to a band of partisans camped in nearby woods. The twelve were permitted to join the group after recounting their terrible ordeal. Word soon spread throughout the area of the strange goings-on at Zhong Ma Camp. Ishii's secret was no longer secure.

Less than a year after the Mid-Autumn Festival escape, the Zhong Ma Camp ammunition dump exploded, and caused significant damage within the compound. No one knew whether the explosion was accidental or whether it was due to sabotage. In any event, the Beiyinhe facility had outlived its usefulness. Ishii pronounced that his experiments there were remarkably successful. He declared that BW was practical as a method for conducting warfare, and that it was destined to be one of the important weapons in future wars.

His Kwantung Army superiors were delighted with Ishii's conclusions. So, too, were his backers in the Army High Command in Tokyo. And so, too, were the intellectual elite within the Japanese scientific community. As a consequence, Ishii announced that he was prepared to embark upon phase two of his project. Of course, he required a much larger facility then Beiyinhe to carry out his plan. He would need more men, more equipment, and much more money to go ahead. Ishii was assured that his needs would be met. Few scientific empire builders could ever have matched Ishii for imagination, gall, or manipulative skills. He was ever resourceful in devising appropriate results from his experimental research in order to convince the most skeptical that his work merited unstinting support.

Ishii abandoned the Beiyinhe facility in late 1937. To ensure that his activities there remained secret, he instructed Togo Unit sappers to destroy most of the installation. They followed their orders so effectively that only a few traces of the facility survived the explosions unleashed. The final act before evacuating the remains of Beiyinhe was to silence anyone who possibly could reveal what had taken place there. Consequently, the remaining prisoners were "sacrificed" in order to prevent them from possibly escaping and revealing the horror of Zhong Ma Camp. Ishii then transferred his men and equipment to a new site, one closer to his headquarters in Harbin. He was about to begin his grand enterprise.

The existence of the Beiyinhe Bacterial Factory, as the Chinese prefer to call it, remained a dark secret for almost forty years. In the early 1980s a Chinese scholar, Mr Han Xiao, Deputy Director of the Ping Fan 731 Museum, made a startling discovery. He stumbled upon the Zhong Ma Camp story while engaged in research upon Ishii's sordid enterprises in Manchuria. This discovery indicates that Ishii engaged in significant human experiments in Manchuria as early as 1932.

Beiyinhe confirms the belief of some scholars that Japan engaged in BW research with humans virtually from the moment it began its occupation of Manchuria. It implies also that prominent figures in Tokyo and among the Kwantung Army conquerors were familiar with Ishii's activities, and, if they did not support him openly, then their silence was tacit consent for him to continue his research. The Beiyinhe story, recounted here for the first time in English, suggests also that Zhong Ma Camp was a prologue to the later activities that would make Ishii infamous in the history of modern science.

4 Ping Fan: the first phase

> It is clear that the human experimentation was bad. However, it is also clear
> that many physicians of conscience and thinking also were a part of "731" and
> similar activities. These are people who would never kill another human being
> in the normal social context. They are the type of people who would be greatly
> troubled if they just injured another person in an automobile accident.
>
> (Tsuneishi and Asano, *Suicide of Two Physicians*, p. 4)

I

The mid-1930s were wonderful years for the young doctor Ishii's military
career. In an era of restricted budgets, Ishii was advanced to the rank of
Surgeon–Lieutenant Colonel on 1 August 1935, just three years after his
earlier elevation to Major.[1] This new promotion was earned, undoubtedly,
because of the claimed initial BW results achieved at Beiyinhe, and the promising possibilities for BW that Ishii trumpeted constantly to his fellow officers
in Harbin and Tokyo.

He was indefatigable in his efforts to promote BW research. Ishii flitted back
and forth between Manchuria and the Home Islands, lobbying the military
High Command, giving lectures at Kyoto Imperial University and at Tokyo
Army Medical College, overseeing the Beiyinhe operation, and supervising
research in his Harbin laboratory. His frenzied professional activities did not,
however, interfere or disrupt his social life. Drinking bouts and dalliance at
geisha parlors continued at a normal level for the ambitious Ishii. He was
never one to permit business to disrupt his pleasures.

In meetings with his superiors Ishii was the professional soldier/scientist,
pleading for his cause with charts, graphs and photographs of some of his
experiments. There was so little literature on BW in the 1930s, in either
Japanese or any Western language, that it was difficult to refute or to even
question Ishii's arguments. And so the forty-three-year-old Lt. Colonel could
freely promise startling results for the military if he were granted the
opportunity to exploit properly BW's tremendous potential. All that was
needed for Japan to achieve BW supremacy was a commitment by the military
of adequate resources and a large contingent of Japan's most up-and-coming
young scientists. Few opposing reasons could be offered by fellow scientists to
dispute his grandiose schemes.

Ishii was given his opportunity one year to the day after his promotion to Lt.
Colonel. On 1 August 1936 he was appointed Chief of the Kwantung Army
Boeki Kyusui Bu. Boeki Kyusui Bu, in literal English translation, stands for

"Anti-Epidemic Water Supply and Purification Bureau,' but it is better known as the Water Purification Bureau. A year earlier, the Kwantung Army experienced a threatening outbreak of cholera which killed an estimated 6000 soldiers before being contained. Intelligence suggested that the flare-up was no common epidemic. Instead, security officers believed that the Chinese enemy was engaging in BW, and somehow managed to pollute water wells, rivers, and streams with cholera pathogens. And if it was not the Chinese, then it was suspected that Soviet troublemakers were responsible.[2]

Ishii was the logical person to head a counter-BW operation. He already was stationed in Manchuria, and continued to enjoy excellent connections both with the top echelon within the Kwantung Army and at military headquarters in Tokyo. The Army doctor/scientist was a longtime advocate of BW research, and, at Beiyinhe, had demonstrated through his experiments some of BW's potential. Most important, he was an expert on water filtration systems.

As early as 1931, shortly after his return from his world tour, Ishii demonstrated publicly a prototype water filter that he had invented. His invention immediately was hailed as a great success, and the Army used Ishii's filter in all operational theaters. Over the years the filter was modified and improved, and was recognized as a significant invention by a creative scientist. Now the military did not need to be concerned whether its drinking supply was forced to rely on polluted or untested river water. Ishii's filter could make any water safe to drink.[3]

Never one to avoid celebrity, Ishii gave a number of flamboyant public demonstrations of his invention. Some of his performances were bizarre and embarrassing on occasion. To the perceptive eyewitness, he was already showing signs of mental instability. Some of his behavior could not be accounted for, except as that of one who was living with increasing stress that could not be controlled without periodic outbursts of unconventional behavior.

At the time of Japan's surrender in 1945, Matsumura Chisho held the rank of Major General and was Vice Chief of Staff of the Kwantung Army. He knew Ishii intimately, and in his memoirs Matsumura paints a remarkable picture of the Army doctor. He remembered Ishii as being a

> manful and resolute military surgeon who possessed great skill in public relations and the ability to execute actions – one who has been referred to as the "army's crazed (wild) surgeon." He has been endowed since his younger times with the ability to do the unusual. In his military Surgeon School faculty days, about 1937, while the writer was on duty with the staff headquarters organization unit, he came barging in and made a forceful request for funds and organization related to epidemic prevention water supply. In doing this, he startled the upper stratum of the staff headquarters by performing such antics before their very eyes, for example, as licking salt that he claimed was recycled from human urine . . . .He was indeed greatly endowed with planning skills and an ability to implement actions.[4]

The Army and Navy chiefs of staff witnessed his turning polluted water into potable liquid during one of his more rational presentations. And Emperor Hirohito evidently observed Ishii's presentation on two occasions, once when he toured the Army Medical College in 1933, and, at another time, while on board a naval ship during a routine Imperial visit. However, it was during one of Hirohito's inspections that Ishii allegedly urinated into one of his filters, and then respectfully offered the concoction to the Emperor to quaff. Hirohito supposedly refused the offer, and Ishii downed with evident delight the urine-turned-water.[5]

The Army scientist also earned a handsome profit from his invention. The filter was manufactured by the Nippon Tokushu Kogyo Kabushiki Kaisha company in a plant that was located conveniently near Ishii's Tokyo laboratory. This company was given an absolute monopoly to manufacture and distribute Ishii's device, and employed Ishii as a "consultant" on production design. His consultancy was worth at least 50,000 yen to the manufacturer, a sizable retainer by the standards of the day. Since bribery was a business way of life with the military, Ishii no doubt received additional sums of money under the table to enable him to continue to enjoy the elaborate living style he adopted as a way of life in prewar Japan. The term "corrupt industrial-military complex" was as yet unknown, but the reference would be appropriate to Ishii's activities throughout his Army career.[6]

II

The Water Purification Bureau was an ideal cover for Ishii. No one could question the value of military units that provided drinkable water to the armed forces. Ultimately, eighteen or more Water Purification branches proliferated in Manchuria and in China proper. All of the units were under the direct control of Ishii Shiro. And virtually every one of the units at one time engaged in secret BW research using human subjects.

The main base of operations for the Ishii network that ultimately emerged from his strenuous endeavors was known as the Ping Fan complex. Ishii discovered Ping Fan shortly before he was appointed to head the Water Purification Bureau. Ping Fan was in reality a cluster of at least ten villages that were located a scant 24 kilometers south of Harbin. Collectively, the land covered by the ten villages, approximately 6 square kilometers, was called Ping Fan. It lay a short forty-five-minute drive from downtown Harbin.

In autumn 1936 several villages in the Ping Fan entity were ordered by Ishii to be evacuated. A total of 120 xiang or 144 acres[7] were involved in this initial effort. The Japanese forced three other nearby villages to be abandoned the following year. On 15 August 1938, according to the Chinese lunar calendar, three further additional villages were requisitioned by the Japanese for their BW facility. In sum, at least eight villages were taken over by the invaders between 1936 and 1938. Seven hundred xiang (840 acres) of cultivated land were appropriated by the Japanese, along with thousands of xiang of meadowland and forest. Seventeen hundred structures were lost by their owners, and a minimum of 600 families were left homeless as a consequence of the Japanese actions.[8]

The Japanese, as was usual in Manchuria, spared no one. The entire population of the sequestered villages were forced to move, abandoning land that they had occupied for generations, giving a final salute to family burial mounds of beloved ancestors, religious sites, and many treasured possessions. Young and old, farmers and small businessmen, collaborators or opponents of the regime were treated alike. All had to obey the dictates of their Japanese masters.

To add to their misfortune, Ishii's cohorts cheated the displaced villagers when they purchased the land from them. One authority[9] estimates that the expropriated land was worth at the time 400 yuan (approximately $20) per xiang. The Japanese paid the villagers an average of 120 yuan, or one quarter its real worth. Moreover, the Chinese living in Manchuria were subject to at least thirty separate taxes, some going directly to the Japanese authorities, while others were used to prop up the puppet Manchukuo government.[10] Consequently, the villagers frequently received less than 100 yuan per xiang once taxes were deducted from the purchase price. New thatched-roof houses were knocked down for 60 yuan, although they were worth much more on the open market. Older homes went for no more than 30 yuan. Sometimes the owner received nothing for his house, the Japanese informing the peasant that the purchase price for his land included the house and other structures on the property as well.

The expropriations usually took place in autumn, while the fields were still ripe from the short summer's growing season. Farmers were not given the opportunity to harvest their crops in order to prepare for the long, cold, bleak, and gray winter ahead. Instead, they left the land with their fields still intact. In the terrible Manchurian winter, the suffering Ping Fan exiles were forced to live in caves wherever they could be found, or in makeshift tents. They subsisted upon wild vegetables, some salvaged livestock, and whatever game could be trapped by the weak and malnourished hunters.[11]

III

Ishii always thought on a grand scale when he planned an operation. But the Ping Fan facility when completed in 1939 was so enormous that the concept truly is astonishing. The Ping Fan blueprint lists at least seventy-six structures[12] in the base compound. These ranged from an immense administrative headquarters building[13] to laboratories, dormitories for civilian workers, barracks, an arms magazine, barns for test animals, stables, an autopsy/dissecting building, a laboratory for frostbite experiments capable of operating year round, a huge farm that produced fruits and vegetables for the staff and was equipped with several greenhouses that were used for plant BW experiments, a special prison that housed human test subjects, a power plant, three furnaces to dispose of discarded human and animal carcasses, and recreational facilities including a swimming pool.

A special railroad spur linked the BW facility to Harbin. And a private airfield was constructed on the base to be used in testing newly developed BW weapons and for other insidious purposes. The base perimeter incorporated more than 6 square kilometers and rivaled Auschwitz-Burkenau in size.

Kwantung Army officals decreed that Ping Fan was to be a "Special Military Region"[14], off limits to all civilians, Japanese or Chinese, unless they received special permission to be in its confines. Absolute secrecy was an ever-present concern of Ishii and his supporters, given their grisly assignment. Therefore, the Japanese authorities prohibited Chinese construction of two- or more story buildings within view of Ishii's domain. Buildings two stories or higher were reserved exclusively for Japanese housing or for Japanese enterprises. No unfriendly eyes would be permitted to peer from their balcony or window onto the death factory.

Airspace near Ping Fan was closed to civilian aircraft. The local civil airline, the Manchuria Airline Company, was cautioned by the authorities that its planes would be shot down by artillery emplacements if one of its pilots strayed into the forbidden zone. The Special Military Region was guarded by three different police forces: the Japanese military police (the dreaded Kempei), the Kwantung Army police, and the local gendarmerie of the puppet Pu Yi government. Japanese soldiers stationed inside the core of the facility were still a fourth line of defense against unwanted intruders.[15]

In order to ensure airtight security in and around Ping Fan, a fleet of Japanese Army planes constantly patrolled the airspace overhead. The air route from the city of Zhoujia to the Simjia airport north of Ping Fan was known as the "60 *li* (30 kilometers) Boundary Line". Any unauthorized plane flying within the Boundary Line was fired upon without warning. Passenger trains routed through Ping Fan were required to have curtains drawn covering all passenger windows. The windows were to be covered at the station before the Ping Fan stop. If any curious passenger was foolhardy enough to move a curtain and peep through a crack, he would be arrested immediately and thrown into prison on spying charges.

Ishii's penchant for security exceeded the boundaries of natural caution one would expect to be taken in order to protect a secret research installation. His concern for security bordered on paranoia. Ishii would not entrust Ping Fan protection to ordinary Japanese soldiers. Only those men who could prove their unswerving loyalty to him and to his cause would be permitted to guard his enterprise. These men usually came from his native village, Chiyoda Mura, and surrounding communities. Many had previously demonstrated their fidelity to the Ishii family, and now they could be given the guardianship of this most important duty.[16]

The death factory headquarters was protected by a complex series of barriers and fortifications. As with the Beiyinhe factory, the headquarters perimeter was surrounded by a deep and extremely wide moat. A tall brick wall at least 5 meters high complemented the moat. Several layers of high voltage wire as well as two strands of barbed wire adorned the wall. Watchtowers were located on each of the wall's four corners. Four gates within the wall provided the only access to the factory. The south gate admitted Ishii's men. The west gate was used solely for emergencies. And the east and north gates were used by Chinese laborers who worked in the facility.

Additional watchtowers were built atop the highest points within the Ping Fan factory. Guards were placed on top of the large chimneys of the plant's power station, since the chimneys were the tallest structures in Ping Fan and offered an unparalleled observation site. Other watchtowers were built on top of the camp's water supply tower and the building known as the "Square Building", the heart of Ishii's BW empire. The Square Building, a huge structure measuring more than 9200 square meters, was surrounded by high earthen walls, and was strictly out of bounds to any Chinese, with the exception of those who were shortly to be required to submit to BW experiments.

IV

Chinese labor built the sprawling death factory over a two-year period. It is estimated that at least 10,000 to 15,000 laborers were recruited to work in Ping Fan from the time construction began in 1936 until its destruction in August 1945 shortly before the arrival of Soviet troops in Harbin.[17] Many of the workers were local peasants from Harbin and the surrounding towns and villages who were forced into working for the Japanese.

The occupation army required that virtually every Chinese male between sixteen and sixty years of age residing in Manchuria devote four months each year to serving their needs. Each household containing three or more males was forced to provide one laborer for one year's duty. Other laborers were beguiled by unscrupulous Japanese middlemen and co-opted Chinese officials to leave their homes in Hebei, Shandong, and other North China provinces for promised well-paying jobs in Manchuria. They, too, ended up by working in Ping Fan.

Sometimes as many as 1500 workers were employed at the base. During the last desperate days of World War II Ishii used more than 3000 laborers in Ping Fan. On average, however, a detail of 750 laborers would be on hand for work at the camp. They ranged in age from a fifteen-year-old named Sun Ru Xue to sixty-year-old Zheng Juang Qi. Most were either illiterate or sub-literate, almost all came from desperately poor peasant families. Work details were arranged in ten-person teams. Everyone in a team was responsible for the behavior of the other members of the group. If, by chance, one person managed to escape from Ping Fan's clutches, the remaining nine members of the team would be punished. They were supervised at all times by retired Japanese servicemen who worked for the Kempei.

Every morning before work the laborers were required to assemble in a large courtyard where they paid respect to their Japanese masters. No sign of disrespect was tolerated during the obedience ceremony, as one Lee Chang learned to his regret. The Japanese loosed their guard dogs upon him because he allegedly violated the rule. Lee succumbed to his wounds shortly afterwards.

Each morning those workers who were permitted to commute to work from off base were compelled to produce their identity cards to the sentries stationed at either the east or the north gate. The men were then subjected to body searches before being allowed to enter the camp. The process was repeated at the end of each working day. But in a further sign of obedience, workers were made to bow to each sentry before leaving for home.

The workers were placed under intensive scrutiny by their Japanese masters throughout the working day. The Chinese were not allowed to look up from their work. They could neither talk among themselves about their tasks nor question other work teams about their assignments. Plainclothes detectives circulated among the men at all times.

Thought control was the norm. No rumor or fact detrimental to the Japanese could be permitted to circulate. In the waning days of the war the Kempei redoubled their effort to prevent bad news from spreading. Two months before the end, some Chinese workers discussed the possibility of a Japanese defeat. They were overheard by a plainclothes man, who detained them in Ping Fan's inhospitable prison. Three days before Japan's surrender, a worker whose nickname was "Dumb Head Lee" told some friends in a restaurant that he had heard news of Japan's imminent defeat. This conversation was overheard by one of the camp's Chinese translators and was duly reported to the authorities. Dumb Head Lee was immediately arrested, physically assaulted, and sent off to prison.

Once employed at Ping Fan, a worker was denied any human rights. He worked from sunrise to sunset or longer. No time off was given for a day of rest. The work week was seven days. No medical care was given to the Chinese laborers. As one guard lightheartedly remarked, "there are lots of Chinese; it does not matter if one or two died." In reality, more than one third of all the workers employed at Ping Fan from 1936 until 1945 died of mistreatment at the camp.

Workers were assigned hazardous tasks with no thought for their safety, since there were others who could replace them, should mishaps occur. In the spring of 1945, Wang Jia Qing, for example, was forced to climb the roof of a building to change some tiles, even though an intensely strong wind was blowing at the time. The guards laughed as Wang was blown off the roof, suffering severe head injuries. Earlier, in 1938, a road-repair detail was engaged in repairing trenches along the road when one of the workers, Xiao Chang Hai, fell ill and could not complete his assignment. His Japanese supervisor proceeded to beat him mercilessly, and then ordered one of the guard dogs to attack Xiao. Countless other stories of Japanese bestiality to the Ping Fan workers have been recorded.[18]

Workers were paid pitifully low wages even by the standards of the day. They earned barely enough to pay for food and shelter. Laborers recruited from outside the Harbin region were worse off than local residents. The rations the Japanese provided daily for the outsiders were a few tiny steamed dumplings mixed together with a handful of pickled vegetables. Housing consisted of tents which offered little protection in winter from the intensely cold and damp climate. All the men suffered from malnutrition.

Those employed locally were able to live at home. Here they could supplement their miserable Japanese-supplied victuals with food grown on their tiny plots of land. Sometimes even the locals became desperate in their hunger, and would raid Japanese trash bins in search for food. In winter 1943, two workers were severely thrashed because they were caught eating some rotten apples they had found among discarded garbage.

The workers dressed in tattered rags in all seasons. Winter, of course, was the most difficult time. The men simply did not have sufficient rags to keep their bodies warm. Many died of frostbite and exposure. The recruits from North China wore clothing salvaged from the workers who died. The camp "tailor" took whatever pieces of clothing he found on the dead bodies, and sewed them together to make garments for the workers. Dressed in the grotesque clothes designed by the "tailor", some men appeared to resemble zebras rather than humans.

Brutal treatment for the workers who built Ping Fan was the norm, not the exception. As a result, many thousands of men died of the callous care meted out to the Chinese. Those who died were buried in wasteland outside Ping Fan's north gate. So many victims were ultimately buried in this common grave that the site became known as the "laborers' graveyard".

Death brought no dignity to the workers. The Japanese graciously provided coffins for the first victims to die. But as time went on and the number of victims climbed greatly, they dispensed with coffins. The bodies were stripped of clothing and whatever little valuables existed. These were turned over to fellow workers who needed them. The naked remains were then dumped into a shallow pit for burial. Initially, just one corpse was lowered into each pit. Later on, four or five bodies were dropped into a common hole, and, as the war rushed to its climax, as many as ten bodies were crammed into a pit. A thin layer of earth covered the bodies, and the decomposing cadavers often cast offensive odors over a wide area.

Japanese personnel were, of course, indifferent to the Chinese workers' suffering and their high mortality rate. But, curiously, they were concerned about the departed souls of the Chinese. Many officers reported hearing strange and queer noises at night that could come only from the "laborers' graveyard". They remembered also those workers who died cursing their masters, calling them robbers and exploiters, and vowing to seek vengance in due course. The superstitious officers, anxious to assuage the vengeful spirits, once each year visited the grave site and offered sacrifices to the dead. Then, reassured of their safety for the coming year, the Japanese would revert once more to their brutal behavior toward the Chinese.[19]

V

The Ping Fan project was an enormously complex and expensive undertaking. In reality, Ishii controlled a huge fiefdom in Ping Fan. He employed thousands of Chinese workers, both unskilled and craftsmen, in the construction and maintenance of his death factory. Many Japanese scientists and technicians were brought to Ping Fan to work on various scientific projects under Ishii's direction. Hundreds of other Japanese served there in clerical and technical support roles. Delicate and intricate equipment, much of it coming from Europe and the United States, and costing tens of thousands of yen, was purchased for the facility.[20]

It was such a huge project that even arrogant Japanese administrators were forced to invent a cover story for Ping Fan. They were usually so contemptuous of, or indifferent to, Chinese public opinion, that the normal procedure was to ignore it. But Ping Fan was simply too large to ignore. Consequently, as an artifice, the local population was informed by Ishii's subordinates that the Japanese were constructing a lumber mill within the compound. And with the exquisite sarcastic "humor" for which Ishii and his colleagues were famous, they referred among themselves to their human subjects as *maruta*, or logs.[21]

Ishii exercised great influence with the local police as well as with the Kempei and the Kwantung Army police. He had also a virtual private army under his command, an army consisting of many home-town boys totally dedicated to their commander. The commandant also had under his wing an air force, complete with a fleet of planes, bombs of different types and dimensions, a dozen or more skilled pilots, a landing strip at Ping Fan, and a test site at Anda, 140 kilometers north of Harbin.

The initial 1936 budget for Ping Fan and auxillary facilities was three million yen "for personnel, two hundred thousand to three hundred thousand yen per autonomous unit and six million yen for experimentation and research."[22] Ishii thus controlled an annual budget of ten or more million yen. But Ishii Shiro in 1936 was a mere Lt. Colonel in the Medical Corps of the Kwantung Army! Some generals commanding many divisions would have been delighted to receive such a princely allocation. It is obvious that Lt. Colonel Ishii could not independently wield sufficient power to initiate the Ping Fan undertaking on such a grand scale. Even his earlier endeavor at Beiyinhe was too expensive for the then Major Ishii to begin on his own initiative.

Someone in the halls of power in Tokyo must have authorized Ishii's BW experiments. Now his patron General Nagata was dead, an assassination victim of one of the infamous coup attempts that marred Japanese politics in the 1930s.[23] But Nagata's successor, or perhaps someone at the Imperial Court, or some group of high-ranking extremist right-wing officers, members of one of the myriad fanatical secret societies of the time, must have been aware of Ishii's grandiose schemes and his ultimate goals, and authorized their implementation. There is the distinct possibility, of course, that all three elements endorsed his BW experiments in Manchuria.

Early on in Manchuria, Ishii bypassed the regular chain of command and reported directly to the Commander of the Kwantung Army. The Chief of the Medical Department of the Kwantung Army also supervised some of Ishii's duties. On sensitive matters he reported directly to "the Tokyo Medical Affairs Bureau and the Section in Charge in the General Staff AO", especially on matters concerned with research and experiments.[24]

The Kwantung Army, as discussed previously, was famous for its vaunted "independence" from Tokyo. The Mukden "Incident" is always cited as an example of Tokyo's inability to control the Army in Manchuria.[25] But the Kwantung Army at no time controlled independent revenue sources sufficient to cover its operating expenses in Manchuria.[26] And Tokyo still held tight control of the military purse strings. Therefore, all road signs point in the direction of the national capital as the source for Ishii's support.

His initial expenditures were too great for the Kwantung Army Command to shoulder. And Ishii, notorious for his extravagances and corrupt palm, could confidently be expected to increase his budget demands greatly. Only powerful champions in Tokyo such as Colonel Suzuki Yorimichi, Chief of the First Section of the Strategical Division of the Japanese General Staff, could provide him with the means to go ahead.[27] Moreover, according to Kajitsuka Ryuji, Lt. General in the Medical Service and former Chief of the Medical Administration of the Kwantung Army, Ishii was given permission to begin the Ping Fan experiment in 1936 by "command of the Emperor." Hirohito's edict, which as yet has not surfaced, purportedly was "sent to all the units of the Japanese Army for information of all the officers." And Kajitsuka "was shown this command and the detachment's personnel list accompanying it, and certified the fact with my personal seal." Later, according to Kajitsuka, in 1939–1940, Hirohito issued still another decree reorganizing Ishii's detachment. "I was acquainted with this decree at the Kwantung Army headquarters approximately in February 1940, signing a pledge of secrecy."[28]

It is clear that Ishii had friends in high places in Tokyo, possibly in the highest place.

5   Ping Fan's version of hell

When we had gone so far ahead
That my master was pleased to show me
The creature that once had been so fair . . .
He stood from in front of me, and made me stop,
Saying, "Behold Dis! Here is the place
Where you must arm yourself with courage."
Oh, how great a marvel appeared to me
When I saw three faces on his head! . . .
With six eyes he wept, and over his three chins
He let tears drip and bloody foam.
In each mouth he chewed a sinner with his teeth . . .
So that he kept three in pain.
To the one in front the biting was nothing
Compared to the scratching, for at times,
His back was stripped of skin.
(Dante Alighieri, *The Divine Comedy*, Canto XXXIV, translated by
H. R. Huse, Rinehart and Co., New York, 1959)

I

In Manchuria, in autumn 1936, the leaves on the trees had long since changed
color; what were gold and red hues had turned a shriveled brown. Most of the
trees were already barren, and looked like giant scarecrows against the ever-
graying, leaden sky that is characteristic of Manchuria in late autumn. Winter
was arriving.

It was so cold by October that former Colonel Sakaki Ryohei (possibly a
pseudonym) recalled in 1952 that his body was already trembling from the
precipitous drop in temperature. However, "indoors, the furnace was working
properly, making it quite comfortable even when one removed outer
garments. Within the newly constituted conference room," Colonel Sakaki
remembered fondly,

> the fragrance of wood intermixed with the smell of fresh paint and a clean
> air smell pervaded – there were the tables aligned in horseshoe arrange-
> ment, and a pot of spectacularly blooming chrysanthemums on a square
> mat in the middle of this stark room having no ornaments whatsoever. In
> accordance with precedence, the conference commenced in the dead of
> night. Sixty-plus attendees were gathered. It was the first conference since
> the full fledged start of the research program.

Unit Commander Nishikawa (Ishii, in reality) rose slowly and spoke solemnly. He addressed the group in triumphant tones:

> The preparation for our research laboratory has been completed. This unit which is referred to as the "remote island" is completely isolated from our surroundings and we have no complaints on the research environment. Compared with the research laboratories with which you are familiar in the universities in the large cities, this facility is inferior to none, and we can be rather proud of the fact that we have several times the equipment. How can anyone, other than those of you assembled here, imagine in his wildest dreams that there exists such a splendid cultural research laboratory in the middle of these expansive wilds. On top of this, we have no worry whatsoever about the availability of research funds.[1]

One quarter-century after the fact, Colonel Sakaki most probably re-created Ishii's speech. But the statement reflected Ishii's views correctly. He now was in a position to fulfill his grand scheme. By imperial edict he controlled his own mini-legion. Although it officially was part of the Kwantung Army,[2] Ishii still retained his entree in the War Ministry in Tokyo and could call upon his supporters for additional resources as needed. The Togo Unit of Beiyinhe fame now passed into history.

The new unit, which consisted of a nucleus of scientists and professional soldiers retained from the old Togo group, and augmented by newly recruited scientists from prestigious Home Islands universities and a praetorian guard of devoted, boorish Chiyoda Mura Ishii zealots, was named the "Ishii Unit" after its leader.[3] In 1941, to further cover up Ishii's BW activities, the unit was given a numerical designation, Unit 731, and it achieved its enduring notoriety under this latter designation.[4]

It was from the chrysanthemum-decorated conference room, in the huge square administration building, that Ishii and his confederates planned the operations that created a living hell for the victims of their twisted concept of "scientific research." No writer of fiction, from the sublime medieval poet Dante Alighieri, to Gothic novelists such as Mary Wollstonecraft Shelley and Robert Louis Stevenson, or modern-day Hollywood–Hong Kong hack science-fiction screenwriters, could possibly rival the real-life misdeeds of Ishii and his fellow researchers. The charnel house that Ishii created at Ping Fan and its satellite facilities throughout Manchuria and China proper is, argu-ably, inconceivable by the most fertile fictive imagination. But, it should be remembered, Ishii was a seemingly normal person with above-normal intelligence who enjoyed gargantuan indulgences.

His co-workers were also average people who were selected for their medical or scientific expertise, and not because they were sadists or evil-minded. They did their job because they were well paid, and because they expected to advance their careers as a consequence of their experiences in the Ping Fan death factory. They participated in, and enjoyed, common pleasures whenever the opportunity presented itself to get away from their deadly tasks. Thus, many would welcome the opportunity to visit Manchukuo's capital city, Changchun, for its recreational opportunities, as well as to resume acquaint-anceships with old friends from the Home Islands who were stationed there. Over cups of potent sake or large tumblers of beer, these hearty comrades would swap stories about their deadly research and play mah-jong for small stakes.[5] And, as a result of the unusual circumstances of the time in Japan, Ishii was permitted to cater to his fantasies, and many of his co-workers were able to succeed in their profession, both during World War II, and in Japan's post-war era of recovery and prosperity.[6]

Ishii's men, for the most part, joined him in Manchuria for an assortment of reasons. Some came out of a sense of adventure. Some were drafted by the military and could not refuse the order to report to Ping Fan.[7] A few came to Ishii in order to assume technical positions of high importance. In 1938, seven faculty from Kyoto Imperial University were lured to Ping Fan by the promise that they would be employed as project directors or, if that were impossible, they would be given other important posts. The Kyoto group were called derisively by their colleagues "the Gang of Seven." One of the "Seven" later recalled that he was forced by his senior professor to join the others. Professor Toda Shozo, President of Kyoto's Medical Department, his voice shaking with anger, told his reluctant assistant that, "if you can't do what you're told, I'll see to it that you're put out of the university."[8]

Others, both civilian and military personnel, knowing what they would be expected to do once they were established in Ping Fan, or in any of the other laboratories under Ishii's jurisdiction, willingly enlisted in his cause because they could pursue research unhindered by either financial or ethical con-siderations. For them, ethics were not an issue. They knew right from wrong. In their minds, however, advanced research was not to be inhibited by ethical restraints. Imbued by a fervent sense of nationalism and a desire to achieve fame and fortune, these men were concerned solely with the final results of their work. They rationalized that the end really did justify the means.

Major Karasawa Tomio may perhaps best illustrate this viewpoint. A Soviet prisoner of war in 1946, and cognizant of the probable fate that lay ahead, Karasawa nevertheless confessed to a continued admiration for Ishii and for the efforts of Unit 731 in the death factories. He admitted that, while "reluctantly a witness for the preparation activities for bacteriological warfare I definitely believed that . . . Ishii had done a great scientific experiment there." He went on to explain:

> I participated in this work and hate to say anything about it, but I will explain it because it will be a burden on my mind if I don't. I had thought at that time that the execution of this work would be explained as a duty of a Japanese officer, but now [in retrospect], I shall explain it as a doctor who engages in the benevolent art.[9]

When asked how he liked working for Ishii Shiro, former pharmacy officer Major Masuda Yoshiyasu replied with some indignation, "We did not think that way. We were working for our country. We did as we were told. I thought General Ishii was a great man, an important man."[10]

For those who may still have harbored ethical doubts, Ishii offered them the perfect answer to ease their concerns. He addressed the issue directly in his speech formally inaugurating the Ping Fan operation. The unit commander exhorted his men to always keep in mind that

> Our god-given mission as doctors is to challenge all varieties of disease-causing micro-organisms; to block all roads of intrusion into the human body; to annihilate all foreign matter resident in our bodies; and to devise the most expeditious treatment possible. However, the research work upon which we are now about to embark is the completely opposite of these principles, and may cause us some anguish as doctors. Nevertheless, I beseech you to pursue this research, based on the dual thrill of 1), a scientist to exert efforts to probing for the truth in natural science and research into, and discovery of, the unknown world and 2), as a military person, to successfully build a powerful military weapon against the enemy.[11]

Hojo Enryo, an Ishii disciple, best addressed the moral question in a lecture in Berlin in 1941, when he observed:

> It is questionable whether in the case of a nation fighting for its honor such an idea of justice as propounded by the League of Nations [the 1925 Convention outlawing BW and CW] will be upheld or not. In the case of a victorious enemy such a moral agreement might possibly be only a dead letter.[12]

Still others brought to their work a dedication derived from a belief that working on human subjects was no different than doing research with plant or animal specimens. Much of their indifference to the suffering of human beings under their care came from an age-old Japanese concept of racial superiority. While Adolf Hitler came to power in Germany in 1933, in part, by promising the German people that he would rid the country of those racially impure elements corrupting the master Aryan race and preventing it from achieving its rightful place in the world, Japan had long since realized that objective.

An island nation, Japan, had been emotionally separated from the Asian mainland and from the outside world at large for hundreds of years. The nation's centuries-old physical isolation bred a cultural isolation as well, and contributed to the development nationally of an extreme racial and cultural xenophobia. By the nineteenth century, if not earlier, most Japanese who concerned themselves with such issues took great satisfaction in the idea that theirs was a racially pure society. With the exception of a 1 or 2 percent aboriginal population,[13] Japan had become a remarkably homogeneous population.[14] It was, and remains, one of the world's most ethnocentric nations.

Even the nineteenth-century so-called "opening of Japan" by Commodore Matthew Perry on 14 July 1853, terminating two centuries of enforced isolation from a world beyond the Home Islands, did not lead to an end to Japanese attitudes of racial and cultural superiority. At mid-century, Japan rapidly began to adapt to Western methods in science and technology, and more slowly in political and military ways. It remained firm, however, in its commitment to traditional cultural and racial viewpoints and values.

The Japanese believed their islands were home to a special race of people who enjoyed a unique and superior culture. They were the lightest-skinned people in East Asia, and disparaged Asians of darker hue.[15] Their religio-political system was older than Christianity, and had stood the test of time for more than 2500 years. According to Shinto belief, the Emperor of Japan was a direct descendant of the goddess who had created the Japanese people, and, as such, he was a living god. Militarists were committed to the concept of a divine origin of the country and the Emperor. Fanatics among the military, and they were numerous throughout the 1930s, joined societies whose objectives were to "establish a government, an economic policy and a culture which shall be based upon the position of the Emperor."

The Soldiers of the Gods, one of more than 500 right-wing groups in the Japan of the 1930s, declared that their goal was "the annihilation of the leaders . . . who are obstructing the progress of the Empire. They shall thereby establish the Imperial Restoration and proclaim the Imperial Rule throughout the world."[16] To protect the nation from corruptive influences, these fanatics did not hesitate to assassinate those in government whom they concluded were unfaithful to their oath of fealty to the Emperor. Thus, on the morning of 12 August 1935, Lt. Colonel Aizawa Saburo entered the office of General Nagata Tetsuzan, Chief of the War Ministry's Military Affairs Bureau, and, as part of a coup attempt, killed him with several thrusts of his sword. He then recalled casually several months later:

> After stabbing his Excellency I went to the office of General Yahaoka. Yahaoka was greatly concerned because my left hand was bleeding badly. He bound up my wrist with his handkerchief and asked what I intended to do. I replied that I had to do some shopping at the Army Club and would then leave for my new post in Taiwan."[17]

Nagata's assassination was one of dozens of political killings and attempted assassinations that characterized Japanese politics during this period. It was in this monstrous environment that Ishii and his loyal adherents flourished. Theirs was a society that believed in being governed by what a latter commentator would define as "hierarchy, loyalty, conformity, duty, and obedience."[18] They were ruthless in eliminating anyone who seemingly stood in the way of achieving these divinely inspired objectives. Their philosophy was perhaps best stated in February 1936 by two mid-level Army officers who wrote, during still another aborted coup attempt:

> With due reverence, we consider that the basis of the divinity of our country lies in the fact that the nation is destined to expand under the Imperial Rule until it embraces all the world. . . . It is now time to expand and develop in all

directions. In recent times, however, self-seeking, refractory men have encroached upon the Imperial Prerogative, obstructing the true growth of the people . . . making our country an object of contempt. . . . Unless we carry out our ultimate duty as his majesty's loyal subjects at this moment, we shall have no chance. Therefore we comrades of like mind and purpose rise together to destroy the villains, to uphold righteousness and to place our land in a position of eternal safety. We, the children of our dear land of the gods, act with pure sincerity of heart.[19]

Some months after Japan's surrender in 1945, Emperor Hirohito finally conceded that he was no longer a divine person by declaring to his loyal subjects:

the bondage between Us and you, the people, is constantly tied with mutual trust, love and respect. It is not brought by mere mythology and legends. It is never founded on a chimerical conception which ascribes the Emperor as a living deity, and, moreover, [regards] the Japanese as superior to all other races of people, hence destined to rule the world.[20]

Thus, in the act of denial, Hirohito acknowledged the pre-1945 Japanese dogma of racial superiority and manifest destiny.[21]

For many, if not all, pre-Pearl Harbor Japanese, it was obvious that a supreme power looked favorably upon the Land of the Rising Sun. This higher power most certainly had great plans for the unique Japanese people by sparing them for so many centuries from both physical and intellectual invasions. Now, in the fourth and fifth decades of the twentieth century, Japanese science in general, and BW specifically, would enable the nation to achieve its role as a world leader. As the 1934 *New Japan Medicine Report* (number 607) succinctly stated:

The Ninth General Japan Medical Conference is a big event on this small archipelago in the Far East. Japan's medicine is now independent from the medical community of the world. We have already kicked off the League of Nations[;] it is the feeling of the people that in the field of science, others will look up to Japan.[22]

Fanatical Japanese racist militarists, and Ishii and several other leading BW scientists posted in Manchuria should be counted among them, knew that Germany under Hitler's leadership eventually would find its *Lebensraum* in territorial aggrandizement in Central and Eastern Europe. Japan, too, would realize its predetermined fate in triumph, but victory would come in China and in Soviet Asia. Nippon's superiority in race and culture would enable this extraordinary community to overcome any obstacle in its triumphant march forward, including the obvious one that the Chinese and the Soviets enjoyed an enormous advantage in population numbers and in natural resources.

The future for the subject peoples was unimportant to those who believed in Japanese racism. The inhabitants of conquered territories were, they assumed, innately inferior to the invaders. Their role was to serve the needs of the master race. As such, they could be exploited ruthlessly to facilitate the goals and aspirations of the Land of the Rising Sun.

Ishii and his subordinates followed these doctrines. Given their perspective, they engaged freely and enthusiastically in BW human experiments because they knew their victims were inferior beings who were being sacrificed for a higher cause. The superior Japanese race would benefit immeasurably from the sacrifices of people who were, in general, of little value to mankind. The world would be a better place in which to live, they reasoned, without so many of the subhumans wasting the planet's limited resources. It does not require the training of an anthropologist to recognize the similarity of these views with those held by the descendants of the Spanish toward the Indians of Central and South America, by Europeans and North Americans to peoples of color throughout the world, by Nazi Germany and Fascist Italy in the 1930s and 1940s, and by some whites in contemporary South Africa.[23]

II

From the conference room, Ishii could look out one of several windows to view an incredible panoramic scene unfolding below. Hundreds of workers milled about carrying lumber and other materials. Large numbers of other workers were erecting brick buildings of different sizes and for specialized purposes. A few laborers, who were being punished for some infraction, could be seen pummeling each other under the supervision of guards with such colorful names as "Big Red Face" and "Talkative Hunchback."[24]

Ishii at times could be an indulgent and caring commander. He wanted his men to be happy and comfortable, and, to achieve that laudable objective, he spent with a lavish hand. No matter that he gave a Japanese construction company a monopoly to build the Ping Fan death factory, and that he authorized the Tokyo firm of Nihon Tokushu-Kogyo Co. Ltd. to supply "every necessary equipment to the Unit,"[25] receiving a handsome kickback for every inflated invoice he authorized. His men were given as many of the comforts of home that the bleak Manchurian landscape would permit.

To make Ping Fan bearable for Japanese scientists, workers, and armed guards, Ishii thoughtfully included in his model death site a city within a city of twenty-two state-of-the-art dormitory buildings for Japanese residents, a 1000-seat auditorium complete with a library and bar, swimming pools, gardens, small bars and restaurants, bathrooms, warehouses to store fish and vegetables, athletic fields, and a brothel to service Japanese personnel. Four bungalows equipped with the latest medical instruments and medicines cared for their medical needs. A large Shinto temple looked after the spiritual requirements of the staff and their family members. And a combined primary and secondary school provided a traditional Japanese education to the children of civilian employees and soldiers.[26]

Of the 150 or so buildings constructed at Ping Fan, none was more important for Ishii's plan than buildings numbers 7 and 8. Known also as the

"Ro" and "Ha" buildings, these two structures were prisons housing the human subjects who were to be the victims of BW experiments. The prison compound was the most heavily guarded part of this most elaborately defended base. No Chinese were permitted to come near the buildings. Even Japanese staff were denied admittance unless they were assigned duty in the Ha and Ro buildings. To make doubly certain that the prison's secrecy remained inviolate, Ishii appointed his brother Mitsuo as prison warden, combining nepotism with security.[27]

The two-story buildings were distinguished by their white-colored exterior and the bristling gun emplacements that surrounded the structures. Each building was approximately 35 to 40 meters long and 20 meters wide. Building number 7 housed male inmates, while building number 8 held members of both sexes.[28] The two structures were constructed with such thick concrete, bricks, steel, and mortar, that at the end of the war the Japanese were unable to destroy 7 and 8 by conventional methods. Dynamite proved ineffective. Desperate to keep the prison's existence secret, even at this late date, Ishii would not entrust the task of demolishing the prison to his engineers. Ultimately, he turned to the most dedicated 731 loyalists, who filled several trucks with 50-kilogram bombs and rammed the buildings, setting off a giant blast which reduced them to rubble.[29]

Victims arrived at buildings 7 and 8 by way of a secret tunnel that led from the administration building to the prison. Other tunnels honeycombed the administration building and the prison, the latter leading to the experimental laboratories and to the crematorium where "sacrificed" casualties were destroyed. Each of the numerous tunnels was roughly 18 meters wide and 3 meters tall. Buildings 7 and 8 were designed to hold up to 400 prisoners, but most authorities believe the prison housed on average about 200 inmates at any one time.

The huge administration building was built in the form of a square, and was known by the local Chinese as "the Square Building." Actually, the Square Building was four interconnected structures, forming one rectangle. The north and south sides of the square were each 170 meters long and approximately 20 meters wide. The east and west buildings were each 100 meters long and 20 meters wide. The buildings on the north and south sides were five-story structures, while the east and west buildings were three stories each. North and south buildings were known respectively as buildings numbers 5 and 3; each building contained a mechanical elevator to haul equipment and personnel to the upper floors. The prisons, buildings 7 and 8, were built within the rectangle, and were thus hidden from outside observation.[30]

Victims came to Ping Fan from a processing location in nearby Harbin. The 20 or so kilometer journey was conducted by one of two methods. Some prisoners were crammed into freight cars which were camouflaged with a layer of wooden logs on top, and then in dead of night were shipped to Ping Fan over the railroad spur that linked the two communities. Others were transported by special vehicles that were under the jurisdiction of the

Kempeitai in Harbin. These were old grayish-green paneled Dodge trucks whose windows were covered with paint to make them opaque. Several air vents to permit breathing were located beneath the truck.[31]

Yue Zhen Fu, a former laborer at Ping Fan, remembers that soldiers drove to the Japanese Consulate in Harbin every other day, and returned usually with eight or more Chinese prisoners for experimentation. Special vehicles brought victims to the camp from other Harbin holding depots on Saturday afternoons. Fang Zhen Yu, still another former Ping Fan worker, remembered quite clearly the day in November 1943 when a "special train" rolled into the camp. Risking his life, Fang peeked out from a small window to see an incredible sight below him. Several Japanese technicians, their white coats flapping in the ever-present Manchurian breeze, ran from the great square building hauling flatbed carts to the train. Tenderly, large objects wrapped in straw were passed from the train to the Ping Fan technicians. They handled the parcels with the care that museum specialists devoted to transporting priceless artifacts from ancient cultures. Instead of marble statues, Fang was shocked to see that two live humans were inside each bag. The bags were so tightly bound that the prisoners head and feet touched each other.[32]

To alleviate local inhabitants' curiosity and fears, Japanese officials informed Ping Fan Chinese residents that the area was being developed as a lumber mill. Therefore, they should not concern themselves with all the construction taking place. Nor should they worry about the late-night roar of train engines chugging into the restricted zone. The Dodge trucks that routinely stormed into the Ping Fan parking lot were none of the locals' concern. They were cautioned by Japanese guards to avoid any sign of interest in the "special transport" vehicles, as they were called, and were told not to be within viewing distance of the trucks when they heard the blare of police sirens. Any disobedience to these instructions would lead to severe punishment.[33]

The *maruta*s ("logs") for the Ping Fan "lumber mill" were, in large part, recruited in Harbin. They were principally Han Chinese, but stateless White Russians (including longtime resident Harbin Jews), Soviet prisoners captured in 1939 and 1940 border skirmishes, Mongolians, Koreans, Europeans of various nationalities accused of an assortment of crimes, including spying, and the mentally handicapped were entrusted to Unit 731's custody. Former Major Iijima Yoshio recalled in 1949 that he was personally responsible for sending "about 40 Soviet citizens . . . to certain death [at Ping Fan]; they all died under the experiments."[34]

All *maruta*s were charged with capital crimes, convicted within a short time after being accused, sentenced to death, and sent to Ping Fan where they were to be used as "experimental material" in fulfillment of their sentence. The Japanese frequently did not bother to engage in the charade of a trial, and sent unfortunates directly to Ping Fan for extermination. In 1939, for example, Major General Shirokura, Chief of the Kwantung Army Kempeitai, issued

Order 224 which sent thirty prisoners on "special consignment" to the death factory.[35]

On occasion, when Ishii required immediate delivery of human specimens, the police would meet their assigned quota by arresting ordinary persons walking the streets of Harbin, then sending them by "special transport" to Unit 731's headquarters. Their license was so broad that it included persons whose "Character of crime gives grounds for assuming that if legal proceedings are taken the person will be acquitted or sentenced to a short prison term and will soon leave prison." Such persons included "vagrant[s]," with "no permanent residence, no relatives," or "Opium smokers." In times of extreme shortage, the police could send to Ishii people who, "not withstanding the minor character of the crime, their release is undesirable."[36]

Former Colonel Machibana Takeo, a top officer in the Kwantung Army Kempeitai, recalled in December 1949 that "Special consignment" persons fell into one of several categories: "persons accused of espionage . . . or suspected of being implicated in foreign espionage . . . so-called hunghutzu, that is, Chinese partisans; then came the category of anti-Japanese elements, [and, finally,] incorrigible criminal elements." While police chief in a small Manchurian town in 1940, Tachibana admitted that he sent "no less than six people" as "special consignments" to Ishii. They "never returned . . . and perished . . . as a result of experiments." Later, in 1943, serving in Kwantung Army Kempeitai headquarters in Changchun, Colonel Tachibana authorized the dispatch of "over a hundred people" to the Ping Fan death factory.[37] There were many other Kempei officers in Manchuria who followed a pattern of conduct similar to Colonel Tachibana.

"Experimental material" candidates were held for preliminary processing in and around Harbin at several different sites. Those suspected of being Chinese communist guerrillas or spies were confined in the basement of the ornate building housing the Japanese Consulate. The Consulate building basement was used as a prison and torture chamber by the secret police, who extracted "confessions" from those detained, then sent them on to their doom. Others were held in the Japanese Scientific Research Institute located in the city's outskirts, before being sent on to Unit 731.[38] And still others were held in Harbin's municipal jail until they were needed for experiments. A magnificent Russian-built mansion located in the heart of the Russian Concession also held special prisoners; here captives were tortured by the Kempeitai, in the splendidly ornate basement, and then transported to Ping Fan or a subsidiary BW laboratory.[39]

The Japanese maintained meticulous, detailed files of the prisoners sent to Ping Fan. A few of the records survived the 1945 destruction carried out by retreating troops, and offer revealing insights into the manner in which Ishii received his human specimens. For example, one folder contains the following data: "*Time*: June 1939; *Commander*: the team leader of the Military Police in Xin Shi Street, Harbin, *Content*: 25 communists seized near Xiang Fang, Harbin, all arrested; *Result*: killed by Ishii Unit with poison injections."

Another folder noted that in a one year period, from August 1942 until the following August, one Harbin police station transferred eighteen "anti-Japanese communists" to Ping Fan, while another jail in the city freed itself of six "communist ideologues," by sending them to the Ishii Unit.[40]

"Logs" were bound hands and feet with shackles throughout the ride to Ping Fan. Once there, they were processed in the administrative building before being sent to either building 7 or 8. The *maruta*, upon entering Ping Fan, were denied their last bit of humanity. They were permitted to keep a few personal possessions, but much of their drab, anonymous clothing was confiscated, and would be used later to disguise Japanese spies when they went into the field. Neither the prisoners' names nor their hometowns were re-corded by the camp's clerks. Instead, each prisoner was assigned a three- or four-digit number,[41] and was known thereafter by that number. The numbers started at 101 and ended at 1500. These figures corresponded to the data recorded on x-ray plates taken of each individual *maruta*.[42] Once the count reached 1500, the next victim would then be given the designation 101, the numbers being repeated until they again reached 1500 as new *maruta*s arrived to be BW replacements.[43]

The numerical system used by Ishii made it impossible for investigators to determine the exact number of "logs" killed by BW experiments throughout Ping Fan's existence. The figure commonly accepted by authorities is 3000 persons exterminated at Ping Fan. However, this estimate is extremely low.[44]

Those selected for BW experiments were provided with excellent care during their short stay at 731 headquarters. The wounds inflicted by the Kempei torturers on the *maruta* were attended with great solicitude by Ishii's doctors. The scientists wanted the candidates to be in good health once the BW investigations commenced. Food provided was far better than an or-dinary citizen in the Home Islands could afford to purchase for his family. The *maruta* were given the same rations as were served the prison guards, sometimes even more than the guards. In fact, Ishii and his colleagues were always on guard against the danger that their prisoners would become obese or develop diabetes, heart trouble, or some other dietary-caused ailment. "Logs", shackled with leg chains and moving under the observant eyes of Ishii's ever-vigilant Chiyoda Mura guards, were given daily periods of exercise in the prison courtyard to ward off the danger of obesity.[45]

Ishii's transient guests were treated with the loving attention that Kobe cattle raisers lavished on their herds in order to develop the tender beef for which they were justly famous. In the spring of 1945, when Japanese resistance was crumbling, and the general population was reduced to eating a combination of grass and bran, an Ishii technician recalled, with some obvious exaggeration, that the *maruta* were served

> all meals through the day . . . on a silver platter. Only at noon was there a small amount of soy bean mixed in . . . full consideration was given to the nutrient value of supplements, and pork was served in a different menu almost every day.[46]

III

Akiyama Hiroshi (a pseudonym) was a seventeen-year-old draftee in 1945 who was posted to Ping Fan in the closing days of the war. In 1956 he published a memoir (*Special Unit 731*) recalling his short service in Ping Fan. With evident rapture, he noted:

> When I set foot on this land which was drenched in the sunlight of spring, I felt as one who had just awakened from a dream and was gazing upon the dazzling light of the grand scenery that lay before my eyes. That brilliance was not due to the sun. It was the sight of rows of modern buildings looming unexpectedly in the middle of a vast plain.
>
> Firstly, the central buildings towering skyward over other buildings in the area, with all square-tiled facades, were larger than any of those I had observed on my trip over, including Osaka, Hsingkiang [Changchun], and Harbin. These buildings reflecting the sunlight glistened in brilliant white and broke into the vast sky. High earth walls were constructed with barbed wire fencing atop. It was obvious that this compound was isolated strictly from the outside world.[47]

Whether the callow Akiyama's bucolic portrait of Ping Fan is accurate is debatable. The compound was not a Japanese version of Camelot, nor was Ishii Shiro King Arthur. What is not in question is that the facility was enormous, and bustled with BW research activity involving human subjects from the moment the first buildings became available for work. Experimentation expanded as the complex grew. The BW death factory went on to achieve its peak of development with the onset of World War II, and operated at full or near capacity until the war's conclusion.

Ishii's unit was formed in 1936 with a complement of men estimated to number roughly 300. By 1940, when the facility was finally completed,[48] approximately 3000 personnel – a tenfold increase – were stationed in Ping Fan. This figure was to remain relatively constant until the final year or so of the war, when casualties on the fighting front led to a reduction in all support units' strength. The five known satellite units[49] (there may have been others) were thought to have a complement of 300 men each, so that the total number of people under Ishii's direct command at one time may have exceeded 5000. The number of doctors and scientists involved was perhaps 10 percent of the total, somewhere between 300 and 500 men.[50] Technical support staff probably amounted to another 15 percent of Ishii's force, or at least 600–800 persons.[51]

From start to finish, Ping Fan was Ishii's nearly all-consuming project. As such, he threw himself into the task of building the complex, and energizing his subordinates to utilize the facilities to their fullest extent. In the nine years that Ping Fan operated, Ishii, while in command, demonstrated fully his vaunted skills as an organizer and administrator. He did try, as best as he could, to make the Ping Fan project the single purpose goal of his career. Shortly after he took command of his unit in 1936, the *Army Surgeon School Magazine* reported that, "Relieved from duty position: Member, Army Surgeon School,

Army Surgeon Lt. Colonel Ishii Shiro."[52] Now, Ishii resolved, he would devote almost his full time to Ping Fan.

But, Ishii being Ishii, his flair for showmanship could not be completely contained, and, on 7 November 1936, in Tokyo, he put on a dazzling demonstration for his fellow medical officers. It was the fiftieth anniversary of the founding of the Army's Medical School, a day for many celebrations. Ishii convinced the school's officials that a demonstration of the feasibility of air drops of medical supplies would be an appropriate way to commemorate the occasion. He and his close collaborator, Masuda Tomosada, took off from Tokorozawa Airfield in an 88-type observation plane, and circled the Medical School.

They made four medical air cargo drops before the delighted observers. Ishii later pridefully wrote:

> The first drop resulted in a complete deployment of the parachute and a successful landing of the cargo; the second drop resulted in a separation of the drop container from the parachute following the cargo drop because of damage to the rope from insects. . . . The fourth drop also resulted in a complete deployment of the parachute and a successful landing.

He assured himself of a warm reception and hearty congratulations from the important dignitaries on the scene by including in the first drop a huge bottle estimated to contain 1400 grams of whiskey. Attached to the whiskey bottle was a note that said, "Presented to all my assigned officers attending the banquet, from his honor the Bureau Chief [Unit Commander] – a toast."[53]

In Manchuria, Ishii combined a flamboyant private life with a somewhat more circumspect professional presence – although he sometimes found difficulty in curbing his extravagant behavior in either role. His Harbin residence was a sequestered Russian mansion. Here he, his wife, and seven children lived in such splendor that daughter Harumi recalled nostalgically nearly forty years later, "It was a graceful mansion indeed, like something out of a romantic movie such as 'Gone With The Wind.' "[54] He commuted to Ping Fan in a magnificent armor-plated chauffeur-driven limousine.[55] Within the compound, he, as commander, stayed in a specially designed suite fitted with all the luxuries the era could provide. At times, his family accompanied him to his headquarters and, unaware of what was taking place nearby, lived with him in the suite.

Between bouts of exhibitionism, embezzlement, and unrestrained drinking and geisha house crawling, Ishii managed to assemble an outstanding team of medical specialists and scientists. Naito Ryoichi, who, in the postwar era, founded the enormously successful ethical drug company known as the Green Cross Company, recalled in 1947:

> Most microbiologists in Japan were connected in some way or another with Ishii's work. He mobilized most of the Universities in Japan to help in research for his unit. In addition to the Tokyo Army Medical College, there

were the Kyoto Imperial University, Tokyo Imperial University, Infectious Disease Research Laboratory, Tokyo, etc.[56]

Many of the men who served Ishii in Manchuria and China later became deans of medical schools, senior science professors, university presidents, and key technicians in those industries that created the country's economic miracle in the postwar era.[57] He also created an infrastructure within the death factory in Harbin's suburb that held together throughout the period of Japanese BW research. He was able, also, to inspire his men with fanatical loyalty to him personally, and to extraordinary dedication to the tasks he assigned them.

In Dante's *Divine Comedy*, the poet divided hell into nine circles. In Ping Fan, Ishii divided his hell into eight subdivisions. Four were given numerical designations. The remaining four, for unknown reasons, were listed without a number. Perhaps the lack of a specific numerical identification was a deliberate effort by Ishii and his confederates to conceal from possible outside auditors some of the work being done at Ping Fan. Or, a possibly less Machiavellian explanation may be that Ishii simply did not think to give or care to give the final four sections of his enterprise a number.

Section I was the facility's research section. Scientists working in this area engaged in research and production of pathogens thought useful for BW. Researchers here worked with every pathogen that conceivably could be employed to destroy potential enemies. They included, but were not limited to, the causative organisms of plague, cholera, typhoid and paratyphoid fevers, dysentery, anthrax, glanders, tetanus, and gas gangrene, "as well as filterable viruses and rickettsiae."[58] These scientists studied tuberculosis and problems relating to frostbite, as well.

This section was favored with equipment that any world-class laboratory would envy. Its principal apparatuses were four boilers, "each of one-ton capacity, for the preparation of the culture medium for the bacteria, and 14 autoclaves [bacteriological pressure cookers] for sterilizing the medium."[59] Each of the autoclaves could hold thirty cultivators that were designed by Ishii. In addition, there were two cooling chambers which held up to 100 cultivators at a time. The size of these units, if the figures are correct (the figures were offered in 1949), must have been enormous. Once peak capacity was reached, the so-called "Ishii cultivators" could produce in the course of one production cycle an estimated "30,000,000 billion microbes," or 30 kilograms of cell mass. If necessary, 40,000,000 billion pathogenic bacteria could be extracted from the cultivators.

This astonishing number of pathogens were pumped out over the short time span of three or four days, and virtually on a non-stop schedule.[60] Pathogen production was so great that the Commander-in-Chief of the Kwantung Army, General Yamada Otozoo, upon an inspection tour of 731 in August 1944, expressed amazement "at the scale on which the work was proceeding." He was so impressed with the facility and its BW potential, that "after inspecting this work, I approved of it and thereby sanctioned its continuation."[61]

Section I was also responsible for the management of buildings 7 and 8, the camp's dreaded *maruta* prison.

Section II was Ping Fan's experimental section. Here scientists and technicians developed and tested the feasibility of various types of BW bombs. They also conducted and managed outdoor experiments at the Anda airfield, some 146 kilometers north of Ping Fan. This section maintained Unit 731's fleet of airplanes. It also was responsible for the breeding of fleas. To produce the fleas, Section II was assigned two boilers of 2 ton capacity each, eight autoclaves (each autoclave contained sixty cultivators), and a distinctively designed refrigerator that could safeguard the finished "product."

In 1949, Major General Kawashima Kiyoshi boasted that when Sections I and II operated at full capacity, they could "manufacture as much as 300 kilograms of plague bacteria monthly." The production divisions could also produce "500–600 kilograms of anthrax germs, or 800–900 kilograms of typhoid, paratyphoid or dysentery germs, or as much as 1000 kilograms of cholera germs." He conceded that "such quantities of bacteria were not actually produced every month," but the division produced bacteria in the quantities needed for the detachment's current work.

Major Karasawa Tomio, a 731 physician, seconded Kawashima's claim, and confirmed that, "The monthly output of the germ-producing division could be raised . . . to about 300 kilograms of plague bacteria."[62] It should be noted also that Unit 731 scientists worked on several dozen different diseases simultaneously. Consequently, the total monthly production of pathogens at the Ping Fan facility alone probably was many times the figure cited by Kawashima and Karasawa.

Section III was known as the Epidemic Prevention Water Supply Unit. Part of its work was to engage in legitimate hospital management and water purification operations. However, from 1944 until the end of the war, the Third Section was assigned the task of manufacturing containers for BW bombs. This latter operation was carried out in a factory located in the heart of Harbin's industrial center.

Section IV was the Manufacturing and Fabricating Division for the unit. Its personnel managed and operated all the facilities dedicated to mass-breeding of an assortment of pathogens. The section was also responsible for storage and maintenance of the enormous quantities of germs that Unit 731 produced at any given time.

The Education Section (V) trained 731's newly assigned personnel. This was an important responsibility since personnel, with certain exceptions, were rotated from the Home Islands to Ping Fan and satellite laboratories on a routine basis. Medical school students as young as fifteen and sixteen years old were trained here. Ishii frequently addressed the students once they completed their course, exhorting them to persevere in the face of all adversity. Typically, in 1941, he cautioned 300 graduates to

pay particular attention to your health when you go to your assignment. Medical corpsmen must not become sick themselves, no matter what. Even more, in the midst of epidemic disease or in a hail of enemy fire, you must not die. You must live, you must survive for the sake of Japan; you must work through your difficulties for the future of Japan.[63]

Section V trained literally many hundreds, possibly thousands, of BW cadres during its existence.

The General Affairs Section (VI) managed the business accounts of the facility. The Materials Section (VII) manufactured BW bombs. It also prepared and stored materials, such as agar-agar, that were essential for the production of pathogens. And, finally, the Diagnosis and Treatment Section (VIII) handled ordinary medical problems that affected Unit 731 personnel. In essence, it was the medical dispensary for Ping Fan.

Ishii, seemingly, had thought of everything necessary for a world-class BW facility.[64]

6   Human experiments: "secret of secrets"[1]

On July 19, 1978, the former commander of military police in Andong County,
China, came to Ping Fan with the fifth Japanese delegation of "Returning to
CHINA Liaison" Committee. He confessed that in 1944 he permitted 20
Chinese to be sent to Ping Fan for bacteriological experiments. He said, "I
killed them. Thus, I have been feeling uneasy for more than 30 years. Now, I
have come to Ping Fan to apologize."
(Quoted in Han and Zhou, "Record of Actual Events of the Bacteriological
Factory in Ping Fan")

Still another confession: "I committed a crime against humanity. I admit that
testing the action of bacteriological weapons on living people by forcibly
injecting them with serious infectious diseases, as was practiced by the
detachment [Unit 731] with my participation, and also the wholesale slaughter
of the experimentees with lethal bacteria are barbarous and criminal."
(Testimony of Kawashima Kiyoshi, *Khabarovsk Trial*, p. 58)

I

Two things happened in 1938 that made Ishii Shiro feel satisfied with his
station in life. He was promoted to Colonel on 1 March,[2] presumably on the
basis of his earlier stunning success with BW research. Later that year, the
Ping Fan complex was finally operational. He was now in a position to
demonstrate to the Japanese military and medical establishments the
practicability of BW. The newly upgraded full Colonel anticipated that his
exploits at the world's finest BW installation would make Japan the pre-
eminent leader in BW, and enable the nation to achieve its rightful leadership
role in East Asia.

Over the next five years, Ishii would redouble his efforts to achieve the
militarists' goals, and at the same time advance his career. Spurred on by a
rapid series of promotions in the 1930s (he was upgraded almost routinely
every three years), Ishii's aspirations continued to soar. His activities in
Manchuria, in China, and in the Home Islands were frenetic and would have
sapped the combined physical strength of several ordinary persons. Instead,
the ambitious Colonel seemingly thrived on the various responsibilities he
brazenly assumed.

He directed the Boeki Kyusuibu (Anti-Epidemic Water Supply Unit) for
the Kwantung Army from 1936 until Japan's surrender. The Boeki Kyusuibu
ultimately expanded to include at least eighteen branches throughout
occupied China, and, later, units were established in Rangoon, Burma,
Singapore, and possibly Manila and the Dutch East Indies. Each section

consisted of a minimum of 120 and a maximum of 500 men, and was led by an officer of the rank of major or lieutenant colonel. The units ostensibly were employed in anti-epidemic work, but they secretly engaged in BW research under Ishii's or one of his subordinates' direction.[3]

Ishii retained his position at the Tokyo Army Medical College throughout his tenure in Manchuria. He would normally spend nine months of the year with the Kwantung Army in Harbin/Ping Fan, and the other three months lecturing, recruiting personnel for BW work, and doing BW research in Japan. His Epidemic Prevention Research Laboratory, established with the help of Dean Koizumi, at the Army Medical College remained a key component in his vast BW enterprise. The Army doctor routinely lectured to young micro-biologists and other potential technical recruits at the several Army medical colleges throughout the country, as well as at Tokyo Imperial University, Kyoto Imperial University, and other prestigious universities and scientific institutes. In his lectures, he frequently employed charts, slides, still photo-graphs, as well as 8 mm motion picture films that illustrated graphically his BW research. The films included, as a special recruiting enticement, close-up views of BW work with human subjects.

An experienced pilot, Ishii handled the controls of several planes placed at his disposal in Ping Fan by the Kwantung Army. He piloted his personal plane to the various Water Purification Units periodically for on-site inspections, and for pep-talk performances to maintain troop morale. The Ishii Unit commander flew missions during BW field tests in China in 1940, 1941, and 1942. He also commuted regularly in one of his planes to his test site at Anda, 146 kilometers north of Harbin. He used a light aircraft for the short flight to Anda if the only passengers were his aides and himself. However, he employed larger planes when the cargo included human subjects to be tested for BW purposes.

Most of the men who served under Ishii adored their commander because of his exuberant personality, daring, and devil-may-care attitude, his obvious intelligence, and his intense patriotism. Ishii's personal weaknesses – the heavy drinking, flagrant womanizing, and manifest embezzlements from the appro-priations earmarked for his unit – were either accepted with resignation or applauded by his loyal followers. His bizarre working habits – Ishii, after a night on the town in Harbin, often called meetings at two or three o'clock in the morning to plan new experiments or a new operation in the field – were condoned by his men as an eccentricity of an extraordinary man.[4]

He continued to have his detractors, such as the Army's Surgeon General. When interviewed in September 1945, Army Surgeon General Lt. General Kambayashi Hiroshi refused to close ranks with his fellow officers. Instead, he castigated Ishii for operating virtually as an independent loose cannon in Manchuria, and for being "an ambitious boaster." Kambayashi was so vigorous in his denunciation that his innocent interrogator was moved to remark in some wonder, "General Ishii is disliked by medical authorities in the homeland.'[5] His opponents remained, however, a minority within the medical and military establishments.

II

The War Ministry, and leading medical specialists such as Dean Koizumi, continued to provide Ishii with all the men and material he demanded, because, seemingly, he achieved concrete results from his research. What set Ishii's investigations apart from most other researches was his heavy reliance upon human subjects for BW analysis. His worth to the military in Tokyo, and later on to both American and Soviet BW scientists, lay in his real and alleged findings from human BW tests. As one authority perceptively noted, Ishii was of little value or interest to any military organization except for his work with human test subjects.[6]

Ishii and Kitano Masaji (Ishii's successor from early 1942 until spring 1945) adopted the shotgun approach to studying potentially useful BW pathogens. They worked with human subjects on diseases that ranged from anthrax to yellow fever. They researched human reactions to plague, typhoid, paratyphoid A and B, typhus, smallpox, tularemia, infectious jaundice, gas gangrene, tetanus, cholera, dysentery, glanders, scarlet fever, undulant fever, tick encephalitis, "songo" or epidemic hemorrhagic fever, whooping cough, diphtheria, pneumonia, brysipelas, epidemic cerebrospinal meningitis, venereal diseases, tuberculosis, salmonella, frostbite, and countless other diseases that were endemic to the communities and surrounding regions that fell within the responsibility of a Unit 731 branch Water Purification Unit.[7] No one has been able to catalogue completely all the maladies that the various death factories in Manchuria visited on human guinea pigs.

Testing pathogens on humans was only a single chapter, albeit a major one, in Ishii's BW enterprise. Other secret research carried out by Ishii and his associates "had the twofold purpose of determining 1) Methods of culture of biological warfare agents; 2) Methods of dissemination."[8] Under the rubric "Defensive Research," unit technicians produced vaccines for eighteen diseases. For "Offensive Research," scientists worked on at least twelve different organisms, including those that cause plague, glanders, anthrax, and typhus.

Those Americans who interrogated Unit 731 personnel in 1946 and 1947 were awed by the "magnitude" of Ishii's venture. At least 20 million doses of vaccine were prepared each year Ping Fan operated. Untold millions more were produced at 731 branches in Dairen, Hailar, Linkow, and Sunyu. Fifty thousand hens and roosters were used at Ping Fan alone to produce fertilized eggs annually just for the preparation of one type of typhus vaccine, R. P. vaccine (*Rickettsia prowazekii*). At least a similar number of rats[9] were required for R. M. vaccine (*Rickettsia mooseri*). Both vaccines were produced in liquid and dry forms.

Ishii crowed that he himself designed the Unit 731 cultivators. He used a duraluminum oven of approximately 14 × 9.85 × 21 inches that weighed

24¼ lb. Individual ovens contained fifteen bacteria-growing trays, while each oven held 6.78 quarts of agar medium to produce the required bacterium. Workers harvested the pathogens by taking scrapings at prescribed intervals. Enteric organisms were produced at 24-hour intervals. Plague, anthrax, and glanders pathogens were cultivated in 48-hour periods. Anaerobes required much more maturation time, and could be gleaned only on a weekly basis. A bacteria-laden artillery shell required 900 bacteria oven cultivators to produce a sufficient quantity of bacteria.[10] Consequently, the bacteria ovens operated 24 hours each day, 365 days each year, from 1939 until the end of the war, in order to keep up with Ishii's and Kitano's insatiable demands for pathogens.[11]

Under the guidance of Ishii, and later Kitano, Ping Fan experts experimented with four different classes of delivery systems:

1. They investigated two different types of artillery shells – a conventional gas shell and a 75 millimeters high-explosive shell with "the bacterial suspension replacing a portion of the bursting charge." Both shells proved to be impractical and were abandoned as biological warfare weapons.

2. Researchers at Ping Fan and at Anda worked with two groups of bombs. A single-purpose high-altitude bomb was designed solely for anthrax spores. Designated the HA bomb, it was a thin-walled steel detonation type, that contained "1500 cylindrical particles immersed in 500 cc of anthrax emulsion." Other steel-walled bombs, designated as either all-purpose Ujis or Uji type-50, were used in extensive tests at the Ping Fan and Anda airfields. Over the span of five or six years, more than 2000 Uji type-50 bombs were detonated in field tests involving humans. Another 4000 Uji type-50 bombs were exploded either in drop tests from airplanes flying at different heights above ground, or in static explosions.[12]

The tests demonstrated that steel-walled bombs were impractical: few pathogens survived the heat-generated explosions on impact. Ishii then turned to ceramics as a substitute for steel. He developed an all-purpose Uji bomb with a porcelain cylinder 27.5 inches long and 7 inches in diameter with a 10.5 quart fluid capacity. Initial tests were totally unsatisfactory. Eventually, he modified the bomb by outfitting the cylinder with celluloid fins to guide its descent, but trajectory remained faulty since the fins never worked properly.[13]

Ishii and his associates also developed the RO bomb, a high-altitude bomb that held two quarts of bacteria-rich fluid. The RO bomb never performed as its architects anticipated, and was abandoned after several fruitless tests. Finally, the scientists designed and built one prototype bomb named the "Mother and Daughters." The Mother bomb was equipped with a radio transmission device conceived to detonate a cluster of Daughter bombs which held the bacteria payload. One of the persons involved in the bombs construction reported that, "The Mother bomb was dropped first, followed by the Daughters. The Daughter bombs were designed to explode when the Mother bomb struck the ground due to the cessation of the radio signal." However, Mother and Daughter bombs were too expensive to construct, and, despite intensive efforts, they could not be developed into a practical weapon.[14]

Researchers engaged in extensive testing of the different forms of bombs over a two-year period, 1941 and 1942.[15] The assorted Uji bombs and the Mother and Daughter bomb were designed primarily to contaminate large areas of land. Analysts noted that "the infliction of infected wounds was secondary." The prototype anthrax bomb, the so-called HA bomb, was planned specifically to cause anthrax-infected wounds. Moreover, it should be noted that once anthrax spores penetrated the ground, their deadly effect would contaminate an area indefinitely and would constitute a near-permanent source of infection.[16]

Interviews conducted by American intelligence personnel with Unit 731 officers in the immediate postwar period (September 1945 to August 1947) suggested that only animals were exposed to the effects of the bacterial bombs during the trials. But other evidence demonstrates conclusively that humans were tested as well. It is known that over 100 horses and 500 sheep were inflicted with anthrax-infected wounds, and a considerable area of ground was contaminated with the stimulant *B. prodigious* during the testing period. A conservative estimate would give human casualties of at least several hundred just in Ping Fan and Anda anthrax and *B. prodigious* tests. Field testing un-doubtedly increased the toll by thousands.

3. Field tests were conducted for the purpose of spreading bacteria over a large area by creating bacterial clouds. Static bombs and conventional bombs loaded with the dye rhodamine and a 2 to 5 percent dextran broth were dropped on a target area and measurements were taken. Studies were made also of the direct dispersion of mists and dusts laced with germs. These aerosol tests employed distinctive equipment Ishii claimed to have designed. Planes were outfitted with specially designed spray nozzles as well as canisters filled with bacteria. Once over the target, the bacteria would be disseminated in a fine mist over a large area. In effect, Unit 731 technicians were engaged in crop dusting, but with pathogens that killed plants, animals, and humans.

Test drops of bacteria bombs were made from altitudes of 4000, 2000, 1000, and 200 meters. To no one's surprise, it was determined that low-altitude drops achieved the best results. Bacterial aerosol spraying was deemed a promising development, but much additional research was required before it could be considered a practical BW weapon. Unit 731 researchers did not perfect a spray device for field use by the end of the war. It was one of many Ishii-inspired BW developments that intrigued postwar American and Soviet investigators.

4. Specially trained volunteers were used as saboteurs to spread BW materials among Chinese enemy forces, among potential enemies such as Soviet military units in border regions, and among the civilian populations. These volunteers were used extensively in 1939 in the so-called Nomonhan Incident, as well as in the field tests in Central China from 1940 to 1942. They caused significant loss of life in Manchuria among the local population during the course of their sabotage training exercises.

III

Human experimentation followed three separate tracks. The most important of these were the laboratory experiments conducted at Ping Fan, at Anda, and at the other Ishii Unit branches in Manchuria and occupied China. A second path was open-air experiments on humans at Anda that were conducted to discover the effectiveness of the prototype delivery systems discussed above. And, finally, there were the field tests in which both civilian populations and military contingents were subject to pathogenic exposure.

Hundreds, if not thousands, of experiments were conducted on humans in the underground laboratories that were a characteristic of all the BW research installations constructed under Ishii's master plans. *Marutas* were dragged from their cells in buildings 7 and 8, or their smaller counterparts in the branch units, and led into the underground testing facilities. Here scientists injected victims with pathogens of differing dosages in order to determine the appropriate quantity of a specific germ to administer to individuals or to a general population. Tests were conducted on the "logs" with separate properties to learn whether certain foods, fabrics, tools, or utensils could be used as germ carriers. Human subjects were forced to eat different foods laced with specific germs. These included chocolates filled with anthrax, and cookies containing plague bacteria.[17] Other subjects were given various fluids (tea, coffee, milk, water, beer, spirits, etc.) to drink, with each liquid containing some specific dose of a pathogen.

Ishii found produce was a valuable conduit for spreading disease, and experimented with a number of viruses injected into different vegetables and fruits. Most of the fruit and vegetable studies were conducted at the Army Medical College in Tokyo under the direction of one of Ishii's brightest disciples, Naito Ryiochi.[18] Naito focused most of his research on "fugu toxin," which he obtained from the livers of blowfish. He reported success with developing a concentrate of toxin sufficient to kill mice, and he believed that he could secure excellent results for man if he were given enough time. However, the "degree of concentration" required to be effective with humans "was not obtained, and further efforts were interrupted by B-29 raids" over Tokyo in November 1944, and "ceased altogether with destruction, by fire, of the Army Medical College in April, 1945."[19]

Each laboratory at Ping Fan contained a large bulletin board that was displayed prominently on one wall. A technician recorded on the board every day data such as: "Specific date; 3 *maruta*, numbers so and so, were given injections of so and so, x cc; we need x number of hearts, or x number of livers, etc."[20] Laboratory technicians would then go to either building 7 or 8, order guards to provide the number of "logs" needed for the next experiment, and prepare the laboratory to receive victims. Some of the tests involved hanging "material" (humans) upside down, in order to determine the time necessary for a person to choke to death. Other experiments were conducted in which air was injected into the subjects to test the rate of onset of embolisms. Horse urine was injected into human kidneys in still other experiments. Mitomo

Kazuo later recalled one experiment conducted in late August 1944, in which he

> put as much as a gram of heroin into some porridge to an arrested Chinese citizen . . . about thirty minutes later he lost consciousness and remained in that state until he died 15–16 hours later. . . . On some prisoners I experimented 5–6 times, testing the action of Korean bindweed, heroin, bactal and castor-oil seeds. . . . I was also present when gendarmes shot three prisoners on whom I had performed experiments.[21]

Some of the tests conducted by "scientists" and "medical doctors" defy imagination today.

"Logs" generally lasted a few weeks before either they succumbed to the experiments, or they were "sacrificed" because they were no longer viable test material. A few somehow remained alive for four to six months, but no longer. There was always a ready supply of fresh replacements.[22] Pathologists inherited the dead *maruta* almost immediately after the conclusion of the test. They would wheel the dead into one of the autopsy rooms, and would go to work by making a large "y"-shaped incision on the "material," and then performing the normal autopsy. After all tests were completed, the pathologists directed orderlies and guards to dispose of the carcasses in one of the several nearby crematoria.

Experiments covered every conceivable approach to spreading disease, and to prevention. A typical laboratory experiment with cholera was conducted in May and June 1940. Twenty prisoners, all between the ages of twenty and thirty, and in good health, were selected for the test. Eight persons were given cholera vaccine injections produced with ultrasonic equipment. Eight others were injected with cholera vaccine manufactured by a conventional method. Four experimentees were not inoculated. Twenty days later, all the victims were forced to drink copious quantities of cholera-infected milk. The four who received no immunization contracted cholera and died. Several of those tested who received conventional cholera injections also became ill and died. The eight who were vaccinated with ultrasonic cholera vaccine showed no cholera symptoms. A similar test with plague vaccines produced comparable results. Ishii then ordered his Vaccine Squad, renamed the "A Team" in 1940, to work only with ultrasonically produced vaccines.[23]

Ishii, Kitano, and the other Unit 731 researchers did not trumpet their activities throughout the scientific world, but neither did they shrink from publicly sharing some of their findings. They just disguised the human experimentation aspect. Researchers published or read more than one hundred scientific papers, both during the heyday of Unit 731's operation as well as in the postwar period. When dealing with humans, the researchers referred to experiments with "monkeys," or "Manchurian monkeys;" animal experiments were labeled with the animals' proper subspecies, such as "long-tailed monkey," "Taiwan monkey," or "Formosan monkey."[24] In "Japanese medical society," their human experiments "were known; that is, [were] an open secret."[25]

Under a cloak of immunity from possible prosecution, the "open secret" became detailed fact in 1946 and 1947. By that time, Unit 731 scientists did not have to resort to deceptive animal terms in describing their work to American scientists eager to gain precious information concerning human BW experiments. Perhaps they were not totally candid with the Americans, but they did provide them with specific details of some of their previous work in the course of lengthy interviews, and in written reports to investigators. The data were allegedly reconstructed from memory, since all records in Manchuria were supposedly destroyed during the Japanese retreat in 1945. However, the documents themselves suggest strongly that many of 731's records survived.[26]

Dugway, Utah, is approximately 10,000 miles from Ping Fan. Yet, here in the barren, windswept desert of western Utah is a United States Army chemical and biological warfare base which houses some of the remnants of Japanese BW research.[27] Among the many facilities to be found at Dugway Proving Grounds, a restricted research center that stretches over 840,911 acres of Utah desert, is a technical library that receives all the latest scientific publications that relate to CW and BW research, as well as general publications.[28] It also stores materials that other research centers no longer want, but that may contain useful intelligence for investigators. Tucked away in an unmarked box in the technical library are more than twenty reports compiled by American scientists from their postwar interviews with Ishii, Kitano, and other surviving Unit 731 authorities. This box contains also three extraordinary autopsy reports that cover glanders, plague, and anthrax. The autopsy reports range in length from 350 pages to more than 800 pages. Each autopsy report contains hundreds of pastel-colored artist drawings of human organs in various states of disintegration. At one time, these reports were designated as Top Secret, but advances in BW research make the findings obsolete, if not arcane. They were declassified in 1978.

At least two dozen BW scientists were interviewed, and the topics ranged from aerosols to typhus. The purpose of the exchanges was to "obtain information necessary to clarify reports submitted by Japanese personnel on the subject of B. W. . . . To examine human pathological material. . . . To obtain protocols necessary for understanding the significance of the pathological material."[29] What follows is a representative selection of the data Unit 731 researchers provided:

Dr Futagi Hideo, in reporting on his experiments with tuberculosis, noted that in human tests with the Calmette bacillus (BCG) "All subjects recovered in this series," but in tests with Cl Tuberculosis Hominis, "all doses produced miliary tuberculosis which was fatal within 1 month in those injected with 10.0 and 1.0 mg. The others were severely ill, lived longer but probably died later." In another test, "death at 1 month occurred following a stormy course with fever immediately post-injection." Futagi experimented with Manchurian children and achieved positive tuberculin results. He received the "original stock" of tuberculum germs from a "natural case. Virulence was maintained by passage through guinea pigs."[30] Dr Futagi Hideo's experiments were particularly hideous because tuberculosis is not an effective BW strategy. Usually it is too slow to have a BW impact. It is reasonable to conclude, therefore, that these experiments were carried out for purely academic purposes at the expense of the lives of those subjects tested.

Dr Tabei Kanau worked on typhoid experiments from 1938 until he was transferred in 1943. During that five-year period he tested perhaps several hundred subjects with different strains and dosages of typhoid germs. Some strains were mixed with sucrose, while others were stirred into milk. In one experiment, "Deaths occurred in 2 cases and 3 committed suicide." In another

> One subject was exposed to a bomb burst containing buckshot mixed with 10 mg bacilli and 10 gm of clay. The buckshot had grooves which were impregnated with the bacteria-clay mixture. Bomb burst 1 meter from the rear of the subject. He developed symptoms of typhoid fever with positive laboratory signs. Laboratory infections occurred in 2 Japanese investigators who seemed to be much sicker than Manchurians although none died. It was the impression of Dr Tabei that Manchurians had more natural resistance than Japanese.[31]

Kitano dealt with many diseases, some of which were exotic, while others were of the common garden variety. His findings on songo fever, tick encephalitis, and typhus were especially welcomed by the Americans. They now could secure data on tick encephalitis that involved injecting mouse brain suspension in humans. One man, according to Kitano's protocol, "produced symptoms after an incubation of 7 days. Highest temperature was 39.8°C. This subject was sacrificed when fever was subsiding, about the 12th day." Another "received similar mouse brain emulsion i. n. in a dose of 1.0 cc. After an incubation period of 10 days the same symptoms appeared." The manifestations of the disease were grim:

> Fever is the first change. When the fever begins to subside, motor paralysis appears in the upper extremities, neck, face, eyelids and respiratory muscles. There are no significant sensor changes. No paralysis is observed in the tongue, muscles of deglutition or lower extremities. After recovery, paralysis may be permanent. . . . Kitano observed it longer than 6 months.[32]

Ishii, as usual, was the star. He was interviewed on his work with human subjects that related to botulism, brucellosis, gas gangrene, glanders, influenza, meningococcus, plague, smallpox, tetanus, and tularemia.[33] Some of his findings were detailed, and covered many typescript pages. Others were as brief as: "Tularemia, Experiments in M were conducted with 10 subjects who were injected s.c. All developed fever lasting as long as 6 months. None died or were sacrificed."[34]

At least thirty-five reports involving human experiments were submitted by the Japanese scientists interviewed,[35] detailing tests conducted upon 801 "logs" plus 30 suicides.[36] This was remarkable, since the interviews took place within slightly more than a one-month period, November–December, in late

1947. Material obtained in such a limited time frame was a fraction of the information Japanese BW researchers realized in China and Manchuria, but even this paltry amount delighted their American counterparts. The Japanese apologetically acknowledged that they maintained autopsy reports on slightly less than 1000 sacrificed persons. Moreover, they regretted that "adequate material" for only 403[37] cases was still available.[38] This, too, was a patent understatement of the true facts, but American scientists rejoiced at their good fortune.

After completing a brief mission to Japan in November 1947, Edwin V. Hill, M.D., Chief, Basic Sciences, Camp Detrick, Maryland, observed, "Evidence gathered in this investigation has greatly supplemented and amplified previous aspects of this field." The data gathered by enemy scientists was secured "at the expenditure of many millions of dollars and years of work. . . . Such information could not be obtained in our own laboratories because of scruples attached to human experimentation." However, thanks to the Japanese, Hill observed, the "data were secured with a total outlay of ¥250,000 to date, a mere pittance by comparison with the actual cost of the studies." Hill noted also that "the pathological material which has been collected constitutes the only material evidence of the nature of these experiments."[39]

The toll of sacrificed *maruta* was much greater than the figures provided to United States investigators. At the 1949 trial of Japanese prisoners in Khabarovsk, USSR, Major General Kawashima Kiyoshi, former head of Unit 731's First, Third, and Fourth Sections, testified that "I can say that the number of prisoners of Detachment 731 who died from the effects of experiments in infecting them with severe infectious diseases was no less than about 600 per annum."[40] Kawashima was stationed at Ping Fan from 1941 until the end of the war. Scholars, using Kawashima's figure of 600 deaths annually, concluded that 3000 people were killed in the BW experiments.[41]

Three thousand deaths is a gross underestimate of the actual number of men, women, and children slaughtered. It does not take into consideration those killed prior to 1941. Ishii, it must be remembered, began human experiments in Harbin in 1932. Hundreds, perhaps thousands, were destroyed during the Beiyinhe venture. Others were killed at Ping Fan from 1938 until Kawashima's arrival there in 1941. Still others were exterminated in the branch camps at Anda, Hailar, Linkow, Sunyu, and Dairen. Many more were murdered in Canton,[42] Peking (Beijing),[43] and, most probably, Shanghai and Singapore (Unit 9420).[44] At least 5000–6000 humans were annihilated in BW death factories not directly under Ishii's control (Mukden, Nanking, and Changchun)[45] during the Japanese rampage in China. Nor does the count include the tens of thousands massacred in August 1945 in order to prevent their falling into the hands of the advancing Soviet or Chinese troops.[46]

Finally, the tally does not account for the 1946, 1947, and 1948 toll of dead in and around Ping Fan. Plague epidemics erupted each autumn and spread throughout the community and to parts of Harbin proper. In 1947, a major plague epidemic broke out in the same area, but ultimately affected much of the northeast. More than 30,000 persons died from plague in 1947 before the epidemic ran its course. A third consecutive annual outbreak (but somewhat diminished in intensity from the previous year) occurred in 1948. In this last case only 6000 people were reported to have died from the disease. Yet, no one could recall a previous outbreak of plague in the region. Chinese doctors became convinced that the epidemics, which caused such a tremendous loss of life, was related directly to the fact that in 1945, during their evacuation, the Japanese released thousands of infected animals, permitting them to run loose among the general population.[47]

Japanese CW activities in Manchuria and in China proper also took a tremendous toll in lives. The Chinese government estimates that at least 2000 persons were killed from coming into direct contact with chemical weapons in the years after Japan's surrender. Tens of thousands of other citizens had their lives disrupted because they lived in such close proximity to toxic agents scattered in bunkers in their communities. These were weapons abandoned by, in the tactful phrase of the Chinese, "a foreign state." Most of these weapons were located in Manchuria, although others have been found in Hebei and Jiangsu provinces. No one knows how many thousands were killed from CW attacks during the Japanese occupation of Manchuria and Japanese incursions into China.

The Chinese figures for abandoned CW munitions and toxic agents in China in the postwar period are truly astonishing. Estimates are that there are currently (February 1992) "approximately 2 million pieces" of chemical weapons buried in China. The munitions are in a dangerous state of deterioration, with many of the weapons "badly rusted" and in an "eroded state." The Chinese destroyed or are in the process of destroying an additional "300,000 pieces." Moreover, Chinese experts destroyed "more than 20 tons" of toxic chemical agents, and have at least "approximately 100 tons" of additional toxic chemicals to eliminate.[48] The true number of BW and CW death factory casualties will never be known. But there can be no doubt that the numbers were far greater than is currently accepted.

IV

The city of Anda lies directly due north of Harbin, roughly two hours by train from Ping Fan. Today it is a fairly prosperous community of 200,000 inhabitants that sits astride the Daqing oilfield, China's largest known petroleum deposit. From 1939 until 1945 Anda achieved another sort of distinction. Then little more than an expanse of empty pastureland interspersed with a handful of villages, Anda was the remote site for Unit 731's proving ground. When a new procedure appeared promising in the Ping Fan laboratory, it was submitted to further tests at Anda. Invariably, humans were used throughout the testing procedure, either in underground laboratories similar to those at Ping Fan, or, more frequently, in above-ground open-air trials.

Nothing remains of the Anda facility. It was destroyed by the Kwantung Army along with the other BW branches in 1945. Unlike other BW branches, however, the Anda ruins were cannibalized by villagers for bricks, timber, equipment, and whatever could be salvaged. The area that once served Unit 731 ultimately was swallowed up into the city that mushroomed in growth after the discovery of oil in the district. No one can now locate the site of this once flourishing death factory.

Scores of tests were conducted with hundreds of human guinea pigs at Anda during the Ishii–Kitano reign. Although there is no exact count of the number of proving-ground casualties, the scope of the enterprise can be gauged from some data disclosed during the postwar Soviet investigation of Japanese BW activities. For example, in the course of the annual inspection of the Anda facility in 1945, a probationary officer in the Quartermaster Corps was asked by a civilian employee for permission to discard some worn blankets. This request offers an important clue for a tally of sacrificed humans, since each year obsolete or worn equipment was replaced with new supplies, if the inspector gave his approval. The probationary officer noticed that "Dried blood was visible on them. These blankets were extremely tattered." There were some eighty badly frayed and blood-encrusted blankets in the pile shown to the quartermaster. When asked to account for the ragged condition of the blankets, the civilian employee replied that they "were used to protect the bodies of experimentees while experiments were being performed on them."[49] It is reasonable to conclude, therefore, that more than eighty persons were killed at the Anda proving grounds yearly during the period it existed.

Anda dealt with the usual laundry list of pathogens. It appears, though, that special emphasis was placed on testing the possibilities of plague,[50] anthrax, and frostbite.[51] As early as June 1941, Anda tested plague-infested flea bombs on humans. Between ten and fifteen captives were fastened to stakes in the ground in one trial, and then an airplane dropped more than ten bombs on the site. The results are unknown, but they must have been promising, since other tests followed that summer.

In the next experiment, fifteen humans were fastened to stakes in the ground. "Flags and smoke signals were used to guide the planes." The planes took off from Ping Fan, and, once over the site, dropped at least "two dozen bombs, which burst at about 100 or 200 meters from the ground." The fleas dispersed, and after waiting a sufficient length of time for the fleas to infect the prisoners, the victims were disinfected and taken back to Ping Fan for observation. Unfortunately, the tests were unsuccessful, disappointing the Colonel in charge of the experiment. He told a colleague that "the experiment did not yield good results." Evidently, the explosive force of the bombs' blasts caused excessively high temperatures, which in turn made the fleas "very sluggish."[52] Shrapnel bombs simply did not prove to be effective plague-dispersal vessels.[53]

Anthrax experiments were conducted periodically at Anda throughout 1943 and 1944. In general, scientists worked with ten *maruta* in each test. The head of Ping Fan's anthrax production team visited Anda on several occasions in 1943 and 1944 to supervise experiments, and observed that the *maruta* tested "looked like Chinese." They, too, as with the plague "logs," were tied to stakes in the ground. Then anthrax-filled bombs were exploded nearby. The anthrax expert did note with some professional pride that "some of the experimentees were infected with anthrax and, as I learned later, they died."[54] Nevertheless, experiments at Anda with anthrax were disappointing. Unit 731 experts failed to develop a viable anthrax delivery system by the end of the war.[55]

Since most germ bomb experiments ended in failure, Unit 731 scientists in 1944 conducted experiments with plague germ contamination through the respiratory tract. They hoped to develop a technique that would prove to be a feasible venue for BW. Accordingly, ten *maruta* were brought to Anda, and, as usual, were tied to stakes in the ground. Each *maruta* was stationed a prescribed number of meters away from his fellow "log." Test tubes filled with an emulsion of plague germs which were bred from the lymph, spleen, and hearts of plague-infected rats were scattered among the *maruta* at predetermined distances. The scientists arranged for the test tubes to burst, and their contents were distributed among the experimentees. The plague emulsion broke into tiny droplets which eventually were inhaled by the test subjects. Despite the hopes of the scientists involved in developing this technique, the test ended in failure. Still other respiratory tract experiments were conducted throughout 1944 and 1945, but they, too, ended in failure.[56]

V

The Kwantung Army High Command, ever anxious to be prepared for the anticipated war with the Soviet Union, extended carte blanche to Ishii to engage in research on the consequences of frostbite, both at Ping Fan and at Anda. The High Command expected that when war came, much of the fighting would take place under sub-zero weather conditions. The scientist responded to the need with his characteristic energy and dedication.

Frostbite tests became an Ishii specialty. Testing in this area became so routine over the years that Unit 731 personnel accepted their assignments to work with half-frozen subjects as being ordinary and commonplace. Naked men were observed through transparent windows in Ping Fan's distinctive frostbite room. Sometimes their bodies were hooked up to special devices designed to measure body reactions to severe changes in temperature. The men, and an occasional woman, were exposed to freezing and sub-freezing temperatures for long periods of time. Then, they were literally defrosted by the use of different experimental techniques.

Testifying in 1949, Nishi Toshihide described in graphic detail what he had been told, and what he had seen of at least one of the frostbite experiments. He remembered:

researcher Yoshimura [Hisato noted] that at times of great frost, with temperatures below − 20 [sic], people were brought out from the detachment's prison into the open. Their arms were bared and made to freeze with the help of an artificial current of air. This was done until their frozen arms, when struck with a short stick, emitted a sound resembling that which a board gives out when it is struck.

A film was made of the experiment, about which Nishi said:

the picture showed four or five men, with their legs in chains, being led out into the open, dressed in warm clothing, but with their arms bare. Then the process of artificially accelerating the freezing with the help of a large fan was shown. Next one saw the men's arms being struck with a stick to test whether they had definitely frozen, and after that the men were brought into a room.[57]

A Unit 731 medical technician recalled that "Experiments in freezing human beings were performed every year in the detachment, in the coldest months of the year: November . . . [through] February." The "logs" were "taken out into the frost at night, at about 11 o'clock, and compelled to put their hands into a barrel of cold water. Then they were compelled to take their hands out and stand with wet hands in the frost for a long time." Sometimes, "the people were taken out dressed, but with bare feet and compelled to stand in the frost." Then, as soon as frostbite set in, "they were taken to a room and forced to put their feet in water of 5°C temperature, and then the temperature was gradually increased. In this way means for healing frostbite were investigated."[58]

Researchers occasionally combined frostbite tests with experiments that related to other BW needs. In January 1945, for example, a test was performed on ten Chinese prisoners at the Anda facility. The primary purpose was to infect them with gas gangrene. But the test took place at a temperature of 20 degrees Celsius below-zero. The subjects were bound to stakes some 10 to 20 meters away from a shrapnel bomb that was loaded with gas gangrene. The object was not to kill the men by exploding the bomb, but to test the effectiveness of gas gangrene as a BW weapon in below zero temperatures. Consequently, "their heads and backs were protected with special metal shields and thick quilted blankets, but their legs and buttocks were left unprotected." Using a remote-control device, the researchers exploded the bomb, and "the shrapnel, bearing gas gangrene germs, scattered all over the spot where the experimentees were bound. All the experimentees were wounded in the legs or buttocks, and seven days later they died in great torment."[59]

Although BW was Ishii's principal forte, he did occasionally experiment with CW. These experiments were done in cooperation with his CW colleagues from Japan's principal CW facility, the Okunoshima arsenal. For example, teams of Okunoshima technicians worked side by side with members of Unit

731 in conducting especially gruesome mustard-gas tests on Chinese prisoners in 1940, and again in 1943.[60]

In other non-BW-related activities, Unit 731 researchers explored the problems attendant to high-altitude flying. A special pressure chamber was constructed at Ping Fan to assist researchers in determining how much pressure the human body could absorb. Test subjects were locked into the chamber, their bodies bearing a host of measuring devices. Pressure was introduced, and increased gradually until the victims collapsed in convulsions and died. Usually death was slow and painful. Cameramen stood by outside the chamber and recorded on motion picture film every moment of the agony.[61]

Occasionally, something would go wrong at Ping Fan or Anda, but the researchers would gain useful knowledge even from disaster. A case in point occurred sometime between May and June 1943. One of the *maruta*, sensing that a guard was slightly inattentive while on patrol in the exercise yard, knocked the guard out, stole his keys, and opened cell doors, freeing at least 100 prisoners. Guards and researchers panicked. The prisoners could not escape from the inner courtyard, but they could not be herded back into their cells without the possibility of doing some harm to persons who were undergoing experiments. The danger was that they could be killed before the experiments were concluded. To prevent such a catastrophe, the researchers flooded the area with what they believed was harmless tear gas, the pesticide chloropicrin. Although low in toxicity, chloropicrin did fearful things to human lungs, and all the liberated *maruta* died of suffocation. One commentator in recording the event observed, perhaps wryly, that "It is said that some of the doctors associated with the experimentation cried tears of regret when their valuable experimental materials were wasted."[62] But there was the consolation that the staff pathologists would gain useful knowledge and experience from the bonanza of dissecting at least one hundred unanticipated fresh specimens.

Still another unintended experiment occurred in August 1940. A cholera epidemic broke out in a village near Ping Fan. Ishii's investigators soon determined that the source of the infection was sewer water that had been discharged from the Ping Fan death factory. The contaminated water apparently was not treated effectively prior to its release into the general water supply. Employing some newly developed vaccines, Ishii's technicians inoculated all the villagers as well as inhabitants of nearby hamlets. They then proceeded to disinfect the sewage source.

Fearful that word would spread concerning the involvement of Ping Fan in the epidemic, and the obvious implications that could be drawn from that fact, Ishii ordered all personnel involved in the operation to maintain total silence. Since blind obedience to a command from the leader was a sacred obligation, the secret was well maintained by Ishii's men. Few people in the unit ever became aware that 731 carelessness caused the cholera outburst until a Japanese novelist in 1983 reported the episode.[63]

VI

Once Anda and other branch units began open-air testing on a meaningful level, the next logical step in Ishii's pursuit of practical BW weapons, and, to a lesser extent, CW, was to investigate their possibilities in the field. He may have begun small-scale probes as early as the Beiyinhe venture. Field tests on a significant scale were commenced no later than 1937.

The long-simmering antagonism between militarist Japan and Kuomintang China had erupted into hostilities with the famous Marco Polo Bridge Incident in July 1937. Some two months later, reports from the battlefield indicated that, in "Guan . . . the enemy succeeded and fought face to face with our soldiers. In the attack, they used choking gas. Many of our soldiers passed out instantly; most died soon after."[64] Another dispatch described a Japanese attack in the Second War Zone in which the enemy employed 30 airplanes and 40 tanks, and "they used irritant gas in their attacks, killing 400 of our soldiers."[65]

Early in the spring of the following year, reports of suspicious enemy practices continued to flow into Chiang Kai Shek's headquarters. A leader from Wu Hu county in Anhui province reported that "poisonous cooking salt" was discovered in three villages within his jurisdiction. Local authorities determined that "there is no difference in color between regular and poisoned salt. However, after frying, the contaminated salt changes color and becomes black and gives off a sulfuric odor. If eaten, the salt causes instant death."[66]

Two months later, a report from Shaanxi province claimed that in the counties of Feng Zhen and Yang Gao the Japanese impressed villagers to act as coolies. The villagers "were given an injection below their throats which made them mute." Then, they were

> transferred to Henan and Anhui [provinces] to work in a factory that produces wire for land mines, as well as to transport the mines to the battlefields. The Japanese injections will cause death within 100 days when the poison in the shot spreads throughout the body.[67]

These early accounts may or may not be true. Some of the statements, as well as later reports, are obviously of dubious value.[68] Several of the incidents, however, were confirmed by independent observers, such as American missionaries in the field and American medical volunteers.[69] More ominously, on 14 December 1938, Chiang Kai Shek received a telegram from Xian that he and others took most seriously. A Fu Zuo Yi wrote that "It is confirmed that an enemy munitions factory in Taiyuan is now producing poisonous bombs solely, and is preparing to use them when they attack our armies in Shaanxi [province]." Chinese spies reported that in November they observed approximately 230 Japanese scientists and technicians, along with "3 German technicians," and "1000 boxes of chemical materials," enter the plant. Fu indicated that the factory produced five different types of bombs and artillery shells capable of delivering both chemical and biological products. He recounted:

the fatal poisons in these bombs and shells are newly invented by German technicians. . . . [Shells] 6 inches long explode and the gas within them chokes people to death instantly. Other shells are about 4 inches long and weigh approximately 5 pounds. These shells, when fired, are followed up by enemy army infantry equipped with gas masks who charge against our lines.[70]

Many more reports of Japanese preparations for chemical and biological warfare attacks, as well as actual strikes, filtered into Chiang's headquarters in 1939. A typical account came from Liu He Hong county in Shaanxi province. Chinese scouts reported that a sulfur factory was now operating once more after undergoing extensive repairs by Japanese technicians. "The machines in the factory have been working day and night. It is confirmed that the products from this factory are disguised as fertilizers, but in fact they are military poisonous products that are used to kill our soldiers."[71] More alarming was the report from Henan province in December that

Recently, in Chang Zhi, [Japan's] Army Division 20 sent a large number of Chinese collaborators (principally children and elderly men) to spread yellow poisonous chemicals and germs into our wells. The chemicals and germs cause death within 24 hours after one swallows the water. In Gao Ping, at least 10 people died after drinking the water.[72]

Stories of Japanese BW and CW attacks were so numerous (*Time* magazine reported that by 1942 the Japanese had launched at least 1000 mustard and lewisite attacks against the Chinese)[73] as the war progressed, that President Chiang was forced to pay them substantial attention. Chiang's public relations people could no longer exploit the reports through a sympathetic foreign press solely for propaganda purposes. Too many people apparently were being killed by enemy BW and CW attacks. Consequently, in late November 1941, one of Chiang's close aides sent a terse telegram to health officials, ordering them "to deal with the fact that the enemy has spread poisonous bacteria and gas in Yi Cang, Ba Wang Cheng, and Qu Zhou." He demanded:

You should organize a delegation consisting of personnel from the Army Medical Corps, the Sanitary Corps, the Red Cross, and foreign doctors. This delegation should journey to those communities affected by Japanese attacks in order to secure documentary evidence. In the meantime, you should conduct research on methods of treatment and prevention. This assignment must be completed immediately. Report all details to this office.[74]

Additionally, President Franklin D. Roosevelt issued a statement in 1943 condemning Japanese BW and CW attacks. Roosevelt declared that "Authoritative reports are reaching this government of the use by Japanese armed forces in various localities of China of poisonous or noxious gases." He warned:

I desire to make it unmistakably clear that if Japan persists in this inhuman form of warfare against China or against any other of the United Nations [,] such action will be regarded by this government as though taken against the United States and retaliation in kind and in full measure will be meted out.

Roosevelt concluded his warning with the observation that "We shall be prepared to enforce complete retribution. Upon [Japan] will rest the responsibility."[75]

VII

It is not easy to determine the extent of either Unit 731 personnel's or Ishii's involvement in these episodes. What is certain is that Ishii did travel extensively throughout the war zones during the period. Several of the reported incidents do bear his operational trademark, but no substantive evidence connects either Unit 731 or any of its scientists to the attacks. Still, the first extensive field test of BW and CW that can be attributed to Unit 731 occurred in 1939.

The tense eastern border between Japan's puppet state of Manchukuo,[76] Mongolia, and the Soviet Union erupted into a series of clashes in May 1939 that led to a short but full-scale mini-war. Fighting continued all summer in the remote desert-like area close to the frontier that separates Inner Mongolia, the People's Republic of Mongolia, Manchuria, and the Soviet Union. Here, along the Halha River, thousands of men on both sides were slaughtered in the confrontation that is known as the Nomonhan Incident.[77] By the time the killing ended in September, it was apparent that the Kwantung Army had experienced a severe drubbing at the hands of the Soviet Army and its incomparable leader, General Georgi K. Zhukov.[78]

Ishii viewed the outbreak of fighting at Nomonhan as a golden opportunity to test the possibilities of BW on a large scale. Shortly after the first clash, along with approximately one half of the Ping Fan technical staff he sped to the Kwantung Army's principal staging site, the city of Hailar, in Inner Mongolia. They brought with them 20 A-type water filters and 50 B- and C-type filters, along with other necessary equipment to provide safe drinking water and to ward off outbreaks of disease for the troops going into combat. Ishii also sent along equipment to be used in the dissemination of BW.

In Hailar, Ishii lobbied Kwantung Army leaders for permission to engage in BW against the Soviet enemy. He immersed himself in his usual tactic of promising startling results if only he were given an opportunity to employ BW properly in battle. He tried flattery, bribery, and sycophancy, going as far as to provide an influential fellow officer, in the closing days of the war, with a bottle of Coty perfume. The officer, about to meet his Soviet counterpart to begin negotiations for an end to the war, "dabbed on some of the perfume to show the Russians 'the fineness of a Japanese officer;' the rest, he saved for his wife."[79]

Unit 731's leader divided his deployment into two groups. The first consisted of some 100 men, split into squads of ten each. They were assigned routine duties as either water filtration experts or anti-epidemic fighters. The second party of approximately 100 men were specially trained in BW, and were formed into groups of twelve or more. These squads were expected to engage in BW sabotage operations, and were known as "suicide squads." Each suicide squad consisted of men who had been tutored in BW operations at Ping Fan's Section II, and were supplemented by a few teenage recruits, primarily from Ishii's home town of Chiyoda Mura, who received instruction in 731's Education Section.

Ishii developed a three-pronged plan for BW operations. He expected to use bacteria-laden artillery shells against attacking Soviet and Mongolian troops. Airplanes loaded with either bacteria-filled porcelain bombs or pathogen-infected animals and food were to be dropped along the west bank of the meandering Halha River, where, it was anticipated, the surviving pathogens would spread epidemics and create other havoc among the enemy. Ishii also expected to dispatch his suicide squads to the west bank of the Halha River to sow pathogens in the river, and in all water wells the saboteurs could locate.[80]

Lt. General Ueda Kenkichi, Kwantung Army Commander, usually a consistent Ishii supporter, initially expressed doubts about the practicability of employing BW in the Nomonhan operation, and refused the Colonel's request. Ueda feared that, once the Soviets realized that the Japanese were engaging in BW activities, they would reciprocate in kind. He voiced concern that the Soviets, if pressed too hard, would wipe out all the Kwantung Army artillery emplacements. Airplane drops were dangerous, too, because the Soviets could shoot down low-flying planes, which then could inadvertently contaminate Japanese troops. Saboteurs would be ineffective in such a tightly guarded area, he worried, since they most likely would be captured before they could disperse their pathogens.[81]

By July, however, the Japanese were in a precarious position, and Ueda gave Ishii permission to attempt BW. On 12 July Ishii dispatched two of his special suicide teams to the Soviet side of the Halha River. The twenty-four-member squad were instructed to drop pathogens in the water, and to return to their base as quickly as possible. Equipped with rubber boats, and 22.5 kilograms of prepared salmonella and typhoid bacteria,[82] the men steered the boats against the current, emptied canisters of germs into the river, rowed ashore, took sample tests of the water, photographed the scene, and left the area silently and in great haste.

One of Ishii's young recruits, at the age of sixty-four, recalled in 1982 still another field test during the Nomonhan conflict. A Mr Tsuruta told a reporter for a Tokyo newspaper that he participated in a typhoid experiment against Soviet forces. Tsuruta remembered:

> It was at the end of August. We were sent out in 3 trucks with extra fuel to take us to the river demarcating the border. During the night, in pitch blackness, the squadron leader gave us the order to spray germs throughout

the area. Across the river we could see the Soviet flares. We could tell where they were camping. We used typhoid germs. I learned later that our squadron leader contracted typhoid and died from the disease.[83]

It is difficult to gauge the effectiveness of these efforts, but, if nothing else, Ishii and his men gained invaluable experience from the venture.[84]

Unit 731 special squads also deployed artillery shells with bacteria-filled warheads against the Soviets. By early June, they had more than 2000 shells stored in Hailar. Each shell contained a steel head, 1.5 centimeters long and 0.5 centimeters in diameter, in which pathogens were lodged. Almost all the shells were launched against the enemy during July and August, with inconclusive results. Plague, dysentery, and cholera did take a serious toll on both Soviet and Japanese troops,[85] but whether those infected contracted their affliction from BW, or rather from natural circumstances connected with the primitive sanitary conditions in the rugged border region, is hard to project.[86]

There is circumstantial evidence that the Soviets also may have engaged in BW during the Nomonhan Incident. In 1942 a Soviet Air Force officer of Balto-Germanic origins defected to the Germans. He claimed to have extensive knowledge concerning Soviet BW preparations. According to his handlers, he told them that BW was given a "practical test in the combats in Mongolia." The deserter alleged that "an extensive plague epidemic broke out" in the region. However, there was no other supporting data included in his interrogators' reports, and so one should approach these statements with some caution.[87]

Perhaps the most interesting feature of the entire Nomonhan affair is that, on 1 October 1939, the Ishii Unit received a special commendation from the Kwantung Army Commanding General. For a medical unit, this was an unprecedented honor. No other such unit in the history of the Medical Corps ever received similar recognition, in spite of the fact that many medical personnel in other units, and in other conflicts, performed heroically in fulfilling their duties.

What makes the commendation even more noteworthy is that, for an organization engaged in so many covert operations, the War Ministry permitted the controlled press to disseminate the news. On 23 May 1940, the Tokyo *Asahi Shimbun* printed Ishii's photograph along with the complete tediously long text of the unit's award. The commendation included the curious statement that "the unit, overcoming all hardships, contributed [by employing BW?] to the securing of an advantageous tactical operation position of a large brigade force." On 29 April 1940, Ishii personally was decorated with the 3rd Order of the Golden Kite and the Middle Cord of the Rising Sun in recognition of his unusual services to Japan during the previous year.[88]

Buoyed by the Nomonhan experience, over the next several years Ishii expanded his field test operations to encompass all of Manchuria and both occupied and free China. From late 1939 through 1942, Unit 731 operatives conducted many tests against both enemy military forces and civilian populations. The logistics required for such extensive trials were so great that Ishii must have received approval to move forward from both the Kwantung Army leaders and area commanders of Japan's invading China forces. Logic suggests strongly that the top War Ministry officials in Tokyo were kept apprised of his operations, and approved them. They were so far-reaching that the devastation and carnage he unleashed brought an outcry from too many sources in China to be refuted as nothing more than lying Kuomintang propaganda.

The tests covered a host of insidious but imaginative artifices. Manchurian water wells were laced with typhoid germs that were remarkably effective killers. It is estimated that more than 1000 wells in and around Harbin were contaminated with typhoid bacilli in 1939 and 1940. Casualties ranged from single deaths to limited outbreaks of typhoid, which devastated entire villages. Mrs Ada Pivo, a native of Harbin, remembered the day her eldest sister died of typhoid fever. The sister belonged to a Harbin Jewish Zionist youth group that went on a field trip in early summer 1940. The day was extremely warm, and on their return home, some of the forty-odd youngsters, thirteen to fifteen years old, bought bottles of lemonade in downtown Harbin. All children who drank the lemonade, which was bottled locally, and contained well-drawn water, contracted typhoid fever and subsequently died. The attending doctors traced the typhoid outbreak to the contaminated lemonade.[89]

Ishii, working with his Changchun counterpart,[90] caused a cholera outbreak in the Manchukuon capital. He descended upon the city in 1940, informed local authorities that cholera was moving in on their community, and that the general population must be inoculated. What he did not tell them was that the "vaccine" he intended to use was a solution containing cholera germs. Innocent people were lined up, given an injection, and possibly some liquid to drink or some contaminated food to eat. In any event, a cholera epidemic spread through metropolitan Changchun shortly after.[91]

In July 1942, Ishii led a BW expedition to Nanking, where he linked forces with local BW death factory personnel. Jointly, they distributed typhoid and paratyphoid germs from metal flasks and glass bottles, dumping the bacteria into wells, marshes, and houses of ordinary citizens. They could afford to be lavish with their dispensation, since Ishii brought along 130 kilograms of paratyphoid "A" and anthrax germs, and an unknown quantity of typhoid, all produced at Ping Fan.[92] Epidemics broke out in the region shortly afterwards, much to the delight of the researchers.

The Nanking trip yielded other benefits as well. Ishii, during his visit to the city, provided special treats for Chinese prisoners of war held in two nearby camps. In addition, he prepared an unusual delicacy for local youngsters, chocolates filled with anthrax bacteria.[93] Three thousand POWs were given, as a special holiday favor, dumplings that had been injected with either typhoid or paratyphoid. The prisoners were then released and sent home, where they acted as unwitting agents for spreading disease. The children gorged themselves on chocolates, with the unavoidable resulting side effects.

Sweet cakes, infused with typhoid and paratyphoid bacteria, were still another Ishii confectionery delight that he used in the Nanking expedition. Japanese soldiers were given 300–400 of the sweet cakes and ordered to leave them near fences and by trees. The idea was to create an impression that the soldiers forgot to take the food with them in the midst of a hasty retreat. It was expected that the local population, always short of food, would be delighted with the opportunity to feast on Japanese provisions. Inevitably, an outbreak of disease occurred shortly after the sweet cakes were ingested. Researchers concluded that "paratyphoid had proved to be the most effective"[94] of the pathogens tested.

In other field tests, Unit 731 saboteurs released, into densely populated areas, rats that were carrying plague-infested fleas. Researchers anticipated that the plague rats would breed with the local rat population, resulting in outbreaks of massive plague epidemics. Unit 731 men found also that germs implanted into expressly modified fountain pens and walking sticks were an effective method for disseminating BW. The germ-encrusted devices were dropped along dirt paths and paved roads, where either the curious or the needy would take them home. An epidemic would develop (plague generally), Japanese soldiers would rush to the affected area, order all villagers to evacuate, and then proceed to torch the villages in order to prevent outsiders from discovering what really took place. These sabotage techniques were so successful that Sir Joseph Needham, the great British scientist stationed in China at the time, noted:

> In the beginning, I felt great doubt about its credibility, but I believe now that the information collected by the Chinese Military Medical Bureau clearly indicates that the Japanese forces have been scattering and are continuing to scatter plague infested fleas in several areas.[95]

Massive BW testing actually commenced with an attack upon an innocent population in July 1940. Two months earlier, Ishii dispatched from Ping Fan a heavily guarded train. Its destination was Hangchow (Hangzhou), the beautiful holiday resort favored by Shanghai's wealthy. The train's cargo was 70 kilograms of typhoid bacterium, 50 kilos of cholera germs, and 5 kilos of plague-infected fleas. The BW target was Ning Bo, a community south of Hangchow. Ning Bo was an important Treaty Port in the nineteenth century, and the birthplace of Chiang Kai Shek.[96] For the next five months, Ning Bo and its environs were subjected to a series of BW attacks.

The methods for spreading disease in Ning Bo varied. Ishii and his researchers devised a host of delivery systems they planned to test on the simple residents of the area. Pathogens were dumped into water reservoirs, ponds, and individual residential water wells. Infected grains of wheat and millet were disseminated by aerial spraying in early October. Later that month, Ishii personally directed the scattering of contaminated wheat and cotton in and around Ning Bo. On 26 November, specially equipped Unit 731 aircraft flew over nearby Jin Hua county, dropping bombs which, on impact, gave off smoke-like objects that later turned a light yellow color.

The final results were that, as a consequence of the five-month campaign, cholera, typhus, and plague spread throughout Ning Bo and at least five surrounding counties. It is known that more than 1000 persons became ill with one or another of the Ishii-produced diseases, and that over 500 people succumbed.[97] Most alarming is that the diseases Ishii unleashed in summer and fall 1940 had long-term effects. Plague ravaged Ning Bo and nearby communities in 1941, 1946, and 1947. Casualties were high.[98]

The Kwantung Army Command and the officers of Unit 731 were delighted with the expedition's achievements. They were so impressed that a documentary film depicting the highlights of the raids was shown to a wide and appreciative audience of scientists and military personnel in both Manchuria and the Home Islands. The film concluded with a shot of a Chinese newspaper, which was translated into Japanese, so that the audience could savor the paper's report of "a severe epidemic . . . [which] had broken out in the Nimpo [Ning Bo] area." The film's final frames were "Chinese orderlies in white overalls disinfecting the plague area."[99]

The following spring and summer, Colonel Ota Kiyoshi, one of Ishii's most loyal and trusted aides, mounted a major BW effort against Chinese resistance in Central China. This time the target was Chang teh, an important railway hub and commercial center in Hunan province. Ota initially was accompanied on the expedition by a contingent of forty or fifty men. This grew later to over 100 persons, including thirty bacteriologists. Ota began the new campaign on 11 April 1941, distributing, by airplane, plague-infected wheat and millet. Eight days later, the first Chang teh resident died of plague. More deaths followed daily.

Later that summer, Ota resumed his attack. This time plague-infected fleas were discharged over Chang teh and the surrounding countryside by aerial spraying. In November, Ota dispatched an airplane to circle Chang teh. The solitary aircraft made three passes over the city, dropping a mixture of wheat and rice balls, strips of colored paper, cotton fibers, and other fabric cuttings. A week later, the first victim, an eleven-year-old girl, died of plague. By December, many Chang teh residents were dead of plague. Overall, as a conservative estimate, between 400 and 500 persons in Hunan province perished from Ota's field tests.[100]

Field trials continued throughout 1942. That winter, the county of Non Gan, Jilin province, was exposed to Unit 731 experiments. A team of saboteurs left Ping Fan in December, and descended upon the unsuspecting district. They toured the county, dropping flasks filled with plague bacteria into water wells and reservoirs, distributing plague-infected fleas throughout wheat and rice fields, and scattering pathogens along paths leading to villages within the region. A few weeks later, plague spread throughout the county. More than 300 inhabitants died from the disease, while hundreds more became ill, displaying plague symptoms. Between 4000 and 5000 families were forced to flee their homes during the coldest part of the year, as the Japanese set fire to dozens of villages in the region in order to control the epidemic.[101]

BW field tests peaked in 1942. Sporadic, half-hearted trials in China, Manchuria, Mongolia, and the Soviet Union continued until the end of the war. However, these later tests never approached the scale of the earlier probes. The exact number of tests Unit 731 conducted is in doubt. United States investigators in the postwar period were told by Ishii and other BW leaders that they carried out only twelve field tests.[102] When all the reported incidents that were verified by independent authorities are tallied, the Japanese figure must be regarded as unbelievably low.

No reasonable explanation was ever advanced by Unit 731 principals for the reduction in field experiments, but certain defects in delivery systems previously noted may have persuaded the leaders that human experiments in the laboratories should be accelerated at the expense of tests in the field. Moreover, specific changes in the command structure at the Ping Fan installation in late 1942 may have had a negative effect on massive testing. Nevertheless, by the end of 1942, the casualty count in the open tests surely fell into the six-figure range.

VIII

After a ten-year posting in and around the Harbin area, Ishii was transferred to Nanking on 1 August 1942, where he assumed the position of Chief of the First Army Medical Department. Ishii's transfer, as with so much else in his career, is clouded in mystery and doubt as to motive. The ambitious career officer one year earlier had been elevated to Surgeon Major General.[103] But, he later explained, if he continued to do research he would be at a dead end in his career. To achieve higher rank, he was required to have field experience.

This is, seemingly, a plausible justification for his Nanking assignment. Yet, in the next breath, Ishii remarked that, "in his opinion," he was given his new job "because 'higher-ups' did not want him to continue BW research."[104] This latter claim is doubtful, since he commenced the Nanking BW field tests almost simultaneously with his assumption of the new command. Moreover, even Ishii conceded that, under his successor "the research continued, to some degree at least."[105]

Ishii's successor was his long-time rival, Major General (later Lt. General) Kitano Masaji. Although they had much in common, their personalities were quite different. They differed also in physical appearance. Where Ishii was tall and slender, Kitano was short and stocky, with a bullet-shaped head. However, he was as quick-witted and as ambitious as Ishii.

Almost nothing is known of Kitano's origins, which suggests that he may have come from the peasant class. He was roughly the same age as Ishii, and attended Tokyo Imperial University at approximately the same time that Ishii studied at Kyoto Imperial University. Both graduated as medical doctors, Ishii in 1920, while Kitano received his degree in 1922. Both entered the Army within days of graduating university.[106] Kitano and Ishii climbed the medical/ military ladder at virtually the same pace, although Ishii's flair for publicity sometimes led him to overshadow Kitano, despite the latter's solid research accomplishments. As Majors in the Medical Corps, Kitano and Ishii were sent to Manchuria in 1932. Here their activities appeared, superficially, to direct them into different areas of responsibility.

Kitano occupied an unusual dual position in the puppet colony. He was jointly a professor of the Manchurian (Army) Medical College in Mukden, and, simultaneously, he retained his commission in the Army. Thus, by some special imperial dispensation, Kitano was both a civilian academic and a career Army doctor.[107] His tenure was so novel, and his authority, consequently, was so powerful, that envious colleagues caustically referred to him as "the emperor."

Ishii's successor was wily and so low keyed that he could be described as almost self-effacing. He lacked Ishii's flair for self-promotion and showmanship, but he was considered to be the better researcher. Kitano published many more scholarly papers than Ishii; his postwar publications, and his later success in Japan's ethical drug industry, support the notion that he was an outstanding scientific investigator. It should be remembered, though, that much of his scholarship was based upon BW experiments with humans. Professor Kitano's sense of medical ethics matched that of Ishii.

Kitano held his post as a professor in Mukden for ten years. During that decade, he and his colleagues in the Medical College killed thousands of Chinese, Koreans, and other "lesser" peoples in the course of experiments that rivaled Ishii's for their bestiality. The litany of experiments and dissections of living persons, as well as of those who were sacrificed, and then dissected, are similar to the Ping Fan horror stories. Despite Japanese last-ditch efforts in 1945 to destroy evidence of their BW work in Mukden, many specimens of their victims were preserved. They are on display today at the Medical College as a testimony to Kitano's work.[108]

In the twenty-two months that he was "Acting" Commander of Unit 731 (August 1942 to March 1945), Kitano demonstrated that he was a worthy successor to Ishii. He actually expanded human BW tests at Ping Fan. Somehow, in spite of the fact that the war had turned badly for Japan, he managed to obtain new equipment from the Home Islands in 1944. The instruments that he provided his men with were "more perfect than the old, and enabled the work of cultivating bacteria to be conducted on the conveyer system."[109] Kitano improved upon Ishii's aerial spraying technique, carrying out a highly successful plague experiment near Shanghai in 1944. This field test was filmed, and its première screening impressed the top echelon of the Kwantung Army Command.[110] His accomplishments during his short tenure at Ping Fan were significant.

IX

All tests on humans, BW as well as the specialized non-BW experiments, were recorded carefully by the Unit 731 scientist or technician in charge of a specific project. The data compiled, both on paper and on film, indicate that Ishii's and Kitano's men recorded every conceivable reaction the human subjects developed during the course of the experiment, until the subject either perished from the effects of the tests, or was no longer a useful specimen and, therefore, was sacrificed. The records accumulated were of enormous quantity, and would prove alluring to both Soviet and American scientists and intelligence authorities in the heyday of the Cold War.

Fortunately for Japan's enemies, neither Ishii nor his fellow researchers ever developed a BW weapon capable of mass production and widespread dissemination. However, they produced certain prototype weapons that in time could have resulted in instruments of mass destruction. If the war had lasted a few more years, it is possible that Ishii, Kitano, and their co-workers could have created a weapon with disturbing potential.

7 Unit 100's BW death factories in Changchun

The veterinarian led us into the west room, an exhibition room with glass windows and photographs on the walls. The photos dealt principally with anthrax, sheep plague, dry leaf rust and smut. . . . The veterinarian then pointed to a photo, remarking that "Generally speaking, nose ulcer and anthrax are not infectious to humans; however, they can cause infection through wounds, resulting in death. This man in the photo, he died of anthrax infection from his being careless while shaving." I examined the photograph and discovered that it was a picture of a Gypsy[1] who I often met in a park. He was always strong and healthy. I had not seen him for about a month, yet he was already dead, according to the photograph. He looked no different than I remembered him, except that he had a black dot under his nose from where, according to the veterinarian, he received the infection.

(Li Ye Guang, "A Visit to the Kwantung Army Unit 100 Camp," in *Historical Material On Jilin History*)

I

The city of Changchun lies 150 miles to the south of Harbin/Ping Fan. Although the name in Chinese means "Eternal Spring," Changchun endures the harsh climate common to central and northern Manchuria. The city does have many attractions, despite the severe winters and warm humid summers. It is, as with Harbin, a relatively new city.

The Eternal Spring city is strategically located in the center of Manchuria. Its original site was on the banks of the important Yitong River. Extensive fishing and trading were carried out by local residents along the river throughout the nineteenth century. However, Changchun's rapid growth commenced at the turn of the nineteenth century with the advance of the Russians into the region, and the coming of the railways. It was the railroad that transformed Changchun into a metropolis. Because of its strategic location, its proximity to Japan's colony of Korea, and its focal point within the Manchurian railway network, the Japanese, in the mid-1930s, made Changchun the capital of the newly created puppet state of Manchukuo.[2]

The metropolis that emerged under Japanese sponsorship was beautiful, reasonably prosperous, and remarkably clean. Light industry was encouraged by the Japanese to come to the community. A vast movie industry thrived in the new capital, and it continues to flourish today as one of China's premier studios.

As befitting a community boasting a population of 500,000 people, Changchun was dotted with many parks and lakes. Enormous public buildings were erected to house the burgeoning bureaucracy of the new Manchukuon empire. Handsome villas were constructed for Japanese "advisors" and Chinese collaborators. Most of the new buildings followed Japanese or European architecture, and the community presented a superficial appearance of being less a Chinese than a Western city. Broad avenues were tree-lined and well maintained.

However, the city's architectural highlight, and the focal point for exercising control over the vast Manchurian domain, was Emperor Pu Yi's imperial complex. In early 1933, the Japanese requisitioned a large plot of land less than a two-minute drive from the main railway station. Here they established the headquarters of the Kwantung Army. Virtually next door, they built a palace worthy of a puppet emperor. These buildings were surrounded with charming gardens, and life appeared to be pleasant for its inhabitants. The Japanese maintained the charade of consulting with the Emperor on every problem that developed. Pu Yi, after considering Japanese advice, dutifully accepted their instructions. Although the nations of the world refused to recognize the new Manchukuo, life for Pu Yi and the royal entourage was one long round of ceremonies, receptions, parties, and occasional tours of the imperial Manchukuon domain.

II

The frenzied building campaign in the new capital did not ignore the city's suburbs. Mokotan, a small village 6 kilometers south of Changchun, was the scene for increased Japanese attention in 1936. Under Japanese direction, local officials commandeered a vast tract of land and "sold" the property to them. Teams of construction experts invaded the area, and using conscripted Chinese labor, erected a huge network of buildings in a short period of time. Unlike the Pu Yi palace enclave, the new complex was not celebrated openly by either the Japanese or their puppets. The Mokotan project had a much more sinister purpose than celebration of the new era of Japanese–Manchukuon collaboration.

This Changchun suburb was to be still another home for military BW research from 1936 until Japan's capitulation. At Mokotan/Changchun the emphasis would be upon research with plants and animals. However, the scientists in charge of the research work did not ignore opportunities to experiment with humans. The Changchun[3] camp became, over the years, one of the most important BW research centers in the entire Japanese BW empire. It was second only to Ping Fan in the scope of its activities, and most probably in the number of humans killed in BW experiments.[4]

A second[5] Imperial decree was issued, in 1936, which established the Kwantung Army Anti-Epizootic Protection of Horses Unit. Ostensibly, this unit was created to enable veterinarians to deal with diseases that might affect horses and other animals useful to the Kwantung Army. Veterinarians there did engage in valuable studies in animal disease prevention. In practice, however, these activities were a cover for the unit's real purpose of expanding research in plant and animal BW. The Anti-Epizootic Protection Unit was completely independent of Ishii's operations, although both organizations were to cooperate in joint ventures over the years.

A relatively obscure veterinarian, Major Wakamatsu Yujiro, was placed in charge of this new organization. Wakamatsu was a career military veterinarian officer who rose through the ranks, eventually achieving the level of Major General in the Kwantung Army Veterinary Service. Unlike Ishii, Wakamatsu never yielded his command to another; he remained in charge of the Changchun operation from its inception until its destruction in 1945.

In keeping with Army tradition, the new unit was known as the "Wakamatsu Unit." Later, when the Kwantung Army decided for purposes of military secrecy to designate BW research agencies with numerical labels, it became known as "Unit 100." Since the unit's principal responsibility was to develop BW weapons useful in sabotage operations, Wakamatsu worked closely with the Intelligence Division of the Kwantung Army. He may have reported directly to both the head of the Veterinary Service and the Director of Intelligence Operations of the Kwantung Army. The Chief of the Kwantung Army Veterinarian Service visited the camp on an inspection tour at least once each month from 1941 until Japan's surrender. He also received oral reports periodically from Wakamatsu.[6]

Funding for Unit 100's operations was both enormous and open-ended. The unit received its money from two sources: the War Ministry in Tokyo, and the Kwantung Army's 2nd Division Headquarters. In the one-year period from 1 April 1944 to 31 March 1945, Tokyo supplied Unit 100 with 600,000 yen, while Kwantung Army sources advanced 1,000,000 yen to the unit. Money was never a problem. As one official boasted, "if necessity demanded, all the money requested would have been granted."[7]

Wakamatsu never achieved the notoriety of Ishii. Unit 100 also did not receive in the postwar investigations the attention accorded Unit 731's activities. Neither investigators, nor historians, nor the journalists researching Japanese BW activities accorded Unit 100 the recognition it deserves. Unlike his Ping Fan counterpart, Wakamatsu did not seek the public attention his more flamboyant fellow officer craved. He preferred to do his work under a protective blanket of anonymity. Still, his lack of medical or scientific ethics rivaled that of both Ishii and Kitano. The veterinarian's exploits in Changchun earn him a notable place in the history of Japan's BW efforts.[8]

Unit 100's campsite occupied an area of approximately 20 square kilometers. This tract of land was off limits to all Chinese, except laborers employed in the camp, and a few invited Chinese specialists. The camp was barred to Japanese who were not part of the research teams, or who were not members of the Kwantung Army.

Much of the land within Unit 100's perimeters was set aside as an experimental farm. Here an assortment of crops were cultivated. After harvesting, they would be subjected to experiments with various types of plant-killing bacteria. The researchers also tested infected crops with different herbicides as well as other chemical pesticides.

The rest of the camp was surrounded by electrified fences at least 3 meters high. Guards patrolled the grounds at all times. No one was admitted beyond the electrified fence without a pass. Everyone entering the compound was subjected to a rigorous physical inspection.

The physical layout of Camp 100 was in many respects similar to that of Ping Fan. Wakamatsu erected a large two-story headquarters building 120 meters or so from the camp's front entrance. The gray concrete building was 1720 square meters in overall size. From east to west it was 12 meters wide, and 60 meters long on its north-to-south axis. This main building reached a height of 6 meters above ground. Laboratories occupied the basement and the first floor. The basement, along with an adjacent underground structure, also contained cells capable of holding thirty to forty prisoners at one time who would be subjected to experimentation when the scientists required their bodies. Each cell was 4 square meters, and was protected by thick double doors 66 centimeters high and 50 centimeters wide. Every door contained a safety lock and a strong bolt to ensure security. Unit 100's headquarters offices were housed on the second floor. Underground tunnels radiated out from the headquarters building to other laboratory sites and to many buildings housing animal research specimens.[9]

Several dozen buildings were scattered throughout the camp, with the structures located about 20–30 meters apart from each other. Three large red-brick stables held fifty horses each. Other stables were used for oxen and for sheep. Smaller buildings housed rats, mice, ground squirrels, and other rodents and small animals. Still other buildings were dedicated to different laboratories and autopsy rooms. Several kilns and a small glass manufacturing factory were also part of the camp's facilities.

Unlike Ping Fan, almost all of Unit 100's scientific and technical personnel lived outside the camp's boundaries. Perhaps the odors emanating from the plant and animal laboratories, as well as the decaying flesh of the sacrificed animals and humans, were too difficult for highly educated and superbly trained men to endure. In any case, they were housed in reasonably decent quarters off base in Mokotan and other nearby communities. The scientists and technicians also enjoyed access to Changchun's cultural offerings as well as its fleshpots and tea houses.

Three crematoria dotted the camp, while a large cemetery catered to those animal and human victims who were not burned to ashes. In spring 1949, peasants planting crops in the area discovered a huge burial site. One of the peasants told authorities that he remembered seeing "human corpses scattered over a 500 meter long area." Another peasant declared that on the site there was "an upper layer of human bodies. Even after digging 2–5 meters deep we found that there were still human bodies."[10]

The camp began operations as soon as the first buildings were ready for occupancy in 1936, while the facility reached its optimum capacity upon its completion in 1939. Under Wakamatsu's watchful direction, Unit 100 employed between 600 and 800 personnel at all times. Of this number, a higher proportion were technical and scientific personnel than were at Ping Fan. Fewer guards were required to protect human specimens in Changchun than the larger number of subjects who were under Unit 731's care further north. Between 1936 and 1945, the cream of Japan's bacteriologists, chemists, botanists, zoologists, pathologists, and veterinarians served tours of duty with Unit 100. Many of these Unit 100 graduates would then be assigned to various Army units throughout Manchuria and China where they engaged in training other personnel in BW techniques.

The unit's internal organizational structure paralleled that of Unit 731. Unit 100's annual budget from 1941 to 1945 averaged 1 million yen. Personnel were assigned to one of four specialized departments or to the one general service department. The first department studied problems relating to horses and to animal blood in general. The second department did most of the research relating to BW. This department was divided into five subsections which studied methods for bacteria reproduction, livestock viruses, especially nose ulcer, sheep pox, ox plague, management and production of animals for future experiments, organic chemistry, with emphasis upon medicines that kill, and finally, viruses that destroy crops. The third and fourth departments assisted the second department in its work, while the general service department concerned itself with design and overall research problems, as well as management of the unit's large experimental crops farm.[11]

Production of bacteria was on a large scale. Unit 100 laboratories concentrated on manufacturing four principal pathogens, although small quantities of other germs were handled as well. The unit leader's primary interest lay in anthrax, glanders, plague, and nose ulcer. It is known that in 1941 and 1942 the laboratories produced annually 1000 kilograms of anthrax bacteria, over 500 kilos of nose bacteria, and possibly as much as 100 kilos of glanders bacteria.[12] Huge quantities of herbicides were also manufactured every year the unit operated.

Wakamatsu established a sixth department in December 1943. This new department was authorized to exploit the allegedly successful plague BW weapons delivery systems previously developed at Ping Fan. The General in command of the Kwantung Army Veterinarian Corps presided at the department's inaugural meeting, and declared proudly that the "establishment of the sixth department has significant strategic importance." Moreover, he personally helped design a plan for housing the new BW weapons in underground storage bunkers.[13] Unfortunately for the Kwantung Army High Command, the delivery systems never achieved the promise Ishii and Kitano predicted.

III

Unit 100's operations were shrouded in the tight security one would expect of a BW research facility. Nevertheless, secrecy was not as well maintained here as around those operations under Ishii's control. Occasionally, presumed trustworthy Chinese collaborators were given an opportunity to visit the Changchun facility. Their reminiscences are useful sources of information on the Changchun operation.

In June 1941, a wealthy Peking woman, who enjoyed a friendship with one of 100's leading scientists, visited the camp. She recalled later that all the research laboratories she visited were numbered. In order to enter one of the cultivating laboratories, visitors were required to pass through five gates. In one laboratory where she was stopped by a Japanese dressed in a white coat, she was told forcefully, "An experiment is in progress, no visitors allowed." She was then informed by her host that "This is a laboratory for infectious corpses [an autopsy room]."

She visited several underground laboratories. Here she was shown numerous humidifiers, large thermometers, and other typical laboratory equipment. She and her host then changed into laboratory gowns, were sprayed with a disinfectant, and were taken to visit laboratories in which different pathogens were being cultivated in a variety of media. She recalled seeing different-sized containers of agar lined up row after row in one room. Her host told her:

> Organic bacillus is a media for acute infectious disease. It grows in a common culture and requires oxygen. If placed in a dark, damp area, it can survive for months, even years. Yet, in dry air, it will die in a day or two. This bacteria [sic] can thrive in rice and cotton. It is resistant to the cold, and can survive indefinitely in a frozen state. However, it cannot withstand high temperatures.

Later, they passed through tunnels to an underground laboratory. "Instantly, an unbearably strong odor choked me. I remember that we passed through a hallway with at least 10 doors on either side. Each doorway was covered with black and red curtains." Suddenly, "a door opened. Three men pushed a surgical bed that contained at least 3 corpses into the hallway. They were covered with a white sheet." Surprised at seeing intruders, "One of the Japanese muttered something to my friend. He was obviously complaining about my presence there since my friend made me immediately leave the building."

Her last stop was a large laboratory. Here she was shown an assortment of equipment. Many of the devices were for formulating a host of vaccines. Others were for cultivating bacteria. "Here no one was allowed to walk around. Everyone was confined to that part of the building where his assigned work was performed." Before leaving Unit 100, her friend told her that human experiments were conducted at the camp. "Japanese military police sent people to Unit 100 for experimental work every week."[14]

Li Ye Guang was a young Chinese who was about to graduate from an Army supply school in Changchun in the summer of 1937. He and his classmates were sent to visit different Army supply depots in and around Changchun as part of their final training before graduation. In July, he was told that he would visit a camp in Mokotan. The next day, after lunch, Li and his classmates were driven to a red-brick walled barracks. Li remembered that on the gate facing north was an attractive sign with black lettering on a white background that read, "Army Horse Epidemic Prevention and Water Supply Department of the Kwantung Army." The brick walls were about 3 meters high, and were surrounded by a deep ditch. "No trespass" signs were posted every 50 meters.

Before being admitted to the camp, all the students were given a physical examination. They were instructed also that

> They must obey their guide explicitly; they were not to speak Chinese; they were to observe, but they would not be permitted to ask any questions; they were not to touch anything during their visit; notetaking or photographs were prohibited; and, finally, no one would be permitted to walk alone during their tour of underground tunnels and underground laboratories.

They were then escorted to a row of buildings that had the appearance of being dormitories. As they approached the buildings, "an ambulance dashed to the gate we had just entered." One of the students exclaimed, "My goodness! Is there infectious disease here?" One of the other students scoffed, saying, "Nonsense! How can infectious disease happen here in an epidemic prevention organization?" The other replied, "Did you not recognize the markings on the ambulance? It came from the Changchun Infectious Disease Hospital. So strange!"[15]

The young men were welcomed by two Japanese Army lieutenants dressed in surgical gowns. One of the men was a medical doctor. The other was a veterinarian. The two lieutenants guided the visitors to a row of laboratories, all containing basements with iron-barred windows. They were greeted with a strong odor of disinfectant upon entering one of the buildings. Here two technicians disinfected them by spraying a combination of cresol and mercuric chloride on their bodies. Everyone was provided with a gauze mask that also "smelled of medicine." Fully disinfected, they were required to walk through a cement ditch filled with a white powder. This ditch separated the first set of laboratories from the second group.

From the outside, the second facility resembled the one they left. The interior, however, was quite different. Adjacent rooms, with closed wooden doors, lined each side of a corridor that ran east–west through the building. Li was especially impressed with the fact that each door was numbered, and he knew that some work was being done behind the closed doors. Yet, "nothing could be heard. Everything was in dead silence."

The veterinarian led the group to an exhibition room. Photographs lined the room's walls. Many of the photos dealt with anthrax, sheep plague, dry leaves, and smut. Their tour guide impressed his audience when he commented that "these plant and animal diseases can be used as weapons of war. They are less costly and more effective than ordinary weapons."

The group visited many laboratories and other buildings. One structure that remained in Li's memory was an animal laboratory. From the "moment we entered, we were almost choked by the foul odor permeating the corridor." The students were shown rows of cages filled with different species of mice and other rodents. The veterinarian cautioned them not to approach the cages, "because the rodents were captured in naturally infectious regions of the country. The animals were brought to Changchun for experimental purposes." The veterinarian proceeded to tell them that they "should pay attention to possibilities of biological warfare." He urged them to study infectious diseases in order to develop vaccines necessary to combat possible BW. Li remembered that "All the rooms in the building were closed and there was an eerie silence throughout the building. Outside two of the doors, armed guards were posted. We did not enter the rooms."

Their tour concluded with a visit to still another exhibition room. Before entering, the veterinarian cautioned them that "Nothing in here is pleasant. All the specimens you will see came from dead bodies of different infected disease carriers. You can look through the open door." The veterinarian opened the door to the frightened youngsters. They observed a "room full of glass jars containing human heads, arms, thighs, hearts, spleens and sexual organs. All the specimens were soaked in formaldehyde."[16]

Their guide had still one more treat in store for his visitors before they were permitted to return to their school. Once outside, he ordered a soldier to bring him a horse. He then fed it some wheat that had been contaminated with a pathogen. "A few minutes later, the horse lay dead." They waited some time for their truck to take them back to the city. While waiting, they observed that "the great chimney was sending out dark yellow smoke that discharged a terrible odor. We thought that the veterinarian gave an order to burn the horse he had just poisoned."[17]

IV

Unit 100's research activities were not confined solely to the Changchun base. As with Unit 731, branch units were established in strategic areas throughout Manchuria. It is known that Unit 100 branches existed in Darien, Hailar, Rako Station, Dalny, Lagu, and Keshan.[18] Later on, other branches were established at Dongan, Jining, Dongning, and Siping. These sub-units also engaged primarily in plant and animal BW research, but they did not ignore opportunities to pursue human BW experiments. All Unit 100 personnel joined with their 731 counterparts in cooperative ventures whenever possible.[19]

The known reports on the nature of Unit 100 human experiments are not as plentiful as those furnished to the United States and the Soviet Union in the postwar period by surviving 731 personnel. Nevertheless, chilling details of the work done with humans by veterinarians and medical doctors at Changchun do exist. These accounts suggest that Changchun personnel viewed their victims with the same lack of compassion as did Ishii and Kitano's men. Wakamatsu's technicians, veterinarians, medical doctors, biologists, micro-biologists, pathologists, and the like, rarely if ever reflected upon the ethics or the morality of what they were doing to fellow humans. To them, these people were not human. They were merely, in the words of one of the veterinarians, "experimental materials." The scientists and technicians were in Changchun to do a job, one that it was hoped would help their country in the war against their enemies.

Laboratory assistant Hataki Akira dispassionately observed in a postwar interrogation that Unit 100

> investigated the action of bacteria by means of experiments on domestic animals and human beings, for which purpose the detachment had horses, cows and other animals, and also kept human beings in isolation cells, which I know from what I saw myself.

Fukuzumi Mitsuyoshi, a veterinarian surgeon, observed dispassionately that the unit was composed essentially of bacteriologists, chemists, veterinarians, and agronomists, whose principal responsiblity was to prepare "for bacterio-logical sabotage and warfare." Unit 100 personnel

> carried on research . . . in methods of employing bacteria and virulent poisons on a large scale for the mass extermination of animals and human beings. . . . In order to ascertain the effectiveness of these poisons, experi-ments were performed on animals and living people.[20]

Ouchi Mamoru, a former blacksmith at Changchun, confessed that, while he did not personally witness human experiments during his tour of duty there, he "heard of the experiments through . . . a photographer who had taken pictures of the experiments." Ouchi did see a picture of one "of the POWs after death and that the POW had been dissected after he died from being injected with BISO [glanders]."[21]

Unlike human BW trials at Ping Fan where *maruta* were subjected to a series of tests with different pathogens, and then ultimately "sacrificed" when they no longer were worthy test materials, Unit 100 "experimental materials" were limited to only a single bacteria or poison. Changchun victims were in general liquidated within two weeks of their exposure to a toxin or pathogen. A sergeant testified, for example, that he witnessed his colonel kill two men after completing an experiment. The colonel then explained that "the ma-terials were no longer worth keeping for further experiments."[22]

Common chemical pesticides, as well as others in the developmental stage, were a favorite weapon tested on humans. Narcotics, such as opium and heroin, were also tried on Unit 100's subjects. In one experiment, in August 1943, seven humans were forced to ingest assorted quantities of heroin. One victim received nearly 1 gram of heroin in his food, collapsed in less than one half-hour after swallowing the potion, and died some fifteen or sixteen minutes later. The other six were given smaller doses, taking longer times to die. Eventually, the researchers discovered to their satisfaction the optimum dosage required to kill people. In another experiment, patients over a two-week period were injected with different quantities of potassium cyanide. All died within the two-week period.

Unit 100 experimented with aerial spraying techniques that resembled those practiced by the Ping Fan researchers. At times, Changchun personnel would test their pathogens at the Anda station. On other occasions, they would use secluded pasturelands near their home base. In one experiment in June 1945, men were tied to stakes in a predetermined pattern. Airplanes then circled the area spraying a chemical that enveloped the men. A short time later, perhaps thirty or so minutes, red spots and swelling began to erupt on the prisoners' skin. White spots appeared on the leaves of plants found in the area. All the exposed prisoners died within a short time of their exposure. The plants withered and died shortly thereafter.[23]

Kino Takeshi was a veterinarian who worked at the Changchun facility from 1938 until the war's end. He, along with virtually every former member of the BW teams in Manchuria, denied to American interrogators that he participated in human tests. While skirting the truth, he did concede that he "heard rumors that experiments of that sort [human BW tests] were being performed." When asked what exactly the rumors were, Kino replied, "I heard others saying that about thirteen (13) persons had been injected with the disease [glanders]." Questioned as to how many of the experimentees died, Kino was startled, and blurted that, 'They all died from the experiment." He identified Wakamatsu as being responsible for the experiments.[24]

The most explicit account of human experimentation at Changchun was disclosed at a trial of Japanese personnel held in Khabarovsk in 1949. Under fierce interrogation by a Soviet prosecutor, one of the Japanese veterinarians yielded startling information in the following colloquy:

Question: What were your functions in the 6th section?
Answer: I was engaged, in the main, in cultivating the glanders germ. I also took part in experiments on human beings. . . .
Question: Tell us what experiments were performed on human beings in Detachment 100.
Answer: . . . I took part once in experiments on human beings.
Question: I am asking you about something else: were experiments performed on human beings in Detachment 100, or not?
Answer: Yes, they were.
Question: Who performed those experiments?
Answer: Four people conducted the experiments.
Question: Tell us all you know about experiments on human beings performed in Detachment 100.
Answer: Experiments on human beings were performed in August–September 1944.[25] These experiments took the form of giving experi-

mentees, without their knowledge, soporific drugs and poisons. The experimentees included 7–8 Russians and Chinese. Korean bindweed, heroin and castor-oil seed were among the poisons used in the experiments. These poisons were put in the food. The poisoned food was given to the experimentees five or six times over a period of two weeks. Korean bindweed was used mostly in soups, I think heroin in porridge, while tobacco was mixed with heroin and bactal (sic). After eating the soup mixed with Korean bindweed the experimentees dropped off into a deep five-hour sleep 30 minutes or an hour later. After two weeks the experimentees were so weak that they could no longer be used.

Question: What happened to them?

Answer: For purposes of secrecy all the experimentees were put to death.

Question: How?

Answer: There was the case of a Russian experimentee who . . . was put to death with an injection of one-tenth of a gram of potassium cyanide.

Question: Who put him to death?

Answer: I made the injection of potassium cyanide.

Question: What did you do with the body of the Russian, whom you had killed?

Answer: I dissected the body at the detachment's cattle cemetery.

Question: What did you do with the body afterwards?

Answer: I buried it . . . in the cattle cemetery, at the back of the detachment's premises.

Question: In the same place where the carcasses of cattle were buried?

Answer: The place is the same, only the pit is different. (There is movement in the courtroom, a low murmur of indignation.)

Question: Do you know of other instances of experimentees being killed?

Answer: Two Russians and one Chinese were shot dead by gendarmes on the same place.

Question: That is, those people were shot dead right in the cattle cemetery?

Answer: Yes.

Question: Why were they killed by the gendarmes?

Answer: I think for purposes of secrecy.

Question: So it would be correct to say that all persons brought to Detachment 100 for experimental purposes were doomed to die?

Answer: That is so.[26]

V

Plague, anthrax, and glanders experiments occupied a considerable amount of the time Wakamatsu's scientists devoted to human experiments. Within the nine years that the Changchun facility operated, hundreds, if not thousands, of "experimental materials" were expended in experiments dealing with these diseases. Pathologists conducted countless autopsies of the dead and, sometimes, the living victims. The autopsies were not typical of those conducted in most hospitals. Instead, these autopsies were so thorough and meticulous, they leave the impression that every cell and every tissue in the bodies on the examining tables was investigated.

Two reports, one on glanders, the other on anthrax, illustrate the incredible degree of thorough study pathologists at Changchun dedicated to their patients and to the diseases under review. The glanders report, entitled "The Report of 'G'," discussed twenty-one cases in 372 pages. This report contained numerous pastel-colored illustrations and hundreds of photographs of body cells. The anthrax report, listed as "The Report of 'A'," analyzes thirty cases in 406 pages, complete with pastel illustrations and photographs of cellular structures.

Case number 54 in the anthrax report reflects one pathologist's dedication to detail. In this example, the person was exposed to a seven-day course of treatment with anthrax spores, and then sacrificed. The autopsy revealed that the principal pathological changes were: "Localized cutaneous ulcers and perifocal phlegmons (r-thigh) . . . Heart: Intense degeneration and interstitial edema. Liver: Hepatitis serosa III, accompanied with some hemorrhagic changes. Kidney: Glomerulo-nephrosis, with vacuolar degeneration of epitheliums. Spleen: Splenitis infectiosa." As for anthrax deaths through peroral infection, "9 cases were infected perorally with some food stuffs, which contain some quantity of anthrax bacillus and all patients died definitely after several days by acute abdominal symptoms and severe hemorrhagic ascites." In other words, the BW scientists kept track almost hourly of the disease as it spread through the victims' bodies.[27]

The glanders report took note of the fact that "Some cases (8 cases of 21 cases) died in acute stage with some septicemic-toxic symptoms and some adjacent septicemic changes of organs. Not yet accompaneid (*sic*) with remarkable organic changes." Case number 224 endured a four-day course of treatment before dying. His autopsy revealed "Traumatic wounds. Congestion in Large-Intestine and Pancreas. Intersitial edema of Kidney. Reactive congestion of lung (slight diffuse Alveolitis)." Case number 180 lasted twelve days. The longest-lived victim in this report, case number 16, lived thirteen days. These longer lived BW experimentees developed the same symptoms as case number 24. In addition, their organs disclosed (number 180) "Miliary glanders-Knots in exudative form, accompanied with some parenchymatous degeneration in the Liver," and (case 16) "Intense parenchymatous degeneration of pancreas" as well as "Metastatic Tonsillitis acuta."[28]

VI

Wakamatsu's unit engaged in field tests from the moment his organization became operational. No limitations were placed by either the War Ministry in Tokyo or the Kwantung Army High Command upon the unit's campaigns. Unit 100 was free to roam wherever it believed a good test site was available in Manchuria and in China, both in occupied territory as well as in areas still under Chiang Kai Shek's command. The men who directed the unit's affairs never hesitated to violate international borders in order to advance BW development.

Consequently, the Changchun BW group entered into even more field trials than Unit 731 ventured during the years of BW testing. These investigations covered a range of BW areas, including primitive attempts at biotechnology in agriculture and animal life, as well as several imaginative undertakings in human BW. Unit 100 participated in joint undertakings on many occasions with Unit 731 personnel and specially qualified persons from other BW units. It operated also on its own whenever the moment appeared propitious. In fact, the principal tests were conducted by Unit 100 as solo enterprises. Wakamatsu was as creative as Ishii and Kitano when it came to apportioning death and destruction to innocent civilian populations, or to the military personnel of countries with whom Japan was not formally at war.

Field trials were conducted as far south as Canton, in cities along the ancient silk trade routes west to Sian (Xian), in and around Changchun, and, in the north, at the Manchurian–Soviet frontier. There is evidence, too, that on numerous occasions daring members of the unit crossed the border into Soviet Siberia. Here they carried out widespread sabotage, spreading disease to animals, humans, and plant life. Respect for international law, international boundaries, or the welfare of foreign nationals and their property did not enter into the calculations of Japan's militarists or the scientists who worked for them.

Field trials occurred routinely from 1939 until the end of the war. No doubt, Wakamatsu and his men conducted many more tests than those revealed to postwar investigators in either Tokyo or Siberia. It was only under intense pressure from the victors that Unit 100 survivors reluctantly disclosed bits and pieces of the field tests undertaken by their Unit. The total count of the number and the size of the tests of this one BW entity perhaps will never be known.

What is clear is that Unit 100 personnel were at Nomonhan in 1939, and assisted Unit 731 in sabotage operations against the Soviets. Wakamatsu's people also conducted attacks independently against Soviet troops, Soviet civilians, their animals and their pasturelands during the conflict. The lessons learned at Nomonhan were put to good use in future campaigns.

BW tests were later conducted in border areas of Manchuria and Mongolia with assorted animals and different soils and crops in the region, in preparation for the expected war with the Soviet Union. In the summer of 1942, for example, animal experiments were carried out "to test the effectiveness of bacteriological weapons under climatic conditions most closely approximating those prevailing on Soviet Union territory."

During the following summer, tests to determine the proper dosage needed to kill horses with different poisons were carried out by Unit 100 veterinarians. Between forty and fifty horses were inoculated with assorted amounts of either potassium cyanide, strychnine, or other poisons. At least ten horses perished. The personnel in charge of the tests were not told the ultimate purpose for conducting such peculiar experiments. Nor did they concern themselves with such questions. They followed orders.

Less than one year later, General Takahashi Takaatsu, Chief of the Veterinary Service, "with the knowledge of the 2nd Intelligence Division . . . of the Kwantung Army," ordered Unit 100 people to deploy into Mongolia, for the purpose of reconnoitering "the roads, summer and winter cattle pastures, the state of water sources and the number of cattle belonging to the local population." The purpose of the expedition was to prepare for the day when the Unit would "conduct bacteriological sabotage against the Soviet Union."

With the war going badly, in early 1945, Takahashi, in a desperate search for a fresh killer weapon, ordered Wakamatsu to test animals with newly devised BW pathogens at Unit 731's Anda proving grounds. He later received encouraging news that "all ten cows that were experimented on died." Emboldened by this success, he directed a subordinate to purchase 500 sheep, 100 cattle, and 90 horses, "which were to be infected with severe infectious diseases and then left in the rear of the Soviet troops" when war was declared. Eighty thousand yen was diverted from the severely limited Kwantung Army budget to carry out the project.

The plan was to infect the cattle with anthrax and cattle plague, the sheep with sheep plague, and the horses with anthrax. The animals were to be liberated and allowed to stray in different directions, permitting them to "wander into the area of the operations of the Soviet troops." At the same time, using aircraft flown by Unit 731 pilots, cattle and horses belonging "to the local population" would be sprayed with cattle plague (for the cattle) and anthrax (for the horses). However, resources were diverted to other projects, and this operation apparently failed to get off the ground.[29]

A smaller project was launched instead. Sometime in spring 1945, one of Wakamatsu's veterinarians stationed in Inner Mongolia purchased ten calves from local farmers. The animals were to be used within the region in cattle plague tests. Snow was still on the ground, and the experimenters conducted what they called "winter manoeuvres." Experiments were launched "under conditions similar to those under which bacteriological sabotage against the Mongolian People's Republic was to be conducted, for it is known that, in Mongolia, cattle gain their food in the winter time by grazing." The tests produced gratifying results.[30]

Tests on a much larger scale were conducted near Unit 100's home base. Counties surrounding Changchun experienced periodic unusual outbreaks of epidemics from 1940 until the end of the war. Some of the communities affected by plague, for example, had not encountered the disease within the memory of local inhabitants. Now, plague seemed to erupt frequently.

A case in point occurred in the summer and fall of 1943. Shinko city and Noan county lie slightly north of Changchun. Plague surfaced in the county in early June. Gradually, the epidemic spread to nearby counties and, by fall, invaded the city of Shinko. Plague was no stranger to Noan county. However, it was virtually unknown in Shinko. The outbreak in Noan county occurred so

abruptly, and under such mysterious circumstances, that a Japanese pathologist, called to the scene to take advantage of the opportunity to study plague
victims, noted with some bewilderment that the June flare-up "occurred
suddenly . . . by some means." Hundreds of people died until the epidemic ran
its course. Shinko city lost eighteen persons to the disease in a few days in mid-
September. The city and Noan county contributed forty-nine patients to the
Japanese pathologists during the period 29 September to 5 November. Many
other victims went to their deaths unrecorded, escaping the skilled post-
mortem examinations of Unit 100's pathologists.[31]

Earlier, in 1940, a series of epidemics struck Nongan county, 50 kilometers
northwest of Changchun. The origin of the epidemics is still uncertain. There
is some evidence that the pestilence may have come to Nongan by accident.
Several scholars believe that waste from the Changchun facility somehow
seeped into the underground water table, and spread as far north as Nongan.
Others are convinced that rats escaped from Unit 100 laboratories, and
brought plague with them to the affected region. Still others are certain that the
Nongan county plague epidemic was nothing more than a BW field test
undertaken by Unit 100.[32]

What is known is that, on 12 June 1940, four young men selling fish
canvassed the western part of the county. Two of the fish peddlers were
obviously ill, and sought medical attention at a local clinic once they disposed
of their catch. The two men died within a few days. Their companions perished
shortly afterwards. The nurse who attended the sick men died a few days later.
The nurse's brother and his wife contracted plague and died within one week
after the fishermen came into the community. Neighbors who had been in
contact with either the nurse or her family became ill and died in a matter of
days. Plague began to ravage the entire county.

One month after the fish sellers appeared in Nongan county, a squad of
doctors and technicians descended upon the community from their base in
Changchun. This was one of Unit 100's Epidemic Prevention Squadrons. The
group, consisting of Japanese and Korean doctors and technicians, numbered
between fifty and sixty men, and took control of the situation quickly.

The Beiguan primary school in Cao Jia Putun became their headquarters.
Here they established isolation rooms for sick patients. Classrooms were set
aside for their doctors to use for medical examinations. Other rooms were
appropriated for laboratories. The rest of the building was used as sleeping
quarters for the squad.

Members of the Japanese–Korean team patrolled the county looking for
sick people. Additional personnel were assigned duties to keep strangers out of
the county and, most specially, out of hard-hit Cao Jia Putun, the county seat.
Casualties were so great that another school, Primary School 21, was
commandeered to serve as an isolation center for sick patients.

Patients with even a slight fever were sent to the isolation wards. Few lived
to tell about their experiences. Pathologists worked fourteen- and fifteen-hour
days, conducting autopsies of the hundreds of persons who perished from one

of several varieties of plague. When finished with, the victims' bodies were tossed out the back of the school house for burial in the woods. Frightened locals joked among themselves that the living entered the Beiguan primary school through the front gates, while the dead exited from the back door. Within six months, hundreds of corpses left via the back door. In August, five traditional Chinese doctors visited the Beiguan facility. After inspecting recently dissected corpses, they were told by the Japanese doctor in charge that "Bacteria is good. It will not kill good people."

By October, plague victims may have numbered in the thousands. Anyone who was ill and who was examined by a member of Unit 100 was certain to die. Either plague would kill the individual, or a Wakamatsu subordinate would conduct in vivo inspections of the person's infected body. The pathologists carved up so many body parts that two blacksmiths were called in to weld together huge iron containers large enough to house all the specimens collected.

The plague attack was so devastating that on one single street in Cao Jia Putun most of the inhabitants were annihilated. On 12 June, forty-five families lived in cramped quarters on Northeast Street. Within six months, thirty-eight residents of Northeast Street were dead of plague.

Panic was endemic throughout the county, but more so in Cao Jia Putun where the Japanese were headquartered. The town was surrounded by soldiers, and placed under quarantine. No one was permitted to leave the community without permission. Every day all the residents of the town were required to submit to a medical examination. People were lined up for inspection beginning at eight in the morning and at three in the afternoon. Residents were desperate to pass the examination in order to be spared the certain death awaiting them in the isolation centers. To appear healthy looking, women wore heavy makeup before entering the medical center. Others placed sliced potatoes or pieces of cabbage under their armpits in the vain hope that such amulets would lower their body temperature and spare them from the isolation ward.

The onset of freezing cold weather, in January 1941, led to the abatement of the plague epidemic. By February, the plague was gone, and residents of Nongan county returned to their normal routines. During the prior six months, 353 citizens of Cao Jia Putun are known to have perished. Many more throughout the county fell victim to Unit 100's experiment. Nongan proved that the plague pathogen could be an effective BW weapon.[33]

Japanese scientists from Unit 100's research section took advantage of the Nongan plague outbreak to test plague as a possible BW weapon by employing a facility closer to headquarters. While attention was focused on Nongan, other scientists from the Unit descended upon a ramshackle slum on the outskirts of Changchun. This desperately poor neighborhood lay 1 kilometer north of Changchun's east gate. Japanese soldiers rounded up the slum's inhabitants for a meeting at which the scientists informed the frightened people that cases of plague had been discovered nearby. They reassured the residents that they all would be inoculated against the dreaded disease. The scientists failed to tell the slum dwellers that they were not being given a vaccine, but that the fluid inserted into their veins contained plague pathogens.

Plague did envelop the community within a short period after the inoculation episode. The 700 families – approximately 5000 people – who lived in the slum were forcibly evacuated to the village of Song Jia Wazi, 2 kilometers away. This was to be their "temporary home" until a new plot of land could be found for permanent habitation. The old slum site was burned to the ground by the Japanese. Although the number of persons who perished in this man-induced plague outbreak is unknown, it is not unreasonable to assume that the death toll must have been high since living conditions in the community were unsanitary and primitive.[34]

VII

The Changchun BW factory and its satellite branches were destroyed by order of the Kwantung Army High Command during the closing days of the war. As with Ping Fan, all buildings were blown up with high explosives. Some expensive equipment, too heavy or cumbersome to transport, was also smashed. The rest of the equipment, and as much data and research material as could be salvaged, was transported back to Japan.

Unit 100 did not abandon Changchun until all prisoners were killed, those infected with pathogens as well as the healthy. No one was spared. Chinese workers at the camp were also eliminated. Prisoners and civilian employees alike were given injections of potassium cyanide. Only a handful of workers managed to survive the dosage given them.

A few lucky ones avoided the potassium ceremony, and lived to tell of some of their experiences. Big Li, a cart driver, was one of the fortunate. In 1943 he raped a Japanese national, and was sent to Unit 100's headquarters. He was so big and strong that the authorities spared him from death by experiment and used his brawn at various work stations. In the chaotic last days of the evacuation, Li was assigned to help pack equipment onto trucks. One of the trucks became stuck in mud. Li and a few other Chinese were ordered to push the truck out of the mud. After doing so, they remained hidden in the gooey mass, forgotten, until the camp evacuation was completed. They then escaped to freedom.[35]

Most of the animals used in experiments were destroyed. A handful were kept alive and were employed for sinister purposes. On 20 August 1945, long after Emperor Hirohito issued his surrender decree, six members of Unit 100 entered one of the horse stables at the headquarters. They proceeded to infect sixty horses with glanders by feeding them oats containing glanders germs. The six men "then opened fences at the base and drove the horses in different directions. All the horses scattered to the near-by villages and along different roads."[36]

Hordes of rats were liberated from their cages at the same time the horses were set free. Some of the rats were infected with a host of pathogens, including plague germs. Soon, a 20 mile area surrounding the former BW death factory was overrun with rats, many of which were disease carriers.

Changchun and environs experienced outbreaks of plague, glanders, and anthrax epidemics in 1946, 1947, and 1951. Casualties were exceptionally high at the time because the civil war then raging in the region left medical facilities limited at best. The death toll was great, and parts of Changchun and the surrounding towns remained uninhabitable until the mid-1950s. Wakamatsu and his fellow veterinarians and scientists left a lasting impression upon the late capital of the Manchukuo empire.

8 Nanking's BW death factory

The people of the unit [in Nanking] called their steel barred cells "rooms that do not open." The cells were patrolled by armed guards at all times. At the 731st, they called these subjects "*maruta*" (logs); but here, they were called "zaimoku" (lumber).

A former member of the Nanking BW unit recalled: sometimes it was tough on the new soldiers and they had no place to go and cry, so they went to the latrine. They would slip out of their beds quietly at night and go. One night when I went, I saw two soldiers dressed in white carrying a stretcher. They took it to the incinerator beyond the latrine. There was a white cloth over the stretcher, but from the way it bulged, it was clear that there was a person under it.
(Quoted in Tsuneishi and Asano, *Suicide of Two Physicians*, pp. 121–122)

I

Nanking (Nanjing) at first glance is a doubtful location to build a BW death factory. Unlike the new Manchurian cities of Harbin and Changchun, it is not positioned in a remote part of the world, isolated from foreign observers. Nanking is one of China's most famous cities, with a long and important history. It is an ancient city that is situated in the heart of China on the lower part of the great Yangtze River.

The city is located in the midst of beautiful natural scenery; lovely green forests and magnificent low-lying mountains, notably the Zijin (Purple and Gold) Mountains, make Nanking one of China's most attractive cities. Nanking's one major drawback is its harsh, brutal climate in summer. Temperature soars into the 100-plus degrees Fahrenheit range for nearly three months (late June through mid-September), and humidity hovers in the 90-plus percentages daily during the period. It is no wonder that Nanking is known as one of the three "hot furnaces" of China, the other two being the Yangtze River towns of Wuhan and Chungking (Chongqing).

Home to a rich variety of agricultural products grown in the fertile areas surrounding the city, this great river port and trading center had been China's national capital several times. It held that honor from 220 to 589 A.D., and then again from 907 to 979. The city's real importance began in 1368 when it became the Ming dynasty's first capital. Nanking played an important role during the British-generated Opium War (1840–1842), and the peasant uprising known as the Taiping Rebellion (1851–1864). It became Chiang Kai Shek's capital in 1927, and remained the nationalist, throughout the era of Chiang's quest for supreme control over all China. He ruled from Nanking until he was driven out of the city by the Japanese in the fall of 1937.

The Japanese onslaught into Nanking is recorded as one of the greatest tragedies imposed on the long-suffering Chinese people, who over the centuries have become inured to disaster and calamity. From 14 December 1937 until 7 February 1938, Japanese troops, with the unofficial blessing of their officers, ran amok through the streets of the city, looting, and raping and killing anyone they could find. Civilians were treated as harshly as any soldiers found still wandering in the devastated community. While the final rape and death count is in dispute (the Tokyo War Crimes Tribunal in 1946 accepted the figure of 20,000 women raped and over 200,000 men slaughtered), a close student of the event estimates that "not less than 100,000 war prisoners and 50,000 civilians were executed within thirty-seven miles of Nanking and that at least 5,000 women were raped, many of them repeatedly or on several occasions."[1] This two-month period of wanton madness is known as "the Rape of Nanking."

Less than fourteen months after shocking the world with their brutal assault on Nanking, Japanese militarists imposed still another horrendous wound on the injured, long-suffering city. On 18 April 1939, the Central China Anti-Epidemic Water Supply Unit established a branch operation in Nanking. The new Unit was known openly as the "Tama Unit," and secretly as Unit Ei 1644. The Unit name or number was unimportant, if not irrelevant. What was crucial was that its operations were expected to be primarily research in BW and secondarily prevention of epidemics.[2]

This Anti-Epidemic Water Unit, as well as all the others scattered throughout China and Manchuria, was the brainchild of the master at Ping Fan, Ishii Shiro. Unit Ei 1644 was the third major link in the BW research chain that Ishii and his supporters erected on the Asian mainland in the mid- to late 1930s. But the reasons for initiating a new station so shortly after completing the massive undertaking at Ping Fan are unknown, and remain a tantalizing mystery.

So, too, with the selection of Nanking as the Unit's home base. Why pick a city that had been in the news so recently, and that continued to remain a newsworthy item in 1939? Indeed, why choose a site that was vulnerable to guerrilla attacks, and was a prime target for Chiang Kai Shek's forces should they ever develop the capacity for a counter attack in what had become a stalemated war of attrition?

One can only speculate. Perhaps the Tokyo militarists' strategy for ending stalemate was to use Ishii's BW weapons – when perfected – as a tool to terrorize Chiang's forces into giving up fighting. Nanking would be an ideal site for launching such a campaign because of its strategic location. Or, there is the possibility that Ishii and his subordinates wanted to test new pathogens in a climate quite different from Manchuria. There is the chance that Ishii, ever the BW empire builder, saw in the newly conquered city an opportunity eventually to move his operations to a more central place, one that would enable his BW scheme to flourish in an area currently of greater concern to the War Ministry at home than the backwater of Manchuria. Moreover, Central

China was a much larger theater in which to prove BW's worth as a military weapon. Consequently, the anticipation of rewards in the form of promotion, greater perks, and the opportunity to extort kickbacks from suppliers, and to embezzle money from the large sums allocated to Unit Ei 1644, could have been the lure that attracted Ishii to the Yangtze River port.

The danger of public exposure, of course, was greater in Nanking than in either Harbin/Ping Fan or any of the other northern branch bases, but security could be controlled if the local authorities were vigilant. Ishii understood that here, as in Manchuria, there were at least three layers of police to call upon to ensure the secrecy of any BW activity. Nanking was ostensibly ruled by an independent Chinese government led by Dr Sun Yat Sen's heir apparent, Wang Ch'in Wei. However, this rival regime to Chiang Kai Shek's in Chungking was nothing more than a creature of the Japanese conquerors,[3] and its police took orders from their foreign masters. They made certain that the local populace remained under tight control. The large force of Japanese paramilitary Kempeitai stationed in the city could be relied upon to act as a support group for the Chinese collaborators should their presence be required. Finally, troops of Japan's First Army were always available if the other forces were inadequate guarantees of the security required for the BW venture.

II

Preoccupied with bringing the Ping Fan death factory to peak operating capacity, Ishii chose Masuda Tomosada to act as his Nanking surrogate. Masuda was an ideal choice to direct a BW facility. He was the exemplary Japanese doctor/scientist of the era: an exceedingly intelligent and talented individual, but one who lacked both scruples or ethics when it came to carrying out experiments with either animals or humans, if it could be rationalized as an act performed in the name of science, or for the needs and objectives of his country's military. A longtime friend and Ishii protégé, he fitted the Ishii mold perfectly.

Their personalities were quite different. A scholar familiar with both men characterized the difference as that which "exists between a man and the horse he is riding. . . . In a word, Ishii was flamboyant, while Masuda was studious and paid attention to detail." Nevertheless, Ishii was to Masuda what General Nagata Tetsuzan had been to Ishii at the outset of his career.[4]

The eldest son of a retired Army doctor, Masuda was blessed with a powerful intellect, enormous energy, a will to succeed, no matter what the cost, and a handsome physique.[5] He was born in Teramachi, Kanazawa city, in Ishikawa prefecture, on 11 January 1901. After receiving the standard primary and secondary school education in Tokyo and its environs, Masuda enrolled at Kyoto Imperial University's Medical School sometime in the early 1920s. He met his first wife – the attractive Masuda would eventually marry four times – while studying at Kyoto, and, in order to make ends meet, he applied for and received an Army reserve scholarship.

Upon entering the military after graduating in 1926, Masuda followed a path remarkably similar to that of his ultimate mentor, Ishii Shiro. Initially, he served as a medical officer in the 4th Regiment of the Imperial Guards in Tokyo, a position reserved for men who were marked for important careers within the Army's Medical Corps. Three years later, he returned to Kyoto Imperial University to begin his studies for a Ph.D. in microbiology. Masuda was awarded his degree in 1931 when the university approved his doctoral thesis, "Sedimentation Quantification in Sedimentation Reactions."

It is unknown whether Masuda came to Ishii's attention while an undergraduate at Kyoto, or only upon his return as a graduate student. In any event, by 1931, when the young Ph.D. joined the Army Medical College in Tokyo, he and Professor Ishii, who had recently come home to Japan from his round-the-world tour, were close friends and collaborators. They journeyed together to Manchuria in 1932 on a secret mission described earlier. While Masuda did not apparently join Ishii in either the Beiyinhe or the early Ping Fan ventures, there is little doubt that, under his mentor's influence, he became an ardent disciple of BW no later than 1932 or 1933.

His approach to BW can best be summarized by quoting from an audacious lecture he delivered to an audience of scientists in Tokyo on 15 December 1942. Billed as an Army Medical Colonel as well as an Instructor at the Army Medical College, Masuda delivered a lecture titled "The Bacteriological Warfare."[6] He began by arguing that the notion of using BW in wartime originated "from the possibilities of introducing artificially created epidemics among the enemy troops" (p. 2). The Colonel then defined BW as "The acts of employing pathogens (sic) to destroy the living matters of the enemy and thereby attaining the more favorable position on our part" (p. 2). Masuda noted that "BW can be used not only against the enemy personnel[,] but all living matters within the enemy territory including the people, livestock, domestic animals, grains, and vegetables." Moreover, "It can be also employed against the neutral countries which manifest signs of becoming the allies of the enemy country" (p. 3).

The career Army doctor discussed dispassionately BW's effect on enemy morale ("Regardless of the results, to disseminate bacteria among the civilized people will affect their morale" (p. 4)), potential economic consequences ("The outbreaks of epidemics at various places will necessitate the country to expend much of its man-power and materials in bringing the epidemics under control and will greatly hinder the nation in carrying out its war" (p. 4)), and various delivery systems ("The offensive tactics can be carried out in forms of bacterial rain or dropping bombs or firing shells filled with bacteria or through spies;" or "It can be used against the enemy not in direct contact with the friendly troops, especially against their navy by contaminating their foodstuffs with typhoid bacteria just prior to their ships leaving port" (pp. 12, 13)).

Masuda concluded his lecture by observing that, "Various countries have been aware of the potential danger of the BW and its usefulness, but it is far from being a simple problem. To cause a great outbreak of epidemics, various

complicated influencing factors must be considered." These could be overcome, he assured his audience in 1942. Employing a not too subtle allusion to
Japan's successful tactic at Pearl Harbor the previous year, Masuda observed:

> It is vitally essential that the BW must be a surprise attack. In defense it is
> impossible to eliminate in advance the danger of BW attacks, but more
> civilized nations can, through their trained scientific personnel and by their
> equipment, keep the epidemics to a minimum, but if unprepared for the BW
> attacks, the subsequent suffering will be great.[7]

Masuda served at the Medical College until 1936, when he joined the elite
staff of the Ministry of the Army Medical Bureau. A year later he was back in
Manchuria. On 1 September 1937, he became Acting Director of the Darien
Anti-Epidemic Center, a branch unit of Ishii's BW operation. He also served
simultaneously as a valued Ishii associate in Harbin, commuting to Darien
when necessary.

The younger man's services to Ishii in Harbin are unknown, but they must
have been greatly valued by his mentor. Ishii could be generous to those whom
he regarded highly. He was to Masuda. It is probable that Masuda became
part of the Ishii coterie who received kickbacks from contractors engaged in
work at Ping Fan and other Ishii-run enterprises. His lifestyle while stationed
in Manchuria was on a scale that is inconceivable if he depended solely on his
Army pay. Masuda's widow later remembered spending three wonderful
months in Harbin, living in a villa once owned by a White Russian. The villa
was lavishly furnished and was staffed with many servants, including a cook.
She was "really surprised that an Army officer could live so well."[8] Two years
later, in 1939, Ishii called upon his loyal friend to take over as Acting Director
of the new BW facility in Nanking.

Ei 1644's home, incredibly, was located in the heart of Nanking, within a
short walk from the Yangtze River. Using an existing Chinese hospital as its
nucleus, the new BW base encompassed a large area along East Zhonsan
Street, an east–west artery that stretched across the city. To the west of the
base lay the Yangtze. The base's north side immediately fronted on the Zijin
mountain, which was always resplendent in spring when its renowned cherry
trees blossomed. A path leading up the mountain to Dr Sun Yat Sen's tomb
lay a brief stroll from this north side.

The Japanese Army's military airport was across the street, providing
military and medical visitors to Ei 1644's headquarters with convenient access.
Almost all the Unit's needs could be provided nearby. The local bar/geisha
district, headquarters for the China Expeditionary Forces High Command,
Military Police Headquarters, the Japanese Consulate, the Army's hospital, a
Japanese movie theater and a Japanese owned and run department store could
be found within a thirty minutes' walk from the camp.

As with all BW facilities, the Nanking base was surrounded by a 3 meter
high brick wall topped with barbed wire. Several strands of electrically
charged wire were also placed along the wall. A special elite police unit was

stationed on base, and patrolled the area twenty-four hours each day. Guard dogs were used as well to prevent escapes and to ward off unwanted intruders. To guarantee that personnel did not reveal BW secrets, every person working in the camp, military or civilian, was required to sign a sacred oath swearing that nothing they saw or heard there would ever be revealed to an outsider. As one officer told his men, "Things that you see here and find out here must never be told to anyone, your parents, your brothers, or even your wife."[9]

The six-story-high former Chinese hospital, lying adjacent to the south gate, was the main building on base. This was the headquarters building, housing the commander's office and the camp's general offices. A four-story annex contained the research facilities and the prison housing humans scheduled to be used in BW experiments. The annex was the heart of the Unit's activities. The camp also contained kitchens, warehouses, barracks for those who were to be trained for BW work, a recreation center, a swimming pool, an auditorium, an armory, a clothing disinfectant station, a library, and an incinerator for disposing of animal and human experiments.

All told, the detachment, which included branches scattered around the city, embraced a complement of roughly 1500 men when at full strength.[10] Officers and important civilian scientists lived off base. Masuda was housed in a luxurious one-story concrete villa that formerly was owned by an expatriate German. The villa was known as the "Momohara Lodge," and was less than a ten minute stroll from East Zhongsan Street. He entertained in an extravagant fashion at the "Lodge," and especially enjoyed heavy drinking bouts with his brother-in-law, Assistant Professor Iijima Mamoru, a fellow BW scientist. A number of small buildings in the grounds provided comfortable living quarters for other high-ranking staff members and visiting officials.

Masuda and his superiors maintained a subterfuge about their work, but their ploy deceived few. They went to the trouble of having a master calligrapher paint a beautiful sign, which they erected at the camp's entrance, proclaiming it to be one of the Central China Anti-Epidemic Water Supply Units. However, soldiers stationed in other nearby Units were not deceived. They sarcastically nicknamed the place the "Nanking Seventh Wonder Unit," or, "the Secret Unit." Rumors flew throughout the Japanese camps in the city that "Sick soldiers who went to the Tama Unit Hospital never returned."[11]

III

Most BW research, including work on humans, was conducted in the annex building, next to administrative headquarters. Here Unit Ei 1644 did not specialize in one or two pathogens that possibly might be utilized for BW purposes. Instead, as with all Ishii led research, Nanking worked with every conceivable disease, the commonplace and the exotic, a medical dictionary full of pathogens, and a collector's fantasy of strange animal toxins used to kill humans. Masuda did stress studies of cholera, typhus, and plague, but he did not ignore snake poisons, blowfish poisons, cyanide, and arsenic.

The annex's first floor gave the appearance of a conventional research laboratory. Scientists and technicians on the first floor worked diligently to produce huge quantities of cholera, typhus, and plague cultures. The smaller research animals were housed on the second floor. Lice, fleas, mice, rats, ground squirrels, etc., were bred in large numbers on this level. Most of the laboratories and research rooms were located on the third floor. The building's upper floor held the prisoners who were undergoing experimentation, or who would shortly be introduced into the realm of BW research.

The fourth-floor jail could house up to 100 persons, but usually only twenty to thirty people were in residence there at one time. Most of the prisoners were Chinese. However, many White Russians, as well as a sprinkling of other nationalities, somehow became experimental subjects for Masuda's scientists. Experiments were not limited to adult male prisoners. Women and young children were also used in the Nanking tests in proportionately larger numbers than in either Ping Fan or Changchun.

Although smaller in size than the BW facilities at either Ping Fan or Changchun, Nanking enjoyed a bacteria production capacity of gargantuan dimensions. The facility's principal incubator room held two autoclaves, about 200 Ishii cultivators, and approximately fifty Koch boilers. Ten other boilers were located in Unit branches. With all the equipment operating, Unit Ei 1644 could produce 10 kilograms of bacteria in each production cycle.

Fleas also were cultivated in large numbers at Nanking. The fleas were bred in approximately one hundred gasoline cans. Hordes of fleas emerged from the gasoline containers within each production sequence. Most of the fleas produced by the scientists were used in plague experiments, a Nanking specialty.[12]

The majority of soldiers assigned to Ei 1644 did not actively participate in human experiments. They knew what was taking place there, or they became familiar with the rumors about what went on within the confines of the fourth floor. Those who actually performed human BW experiments were few in number. They were the Unit's doctors and high-level technicians. Nevertheless, in a three-year period, 1941–1943, Major General Sato Shunji, chief of the detachment, noted that 'Under my direction . . . the Training Division every year trained about 300 bacteriologists with the object of employing them in bacteriological warfare.'[13]

Masuda instilled a strong degree of personal loyalty into this latter group. Professor Yamanaka Futoki, forty-seventh Director of the Japan Bacteriology Association, and an alumnus of Ei 1644, recalled with nostalgia forty years later that Masuda enjoyed driving fast cars. He remembered that his leader took him driving on several occasions. For Yamanaka, Masuda "wasn't a bad guy."[14] Masuda's brother-in-law, Iijima Mamoru, fascinated by the Unit Commander's personality, worked at Ei 1644, despite holding grave misgivings about the nature of his BW work assignments. Iijima was a Christian and a socialist. He harbored strong feelings about a doctor's role being that of a healer, rather than that of a killer. Nevertheless, under the force of Masuda's persuasive influence, he continued to labor in Nanking while growing increasingly guilt-ridden about his work.

The average Japanese soldier's experience within the Unit is perhaps best described by one ex-draftee who told an interviewer, long after the event, of his duties there. This former private came to Unit Ei 1644 in early 1944 where he was placed in a "training unit," and given rudimentary scientific training. Each training squad consisted of ten persons. The trainees were taught how to cultivate bacteria and lice, the methods for examining water for different germs, etc. All personnel while at work wore candy-striped rubber boots and rubber gloves that came up to the shoulder. They also wore white surgical clothing, and covered their mouths with a surgical mask at all times while employed in the laboratories.

Soldiers were not permitted to take photographs while on base. They could not mention Ei 1644 in letters sent to their loved ones. Mere reference to their being attached to an anti-epidemic unit was banned by their officers. All mail was censored by their superiors.

The men were confined to the camp as much as possible[15] in the hope that information concerning 1644's activities could thus be suppressed. These security efforts may have been partially successful in keeping the local population ignorant of Masuda's activities, but his subordinates quickly learned of the real nature of the camp's work. The ex-private remembered:

> After quite a while, I found out that there were prisoners kept in the unit. My superior officer said to me: "There is a lumber storage facility on the fourth floor. You never go above the second floor, you got it."

Sometime later, another officer told him that the camp incinerator, which was surrounded by a high fence, a locked gate, and a sign saying "No Entry," was used to cremate discarded "lumber." He "said that prisoners killed in the experiments were incinerated using the oil burner, then the bones were crushed and buried on the grounds." Incineration routinely took place late at night, usually between the hours of 11 p.m. and 1 or 2 a.m.[16]

Another former member of Unit Ei 1644, a corporal, recalled that his initial assignment with the Unit was in the mice-raising laboratory. One day in 1944,

> We had to fall out on an emergency basis. We formed up with our weapons. I was put as a guard near the front gate. A military police car then came through the gate and let out a prisoner. His head was covered with white cloth, but he seemed to be a Chinese male. . . . I had not participated in human experimentation myself, but it was common knowledge that human beings were used in place of guinea pigs for the bacteriological testing. . . . I had been given the job several times of guarding "the rooms that did not open" on the fourth floor. When we lost the war, the officers panicked and incinerated the mice and took ping pong tables up to the 4th floor. I don't know what happened to the prisoners at that time.[17]

Unit Ei 1644's crowning achievement in human BW research occurred in 1941. The undertaking was so enormous that it had to include staff from other technical units in order for the project to be viable. Ultimately, Masuda collaborated with the Ninth Army Technology Research Institute, or Kyu-Ken, in a series of experiments that ran the gamut of human imagination in depravity.

The Kyu-Ken was headquartered in Kanagawa prefecture. Here, on a picturesque plateau overlooking the Tama River and the nearby city of Kawasaki, the Kyu-Ken engaged in the development of secret weapons. Sometime that year, a Kyu-Ken colonel, who headed the Unit's Technical Second Branch, and seven of his best people (five technical officers and two assistants), left by ship for Nanking. They carried with them an enormous variety of toxins that were to be used in the forthcoming human experiments. These included nitrile prussiate, acetone, cyanide hydric, arsenite, poison taken from Taiwanese snakes such as cobra, habu, and amagasa, as well as crystallized blowfish poison and refined "trikabuto" poison. For good measure, they brought along also a collection of different types of bacteria.

In Nanking, the Kyu-Ken joined with Ei 1644, employing the Unit's facilities and two of its doctors and an interpreter. For a little over one month, prisoners under close guard were daily taken from the fourth floor to the third-floor laboratories. Once in the third-floor laboratory, they were placed on beds, and told by the interpreter not to worry. The men in white gowns were doctors, the interpreter reassured them, and they were in Nanking to "give you medicine to heal your bodies." The victims were then quickly injected with snake venom or prussic acid, or some other poison, and the doctors and technicians settled down to observe the subjects' reactions. One of the Japanese technicians who participated in the experiments recalled that "We didn't want them to catch on and thrash around so I gave them the injection very quickly." Shortly after injecting one patient, the technician remembered, the victim's "body went limp, but it took several minutes for his heart to completely stop beating."

In order to test the validity of the thesis that arsenite causes cardiac arrest, the technician who injected the poisons into humans was given the assignment of feeding arsenite to the victims. The ever-helpful technician fed six people dumplings filled with arsenite. Unfortunately for him, the six did not fall ill. Frustrated, the technician increased the dosage, but to no avail. He gave up in disgust after a tenfold increase in the dosage failed to produce the desired results, commenting that "You can't depend on the literature. No matter how much I fed them, it would be excreted by them a few days later." The technician's interviewer was moved to observe that "Mr A talked of these things lightly, seemingly with no sense of guilt."[18]

The joint Kyu-Ken–Masuda experiments concentrated on BW, but they did not ignore CW. Unit Ei 1644 possessed a gas chamber fitted with an observation window in which CW experiments could be conducted, and it was put to use shortly after the Kyu-Ken contingent arrived in Nanking. Japanese researchers were most interested in the effects of prussic acid as a potentially effective CW weapon, especially in tank warfare. To test their theories, prisoners were brought to the gas chamber and strapped into chairs in the room. A doctor wearing a gas mask would then join them, strip the seals from a container filled with prussic acid, and proceed to record the death throes of the human subjects. These CW experiments were conducted at the same time, or shortly before, those that Ishii was carrying on along the Soviet border.

The joint Nanking tests killed many people (just how many is uncertain),[19] but the results were largely unsatisfactory. One former member of the test team noted ruefully that "Having them drink snake venom was no good. Effects were better when it was injected." Another stated that "Anthracnose [possibly a mistranslation for anthrax] bacteria had been one which caused illness in cattle and horses. We were trying to infect people by having them drink a culture solution, but it did not kill them." These failures did not matter in the long run. The prisoners were killed to keep them from talking, and the pathologists gained useful knowledge for their profession by dissecting the bodies, studying the organs, and disposing of the remains in the ever-busy Unit Ei 1644 incinerator.[20]

IV

Masuda's Unit exercised little independent control over its activities. Unit Ei 1644 essentially was a support component for Ishii's Unit 731 projects. The Nanking venture may on occasion have engaged in field trials or some other activity on its own initiative, but its basic responsibilities were to produce pathogens, test the products on "lumber material," and assist Ishii whenever he called upon the Unit for help.

Unit Ei 1644 actively participated in the three most notorious BW field trials Ishii conducted in Central China. Nanking produced many of the fleas used in these tests, as well as pathogens employed in the same probes. Masuda also loaned Ishii some of his best men for the expeditions, and assisted his friend and benefactor in whatever way that he could.

Nanking played a role in the 1940 Ning Bo BW operation, furnishing the bulk of the fleas used in spreading the devastating epidemic that ravaged the area. In 1941, the Unit once more proved its value to Ishii by providing him with fleas and pathogens that were used in the massive field test conducted in and around Changteh. Scientists from Nanking flew in some of the Ishii-operated planes, assisting their Ping Fan brethren in aerial spraying of lethal doses of various germs on an unsuspecting population.

The Chekiang campaign in the summer of 1942 demonstrated Nanking's worth to Ishii and his BW efforts. This Central China province was a thorn in the side of the Japanese military, and the High Command determined to clean out pockets of Chinese resistance in the area by the use of conventional military methods as well as by the employment of BW. Chekiang province was going to be used as an example of Japanese retribution levied on any part of China resisting the New Order.

Ishii, in late August 1942, came down from Ping Fan to Nanking to participate in the coming campaign. Traveling in style, he arrived in the city with approximately 120 military officers and civilian employees. Some thirty other Ping Fan experts ultimately joined their confederates before the operation started. Ishii also brought with him over 100 kilograms of anthrax and paratyphoid germs. After making certain that his men and equipment were properly housed, he then called on Masuda for back-up support, since even his great resources could not provide all the men and material required to mount the massive maneuver being planned.[21]

Masuda complied readily. He played the gracious host to his important guests, providing them with all the comforts they required. He also furnished Ishii with additional supplies of pathogens, along with scientists and technicians to fill in the gaps in Unit 731's ranks.

One of the expedition's first objectives was to contaminate all water sources available to the enemy. In Ping Fan, typhoid and paratyphoid germs were placed into peptone bottles labeled "Water Supply," and transported by aircraft to Nanking. They were then brought to Unit Ei 1644's base, where the contents of the bottles were placed into metal drinking canteens or into small glass bottles. These were flown to Chekiang province, along with technicians and scientists from Units 731 and Ei 1644. The flasks and bottles were given to soldiers entrusted with the responsibility for dropping them into wells and marshes, and in people's homes. It was during this campaign that the two units distributed to Chinese prisoners the pathogen-laced sweet cakes described earlier.

In one sense, the Chekiang campaign was an enormous success. Epidemics ravaged the region in both 1942 and 1943. The number of Chinese civilians and military personnel affected by epidemic outbreaks is unknown, but most sources agree that the death toll alone was in the many thousands.

Ishii, as was his habit when dealing with anything he led, called the operation a total success. But was it? It is now known that Japanese troops became victims of the epidemics the master BW exponent produced. Casualty figures among the troops were extremely high, with one estimate suggesting that at least 1700 men died and another 10,000 became ill for a time. Chekiang, perhaps, was not the unalloyed triumph Ishii claimed.[22]

It was at this time that both Ishii and Masuda were transferred to new posts. Whether it was due to the questionable outcome of the Chekiang test, or not, is unclear. Masuda left his command in Nanking and went to Burma to head a new epidemic prevention center in Rangoon. The epidemic prevention organization, was, of course, a cover for BW research in tropical diseases. Ishii, as we have seen, took over as head of the First Army Medical Corps in Nanking. He also kept a benevolent and watchful eye on the research conducted on East Zhongsan Street. The new commander of Unit Ei 1644 was Colonel Ota Kiyoshi, still another Ishii protégé.[23]

Changes in command did not alter the daily routine of Unit Ei 1644. Life went on in the same manner as before. The facility continued to produce huge amounts of pathogens on a regular schedule. If anything, production increased significantly with Masuda's departure. Scientists and technicians proceeded with their experiments on humans at the same pace. Each week between ten and twenty persons were exposed to poisons, germs, and different gases. Scientists killed ten or more persons weekly as the human subjects lost their value to the researchers.[24] The victims were dispatched with lethal injections, exposure to a variety of gases, or a bullet in the head. Corpses were autopsied with the same businesslike manner as under Masuda, and the remains were disposed of in the efficient oil-burning incinerator which continued to operate at peak capacity.

With Japan's impending defeat in August 1945, the High Command in China issued orders to the BW death factories similar to those released by the Kwantung Army leaders in Manchuria. All BW facilities under its command were to be destroyed. Nanking followed the order with the promptness it had demonstrated in earlier and happier research days. All "lumber" materials on hand were murdered. The East Zhongsan Street complex was leveled with explosive charges. All equipment and BW research data were allegedly destroyed.

Leading Nanking scientists and technicians managed to return to Japan before the advance of Chinese troops into the city. Masuda, then stationed in Harbin, fled home before the Soviets could catch him. Ota and other high-ranking colleagues also avoided capture. However, the powdery ash of the bones of BW victims remained in the ruined complex: a silent reminder of what took place at that site during the previous six years.

9 BW experiments on prisoners of war?

Some veterans today – veterans captured and imprisoned in World War II's Pacific theatre – have a story to tell and an agonizing chapter of their lives to resolve. These veterans . . . have not received justice. . . . These men are victims of a terrible secret, born 44 years ago deep in Manchuria in Japanese POW camps. Theirs perhaps has been the longest and best kept secret of World War II, long denied by Japan and long concealed by the US government.

Bit by bit, and year by year, despite our government's public statements of ignorance, the truth has been leaking out. We know now that Mukden was more than just another Japanese POW camp for Allied soldiers.

Operated by Japanese scientists from Unit 731, Mukden was the site for deadly chemical and biological experiments, for injections, body dissections, blood and feces tests, freezing of body parts, infection of wounds with anthrax, the applications of plague bacillus, cholera, dysentery, and typhoid.

That . . . was what was waiting for many of the American fighting men who survived the Bataan Death March. Along with our soldiers at these terrible camps were also men from China, Great Britain, Australia, and the Soviet Union. We don't know how many survived, but we do know that the US government knew of the experiments at the war's end.

(Statement of Congressman Pat Williams, Dem., Montana, before the Subcommittee on Compensation, Pension, and Insurance of the Committee on Veterans' Affairs, House of Representatives, Ninety-Ninth Congress, Second Session, 17 September 1986, Serial No. 99–61, p. 3)

I

On Tuesday evening, 13 August 1985, British television aired a documentary on General Ishii Shiro and Japanese BW experiments in Manchuria. Broadcast on Independent Television, the program was preceded by a barrage of sensational newspaper accounts of what the program would contain. The London *Standard* noted that, "Finding out about Unit 731 and the 3000 Chinese, Russian and American prisoners they used sounds like the unravelling of a thriller plot."[1] The tabloid *Sunday Mirror*'s page 1 blared that "A shock TV documentary about Japanese experiments on British prisoners of war is to be shown this week. . . . British POWs were exposed to the ravages of anthrax, typhus and tetanus and often dissected while still ALIVE."[2] *The Sunday Mail* front page headlined its lengthy account with a 2 inch banner: "EXPOSED: LAST HORROR STORY OF THE WAR THE EVIL DOCTORS OF DEATH."[3] Even the responsible *Guardian* reported that the documentary producers had sent a copy of the film to Japanese officials in London, and to the British Foreign Office, for preview and comment. It reported also that "the film claims that British, American and Australian prisoners of war were victims of a series of experiments by Japanese scientists of Unit 731."[4]

The documentary, *Unit 731 – Did the Emperor Know?*, was produced by two veteran television journalists who spent several years researching the subject in archives and in interviewing ex-POWs and former Unit 731 personnel.[5] The result was a one-hour program that stated baldly that American, British, and other Western allied POWs were victims of human experimentation. More-over, the documentary's narrator-producer hinted broadly that Emperor Hirohito was aware of the human BW experiments in Manchuria. Perhaps the hour's most dramatic moment occurred in an interview with retired Lt. Colonel Murray Sanders, an American microbiologist. Sanders claimed that General Douglas MacArthur authorized him to make a deal with the Japanese responsible for these atrocities. According to Sanders, the ultimate arrange-ment was that the scientists would be forgiven their crimes in return for their cooperating with American BW scientists.[6]

The broadcast made an impact in both Great Britain and the United States. The full one-hour program was not shown in the United States. However, the American Broadcasting System's popular weekly news feature program *20/20* ran the segment of the show which featured interviews with American POWs and Murray Sanders. The excerpt drew wide audience reaction.

II

The charge that Ishii and his confederates used American and other Allied POWs as human guinea pigs was not new. As early as 6 January 1946, the American Armed Forces newspaper *Pacific Stars and Stripes* had carried a story attributed to Japanese communist sources that Americans were among Ishii's BW victims. The report claimed that Ishii directed human BW tests with Americans and Chinese at Mukden and Harbin. The *New York Times*, citing the same sources, indicated the POWs were inoculated with bubonic plague bacterium.[7] Six days later, having expressed initial faith in the allegations, investigators ordered Ishii "arrested for questioning . . . by American Counter-Intelligence authorities."[8] At the same time, a Japanese newspaper noted that Ishii "is to be questioned on technical matters of medical treatment,"[9] and, curiously, that "The Japanese Government has been ordered *not to have Maj-Gen. Ishii interned at Sugamo Prison but to leave him in such a state where he can be temporarily questioned by GHQ*."[10]

Eight months later, Allied Headquarters in Tokyo received a letter accusing three Ishii associates by name of having "dissected many war prisoners of the Allied Forces at the outdoor dissecting ground of Unit 100 Army Corps at Hsingking [Changchun], Manchuria, at their inspections [the results stemming from injections] of the cattle plague."[11] Still later, in 1947, United States Intelligence compiled a lengthy report on Ishii's real and alleged activities. The report observed, typically, that on

10 February 1946, an individual giving his name as Takeshi Kino . . . directed a letter to Legal Section reflected that certain residents of Hagishiji . . . were responsible for using Allied POW's as human guinea pigs at an experimental station at Mokotan, Hsingking [Changchun] China.

It quoted a letter, dated 4 October 1946, in which a Hiroshi Ueki wrote to General MacArthur charging that during the recent war "Lieutenant General Shiro Ishii . . . executed brutal experiments on many Allied POWs." Others charged that the scientists infected "Prisoners of War with glanders for experimental purposes." In all, the 1947 report included extracts or summaries of statements supporting more than twelve separate allegations that Ishii or his co-workers engaged in BW experiments on POWs.[12] Later that year, in still another intelligence memorandum, it was noted that

> Legal Section, SCAP, stated in cable No. C53169, dated 7 June 1947, that the Japanese Communist Party alleges that Ishii BW group conducted experiments on captured Americans in Mukden and that simultaneously research on similar lines was conducted in Tokyo and Kyoto.

Some members of the intelligence community accepted the charges completely. A United States government document observed in August 1947:

> it should be kept in mind that there is a remote possibility that independent investigation conducted by the Soviets in the Mukden area may have disclosed evidence that American prisoners of war were used for experimental purposes of a BW nature and that they lost their lives as a result of these experiments."[13]

Moreover, "such evidence may be introduced by the Soviet prosecutors in the course of cross-examination of certain of the major Japanese war criminals."[14]

Nine years later, in 1956, the Federal Bureau of Investigation continued to accept as fact that United States POWs were used in human experiments. In a "Confidential" FBI internal memorandum of 13 March sent to Director J. Edgar Hoover, an agent states:

> Mr James J. Kelleher, Jr, Office Of Special Operations, DOD [Department of Defense], has volunteered further comments to the effect that American Military Forces after occupying Japan, determined that the Japanese actually did experiment with "BW" agents in Manchuria during 1943–44 using American prisoners as test victims.

Kelleher added the comment that "information of the type in question is closely controlled and regarded as highly sensitive."[15]

The BW–POW issue was ignored in the 1960s by the media, both in the United States and in Japan. But the decade of the 1970s brought renewed interest in Japan. Japanese investigative reporters began to focus attention on the dark side of the war effort, and, inevitably, Ishii and Unit 731 became prime subjects for investigation. On 2 November 1976, Tokyo Broadcasting

System televised a one-hour documentary entitled *A Bruise – Terror of the 731 Corps*. The documentary producer, Yoshinaga Haruko, spent three years doing research on the subject and became convinced that American POWs were among Ishii's victims.[16] Several weeks later, the *Washington Post* ran a front-page story on Yoshinaga's broadcast. The *Post*'s story did cause a temporary stir in the United States, but little of substance developed.[17]

It was the decade of the 1980s, however, that brought the greatest attention to the topic. The decade opened with the publication in Japan of Seiichi Morimura's *The Devil's Gluttony*. A powerful work of fiction based on extensive research, Morimura's runaway bestseller[18] included the assertion that Allied POWs were Ishii's test subjects. Morimura in a subsequent interview maintained that "The victims were mostly Chinese, Koreans, and White Russians. But I have learned from various sources that they also included Britons, Dutch, Australians, New Zealanders and Americans."[19]

Morimura's revelations were followed by a path-breaking article in the October 1981 issue of the prestigious periodical, the *Bulletin of Atomic Scientists*. Written by the veteran journalist John W. Powell, Jr., "Japan's Biological Weapons: 1930–1945, a Hidden Chapter in History" contained sensational allegations that were backed with impressive documentation. Powell alleged, among many other charges, that "among the human guinea pigs were an undetermined number of American soldiers, captured during the early part of the war and confined in prisoner-of-war camps in Manchuria." Moreover, Powell claimed that "Official US reports reveal that Washington was aware of these facts when the decision was made to forgo prosecution of the Japanese participants."[20]

Powell's findings were reported widely in the United States, in Europe, and in the Far East. He became once again an instant celebrity.[21] His comments on BW and on POW victims were carried on the popular CBS weekly television program *Sixty Minutes*.[22] They were also featured in the mass-circulation *People Magazine*.[23] A year after the Powell article appeared, the editors of the *Bulletin of Atomic Scientists* were moved to comment that "Rarely has an article in these pages generated more interest and concern."[24]

The Powell article, and Morimura's novel, led to such an uproar in Japan that the government was forced to comment. It acknowledged in the Diet for the first time that Unit 731 had existed, and that it had committed heinous war crimes. The government, in the course of the debate, quite casually revealed that Ishii had been given a handsome retirement pension, despite government knowledge of his BW experiments. In the course of this unusual debate, a government spokesman did not acknowledge that Americans were among Ishii's victims, but by the same token, he did not deny the charge. The *Washington Post*, in reporting the Diet discussion, observed that Ishii's Unit 731 "allegedly killed more than 3000 people – perhaps including American GIs. . . . there have been persistent rumors a small number of American prisoners of war also died in the experiments." It also quoted a Japanese government official as commenting that the atrocities "occurred during the most extraordinary wartime conditions. It's most regrettable from the point of view of humanity."[25]

The rising interest in the topic led the then US Army Chief Archivist, Dr John H. Hatcher, to comment:

Allegations of biological experimentation upon Americans and other nationals held prisoner of war in Manchuria during World War II have been the subject of speculation since at least 1956 and recently caught the attention of the television documentary industry in both the United States and United Kingdom.

He noted with some amazement that, "Even the Japanese, have published some accounts of it though I do not believe any of them are available in English." And, "From all these sources, this subject has fired the popular imagination."[26]

III

With the print media and television focusing increasing attention on the subject, it was inevitable that the issue of American POW victims of Ishii would reach the halls of Congress. Everyone previously interested in the subject had concentrated primarily upon the treatment accorded Allied POWs at the Mukden, Manchuria, POW camp. Congressmen followed suit.

Pressured by several concerned constituents, Montana Democratic Representative Pat Williams lobbied fellow Congressmen over a period of several years to hold a hearing. Forty-seven years after Japan's surrender, a House Veterans' Affairs Subcommittee met in Helena, Montana, to hear testimony from ex-POWs and other interested parties. The hearing lasted less than one full day, but it enabled some of the POWs to tell their story.

Warren W. ("Pappy") Whelchel of Tulsa, Oklahoma, told the subcommittee of the truly terrible conditions to which he and his fellow prisoners were subjected during their three-year incarceration in a Mukden POW camp. Food was scarce, and what was available was badly spoiled. The guards were especially brutal. Medical services were primitive at best. Prior to their arrival in Mukden, he, along with approximately 150 other very sick Americans, was sent to a hospital in Pusan, Korea. Although they received no treatment, those who survived were then sent to the Mukden facility.

Whelchel and the others were at first segregated from the rest of the prisoners. Sometime later, five or six Japanese doctors interviewed these men. The doctors "gave the Americans various shots discriminately; not all the prisoners were given the same type of shots." The men became quite disturbed, since "we felt that we were being tested for bacteriological immunity for their possible use of bacterial warfare against the Allied troops in the Far East."

The Oklahoman recalled:

Some persons were checked for oral and rectal temperatures, some for whelps the shots caused, rectal tissues from some, rectal smears from others. All the personnel were sprayed in the face by some kind of spray from a spray instrument similar to our Flit spray guns.

The segregated group was then permitted to integrate with the other prisoners. Whelchel stressed that "the Japanese medical personnel were keeping accurate records of each and every one of us in this one barracks."[27]

Gregory Rodriguez, Jr, testified on behalf of his father and other former Mukden POWs. Rodriguez, Jr, described the many years he had spent in amassing documents to help the case of his father and others who claimed that they were victims of Japanese BW experiments, and their postwar suffering from lack of sufficient care and compensation from the Veterans Administration. He charged flatly that "the Pacific War was a racial war. American prisoners of war were experimented upon by the Japanese at Mukden." Then, in a statement certain to arouse the ire of committee members, he indicted the top American leader of the Occupation forces. Rodriguez, Jr., stated:

I have refused to bow before circumstances and keep truth behind closed doors. General Douglas A. MacArthur left his men in 1942 and sealed their fate in May of 1946 by promising the war criminal General Ishii immunity from prosecution if he would surrender the records of Unit 731. This collaboration between MacArthur and Ishii is unsavory to say the least. The lives of the American FEPOWs [Far East Prisoners Of War] experimented on by Unit 731 at Mukden were forfeited in the name of national security.[28]

Unfortunately for Rodriguez, Jr, his mixture of fact with conjecture was not substantiated at the hearing. In fact, Yoshinaga Haruko, the Tokyo Broadcasting System documentary film maker who had earlier created a sensation with her 1976 film, *A Bruise – Terror of the 731 Corps*, submitted a statement to the Subcommittee that undercut some of his claims. She noted:

Currently we are trying to find out and [re]cover where the valuable and enormous amount of research findings of 731st Unit accumulated as the result of living body experiments went after the War was over. As to the living body tests which were said to be conducted on American POWs, we still have not made much progress.[29]

The hearing ended with comments by members in support of veterans' rights, but little more. Subcommittee Chairman Sonny Montgomery, of Mississippi, indicated sympathy for the POWs, and mildly rebuked young Rodriquez, Jr, by saying, "for the record . . . I disagree with your statement on General MacArthur."[30] No report was ever issued. No further hearings were held. No investigation was ordered to determine the validity of the charge that American POWs were exposed to BW tests. The issue, as far as the Congressmen were concerned, was closed.

Four years later, on 17 September 1986, another House of Representatives Veterans' Affairs Subcommittee held a one-day hearing on the subject. This new airing of the topic was due solely to the persistent lobbying of Gregory Rodriguez, Jr, Congressman Pat Williams,[31] and several of his POW constituents. To many observers, it seemed that if the issue were left to the Representatives on the Committee, the question would long since have been abandoned. However, due to Rodriguez's determination, and the increasing media attention, Congressmen responded to the pressures.

The hearing was held in the nation's capital, under the tight supervision of the Subcommittee Chairman, Democratic Representative Douglas Applegate, of Ohio. He wanted a limited hearing, one that would focus exclusively on veterans' benefits, and not one that could wander into sensitive areas such as possible cover-ups, or the role allegedly played by General MacArthur, or Emperor Hirohito, in the BW controversy.[32] Applegate reinforced this view forcefully in his opening remarks. He began by observing that "This committee does not have jurisdiction on the matter of war crimes." Furthermore:

> I want to make it clear that the issue before the committee today is whether or not Americans held at Camp Mukden have suffered, or are now suffering, from events which occurred at the camp. . . . We do not look to the cause of such conditions. . . . our main objective in holding this hearing is simply to get information on whether former POWs held at Camp Mukden have demonstrated any medical symptoms which could be reasonably traced to their period of military service.[33]

Some Committee members appeared to take a more open-minded approach than Applegate. New York Republican Representative Gerald Solomon, in his remarks, stated that "If it can be established that the Japanese were, indeed, conducting some kind of germ warfare experiments on American prisoners of war there, we then should address whether any harm resulted to those men."[34] Pat Williams, who was not a Committee member, was permitted to make a statement as well. Williams, in a forceful declaration, charged that the government knew that Americans were BW victims, but covered up the facts in order to secure Japanese BW data. He noted that Greg Rodriguez, Sr. Mukden prisoner 768, was "a subject of the germ warfare experiments." "Pappy" Whelchel, who died shortly before the hearing, was "experimented upon," and although the Veterans Administration denied Whelchel's assertions, "an autopsy was performed and finally revealed the truth of his claims."[35] Finally:

> I understand that our Government consistently has denied any firm knowledge that any Americans were experimented upon. But today you will hear from a POW who was experimented upon. To deny that truth is to deny the existence of that POW.[36]

Testimony before the Subcommittee – with one notable exception – was much as that presented at the 1982 hearing. "Pappy" Whelchel was dead, but he was replaced by Frank James of Northern California, still another former

Mukden POW. James' story was as harrowing as Whelchel's. He charged that initially the Japanese did not accord their prisoners POW rank, but instead treated them as "captives." It was "During the period we were held captive [1942 to early 1944 when the men were given POW status] was when we were used as guinea pigs for the biological research Unit 731.³⁷"

James had arrived in the Mukden camp on 11 November 1942. Upon entering the camp, he and the other prisoners were met by a team of Japanese medical personnel. Wearing masks, the team proceeded to spray "liquid in our faces and we were given injections." Earlier, en route from Pusan, Korea, "we had glass rods inserted in our rectums." In Mukden, James was assigned to the burial detail, where he was kept quite busy. In winter, the ground was too hard to be opened for burials, and the dead were stacked in an old wooden building where, in the sub-zero weather, they remained in good condition.

With the spring 1943 thaw, James and another prisoner were assigned to assist the Japanese in preparing for burial the 200 or so men who had perished earlier. He recalled that "A team of Japanese medical personnel, Unit 731, arrived with an autopsy table for taking specimens." James and the other prisoner were given the task of lifting "the bodies off the tables, those bodies that had been selected. . . . Then the Japanese opened the bodies – the head, chest and stomach – and took out the desired specimens, which were placed in containers and marked with the POWs number." The specimens were then removed from the camp.

Sometime later, the group returned to Mukden, and proceeded to perform what "seemed to be a psycho-physical and anatomical examination on selected POWs. I was one of them." The men selected were

required to walk in footsteps that had been painted on the floor, which led to a desk, at which the Japanese medical personnel sat. . . . We were also asked questions about our national origin, and "American" was not an acceptable answer. It had to be Scotch, French, English, or whatever.

Injecting some black humor into the hearing, James recalled that he was "asked was I getting enough steak, and I answered, 'what's that?'." The Japanese doctor also "measured my head, shoulders, arms and legs with calipers, and asked many questions about the medical history of my family."³⁸

These alleged BW tests were not publicized by James or fellow POWs after their liberation in 1945, because

We were required, when we came to the depot at Manila, on the way back from the prisoner of war camps, we signed a statement by the Army stating we would not tell before our experiences or conditions, what happened to us in the prison camps, before any audiences or the newspapers, under threat of court martial.

James reasoned, "This was an attempt to harmonize the American public to get to like the Japanese." He felt that "They [the Army] didn't want us to go back and stir things up."³⁹

Gregory Rodriguez, Jr, testified once again. His accusations were more detailed and more pointed than before (although General MacArthur was not cited). Perhaps his most controversial statement concerned a conversation he had with Murray Sanders, the so-called point man in the "deal" he alleged that Sanders and General MacArthur had made with Unit 731 leaders. Rodriguez testified:

There is proof of the experiments at Mukden. Dr Sanders told me that he was aware of the experiments at Mukden, but not until after he cut the deal. He said he would never have cut the deal to grant Ishii immunity from prosecution if he had known Americans were experimented on.[40] But he said that an American officer of high rank, "whom I pledged to never reveal his name," had told him that the Americans at Mukden were guinea pigs.[41]

Sanders died before the hearing took place, and, therefore, could not corroborate this serious allegation.

Unlike the 1982 hearing, the United States Army presented testimony before this panel. Its spokesman was John H. Hatcher, Ph.D., retired Army Lt. Colonel. Bearing an impressive series of titles – Chief, Army Records Management, Department of the Army, and Archivist of the Army – Dr Hatcher began by observing that he was aware that the Subcommittee had "weighty issues . . . to be wrestling with. They are emotion-charged and they commence to fall into the category of ancient history."[42]

Hatcher claimed that he had searched the appropriate Army files, but had come up virtually empty handed. He did find a few documents, "certainly not conclusive," but no "primary materials."[43] He conceded that "It is possible that in one brief period we may have had some of those materials." In the months following Japan's surrender, United States Intelligence had seized all relevant Japanese archival material and sent the documents to Washington where the bulk of the material was housed in the National Archives. After a "number of years," the documents were

finally boxed up and sent back to Japan, because the problem of language was too difficult for us to overcome. It was written in many dif.erent dialects, many different alphabets, congu or conji,[44] all of those things. . . . In fact, they were so difficult that *we did not even copy them*.[45] I think we boxed them up and sent them back to Tokyo.[46]

As a consequence of this action,

The fact remains that we simply have no identifiable body of records anywhere in the Army's holdings that have subsequently been passed into the National Archives, that would tend to either support or, on the other hand, to refute the claims that are being made.[47]

Hatcher's statements were so remarkable that Subcommittee members, all fervent supporters of the military, were either stunned or incredulous. Representative Applegate asked Hatcher whether the Army had ever held files on Japanese BW or on Mukden. The archivist replied, "No, sir. We do not presently have . . . We have no evidence that we ever held any material from those camps."[48] An exasperated Applegate then asked Hatcher, "Do you know if the material that was returned to Japan might have been microfilmed before it was returned?" Hatcher: "No sir, it was not. . . . It was simply packed up and sent back."[49] Applegate: "Don't you always keep a file of things you send out?" Hatcher:

> The problem here is, with the language it was written in, we simply could not get enough translators and interpreters to tell us what we had. . . . It was a joint Defense and State Department decision at the time, that these materials would be repatriated without retaining copies.[50]

Applegate:

> Lastly, your conclusions. What you say is, "Based upon the manner in which records pertaining to American prisoners of war were generated . . . the absence of such records suggests that Americans were not subjected to biological experimentation as alleged." You don't think there was any supportive materials in what was sent back?

Hatcher: "It might have been . . . we really don't know the content of the materials that were repatriated."[51]

Representative Solomon was equally astounded at some of Hatcher's testimony. He cited an old bureaucratic motto that "the definition of a bureaucrat is one who shoots the bull, passes the buck, and makes six copies of everything." Consequently, he found it "hard to believe that we packed up all this information and sent it back and we don't have copies of it."[52] Solomon: "Did we send it back to Douglas MacArthur?" Hatcher: "No sir. We returned it to the Government of Japan." A stunned Solomon: "The Government of Japan?" Hatcher: "Yes. . . . I'm sure it still exists. I mean, the Japanese are good record keepers."[53] Ultimately, Solomon threw up his hands, literally, commenting that there were countless loyal Japanese Americans who had fought in World War II, and who could read and speak Japanese. He felt that "It just seems to me that after the war was over . . . to say that we didn't have the expertise in this country to translate those records is almost incomprehensible."[54]

The skeptical and pointed questions addressed to Hatcher suggested that Subcommittee members believed either that the Army was engaged in a cover-up of the charges, or that Army and State Department personnel were unusually inept, or perhaps both. Hatcher's comments were considered to be evasive, superficial, or, in some instances, unbelievable. Nevertheless, the Subcommittee adjourned without taking further action. No report was issued. No remedial legislation was recommended. No investigation of Army record-keeping practices was either urged or undertaken. The Mukden POWs were thanked for their service to their country, and sent on their way home.

Still, the issue of POW/human experimentation would not die. The nationally syndicated investigative reporting team of Jack Anderson and Dale

Van Atta summarized the charges once again in a 1987 newspaper column.[55] They quoted Rep. Williams to the effect that "he had encountered cover-up, denials and an intolerable cloud of secrecy." One year later, an Australian academic, Yuki Tanaka, charged in the *Bulletin of Atomic Scientists* that "There is also evidence that these special military groups [Units 731 and 516] conducted experiments with poison gases and bacteria on Chinese, Russian, American, and Polish prisoners."[56] And, in August 1990, The *New York Times* front-paged a story concerning the discovery of thirty-five non-Japanese "human skulls and thighbones that appeared to date to World War II." The discovery was made "just steps from the site of the wartime laboratory of Lieut. Gen. Shiro Ishii." The story noted that, "Under General Ishii's direction, prisoners of war – primarily Chinese, but by some accounts Americans and Russians as well – died gruesome deaths in secret camps set up in Japanese occupied territory."[57]

IV

What happened in Mukden, Manchuria, from 11 November 1942, when the first Allied prisoners arrived in the prison camp, until the survivors were liberated in August 1945 by some members of the Office of Strategic Services (OSS)[58] and an advancing Soviet army[59]? Did Ishii, or Kitano, or other Unit 731 members use these prisoners for their experiments? If not Ishii and his colleagues, did persons from the Mukden Army Medical College – where Kitano conducted human BW experiments for a decade – find experimental material in Camp Mukden? Or did the frail and elderly POWs who appeared before Congressional subcommittees or on British television contract their infirmities naturally, and, through the power of psychological suggestion, associate their assorted illnesses with Ishii and BW?[60]

The passage of time, the seeming negligence on the part of the Army in not providing the liberated prisoners with exhaustive physical examinations and detailed debriefings, and the paucity of available records make it almost impossible for the modern researcher to offer a definitive answer. Significant records may exist, but key American agencies (the CIA, the Veterans Administration, and the FBI) are uncooperative or evasive when questions concerning the POW–BW issue are addressed to them.[61] However, some of the survivors do have memories of their experiences that can be substantiated with documentary evidence, and their comments, therefore, can be given a degree of credence.[62] Moreover, certain documents dating from the era are available to offer clues as to what most probably occurred in Mukden. Of these, two diaries, one maintained by the highest-ranking British officer in the camp, Major Robert Peaty,[63] and the other, by a remarkably perceptive and sensitive twenty-three-year-old American Air Force private, Sigmund "Sig" Schreiner, who hailed from New Britain, Connecticut, provide adequate information to make a reasonable determination of the issue. Peaty's diary records daily activities in the camp from the perspective of a high-ranking officer who received detailed information from his men of what was happening throughout the camp. Schreiner's diary is that of an uncommon young man who was determined to record for posterity every incident of daily life in the camp. His diary is a testament to his skills.

Japan invaded the Philippine Islands on 10 December 1941, capturing the bulk of the combined American–Filipino armed forces on the Bataan Peninsula on 9 April 1942. Corregidor, the once impregnable rock in Manila Bay, surrendered on 6 May, with a loss to the Japanese of an additional 12,000 soldiers. Nearly 90,000 prisoners of war were then subjected to the infamous Bataan Death March. Of those who survived, perhaps several thousand were crowded aboard an ancient Japanese cargo vessel, the *Totori Maru*, in Manila harbor on 6 October 1942. Roughly 1000 Japanese soldiers, who were being reassigned, were given the task of guarding the prisoners on the journey. The ship's destination was unknown.[64]

It was a strange forty-day odyssey. The prisoners were crammed so tightly into the ship's holds that "you couldn't put a piece of paper between the bodies."[65] Sometimes a day's rations consisted of little more than a loaf of bread. At other times they were given Japanese dry provisions known not so fondly by the prisoners as "dog biscuits," as well as one meal of rice each day. There was only one latrine with a capacity for five men available. Two large water tanks served as the total water supply for the passengers until the ship reached port. Men became ill with dysentery and other dietary diseases almost at once.

The *Totori Maru* was attacked by an American submarine the first day out of port, but the two torpedoes aimed at the ship passed wide of the target. Otherwise the trip to Formosa, their first stop, was uneventful, except that "once in awhile the Japs would throw cigarettes down at us. Just to see us fight over them."[66] Taking on coal and water, the ship sailed once more for its final destination, Pusan, Korea. The men's quarters became unbearable. The "air was foul and the lice situation in terrific state." Later:

> most of us had diarrhea and other intestinal diseases. . . . The number of cases suddenly started to increase rapidly. Finally the reason for this was discovered when someone happened to glance into the water tank and saw a pair of dirty shorts floating around.

The tank was cleaned, but "we didn't have any medicine to administer. A few men died and were thrown over the side with a piece of scrap iron tied to their feet."[67]

The *Totori Maru* docked eventually at Pusan on 8 November. Two-thirds of the prisoners disembarked, were deloused, issued Japanese cotton clothing, and then assembled in columns of four. They were marched through the center of town, one "of those marches to show the populace how the superior race had captured the degenerates," to the railroad station. Here they boarded a train for the three-day journey to Mukden.[68] Along the way, they picked up a batch of British soldiers who had been captured at Singapore. The men arrived at their final stop on 11 November 1942, Armistice Day.[69]

The American, British, Australian (also captured at Singapore and in Hong Kong), New Zealand, and Dutch (captured in the Dutch East Indies) prisoners were housed some two miles from the South Manchurian Railway line in an old army camp that had been built during the Russo-Japanese War. There was a plaque mounted at the entrance celebrating the camp becoming operational in 1904. The camp was not a pretty sight; in fact, "The first glimpse . . . was down-heartening as it was a sea of mud." The barracks were built in the Chinese style, partly underground. The walls were filled with dirt for insulation. Heating facilities were minimal. In all, the camp contained nineteen barrack buildings for the more than 2000 Allied war prisoners.

Discipline was strict, the guards (many of whom spoke English) were brutal, and sanitation facilities at best were primitive. At first, food was adequate, but supplies became increasingly scarce. Within a few months, the daily diet was pitiful. A day's rations (30 April 1943) consisted of "Breakfast -Delicious Purple Maize. Dinner – Soy Bean and Onion soup – something new. Supper – Soy Bean Soup Period." The following day's fare (1 May 1943) was "Breakfast – Soy Bean and Maize Soup – just wonderful, bah. Dinner – Soy Bean soup. Supper – Get a load of this – Carrot, maize and soy bean soup."[70]

Living conditions in the camp were so difficult that by late November 1942 the death rate averaged one man each day.[71] By December, the fierce Manchurian winter, the inadequate food, and the poor sanitary conditions in the camp began to take a greater toll on the men. Near Christmas, Schreiner noted in his diary that "Eight men have died in the last few days. The doctors predict that many more will die before the end of the month. The utility shop has an order for seventy-five caskets."[72] The caskets would be put to use later, because:

> Four men died yesterday. The ground is frozen so hard. Almost impossible to dig. Japs decided to store the bodies in the warehouse until spring. To date it's almost full. This warehouse is diagonally across from the kitchen. It is of flimsy construction. One can see through the building in spots. Because of the cold weather the bodies are kept in good shape.[73]

The sick were tended to by a team of at least eight American doctors and an Australian M.D. American hospital corpsmen were available as well. The camp doctor was a young Japanese with the rank of first lieutenant. He treated only the most severely ill, and then frequently with the assistance or advice of an American doctor. Those who were desperately ill were sent to a hospital in Mukden. Some of these men, at least, "consented to let the Jap doctors operate" in the hope of their obtaining some relief from their disorder.[74] At other times, American doctors accompanied their patients to the Mukden hospital and performed the needed surgery.[75]

Camp routine, which consisted of the men working in either a foundry, or a textile mill, or a leather tanning factory, scrounging for food in their spare time, and gambling, was disrupted in early February 1943 when a team of Japanese pathologists came into the camp. Schreiner was quick to note in his diary that "They are going to perform autopsies on all the dead men in the warehouse. They look young to me, probably interns from the Mukden hospital." The next day, the pathologists began their work. There was nothing secret about their activity. The building housing the dead was roped off, and the guards would "not allow any prisoner within 50 feet of the building." Nevertheless, Schreiner "watched them from one of the windows in the kitchen. After they finished with a body it's thrown in the wooden box and nailed down."[76]

Health conditions continued to worsen. In late February 1943, Schreiner noted:

> The fellow in the hospital that can't urinate had 2 drains put in each of his legs today. Two other men had amputations . . . both had gangrene. We all had stool tests this morning. In the afternoon, a lot of men were being hospitalized as dysentery germs were found in their stools.[77]

In June 1943, a Japanese psychologist came into the camp. His assistants took measurements of each prisoner's height and weight. Then:

> we stripped naked and went into a small room. Here the doctor sat at a desk on the other side of the room and asked a lot of questions. Examples – "Would you like to go home?" "What do you think?" "Are you a peaceful man?"

Schreiner noted drily that the interview lasted fifteen minutes, and that 'Personally I think the man is cracked. After this, we got a so-called dysentery injection."[78]

The Japanese were not eager to deal with sick prisoners. On 7 June 1943 Schreiner felt feverish. He went to see

> [Dr.] "Handle Bar" Herbst [Schreiner's favorite American doctor]. . . . He took my temperature. It was 104. I had to wait 3 hours in the office till the Jap doctor came. He examined and finally admitted me to the hospital. This was after Dr Herbst argued with him for a while.[79]

Later that year, Schreiner noted bitterly in his diary that "There is a few cases of pneumonia in the hospital. The Japs won't admit you in the hospital till it's almost too late. Most of the men are doctoring themselves."[80]

In July 1943, the prisoners were removed to a new camp in what was then a suburb of Mukden. Nothing much changed. The buildings were of brick, toilet facilities were somewhat improved from those in the old camp, and the hospital was a little better equipped. The new guards and the officers were as brutal to the men as their former jailers.[81] The food continued to be pitiful. Fewer prisoners died in the new camp because the Darwinian principle began to work: the fittest were surviving. All the prisoners could do was to wait for the war to end.

At no time did Schreiner ever see or note anything untoward in the area of BW human experiments. The men were mainly cared for by American doctors and the Australian physician. Periodically, the Japanese X-rayed the prisoners, provided them with dysentery shots and other vaccines that were supposed to deal with smallpox and the different diseases that from time to time ravaged the camp. On only one occasion did high-ranking Japanese doctors seemingly ever visit the camp. None of the prisoners were spirited away to Mukden, never to be heard from again. In early July 1943, three American prisoners did escape from the camp. However, they were recaptured, and later executed and buried in an unmarked grave within the camp's cemetery.[82] They had not been sent to Ping Fan or to Changchun, or to the Mukden Army Medical College as candidates for BW tests.

The injections the prisoners received were painful. Schreiner complained of the needles used to inject the assorted fluids into the body as being exceedingly long, and the tips very dull, which caused excruciating pain. Other POWs later recalled the long blunt needles.[83] The equipment may have been primitive by American standards, but there is nothing in Schreiner's commentaries that suggest a link with BW experiments.

British Major Robert Peaty's diary echoes Schreiner's entries. The British, not having to endure the Bataan Death March, arrived in camp in better health than the Americans. Thus, he recorded a constant stream of American deaths, but no British losses: "11.11.42. Arrived at Mukden. . . . One American died the same evening." "14.11.42. There is a large incidence of dysentery among the Americans." "15.11.42. Sickness due to exposure is increasing." "17.11.42. One American died."[84] "16.12.42. Two Americans died in hospital." "17.12.42. Two Americans died in hospital." "18.12.42. Four Americans died in hospital." "20.12.42. Six Americans died in hospital." And so on.[85]

The high incidence of American deaths evidently alarmed the Japanese authorities, and an investigating team was sent to the camp in February 1943. The team spent several days touring the facility, interviewing personnel, and inspecting the available amenities. On 24 February, Peaty wrote that "The Medical Investigation is completed." The findings are "that ordinary diarrhoea, not usually fatal, plus malnutrition and poor sanitation, and insufficient medicine, have proved a fatal combination of circumstances."[86] One day earlier, Peaty entered the mournful note in his journal that "Funeral service for 142 dead. 186 have died in 105 days, all Americans."[87]

Peaty, on the last day of the year in 1943, summed up all the causes for the high American death rate. He observed that, "Food has been lacking in variety, and in essential vitamins all this year." The men "never had meat more than once a week for months, and then only about an ounce." Fish occasionally was substituted for meat, but "we have had none for five weeks." Medical treatment was very bad, and accounted in large part for the death toll. He noted:

Lack of medicine and equipment plus incompetence, on the part of the Japanese doctor, have been the chief complaints. There was only one bedpan between a hundred dysentery patients last winter, and many men died of pneumonia through having to get out of their blankets to go to outdoor latrines with the thermometer at a sub-Siberian level.[88]

After the war, Peaty tempered some of his ill-feelings toward his captors. He wrote in an addendum to his diary: "Atrocities. I have no knowledge of any." He felt that "From our point of view, the medical facilities were of a deplorably low standard." And:

Much as I grew to hate them, I must state the facts as they appear to me, and though our food was low in calorific value and lacking in vitamins, so that deficiency diseases were prevalent, yet we had more to eat than the civilian population. . . . We were hungry, but they [Manchurian Chinese] were starving.

In summary:

I often thought we were being badly treated at the time, but after having met officers and men who were in Formosa, Japan and Siam, I found that we had been better off than many, with the possible exception of those at Koijo, Korea, where the treatment seems to have been much the same as in Mukden.[89]

Recent scholarship tends to support Major Peaty's temperate assessment of conditions at Mukden. It is now reckoned that "at least 27 percent" of Japanese-held POWs perished in captivity. By comparison, only "4 percent" of European-held POWs died. Camp Mukden's death rate was approximately 12 percent, with almost all those who died there being Americans.

The mortality rate in Japanese camps was greatest at the beginning of the war. But once survivers made "a successful reversion to a primitive level of existence. . . . a condition of relative balance resulted, morbidity stabilized, and mortality rates fell."[90] One British medical officer, who was a former Japanese-held POW, wrote in 1946 that he was actually surprised that casualty rates in Asia were not higher, since they had been "living as it were on the edge of a precipice"[91] for such a long time.

Schreiner and Peaty both record that rectal examinations with glass tubes were conducted at the camp periodically.[92] Feces smears from prisoners were also taken routinely by Japanese doctors. Blood samples were taken occasionally, and they may have been used in an attempt to ascertain possible American immunity to various diseases. These latter tests are the only known potentially reasonable tie to a BW connection, and even this supposition is based upon one single reference in the 1949 trial of Japanese captives in Khabarovsk, Siberia, and the one line entry in the Peaty Diary, "12.9.43 Blood tests taken of every man in camp."

At the Khabarovsk trial, during cross-examination of the witness, Major Karasawa Tomio and the Soviet prosecutor engaged in the following exchange:

Question: Please tell us, did Detachment 731 study the immunity of Americans to infectious diseases?

Answer: As far as I can recall, that was at the beginning of 1943. I was in
hospital at the time in Mukden, and Minato, one of the researchers of the
detachment, came to see me. He told me about his work, and said that he
had come to study the immunity of Anglo-Saxons to infectious diseases.
Question: And for this purpose tests were made of the blood of American
war prisoners?
Answer: That is so.[93]

Nothing more concrete was elicited from either Karasawa or any of the other
defendants.

Still, taking blood tests of prisoners of war in order to study possible im-
munities to infectious diseases is something that all powers appeared to accept
during World War II.[94] The United States began testing POWs on a wide scale
as early as August 1943. The novelist John P. Marquand, then a high official in
the OSS, sent a memo from Algiers noting that "The blood sampling project is
being set up in London and in the African theatre." A colonel in London was

> arranging to draw specimens from the few thousand German prisoners in
> England. . . . This laboratory can also take care of specimens from the
> African Theatre . . . but Lt. Colonel Stone who will set up the project here
> believes he has adequate laboratory facilities. He proposes starting with
> wounded prisoners and enlarging the program.

The British, who were informed of the project, reacted coolly. Paul Fildes,
one of their leading BW experts, observed on 8 September that "No attempt
has been made to examine the blood of prisoners." He felt it was a waste of
time. "Our general view has been that our depleted medical services could
hardly be asked to undertake a job so unlikely to be productive, but if it is true
that [an American] could undertake it, we should be very interested."[95]

The Americans proceeded with the project, despite Fildes's reservations. In
a 23 October 1944 report to officials at Fort Detrick, Maryland, BW
researchers indicated that since 1 April 1944 a total of 270 POWs were tested
for two anti-toxins, "101 sera were from German prisoners and 169 were from
Japanese prisoners."[96] A second test was conducted upon 76 Japanese and
German prisoners, but, as Fildes predicted, "None of the sera showed any
measurable anti-toxin."[97]

V

The bulk of POWs were still alive at the time Camp Mukden was liberated in
1945. According to current estimates, 80 American officers and 1038 enlisted
men were among the survivors. In addition, there were 176 British officers and
108 enlisted men, 58 Dutch officers, 7 enlisted men, and 4 civilians of unknown
nationality who were among those freed. Two hundred and thirty-eight
POWs, all but two American, were buried in the camp cemetery.[98] In all, there
were 1671 individuals[99] who could indict the Japanese for human BW experiments. No one apparently did.

The Americans received numerous physical examinations from the time they left Mukden until the day they headed home from the Philippines, months later. During repeated meetings with medical personnel, they were not questioned to any extent about their POW experiences.[100] They evidently were never interviewed by American intelligence sources.

The question remains, were American POWs in Mukden subjected to human BW experiments? The evidence, while inconclusive, suggests strongly that they were not. There are several reasons for this conclusion.

1. Perhaps the least important point is that General Ishii denied the charge vehemently. To American interrogators, Ishii in 1947 "stated positively that no American or Russian prisoners of war had been used at any time except that the blood of some American POW's had been checked for antibody content."[101] Ishii was notorious for telling people what they wished to hear in order to save his own neck. However, once he was granted immunity from prosecution in 1948, he admitted candidly to using Soviet prisoners, but clung persistently to his 1947 denial concerning Americans.

2. Camp Mukden, despite the horrendous treatment meted out to POWs, was regarded by the Japanese authorities as a "model" prison. Propaganda teams visited the camp so frequently, photographing the men playing baseball and performing at concerts, that Major Peaty petulantly recorded in his journal on 18 December 1943, "The Propaganda Corps is back again. I think this camp must be a 'propaganda camp'."[102] Four months later, Sig Schreiner wrote, "Rumors – The propaganda Japs coming into camp in the near future. This camp is supposed to be the model prison camp. That's the reason for the frequent visits by the slap-happy cameramen."[103] In addition, Red Cross representatives visited the camp routinely, and enjoyed fairly free access to the inmates. There is no record of any Red Cross complaints. It is doubtful that BW experiments would be undertaken in a facility in which so many outsiders enjoyed frequent access.

3. Most important, 1671 men survived at Mukden. In the closing days of the war, the Japanese killed every prisoner in every camp in which human experiments were performed. Some experts believe the Americans at Mukden were spared because the Japanese feared retribution at the hands of the victorious United States.[104] However, Ishii's men killed all Chinese and Soviet prisoners at Ping Fan, even though the Chinese guerrilla armies, as well as a large Soviet force, were nearby. Fear of Soviet or Chinese punishment did not stay the hands of the BW officials.

The possibility in 1945 of the American military coming to Manchuria was remote. Besides, Ishii and his confederates, as we have seen, were completely ruthless, never hesitating to take extreme measures when they were deemed necessary to ensure the success or safety of an undertaking. It is inconceivable that Ishii, Wakamatsu, or any of the other BW project leaders would have had any scruples, or would even have paused for a moment's reflection, before ordering the elimination of a single Allied POW if that individual were exposed to BW tests. Thus, there is little reason to doubt that officials would have liquidated all witnesses to BW tests at Mukden, if any had taken place there. American POWs may have been victims of BW tests, but there is no substantive evidence available to prove that the experiments took place at Camp Mukden.

10   Who knew?

Q: Was the Emperor informed of BW Research?
A: Not at all. The Emperor is a lover of humanity and never would have consented to such a thing. (Interrogation of Lt. General Ishii Shiro in Tokyo, 8 February 1946)

Q: What does the Japanese General Staff think of BW as a weapon?
A: We had no idea of its possibilities because we did so little work in that field.
Q: Would it be possible for independent BW research to be carried out by individual Army units, e.g. Kwantung authorities?
A: We are responsible for the general directions of research and I made budget estimates for all divisions. BW was not included.
(Interrogation of Lt. Colonel Seiichi Niizuma by Lt. Colonel Murray Sanders, 1 October 1945, typescript "Report on Scientific intelligence Survey in Japan September and October 1945," Volume V, "Biological warfare," 1 November 1945,[1] Document 003, Fort Detrick Archives, Frederick, Md.)

I

The June 1989 issue of *Days Japan*, a slick upscale populist magazine published in Tokyo, featured an article[2] which at first glance appeared to be just one more story about the men who helped create Japan's postwar miracle of economic success. The fifteen-page spread was titled dramatically "Black Blood and White Genes." It contained dozens of photographs of men of science who had assisted in making the Green Cross Company, Japan's preeminent blood-processing facility, one of the great international success stories of the past forty years. "Black Blood and White Genes" also displayed a montage of photographs of nine past presidents of Japan's prestigious Institute for Preventive Medicine.

A closer view discloses that the article was a devastating exposé of the relationship between respected scientists, fanatical militarists, and the human BW experiments in China and Manchuria. These men had several things in common. They were graduates of either Tokyo or Kyoto Imperial Universities. They were all also alumni of Unit 731. Each of these distinguished men of science had received significant training in the death factories of Ping Fan, or in one of 731's satellite units in Manchuria. Using the expertise they acquired under the tutelage of Ishii and Kitano while working in the experimental BW facilities, the Green Cross Company scientists joined with other past members of Unit 731 to become outstanding leaders in modern Japan in their scientific specialties.

The Green Cross Company was not the sole industrial enterprise to use Unit 731's personnel. Nor was the Institute for Preventive Medicine the only scientific agency to utilize the expertise gained at Ping Fan. Many of Japan's leading ethical drug companies in the years following the war employed former 731 personnel, placing them in key leadership positions. They included the Takeda Pharmaceutical Company, the Hayakawa Medical Company, and the S. J. Company Ltd., as well as several smaller but important enterprises. The faculties of Tokyo University, Kyoto University, Osaka University, Kanazawa University, Showa University of Pharmacology, Nagoya Prefecture Medical University, Osaka Municipal University's School of Medicine, Juntendo University, and other less prominent universities and medical schools were staffed with Unit 731 associates.

Many of 731's leading personalities later achieved great distinction in public health careers. One became Chief of the Entomology Section of the Health and Welfare Ministry's Preventive Health Research Laboratories. Another became a director of Japan's National Cancer Center, and, later, a president of Japan's Medical Association. A third became Surgeon General of Japan's reformed armed forces. Still others served as Yokohama's Director of Hygiene, president of Japan's Meteorological Society, and heads of various divisions of Japan's National Institute of Health. Kitano Masaji enrolled in Naito's Green Cross Company, and became the director of the Tokyo branch. Unit 100's commander, Wakamatsu Yujiro, joined the National Institute of Health, and pursued studies on streptococcal infections in young children.[3]

Many of these men received their nation's highest awards for distinguished scientific achievements. Others were accorded international recognition, receiving honorary degrees from numerous prestigious universities, and citations from world scientific bodies. Several worked in important posts in international scientific agencies. Their past history was either unknown or ignored.

Others preferred to live a life of modest obscurity. Those with medical or veterinarian degrees entered into private practice after the war, eking out a comfortable living in little-known communities. Those who had received technical training found employment in different professions, ranging from house painting to typesetting or writing specialized manuals. The ordinary soldiers who guarded Ping Fan and the other facilities went back to their home towns and villages, and were absorbed into the general population as farmers, truck drivers, etc. In all, many thousands of former BW operatives, all with some knowledge of the work performed in Manchuria and China proper, lived with their knowledge for many years in the new Japan.

II

In the days and months and years following Japan's surrender, intensive efforts were made by Allied intelligence and scientific investigators to learn something about the nature and extent of Japanese BW activities. They were keenly interested in discovering the organizations and individuals who were responsible for creating and supporting the vast BW enterprise whose outlines American intelligence pieced together during the war. The search began within days following General Douglas MacArthur's triumphal entrance into Tokyo in September 1945. The hunt was pursued for three years, until official interest in the topic ceased with the conclusion of the War Crimes Trials in Tokyo in June 1948. Investigative journalists and academics on both sides of the Pacific Ocean, however, continued to pursue the question.

Key Japanese officials, in 1945, dealt with initial BW investigations by erecting a stone wall of ignorance, either real or feigned. No one in authority appeared to have the slightest information about BW research. Every military leader, except for one individual, Masuda Tomosada, denied that Japan had engaged in offensive BW research. All parties interviewed in the early days of the occupation agreed either that Emperor Hirohito was uninformed of BW research[4], or that it was done without his approval.[5]

The Japanese Navy denied any responsibility for offensive BW research, or even any interest in the issue. Civilian scientists also disclaimed knowledge of the subject. The principal investigator responsible for the first detailed study of Japanese BW, Lt. Colonel Murray Sanders, accepted the thesis that "BW seems to have been largely a military activity, with civilian talent excluded in all but minor roles."[6]

Sanders, a promising microbiologist, held entry-level positions of lecturer and assistant professor at Columbia University's world-famous College of Physicians and Surgeons from 1940 to 1943, when he entered the United States military. Commissioned as a major, Sanders was assigned to do research in his field at Fort Detrick. At the time of his posting to Tokyo, Sanders was a Section Chief and had been promoted to Lt. Colonel. Young, intelligent, and movie-star handsome, Sanders was ambitious but naive. He lacked the experience or the toughness to ferret the truth from those who were prepared to conceal it from him. As a junior academic, he was in awe of men who held impressive titles, especially those who were highly placed in powerful positions in the military hierarchy. He was not forceful or trenchant with such individuals. In fact, Sanders tried not to offend such important people, but, instead, to win their trust and confidence.[7] It was this personality trait that would lead Sanders to make some unfortunate assessments in the course of attempting to complete his critically important task.[8]

To Sanders, after a cursory investigation of the BW program, the Japanese Army appeared to be the prime culprit. As a result of lies told to him by some of the people he interviewed, Sanders concluded that within the Army, responsibility should be shifted from the military leadership in Tokyo to Lt. General Ishii Shiro in Manchuria.[9]

No one in the capital seemed to know anything about BW programs. The Kwantung Army had operated with a high degree of independence, and according to the Japanese officers Sanders interviewed, Tokyo wielded minimum influence over its command. Since Sanders lacked any background about the true chain of command within the Japanese Army, he accepted readily the argument that only the so-called ruffians in the Kwantung Army would engage in BW research.[10]

Sanders concluded that the Army's Medical Department "exercised no control" over Ishii's operations.[11] Colonel Saburo Idezuki, Chief, Division of Preventive Medicine, Tokyo Army Medical College, claimed that "The offensive phase of BW was never studied"[12] in the Home Islands. Colonel Takatomo Inoue, Chief, Bacteriological Section, Tokyo Army Medical College, indicated that "no type of artificial infection experiment had been carried out [in his laboratory] and that the approach to the problem of BW was based on general medical concept[s]. Furthermore, 90 percent of their efforts had been expended toward the improvement of vaccines."[13] Lt. Colonel Seiichi Niizuma, whose position, according to his own testimony, controlled "all technical research work for the Japanese Army," disavowed having any knowledge of BW studies. He even denied that the Army had possessed BW protective clothing.[14]

The Army Surgeon General, Lt. General Kambayashi Hiroshi, should have known something about the Manchurian BW venture. As Surgeon General, he was responsible for all medically related activities within the Army. Nevertheless, when interviewed on 25 September 1945, Kambayashi steadfastly denied possessing knowledge of any offensive BW studies carried out by the Army. He did admit of the possibility that "certain offensive activities might have been carried out in relation to defensive evaluation."[15] Everyone in authority denied knowledge of BW research. All blame or responsibility for offensive BW lay, according to the top Japanese military-medical leaders, with what they labeled "that loose cannon," Ishii Shiro.[16]

This initial investigation was flawed from its inception. Murray Sanders was given an assignment by his superiors at Fort Detrick that was beyond his capabilities. Japanese subjects interviewed by Sanders were at best disingenuous in their responses to his questions. He was so misled by those he interviewed that he declared in an interim report, "We have uncovered absolutely no evidence of offensive BW activities . . . but I can assure you that every effort will be made to continue this search." On BW in general, "It is my impression that Japanese BW was not a major activity and that it will not be necessary to extend this investigation as originally planned."[17]

Moreover, on his arrival in Tokyo in September 1945, Sanders immediately fell under the influence of still another of Ishii's protégés,[18] the energetic, English-speaking Lt. Colonel Naito Ryoichi, future founder of the Green Cross Company. Naito sat in on many of Sanders's interviews, leading the questions and the answers in the direction that he, not Sanders, wished the investigation to take. He plied Sanders with selective data, giving him on 4 October 1945 a twelve-page handwritten statement that was both self-serving and protective of his superiors. Naito prevaricated if he felt it necessary. When asked, for example, whether prisoners had ever been used as experimental guinea pigs, "The informant [Naito] 'vows' that this was never done." Sanders accepted Naito's views almost completely.[19]

The final result was a report written by Sanders that contained some useful information concerning the general nature of Japanese BW research. The report gave few details on those individuals who did BW work or their findings. It was a report full of contradictions. In his summary page, Sanders stated firmly that "from 1936 to 1945 the Japanese Army fostered offensive BW, probably on a large scale."[20] Then in an appendix, he comments, "On the basis of the material previously provided by officers responsible to the Surgeon Generals of Army and Navy, a tentative conclusion had been drawn that Japanese BW activities in the military program constituted an unimportant minor activity."[21] Sanders compounded this incongruity by observing:

> It was further pointed out to the Surgeon Generals that the investigating officer [Sanders] was perfectly willing to accept the Japanese version on BW, but that in view of the complete absence of offensive data, it would be difficult to convince others that the whole story had been told.[22]

A second Fort Detrick-sponsored investigation was launched in April and May 1946. Lt. Colonel Arvo T. Thompson, a veterinarian well versed in BW research, was sent to Japan to follow up on Sanders's findings. Thompson was far more sophisticated than Sanders. He was also less impressed with the fact that his assignment involved interviewing persons who previously had held high rank and great positions of power in the defeated enemy's armed forces. His interviews were forceful and hard hitting. He did not hesitate to press his subjects for honest answers, refusing to accept evasive or skirted half-truths.

Thompson enjoyed several other advantages. He did not have Naito hovering over each interrogation session, orchestrating questions and responses. And the elusive Ishii Shiro, brought to ground in January 1946, and placed technically under house arrest, was available for questioning.

Consequently, Thompson's report was significantly more detailed than the previous finding. But Thompson noted that the full story remained to be told because most of the persons interviewed either lied, pretended to be uninformed, or consulted with fellow officers, rehearsing their responses, before meeting with him. In effect, he ran into the same deceptions as did Sanders six months earlier.

Ishii attempted to fool Thompson during a series of interviews, but Thompson remained suspicious. The investigator observed that "On the subject of BW research and development, Ishii's replies to questions were guarded, concise and often evasive."[23] Thompson noted, also, that despite Ishii's pretense that all BW records were destroyed, the

> technical information obtained from Ishii, however, indicates an amazing familiarity with detailed technical data. It leads one to question the contention that all records pertaining to BW research and development were destroyed. In all probability, much of the information Ishii presented was compiled with the assistance of his former associates at Ping Fan.[24]

Thompson's conclusions were more sophisticated and closer to the truth than earlier findings. Despite Japanese efforts to downplay BW research, Thompson understood its potential significance for the Japanese war effort. He made the point that

> While Ishii maintained that no official directive existed for the prosecution of this activity and that it was conducted as a phase of military preventive medicine, it is evident from the progress that was made that BW research and development in all its phases was conducted on a large scale, and was officially sanctioned and supported by the highest military authority.

He understood also that BW research was carried on at facilities other than Ping Fan, remarking that "Work in this field was also carried on in the Army Medical College in Tokyo."

Thompson failed to discover significant civilian BW activity. He reasoned that "BW being a military activity and highly classified for security reasons, civilian scientists and facilities of civilian research institutes were not utilized for this activity."[25] He was mistaken. Civilians did play an active role in offensive BW research.

Despite his insight, Thompson's report could deal basically only in generalities. He could offer few names other than Ishii's. The Emperor's cloudy role in the BW operation was protected totally by Ishii and the others. Thompson returned to Fort Detrick a somewhat frustrated investigator. He had tried to find the truth, but was only partly successful.[26]

Other American intelligence officers in this period pursued the subject, and ultimately found new and significant material. A 30 March 1946 Army Military Intelligence report identified five BW principals and three BW research locations.[27] War crimes investigators in Tokyo located ex-731 personnel, and, in interviews in 1946 and 1947, pieced together a detailed and reasonably accurate composite of Japan's BW program and the names or official titles of those who either had supported the project, or had participated actively in BW research.[28] These findings were complemented by revelations disclosed in 1949 by the Soviets in Khabarovsk, Siberia, during the course of a war crimes trial of captured Kwantung Army personnel.[29] By 1950, it was no longer difficult for persons with access to American and Soviet archival resources to identify the BW principals.

III

It is now known that Ishii's "secret of secrets" was not as closely held as he suggested to others. Knowledge of BW research activities, including human experimentation, was shared by many Japanese who belonged to a certain stratum of society. The military, the scientific community, key elements within the Diet, and members of the extended Royal Family were privy to the secret. Over the years, thousands of persons in Japan had become familiar with the developmental activities being done with BW. Few among them had refused to participate in the projects, or raised moral or ethical concerns.

Ishii and his BW collaborators would have been unable to conduct such a vast undertaking without the support and encouragement of high-level officers in the Army. The BW proponents were given encouragement by leading Japanese militarists beginning in 1930. Emperor Hirohito's favorite military officer in the early 1930s, General Nagata Tetsuzan, Head of the Military Affairs Bureau until his assassination in 1935,[30] was one of Ishii's earliest patrons. Nagata knew his protégé's aspirations, and helped him advance his career. All of Nagata's successors in the Military Affairs Bureau became familiar with the BW program in Manchuria, and they all promoted its development.

Tojo Hideki, a close Nagata associate,[31] and wartime Prime Minister, was posted to Manchuria in the mid-1930s. There, he, along with other high-ranking Army officers, viewed some of Ishii's early motion picture films showing human experiments. A Tojo associate recalled that Tojo developed "an aversion" to attending screenings of Ishii's subsequent movies.[32] Yet despite his evident distaste, Tojo, when War Minister or Foreign Minister, or as Prime Minister, never sought to restrict the BW program.

Every military leader appointed to serve in the revolving Japanese Cabinets in the 1930s was cognizant of what was taking place in Manchuria. The General Staff planners and their superiors were familiar with the Ishii, Wakamatsu, and Kitano projects, supporting BW in 1944 to the extent of sending scarce high-technology equipment to Manchuria's death factories even after the war turned badly for Japan.[33] The officers responsible for developing Army budgets, and for allocating funds for the various enterprises approved by their superiors, were aware of what was happening in Manchuria, as were the respective Army Surgeons General.

Thousands, perhaps tens of thousands, of Army medical doctors, veterinarians, biologists, chemists, microbiologists, technical staff, and the like, were rotated regularly to Manchuria and to occupied China. Many of these people were employed in the human experiment stations, and either participated directly in the experiments, or were told about them by others who did work with humans. At the least, they heard rumors concerning offensive BW work with humans conducted in their workplace.[34]

In Manchuria, the entire High Command was kept informed of Ishii, Wakamatsu, and Kitano's activities from the beginning of the Japanese occupation until the end of the war. General Umezu Yoshijiro, Commander-in-Chief of the Kwantung Army during much of World War II, was fully briefed on the subject.[35] Yamada Otozoo, Umezu's successor, confessed that "I learned . . . in July 1944 . . . that bacteriological detachments 731 and 100 were engaged in devising and in the mass production of bacteriological weapons." He visited Ping Fan in August 1944, and during his inspection tour of the facility, Yamada was "amazed at the scale on which the work was proceeding."[36] The Chief of the Operations Division, Major General Matsumura Tomokatsu, was sufficiently informed of BW projects, as was his counterpart in the Home Islands.[37]

Within the Kwantung Army Medical and Veterinarian Corps, almost everyone with the rank of major or above apparently knew something of these operations. Takahashi Takaatsu, Chief of the Veterinary Service of the Kwantung Army (1941–1945), supervised Wakamatsu and Unit 100's research. Lt. General Kajitsuka Ryuji, Chief of the Kwantung Army Medical Administration from December 1939 until the war's end, nominally oversaw Ishii and Kitano's work.[38]

The various BW research units eventually grew so large that the Kwantung Army leaders were required to appoint special commissions to supervise their performance. These commissions consisted of the Kwantung Army Chief of Staff, the Chief of the Operations Division, and either Ishii, Kitano, or Wakamatsu. The head of Unit 731 attended meetings when his organization was under review. Unit 100's chief attended when his group was considered. The respective commissions' recommendations were transmitted to the Kwantung Army Commander-in-Chief, "and after he endorsed them," they were forwarded to "the Japanese General Staff," who, in turn, "informed the Kwantung Army headquarters what method had been put in commission." Orders were then issued to the appropriate BW facility to proceed with the desired work.[39]

Ishii, as we have seen, openly promoted offensive BW programs among his fellow officers and scientists. Over a fifteen-year period, 1930–1945, he and others spoke frequently to large audiences, both at Army medical colleges, civilian universities, and scientific conferences, making little secret of the fact that BW research involved the use of humans in experiments. In their talks, they used exhibits which, on occasion, included preserved human parts in order to illustrate points they wished to make. For example, Army Technician Yoshimura Hisato gave a "Special lecture" at the Harbin branch of the 15th Manchurian Academy Conference, 26 October 1941, in which he barely disguised the fact that he used humans in frostbite experiments to support his thesis.[40] Kitano, in his many lectures in Mukden and elsewhere, brought with him some of the hundreds of specimens he had preserved in jars. Ishii, in his talks, favored still photographs and motion pictures taken of human experiments.

Kitano, Ishii, and top-level scientists in the BW research stations published many of their findings in Japan's leading technical journals.[41] The BW experts enlisted the help of Japan's most influential professors to assist them in recruiting the best civilian scientists for the BW laboratories. Professor Oshima Saburo of the Tokyo University Medical Research Institute, for example, visited the Nanking BW facility on a number of occasions beginning in 1941, and encouraged his students to volunteer to work there.[42] Earlier, Ishii visited Oshima's institute to recruit promising students for service in Manchuria. A former Oshima student remembered seeing Ishii "frequently in the halls in his military uniform," hurrying in and out of the Director's office.[43]

At Kyoto Imperial University, Ishii spoke to the assembled medical students every year. His topic was, usually, "How Physicians Could Help the

Military." The BW authority was eloquent and persuasive. In 1938, he sent seven of the best young Kyoto Imperial University research professors in hygiene and pathology to Ping Fan. Here they were known officially as Military Technicians, and, unofficially, as "the Gang of Seven." The new members of the BW team were given important jobs at Ping Fan as project directors on research assignments dealing with bacteriology, pathology, and frostbite. All worked with human subjects.

Ishii was helped in his talent search by Professor Toda Masaro, president' of Kyoto's Medical Department, and an ardent disciple of BW research. Masaro's expressed philosophy was, "Research which is not beneficial to the state should be abandoned." Professor Masaro used blandishments and threats to enlist researchers. It will be recalled that in the case of one of "the "Gang of Seven" who was reluctant to go to Manchuria, Masaro "ordered me to go." He would not accept any excuse, telling the doubter that "if you can't do what you are told, I'll see to it that you're put out of the university."[44]

One way or another over the years, Ishii and his colleagues secured the services of civilian researchers from the most important Japanese universities. Their work became known to others, and through their success Ishii was accorded by his peers the acknowledgement that he was Japan's leading BW expert. An associate observed of Ishii that "he was very famous among the professors in Japan. . . . Most microbiologists in Japan were connected in some way . . . with Ishii's work."[45] Moreover, "it was common knowledge among the microbiologists in Japan, all of whom were connected to Ishii, that humans were used for experimentation at the Harbin installation."[46]

Japan's faction-ridden parliament, the Diet, was known in the 1930s for its support of the military. Its members may have disagreed with each other on many issues, but not when it came to military requirements. The Diet became even more responsive to military demands after Pearl Harbor. The Cabinet, throughout this era, was equally sensitive to the needs of military leaders and the Royal Family.[47] Civilian government, after 1936, became subservient to military factions who planned various campaigns designed to expand Japan's role in East Asia.

Few civilian members of the Diet or of the Cabinet were familiar with all the details concerning the BW program in China and Manchuria. Fewer still were apprised of the human experiments.[48] The funds appropriated for Japanese BW research were hidden in different categories within the Army's budget, so that anyone reading the budget figures would not find an item labeled "BW."[49] To secure passage of budgets larded with covert funds required that some influential members of the two-housed Diet be given enough information, periodically, by informed Army officials to motivate them to vote necessary appropriations.

Key individuals of the numerous Cabinets were also aware of BW programs. The War Minister undoubtedly knew of the BW research. Various Foreign Ministers and Prime Ministers must have been informed of the BW operations (at least in outline), if for no other purpose than to be able to respond intelligently to the outcry from China after the commencement there in the mid-1930s of CW and BW field tests.

At times, Ishii impressed Cabinet officers of his needs by his own unique methods. According to an informant regarded by United States investigators as "very reliable," Ishii raised money from a Cabinet Minister in the early 1930s by bizarre threats and forceful oratory. Never loath to using strong-arm methods when he thought they were feasible, Ishii one day approached the Finance Minister in the Inukai Cabinet, and demanded a huge sum of money for his BW research. The Finance Minister refused the demand. Ishii then went to

> the private house of [Minister] Takahashi with a huge flask of cultured cholera bacilli and tried to blackmail [him]. The intransigent liberal Minister did not succumb to the blackmailer who menaced him, saying he would pour the content of the flask in the kitchen of the Minister's house.

The Minister would not bend. Then, according to the "very reliable" informant, "the crooked surgeon began a 24-hour sit-down strike in the Minister's salon." Ishii "changed his tone from that of blackmailer to that of cool scientist, citing the other countries as eagerly studying the germ strategy." The Minister was impressed with Ishii's arguments as well as his persistence, and granted him a huge sum of money from a "secret appropriation."[50]

The clever and capricious Prince Konoye Fumimaro, an Imperial favorite who headed several governments from 1937 through 1941, was probably aware of the BW program. Konoye was involved in the China affair from the start. He was the Imperial go-between in government throughout the 1930s and during World War II. He knew most of Japan's secrets, and was a hard-liner on China. The military trusted him because it understood that, despite his often contradictory public comments over the years, he would comply with whatever programs it proposed.[51]

The Privy Council, a group of twenty-six senior statesman appointed by the Emperor with the counsel of the Prime Minister, exerted great influence with Hirohito. Several of these men held close ties with the military and were familiar with the various expansionist plans considered during the 1930s. Members were certainly aware of what was developing in Manchuria in the area of BW projects. The most powerful member of the Privy Council from 1937 until 1945 was Marquis Kido Koichi, the Emperor's trusted advisor and a member of his inner circle. It is probable that Kido knew of the BW experiments, but he makes no mention in his extensive diary of either BW or CW.[52]

Of the extended Royal Family, several members either participated in the BW program, or were familiar with its objectives and the research techniques used in order to accomplish the goals. Two of the Emperor's brothers had contact with Ishii and the other leading BW specialists. One of Hirohito's cousins, and a close confidant, worked at Ping Fan for a time under an alias. The Emperor's uncle and long-time friend, Prince Higashikuni Naruhiko, enjoyed an intimate working relationship with the Kwantung Army leaders throughout the period of the Manchurian occupation.

Higashikuni, in earlier times, had toured the Ping Fan facility.[53] Other members of the Royal Family also visited Manchuria from time to time, gathering information on the general condition of the colony. Some of the royal party probably surveyed the BW laboratories at Mukden, Changchun, and Ping Fan/Harbin.

On 9 February 1939, Hirohito's younger brother, the exuberant Prince Chichibu, attended a two-and-one-half-hour Ishii "spell-binding" lecture in the War Ministry's Grand Conference Hall in Tokyo. The BW expert was so well known by then that "the vast grand conference hall was completely packed, a 'standing room only'" audience had gathered to hear him. The audience consisted of "practically the entire complement of personnel from general officers and down, assigned to the Ministry of Army and the Headquarters Staff." This was in itself an unusual tribute to a military doctor who was then only a colonel in the Medical Corps. More unusual was the fact that "his Imperial Highness, Prince Chichibu, broke away from his busy military responsibilities and honored the meeting with his royal presence and listened most intently to the proceedings."[54]

The Emperor's youngest brother, Prince Mikasa, evidently visited Ping Fan and toured much of the facility.[55] Unit 731's official photographer remembered the visit vividly, because he had produced an unclear photograph taken of Mikasa during his stop. Ishii had upbraided the photographer, saying, in effect, that with all the scientific expertise available at Ping Fan, surely something could be done to make the photograph more attractive.[56] Mikasa, in his memoirs, remembered seeing "films where large numbers of Chinese prisoners of war brought by cargo trains and lorries were made to march on the Manchurian plain for poison gas experiments on live subjects." He also recalled:

A high ranking military doctor [Ishii?] who took part in these experiments was telling me prior to this, at the time when Lord Lytton with his group was dispatched by the League of Nations [1932, at the time Ishii began his BW work in Manchuria] in order to investigate the Manchurian Incident, they attempted to give this group some fruit infected with cholera, but did not succeed.[57]

In April 1964 the (Tokyo) *Japan Times* profiled Hirohito's cousin, ex-Prince Takeda Tsuneyoshi, Japan's "sporting prince." The *Times* noted that Takeda, who was "well-favored in build and presence," was "chairman of the Japan Olympic Committee, vice chairman of the Tokyo Olympic Organizing Committee, president of the Japan Skating Union, president of the Japan Modern Pentathlon, and honorary president of the Japan Equestrian Federation." The reporter described Takeda's prewar lifestyle, and concluded the lengthy story with the observation:

1. Ishii Shiro, *c.* 1940

2. Members of the Ishii family. Ishii Shiro is third from
the left in the top row

3. Ishii Shiro, *c.* 1943

4. Kitano Masaji

5. Naito Yoshikazu, successor
to Ishii Shiro as Dean of the
Institute of Epidemic Prevention
(secret BW research) of the Army
Research School, Tokyo

6. 1943 group photo at Ping Fan of General Yoshimi Haruo, Commander of the Kwantung Army, and his top commanders

7. Mansion in Harbin used by the Japanese to interrogate candidates for Ping Fan BW experiments

8. Sentry post at the southern gate of the Ping Fan complex

9. Section of track of special rail line that led directly from Harbin to Ping Fan

10. Instruments of torture used by Unit 731 to discipline Chinese workers

11. Nanking headquarters for Unit Ei 1644

12. Remains of the boiler room of the power station at Ping Fan

13. Youthful recruits serving in Unit 731

14. Two Chinese victims of Unit 731 BW experiments

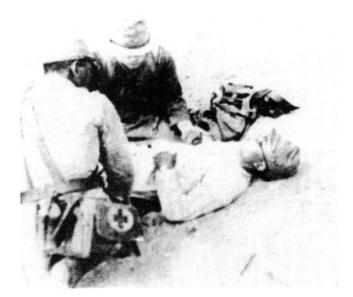

15. Japanese victim of a misdirected BW field test

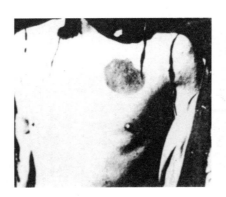

16. Some results of CW and BW human experiments

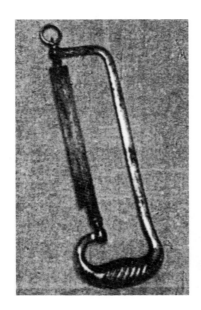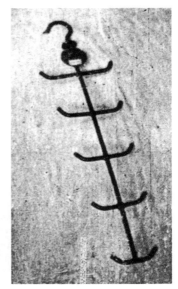

17. Implements used by pathologists to dissect BW victims

66

18. Remains of one of several crematoria at Ping Fan

19. Pathologist at work after a BW field test

20. Plague victim near Ping Fan, *c.* 1946

21. Aerial view of Unit 731's Ping Fan complex

22. 1939 group photograph of Unit 731's leading scientists, taken at a banquet in Harbin

If it were possible to sum up Takeda in a single word, the adjective for him would be "relaxed." Completely free from self-consciousness and tension, he breathes genuine warmth and generous friendliness. A text by his desk urging adherence to truth, fairness, and goodwill in everyday actions suggests the principles by which he is guided in life. If you wanted to espouse the cause of royalty, you need look no further for the perfect model for your argument than Tsuneyoshi Takeda.[58]

The article, despite its length, did not cover an important part of Takeda's experiences. Takeda had served for several years in Manchuria during the period of Japanese occupation. There he held a prominent wartime position in the Kwantung Army as Chief Financial Officer. As such, he handled the monies allocated to all the BW stations in Manchuria. He visited Ping Fan frequently, under the disguised name of Colonel Miata Suneyochi. It is probable that Prince Takeda/Colonel Miata inspected the other Manchurian death factories, as well, in the course of fulfilling his duties.

Takeda held other more direct links with the BW stations. He was a staff member of the special committee established by the Kwantung Army Command to oversee the operations of Units 731 and 100. His most important responsibility as a staff member was to determine who would be granted permission to visit Ping Fan and the satellite facilities. Even so powerful an individual as the Kwantung Army Chief of Medical Administration was required to solicit a pass from Takeda/Miata before being admitted to Ping Fan. When the Commander-in-Chief of the Kwantung Army, or his immediate subordinates, visited Unit 731 laboratories, Takeda personally escorted them on their tours.[59]

Despite his outward pacifism and good works in the postwar period, citizen Takeda[60] remained a firm believer in BW. He retained a conviction that BW was nothing more than another instrument of war. As late as 1983, Takeda told an interviewer regarding BW, "I believe we needed to study all means of waging war."[61]

IV

With so many of his closest associates, advisors, and relatives aware of the BW program, the question of the Emperor's role must be considered. Did Hirohito know what was happening in Ishii's, Wakamatsu's and Kitano's domains? The issue is a vexing and sensitive one to raise.

The Emperor was the central figure in the Japanese hierarchy in the prewar period, and, until his death in 1989, continued to play a large role in the new Japan. For the believer, he was regarded as a god. Significant numbers of ordinary people saw him as a god-like figure. Virtually all citizens recognized him as the unifying force in Japanese life, the one individual who represented to them and to the outside world the Japanese character and persona. It was inconceivable to most people that traditional Japan could exist without his presence. To link the Emperor to BW, even in a tiny or peripheral way, would be an aspersion many Japanese would resent.[62] And, in fact, no evidence connecting Hirohito directly to BW is currently available.

Edward Behr, a late-twentieth-century British journalist turned biographer, who portrays Hirohito in unflattering terms, concedes that, in his words, "'Guilt by association' is an unacceptable concept in the West." Yet Behr found so many tangential ties between the Emperor and BW that he concluded Hirohito knew something about the project.[63] Other contemporary British journalists-turned-historians see Hirohito as an integral part of the Japanese war machine, and do not discount the possibility of his knowledge of BW projects.[64] Most American researchers and some professional British historians,[65] on the other hand, view him as a basically humane individual, nationalistic, eager to see Japan achieve a dominant role in East Asia, but one who would shrink at employing unconventional weapons such as BW and CW to achieve his nation's objectives. These scholars portray him as playing a restraining role on the more aggressive members of the military hierarchy. They say, in effect, that he functioned as a benign character.[66]

In fact, Hirohito was neither an absolute ruler, nor was he a figurehead emperor similar to the role the British monarch plays. Hirohito was an intelligent leader who immersed himself in the details of government affairs during his long reign. He was not a decision maker, but he could, when he chose to, play a restraining role on matters of state. In the case of most military decisions, however, from the invasion of Manchuria, to the China Incident, to Pearl Harbor, the direct descendent of 2500 years of Japanese rulers played a passive role. The only time that apparently he intervened forcefully with the military was to insist in August 1945 that the war with the United States should be terminated.[67] No matter which Hirohito scenario one accepts, however, a massive weight of circumstantial evidence exists that must be considered when evaluating the Emperor's position.

It was noted earlier that both Ishii's and Wakamatsu's units were created in 1936 by Imperial edict.[68] Some belittle the significance of this action,[69] observing that the Emperor's seal was placed upon thousands of documents, with Hirohito's underlings actually deciding the issue at hand.[70] Others argue that Hirohito expressed a keen interest in CW and BW even prior to his accession to the throne in 1926,[71] and should have known, therefore, what these units were intended to become. What cannot be discounted is the fact that the Ishii and Wakamatsu units were the only units established by royal decree during Hirohito's long reign. All other units were created, as necessity required, by the appropriate commander within the Army.

The Emperor knew Ishii personally. He met him on at least two public occasions in the 1930s.[72] At one meeting, Ishii's somewhat unorthodox performance, while demonstrating his water purification device, must have made a lasting impression on Hirohito. Ishii, it will be recalled, offered the Emperor a drink of urine converted into purified drinking water.

Wakamatsu and Ishii received high government honors bearing the Emperor's seal as a reward for their services during the Nomonhan Incident.

Their units were awarded meritorious citations by the Emperor for their heroic deeds during the same engagement. This was, once more, a singular honor. Other medical units performed bravely in Japan's wars. Nevertheless, no other medical unit in the twentieth century received an Imperial citation for its accomplishments. It is reasonable to suspect that Hirohito may have made some inquiries before granting these honors.

Hirohito was a hard-working ruler. He is known to have consulted with his military advisors almost daily, and to have studied their reports avidly. His attention to military details increased greatly after Japan attacked the United States and European colonies.[73]

The Emperor was known also for his frugality. He constantly expressed his concern that government expenditures not be wasted on useless or frivolous projects.[74] The BW program represented an enormous drain on the nation's resources. During World War II, the main bases of Ping Fan, Changchun, Mukden, Nanking, and the numerous satellite facilities must have operated on an annual budget of at least 15 to 20 million yen, and probably more. The stationing of thousands of scientists and technicians in Manchuria and China proper, along with their many thousands of support and security personnel, would have been of concern to the Emperor as he pored over the military budget. Hirohito also had a secret Imperial fund earmarked for special weapons research, which may well have been used in Manchuria and China for BW research.[75]

Hirohito was an avid student of science. His passion for marine biology is well known. Critics charge that his scientific interests went much beyond marine biology. They assert that early in his career he became interested in the study of disease-carrying fungi, bacilli, and various culture tissues.[76] One critic insists that the institutes the Emperor funded, and the comments he made to advisors, demonstrate that "he believed in science as a practical tool, a necessary tool of warfare," and this tool included CW and BW.[77] Another states without equivocation that, "recently-declassified documents put it beyond doubt" that Hirohito "personally monitored the progress of the section's [Unit 731] researches."[78]

These extreme charges cannot be substantiated, at this time. The declassified documents currently available at the National Archives in Washington, DC, or in the other known United States and Chinese archives, do not support the claims. Unless stronger evidence surfaces in the future, these charges remain unproven.

Still, the disturbing question remains, did the Emperor know of human experiments? The answer: probably not. There was, after all, no need to provide him with intimate details of the BW studies. If the question should arise, he could be informed in general terms of the progress in BW research. Encouraging developments in BW research, not the fate of *maruta*, was the important point to make with the sovereign.

Did Hirohito know of BW research? Probably. The project was simply too large to conceal from the Emperor. Expenditures were too great to escape his keen interest in government costs. If Naito Ryoichi can be believed, the Emperor was aware of the CW program, but did not like it. With that in mind, the General Staff, according to Naito, "insisted that the work on biological warfare should not refer to offensive preparations. They . . . referred to all work on BW as being purely defensive."[79]

Too many people who had intimate contact with Hirohito were aware of the magnitude of the program. He was bound, eventually, to have heard something concerning the policy. And, finally, in Imperial Japan, policy decisions were made at the highest levels of government, and not at the whim of Army generals.

Nevertheless, it should be reiterated in fairness to the Emperor that Hirohito was not an absolute monarch. Despite Ishii's and the General Staff's assertions in the postwar period to the contrary, the Emperor would not have been able to peremptorily command the cessation of BW research, defensive or offensive. His was essentially a passive role in state matters. Moreover, in all probability, the fanatical militarists who dominated the Army throughout the 1930s and in World War II would have ignored an Imperial command ordering a halt to BW studies, if Hirohito had the temerity to issue such an order. The militarists were determined to create a viable BW weapon at all costs. They would have gone ahead despite the wishes of anyone in civilian life, even of the Emperor of Japan.

In light of all the evidence available today, however, perhaps the question raised at the top of this chapter should be changed to read, who among the prewar and wartime ruling Japanese elites *did not know of the BW program*?

Part II
Cover-up

Policy of the United States in regard to the Apprehension and Punishment of War Criminals in the Far East

1. The term "war crimes" . . . includes:
    . . . B. Violations of the laws or customs of war. Such violations shall include but not be limited to murder, ill-treatment or deportation to slave labor or for any other purpose of civilian population, of, or in, occupied territory, murder or ill-treatment of prisoners of war . . . plunder of public or private property, wanton destruction of cities, towns or villages or devastation not justified by military necessity.
    C. Murder, extermination, enslavement, deportation and other inhumane acts committed against any civilian population before or during the war . . . in execution of or in connection with any crime defined herein whether or not in violation of the domestic law of the country where perpetrated.

2. The offense need not have been committed after a particular date to render the responsible party or parties subject to arrest but, in general, should have been committed since, or in the period immediately preceding the Mukden incident of September 18, 1931.
(Department of State to the British Ambassador in Washington, 18 October 1945, Pritchard, R. John, and Zaide, Sonia M., *The Tokyo War Crimes Trial: The Complete Transcripts of the Proceedings of the International Military Tribunal for the Far East* (New York: Garland, 1981), vol. 1, pp. xiv–xv, xxvii)

11 The United States BW program

It is . . . apparent that the question of whether chemical munitions will be used or not, and whether bacterial warfare will be used or not, will depend on their practicability rather than on the sentimental reactions of pacifists. I consider that it is highly questionable if biologic agents are suited for warfare. Certainly, at the present time practically insurmountable technical difficulties prevent the use of biologic agents as effective weapons of warfare.
(Major Leon A. Fox, M.C., United States Army, "Bacterial Warfare: The Use of Biologic Agents in Warfare," *The Military Surgeon*, vol. 72, No. 3, March 1933, p. 18)

The likelihood that bacterial warfare will be used against us will surely be increased if an enemy suspects that we are unprepared to meet it and return blow for blow. . . . It seems self-evident that adequate knowledge of the possibilities of bacterial warfare demands investigation of both the offensive and the defensive aspects of the subject. Effective defenses cannot be erected without an understanding of the weapons against which they are meant to protect, and of the means by which those weapons are to be used.
(Theodor Rosebury and Elvin A. Kabat, with the assistance of Martin H. Boldt, "Bacterial Warfare: A Critical Analysis of the Available Agents, Their Possible Military Applications, and the Means for Protection against Them," *Journal of Immunology*, vol. 56, No. 1, May 1947, p. 11)

I

The decade of the 1930s offers an interesting comparison between military preparations in Japan and in the United States. The Japanese military increased its influence in government, created a large war machine that included the immense BW program previously described, and engaged in adventures in Manchuria and China, and in border skirmishes with the Soviet Union. The United States, by contrast, retreated further into the isolationist mode it had adopted in the previous decade. The American military, always regarded as little more than a pesky necessity in peacetime, was pared by Congress to a tiny size. Military research was largely neglected. Army and Navy leaders' requests were ignored generally by Congress and Presidents Hoover and Roosevelt.

Appropriations for the military were reduced further through much of the decade. This was in response to the severe economic difficulties the United States endured in reaction to the era's Great Depression. Money was spent on social welfare programs, not on exotic weapons.

Development of a viable American BW program appeared to be out of the question during the decade. The limited funds available for weapons programs were too scarce to expend on something as uncertain as BW. Besides, American military planners were skeptical about the practical application of BW in war.

Major Leon A. Fox, Chief of the Medical Section, US Chemical Warfare Service, published a paper in March 1933[1] that promulgated the current thinking of American military planners as it related to BW. Fox was a brilliant scientist whose views profoundly influenced American military tacticians throughout the decade, and well into World War II. He could on occasion wax lyrical in his writings on war.[2] However, it was his clear and penetrating insight into the problems and potential of BW that brought him lasting fame. His eighteen-page article was a dazzling overview of the subject, and was read by military strategists throughout the world.[3]

Fox concluded that BW was an impractical weapon of war. He believed that BW would be ineffective in advanced countries because populations there could be immunized against most pathogens. There were also technical problems concerning delivery systems. These problems were so massive and complex that Fox did not consider them solvable in the near future. Fox's stance on BW remained the dominant view of American planners throughout the decade.[4]

The popular press during the period carried many stories and articles dealing with BW. Wickham Steed, a British journalist, published a series of sensational articles in 1934[5] that claimed the Germans were planning to introduce BW into the ventilating systems of the Paris and London underground systems.[6] Other journalists and popular science writers produced copy dealing with potential enemies infecting numbers of people in public places with invisible pathogens, or contaminating food and water supply systems. Animals were not spared either. The press featured articles on how simple it would be to infect animals by inoculation with diseases that were contagious to man.[7] These stories were written, for the most part, by Europeans, and were disseminated throughout the continent. Few American writers were attracted to the topic.

The War Department in Washington did take note of the press reports, but put little credence in the stories. In 1937, Lt. Colonel James S. Simmons, of the Medical Corps, wrote a report that suggested the possibility of enemy BW against the United States. His idea was that enemy agents would disperse infected insects throughout the country. The insects would then cause the outbreak of epidemics, thus weakening the US war effort. Simmons's report was received with passing interest.[8] Major Fox's assessment remained the official War Department position.

II

Interest in BW's potential increased among American strategists beginning in February 1939, as several disquieting reports filtered in to Washington. Initial suspicion fell upon the Japanese because some of their scientists, including young doctor Naito Ryoichi, approached the Rockefeller Institute in New York seeking to acquire the virus of yellow fever. The request was denied. A Rockefeller technician was then offered a $3000 bribe to provide the Japanese with the virus. This approach failed also. In August 1939, a Japanese bacteriologist who was world famous, Dr Miyagawa Yoneji, approached Rockefeller's laboratory director, Dr Wilbur Sawyer, to solicit a supply of the virus. Sawyer refused to comply. However, the incidents were reported to Washington.[9]

Eighteen months later, Washington heard that Japan was stationing a BW-trained battalion of soldiers with two of its chemical warfare regiments. More frightening was the May 1941 report from the American Military Attaché in Berne, Switzerland, that the Germans were working on BW toxin in occupied France. The Attaché stated that the Koch Foundation laboratories near Paris, France's premier BW research facility, were being utilized by German experts along with French collaborators to develop botulinus toxin in an inert container that could be dropped in bombs from airplanes.[10]

Interest in BW accelerated in August 1939 as war in Europe impended. Several members of the Army Technical Division visited a Dr I. Silverman in Washington. Dr Silverman had no "real evidence" that the Germans were planning BW, but he was convinced that "nothing would deter the Germans from carrying out bacterial warfare . . . if that method offered promise of securing effective results." He urged the Public Health Department, in cooperation with the Army, to put six to eight trained personnel to investigate the subject. Their work should be done in secret, and should concentrate on countering potential German attacks. The Army was persuaded with his reasoning, but not with Dr Silverman, since they were "impressed with his sincerity and lack of real knowledge of the subject."[11]

On the same day that an investigator met with Dr Silverman, the Chemical Warfare Service circulated "Technical Study No. 10" to selected personnel. The report dealt with the potential BW threat to the United States. Its most important finding was "that attack by airplane dissemination of infected insects and other bacteriological materials is a possibility not to be ignored, especially when parachute troop landing can be expected."[12]

Two weeks later, Lt. Colonel G. C. Dunham, Director, the Army Medical Corps, sent a three-page memorandum to Colonel C. C. Hillman outlining current thinking on BW. Dunham concluded that BW was not a potentially significant military weapon. He felt that in time of war BW could be important for the propaganda effect it would have on civilian populations. This in turn would have a possible deleterious effect on the war effort. Dunham recommended that, should the United States be involved in war, the intelligence authorities go on alert for enemy attempts to engage in BW. He urged also that a group of experts be appointed to work on control measures to counter enemy BW propaganda.[13]

Throughout 1939 and 1940 military planners devoted increasing attention to BW. The various studies undertaken offered cautious and skeptical conclusions. An 8 September 1940 letter from the Chief of the Chemical Warfare Service noted that "there was little danger from any possible enemy use of bacteria or bacteria carriers," but that BW should not be dismissed out of hand. A further study should be made. By December 1940, a committee headed by Dr Irvin Abell, Chairman of the Health and Medical Committee of the Council of National Defense, and Dr Vannevar Bush, President of the Massachusetts Institute of Technology, concluded that BW would have little more than "nuisance value in impeding defense," and that "probable results would be less potent than generally assumed."

In April 1941, the Chief of the Chemical Warfare Service stated that "while the danger of enemy use of bacteria or infected insects, disseminated by airplane or parachute troop landings, is relatively small, the possibility should not be ignored." As late as 9 May 1941, seven months before Pearl Harbor, and long after Ishii began his BW field tests in China, the Adjutant General remained extremely cautious about BW. He circulated a letter to interested parties in which he noted the "futility of bacterial warfare from present knowledge." Still, he recognized that "the possible potential danger of it dictates constant alertness and study of its use by or against us and of defense against it."[14]

On 15 July 1941, the Surgeon General of the Army offered the suggestion that a committee of scientists be instituted to review the possible dangers of BW.[15] One month later, on 14 August, Colonel James S. Simmons of the Medical Corps sent a comprehensive memorandum to Harvey H. Bundy, Special Assistant to the Secretary of War, summarizing the data compiled in the Surgeon General's files. Simmons, one of a handful of early supporters who believed in the notion that BW was feasible, reported that experts were now beginning to believe that "the possibilities of biological warfare are potentially important enough to warrant a further careful study of all phases of the subject."

Events had moved so rapidly that Simmons now offered comments on the advisability of developing offensive BW weapons. He felt that it was "important to continue to study all aspects of biological warfare," including "any effective methods which may be developed offensively." He noted:

> it is the opinion of the Surgeon General that since the primary function of the Medical Department is to preserve life rather than to destroy it, should it be deemed advisable to develop facilities of this type of warfare, this should be accomplished through the activities of some branch of the services other than the Medical.[16]

Bundy was sufficiently impressed with the Simmons memo, as well as the 15 July memo of Lt. Colonel Jacobs, to call a meeting on 20 August 1941 of representatives from the Office of the Surgeon General, Chemical Warfare Service, National Research Council, G-2 (Military Intelligence), and the

Committees on Medical Research of the Office of Scientific Research and Development. This was a momentous meeting since it was held to consider "initial steps in the development of defensive aspects of biological warfare." The debate on BW had come full circle. United States military planners had gone from Major Fox's negative view of BW, to skepticism concerning its practicality, to a need to develop defensive BW.[17]

The Committee went beyond the consideration of defensive BW. It was agreed, after some discussion, that offensive BW should be studied as well. Of course, the minutes recorded, "It is fully understood that the Surgeon General and Medical Corps of the Army can take no part in offensive developments in this field." They would go along with a civilian committee that would concern itself with preventive care in the event of offensive BW attacks. At the same time, it was revealed that the Chemical Warfare Service had already requested of the National Research Council that it establish a committee to "survey the offensive possibilities of biological warfare."

The Committee concluded its deliberations by agreeing to establish two committees, one to handle defensive BW, and the other one holding the exclusive mandate on offensive BW. However, the two committees would "in effect be one." It would, "contain civilian experts not only in fields of human and veterinary medicine but also in entomology, plant pathology, toxicology and soil chemistry." Representatives of the interested branches of the Army and Navy should attend all meetings, "but should not be members." To satisfy the evident moral dilemma of the Surgeon General, the Committee agreed also that separate reports would be prepared dealing with offensive and defensive BW. The offensive reports would be addressed to the Chemical Warfare Service and the General Staff. Defensive reports would be sent to the Surgeons General of the Army and the Navy.[18]

On 1 October 1941, Secretary of War Henry Stimson wrote a letter to the President of the National Academy of Sciences requesting him to arrange for the personnel to be appointed to a special civilian BW Committee.[19] This ultimately became the WBC Committee, and consisted of nine of the most distinguished American biologists.[20] The initials WBC were a transposition of BWC, but whether this was accidental or by design was never disclosed. The WBC initiated immediate research on BW, and established liaison with both its Canadian and British counterparts. The Committee submitted a series of reports to the Secretary of War in early 1942 that recommended "a study of both offensive and defensive methods" of BW.

In one report, these eminent biologists determined that, "biological warfare is regarded as distinctly feasible." They reminded the Secretary that "the value of biological warfare will be a debatable question until it has been clearly proven by experience." Therefore:

> The wise assumption is that any method which appears to offer advantages to a nation at war will be vigorously employed by that nation. There is but

one logical course to pursue, namely, to study the possibilities from every angle, make every preparation for reducing its effectiveness, and thereby reduce the likelihood of its use.[21]

This new civilian committee concluded in February 1942 that BW was feasible. It urged that steps be taken to make the United States invulnerable to BW attacks. Secretary of War Stimson responded positively to the WBC's recommendation. He believed that BW was "of course, 'dirty business,' but . . . I think we must be prepared."[22] Consequently, he forwarded their recommendations to President Roosevelt, who accepted all their suggestions.[23]

A civilian committee, the War Reserve Service (WRS), was created in August 1942, headed by George W. Merck of the Merck pharmaceutical company in New Jersey. The WRS acted as the coordinating body for all BW work. To ensure that the WRS's work would be conducted in complete secrecy, this new organization was attached to the Federal Security Agency, a social service organization that handled Social Security, among its other responsibilities.[24]

Still another civilian committee emerged during the formative months of the American BW program. In response to a plea by the WRS for assistance from the National Academy of Sciences, the Academy, on 16 October 1942, appointed a National Research Council Committee of advisors, code name ABC Committee. The ABC Committee consisted of nine distinguished academics from such notable universities as Johns Hopkins University Medical School, University of Illinois, Columbia University Presbyterian Hospital, the Mayo Foundation, Vanderbilt University School of Medicine, University of Chicago, and Yale University School of Medicine. The government was represented by senior Army and Navy officers, and one representative each from the US Public Health Service and the US Department of Agriculture. Dr W. Mansfield Clark, Member, National Academy of Sciences, Chairman, Division of Chemistry and Chemical Technology, National Research Council, and faculty member of the Johns Hopkins Medical School, was selected as ABC's Chairman.[25] ABC now became the successor to WBC.[26]

III

With the principal players and committees in place, the American BW program in late 1942 (twelve years after Ishii had commenced his BW efforts) began an astonishingly rapid development. BW research was launched with an initial grant of under $250,000 from President Roosevelt's Special Emergency Fund,[27] a modest sum by wartime standards. WRS, as a coordinating body, remained a small organization. George Merck continued as its head; Dr E. B. Fred, soon to become President of the University of Wisconsin, became Director of Research and Development; and John P. Marquand, the novelist, directed Information and Intelligence. A few technical assistants and a secretarial pool completed the roster.

WRS did not actually conduct BW research. This work was assigned to the United States Army Chemical Warfare Service (CWS) in November 1942. Initially, all BW work was confined to the CWS's Edgewood Arsenal in Maryland. It soon became evident to the CWS leaders that the facility was too small and too exposed to handle a massive increase in BW research. After scouting for a more adequate location, in early 1943, CWS chose a 500-acre National Guard airfield with a single hangar, Camp Detrick (later renamed Fort Detrick), Frederick, Maryland, as the site for its principal BW research center.

Detrick was within easy commuting distance from Washington, but was located in such a rural and historical area[28] that it was assumed the facility could retain an anonymous character, free from enemy surveillance. Construction of BW facilities began at Detrick on 5 April 1943. Fifteen days later, Camp Detrick was formally activated. Research on a large scale was already underway within eight months of Detrick's activation.

Camp Detrick and other BW installations were directed by the Special Projects Division of the CWS. At their peak, all American BW facilities involved approximately 3900 people, about 25 percent more personnel than the Ping Fan research center at its maximum strength. Personnel were divided into three categories. Two thousand eight hundred servicemen came from the Army. The Navy supplied roughly 1000 men. One hundred civilians worked on contracts, principally at their university affiliation.[29]

Three other major installations were established to help Detrick with its work. A field test site at Horn Island, some 10 miles south of Pascagoula and Biloxi, Mississippi, was acquired in March 1943. It was discovered shortly after construction began at the island that it was not a desirable place to locate a BW testing complex. Shipping in the Mississippi River near Horn Island was on the rise, and it was too dangerous to test BW weapons so close to large concentrations of humans. As a result of this finding, the Mississippi location was restricted to testing only two toxins, botulinus toxin and ricin.

A far more important test site was established at Granite Peak, Utah, in June 1944. Granite Peak was 35 miles away from Dugway Proving Grounds, a small distance by Utah standards, and became a substation for the larger facility. In comparison to Horn Island, Granite Peak was enormous. Here, in the isolated desert and scrub-brush country of Utah, large barracks for personnel were constructed, as well as 22 miles of surfaced roads, an airplane landing strip, sewers, septic tanks, power plants, and electricity, steam, and water distribution systems. All were equipped with special devices necessary for BW testing. Granite Peak was a tribute to the daring, energy, and imagination of American BW planners. Construction began on 10 July 1944. The massive complex was completed seven months later on 30 January 1945.[30]

The fourth component of the BW program was the Vigo, Indiana, production facility. The CWS originally planned to produce BW agents at its

Huntsville, Alabama, depot, but that would have involved expensive outlays for new construction. To save money, CWS turned to the pre-existing Vigo Ordnance plant, located 6 miles from Terre Haute, Indiana. Vigo, built in 1942, was turned over to the CWS's Special Projects Division on 8 May 1944. A few new buildings to meet the unusual needs of a BW facility were constructed, but many of the ordnance structures were converted rapidly for BW use.

The plan was to use the Vigo plant to manufacture BW agents and biological vaccines. In addition, it was expected that Vigo would fill and load biological munitions. It would also be the home for breeding laboratory animals. Its principal mission, however, was to manufacture and load a material code-named INK-B, which in reality was anthrax bacteria.

By spring 1944 BW developments were advanced to the point that plans were drawn to load the anthrax bacteria into British-designed and manufactured 4-pound bombs. Initial plans were to prove the feasibility of anthrax bombs through every phase of production by filling the bombs first with water, then with an anthrax simulant, and, finally, with simulated explosives. Careful testing of the filling and loading operations would be conducted before the bomb would be declared operational. Limited production of the bomb would begin once it was determined to be a practical weapon.

The Special Projects Division considered Vigo to be nothing more than a pilot project. No one in 1944 knew whether BW would be workable, and Vigo was to be the prototype for many other BW factories once the concept was proved. Vigo's scale of operation was confined to a minimum. It was decided to recruit and to train sufficient personnel in order to operate the plant at only a 10 percent capacity. Nevertheless, the potential scale of operation at Vigo alone was quite large. If permitted to operate at full capacity, by 1945 the Vigo plant was expected to be able to produce on a regular basis fully assembled 4-pound bombs filled with 4 percent anthrax slurry at 500,000 units per month.

By April 1945 the water testing phase of the operation was completed. Two months later, Vigo began to produce the anthrax simulant, *Bacillus globigii*. At the time of Japan's surrender, Vigo had on hand nearly 8000 pounds of the agent. The first shipments of bomb casings from the British company Electromaster were ready to be filled when orders were received to halt production. The bombs were then placed in storage until a determination could be made as to what to do with them in the postwar period.

Those responsible for planning BW operations expected to use the anthrax bomb extensively. Orders to procure one million 4-pound bombs were placed with the British, with a delivery schedule of 125,000 per month beginning in March 1945. One half of these bombs were to be set aside, unfilled, for use later by the British Air Command. The other half would be for the CWS. It was expected that Vigo would begin on a small scale, producing 50,000 bombs each month, or 10 percent of capacity. These bombs would be used for testing purposes and for "surveillance."[31]

IV

Detrick did not confine its work solely to anthrax research. Instead, the scientists at Detrick unwittingly followed the Japanese research pattern of studying a host of biological agents that held potential BW application. Scientists were assigned to study botulism, brucellosis, glanders and melildosis, tularemia, psittacosis, coccidioidal granuloma, neurotropic encephalitides, shellfish poisoning (special emphasis was placed upon mussel poisoning), plague, rinderpest, Newcastle disease and fowl plague, rice brown spot, rice blast, late blight of potato, southern blight, chemical plant growth regulators, and chemical defoliants. It is probable that other possible BW agents may have been examined by Detrick personnel. As George W. Merck reported, "All possible living agents, or their toxic products, which were pathogenic for man, animals, and plants were considered."[32]

The Maryland facility worked on defensive BW as well, devising a variety of materials and devices to provide physical and chemical protection to both military and civilian populations. Technicians developed effective biological masks and protective clothing. Ointments and decontaminating agents were other areas investigated.

In munitions development, Detrick people worked on a bomb labeled the SPD Mark 1 bomb and other burster-type munitions. Research was done also on a gas-expulsion bomb, an SS bomb, the SPD Mark 2 bomb (successor to the Mark 1), and a co-agent bomb. Special studies leading to the development of unusual devices were inaugurated at Detrick. Work was done on the British Cloud Chamber. An American version was also underway by the war's end. Bacteriological and chemical laboratory studies on a massive scale were a Detrick mission.[33]

V

The United States was the last of the major powers to inaugurate a BW program. It lagged behind even many of the smaller nations in BW research. Japan was the leader in researching BW. But other signatories to the Geneva Convention also ignored its provisions and supported significant research programs throughout the 1930s. The Soviet Union had a massive program underway during the period. Great Britain was deeply involved in BW research at its Porton Down facility in the charming rural countryside of Salisbury Plain. France had a major BW facility on the outskirts of Paris. Germany, despite Hitler's distaste for BW, did engage in BW research during his rule, and tested pathogens on concentration camp victims. Canada, Belgium, and Holland employed many specialists in BW research before World War II, as did Poland, Italy, and several other small European countries.[34]

Under the circumstances, the United States' BW achievements in less than three years are impressive.[35] George Merck recalled that, during this short period (1942–1945), "Apart from the military objectives attained in this work, much information of great value to public health, human and veterinary medical science, the fundamental sciences, industry, and agriculture was derived from the research and development work performed."[36] Detrick researchers developed methods and facilities for the mass production of microorganisms and their products. Techniques were developed for "rapid and accurate detection" of small quantities of disease producing agents, including airborne agents. Various toxins to counteract potential enemy use of BW were also perfected at Detrick. Immunity vaccines against certain infectious diseases common to humans and animals were also discovered in the laboratories. Protective equipment and clothing to ward off infectious diseases were created by Detrick scientists. Special photographic techniques to study airborne microorganisms were generated during the course of BW research. Finally, the BW researchers obtained information on the effect of more than 1000 chemical agents on living plants.[37]

The BW program was the second most important wartime scientific undertaking in United States history. BW administrators were given carte blanche by the government. They were provided with all the funds they required to do their work. Any person deemed necessary for the BW program was at the disposal of the appropriate BW official. No other agency of government had priority over that individual, not even the military.[38] Only the Manhattan Project and the atomic bomb it produced exceeded the efforts of the Detrick scientists. The Manhattan Project involved many more people and expenditures of over two billion dollars. The BW program required far fewer persons, and cost about sixty million dollars.[39] BW was cheap, simple to produce, and it was deadly.

Would the United States have used BW if the war had lasted longer than it did? The answer is: probably. There is little doubt that most of the Detrick scientists would have supported using BW. While some researchers had delicate feelings concerning offensive BW, Theodor Rosebury noted in 1963:

> We were fighting a fire, and it seemed necessary to risk getting dirty as well as burnt. . . . We resolved the ethical question just as other equally good men resolved the same question at Oak Ridge and Hanford and Chicago and Los Alamos.[40]

Few presidential advisors appeared to question the issue. Those closest to President Roosevelt evidently were either indifferent, or mildly supportive of BW use. Only Admiral William Leahy, Military Chief of Staff to the President, strongly opposed deployment of BW.[41] Leahy felt that BW "would violate every Christian ethic I have ever heard of and all of the known laws of war."[42]

The military surely approved of the project. It was planning to produce one million 4-pound anthrax bombs alone for use in the later stages of the war. Most assuredly, the military would have authorized the production and deployment of other viable BW packages once Detrick researchers produced the necessary technology.

One clue to military thinking at the time is a May 1950 position paper which summed up plans for the use of toxic chemicals in the Pacific War. The paper stated that "Southwest Pacific Theater had limited stocks of all types of toxic munitions except 4.2″ mortar toxic shell." The paper's author noted that, "Readiness for gas warfare was reported on periodically by the US Chemical Warfare Committee." He reported also that "OC-CWS prepared a study of gas requirements for major gas effort in operation OLYMPIC (capture of Kyushu)," and "The final action was a very carefully prepared statement on the strategic possibilities of gas to terminate quickly the war in the Pacific. This was turned over to General Somervell just prior to the Potsdam Conference."[43]

President Roosevelt was seemingly non-committal when the issue arose.[44] However, he never questioned either the funding, or the need for the program, from the time Stimson approached him in 1942 until his death in early 1945. His successor, Harry S. Truman, evidently left no paper trail as to his attitude toward BW.[45] Truman, however, was a simple but strident patriot. He believed that, when his country was in a life-and-death conflict, the armed forces should use any weapon available to defend American freedom. He did not hesitate to authorize the use of the atomic bomb against Japan in August 1945. In order to save American lives, there is little reason to doubt that he would have authorized the utilization of BW or toxic chemical attacks in the planned invasion of Japan when the time arrived.

12   Discovery of the "secret of secrets"

The Japanese are using a BW weapon that is more deadly, far vaster than that which killed sleeping Americans on December 7, 1941. This attack would strike not only at outposts of empire but even at the life-blood in the very veins of the nation. Its effects would be visited on generations. A crude type of this secret weapon speeded the fall of Bataan.
(Newman, Barclay Moon, *Japan's Secret Weapon* (New York: Current Publishing, 1944), p. 2)

I

Fear of Japanese success with BW was not a motivating factor in compelling American leaders to begin work on BW projects in 1942. It was apprehension of Germany and its vaunted scientific prowess that motivated them. The Germans were known to be masters of technology, especially technology associated with a potential military application. Even in the closing months of World War II, with France and Belgium having been liberated, and with Germany reeling to certain defeat, the United States remained wary of German BW capabilities.[1]

American leaders were aware that Germany had introduced widespread submarine warfare in World War I, and this new weapon had almost led to victory. They recalled that Germany was the first nation in the twentieth century to employ chemical warfare in battle, creating havoc with Allied strategy in 1915, and causing tremendous losses among the combined British–French armies that confronted them in that harsh war. Rumor had it that in 1917 German agents in their Bucharest, Romania, legation imported large quantities of the glanders bacterium with the intention of spreading the disease among horses in the Romanian cavalry. These rumors surfaced once more in 1939. Some Americans suspected as well that in World War I there were German attempts to spread glanders among the cavalry services of the United States and of France. Other rumors at the time blamed German BW for the Spanish flu epidemic of 1918 which killed millions of people throughout the world. The United States Army Surgeon General became convinced in 1918 that German agents had poisoned wells with cholera germs, and were responsible for several cholera outbreaks near American encampments in Europe.[2]

If Germany could engage in such inhuman warfare under the civilized government of the Kaiser, what could the world expect from a Germany under the ruthless dictatorship of Adolf Hitler? With hindsight, it is now known that Hitler opposed BW, and that he supposedly issued orders prohibiting BW research. German scientists, with the support of high-ranking Nazis, defied the alleged ban, but their work lagged far behind that of other countries.[3] The nations fighting the Nazis were unaware of this lapse, and operated with the belief that Germany was in the forefront of BW investigations. Canada, the United States, and Great Britain all predicated their BW programs on the premise that they must counter the German menace.[4]

II

The potential Japanese BW danger was either ignored or discounted by Western experts as late as 1942. These attitudes can be explained in part by recognizing that Japan's BW program in Manchuria was a tightly controlled secret. Europeans and Americans were restricted in their movements there, making hard intelligence difficult to ferret. The principal reasons Allied specialists rejected Japan as a creditable threat, however, were geography and patronizing racism, and not their ignorance of Japanese BW progress.

Japan's employment of BW in the field in China had been extensively reported in the press as early as 1937. But China was more than ten thousand miles from Washington, DC, London, and Ottawa. It seemed obvious to those who watched events develop in that distant part of the world that Japan did not possess a delivery system capable of causing significant public health problems in the United States, Canada, or Great Britain. Consequently, even if the Chinese reports of Japanese BW attacks could be confirmed – and many could not – they seemed to pose no danger to the West. Moreover, even after relations between the United States and Japan began to deteriorate badly in 1940, Americans viewed Asia as a secondary interest. Their primary concern was focused on the North Atlantic and the Nazi menace.

Throughout the 1930s, and long after the attack on Pearl Harbor, Western racist attitudes resisted the notion that Japanese scientists operating on their own initiative would be sufficiently accomplished to produce anything significant. Japanese technology, in the opinion of many officials, was simply incapable of achieving the technical expertise required for developing an effective BW program. The Japanese stereotype in the West was that of an industrious people who were hard-working and disciplined, but lacking in imagination or creativity. They did not innovate. They copied the achievements of others. Japan was known for producing shoddy merchandise and cheap gimcrack items. Most Western analysts believed that Japanese technology lacked the sophistication required to mass-produce quality goods. It seemed unlikely that Japan could develop a corps of scientists capable of creating advanced weapons.

Western arrogance toward Japanese intellect was such that it was deemed inconceivable for Asians to create a viable BW procedure. To accomplish their ends, it was thought, they would need the help of Europeans or North Americans. Racism was so endemic, however, that on 10 December 1941, when an individual appeared at the Milwaukee, Wisconsin, office of the FBI, the information he divulged was deemed sufficiently important for the Special Agent in Charge to dispatch a report of the interview to Director John Edgar Hoover.

Hoover was so impressed with the information he received that he sent copies of the report to the Director of Naval Intelligence and to Paul V. McNutt, Head of the Federal Security Agency and front man for the WBC. The unnamed informant revealed that while serving in Japan in 1925 he concluded that war between the United States and Japan would occur within fifteen years. During his posting in Tokyo, he and his wife associated with a small group of "white persons," including several German doctors. One of the Germans, while drunk, blurted out one day that the German doctors were in Japan solely to "teach Japanese the art of bacterial warfare and that some day Germany would get its revenge over the United States through the use of that mode of warfare." The informant recalled, sixteen years after this drunken conversation allegedly occurred, that the German mentioned specifically the use of "anthrax bacilli [,] dysenary [sic.] and typhus germs as some of the methods to be used." He added that, "the human mind is incapable of visualizing the means to which the Japanese would resort to achieve their ends."[5]

After the attack on Pearl Harbor, racist paranoia was so great in the United States, especially in the western regions, that it affected even the most sensible people. While Ishii, Kitano, and Wakamatsu intensified their BW efforts in Manchuria and China, the FBI investigated Japanese-American pharmacists for their possible culpability in waging BW against their fellow Americans. In February 1942, an agent interviewed an official of a large San Francisco wholesale drug company. The official reported that Japanese druggists in the rich farming community of Salinas, California, were buying large quantities of typhoid serum. One of his salesmen had received an order for "50 vials at one drug store." The official asked his salesman to report the incident to the appropriate authority, but the salesman refused, arguing that "he was interested in selling supplies and receiving his commission, rather than reporting unusual activities to the authorities."[6]

The FBI ordered numerous agents to investigate Japanese and Japanese-American pharmacists living in the San Francisco area, as well as in farming communities throughout the San Joaquin Valley, for possible BW activities. Agents devoted countless hours to this task, contacting numerous wholesale drug companies in San Francisco, enlisting drug salesmen as informants, and personally interrogating pharmacists and other individuals to learn of any unusual purchases of vaccines that could be used as possible antidotes for BW sabotage attacks. The hunt was so intense that one informant urged the FBI to make a check on "Japanese research doctors and workers employed in state, municipal and university laboratories, as it would be possible for those people to obtain Shiga Dysentery cultures and cholera cultures."[7] Agents were so diligent that one submitted a report deemed so sensitive that only one paragraph of nine survived the FBI's censor in 1990. The surviving paragraph states, "In this connection the following supplied upon reliable information reveals a subversive rumor is circulating in Alameda, California, that commercial rice has been poisoned. In consequence of this rumor civilians are refusing to purchase rice."[8]

The diligence of the FBI in its hunt for possible Japanese BW saboteurs is perhaps best exemplified by an incident that occurred in Ecuador in the closing months of 1942. An agent in Guayaquil learned that a Japanese national possessed laboratory facilities and "knowledge." The agent was given permission by the Ecuadorean government to search the laboratory's premises, but found no evidence there of BW preparations. Consequently, the agent concluded that "Subject had advance information on proposed search of laboratory . . . indicating a leak in the office of Security."

It was subsequently discovered that this Japanese national, apparently "Ecuador's only Japanese," had another laboratory in the remote flea- and mosquito-ridden community of Maldonado. Another agent was dispatched on horseback to Maldonado, with instructions to search the reported laboratory. One misadventure after another struck the FBI agent. Trying to save time, he ordered the rental of horses in the town of Torfino, along with the requisitioning of supplies of canned food, blankets, and other necessities. The agent rented a taxi to take him to Torfino, but the taxi became "stuck in a mud hole and after long and futile efforts to extract it culminating with the failure of three yoke of oxen" to loosen the taxi, "agent proceeded a [on] foot until a hacienda was reached that would rent horse for Torfino." The delay forced the dedicated agent to spend the night in Torfino, "sleeping on the floor of the Tomiente Politico's office."

The agent eventually made his way to Maldonado. Here, he found the alleged Japanese BW scientist. However, the person was not what the agent expected. The unfortunate individual turned out to be a half-starved Japanese national who was living in one room of a tiny house inhabited by a large family. The "scientist" was in such dire straits, the agent reported, that he was "living on the charity of this family, for he is absolutely without funds." The agent reported that the suspect "has absolutely no laboratory equipment of any kind." He did have an improvised bunsen burner that he used to illuminate his room. He owned only one book, a Japanese–English grammar, and since he could find no work, he spent most of his time studying English. The purpose behind his intensive study of his enemies' language was "in hopes of getting into a concentration camp in the US." The man was "heartily sick of Maldonado [a village of eight houses stuck midway up a canyon wall] and is very desirous of getting to a concentration camp in the US where he has learned that the Japanese are well treated." He saw in the FBI his salvation and urged the agent to arrest him. Otherwise, he threatened to go to Tulcan "and get himself thrown in jail. He stated that one would be better off in jail than Maldonado."[9] The poor man did not get his wish. The FBI agent returned alone to Guayaquil, leaving him to find his destiny in either Maldonado or a Tulcan jail.

III

Those responsible for security matters in the United States, including the FBI, began by summer 1942 to place greater emphasis on the possibility of a Japanese external BW threat, rather than as an internal danger to the country's well-being. The FBI, to be sure, continued to keep an eye on Japanese-American and Japanese pharmacists in central and northern California as late as November 1942.[10] Fear that agents of Japan were about to contaminate large parts of the Golden State with typhoid germs led the FBI to investigate leads in Salinas and Oakland in August and November that year, but the investigations turned up nothing unusual.[11]

At the same time, information and analytical papers dealing with possible Japanese BW efforts that previously were either discredited or ignored were now resurrected and considered more carefully. A 12 June 1942 study prepared by a researcher in Hawaii that analyzed possible Japanese and German BW efforts was first seriously evaluated by the FBI thirteen months later, in July 1943. The report contained a useful review of pathogens that could readily be converted into instruments for BW in Hawaii. However, the overall assessment was flawed by the author's rabid racism and worst-case-possible scenarios that lent themselves more to science fiction than to reality. Nevertheless, the individual who formulated the study did point out that "In the present war the Japanese are reliably reported to have used the bacillus which causes bubonic plague against their Chinese adversaries." Moreover, "Can we believe," he asked, that "when an Axis victory becomes a matter of great doubt, the Germans and Japanese will shrink from using, in desperation, this trump card of theirs [BW] against" the United States? The writer urged that "we face this problem realistically and prepare now to resist any attacks by bacteria which the enemy may attempt." He exhorted those who read his report: "Let it never be said that the enemy surprised us twice, first with bullets and second, with bacteria."[12]

At least one American medical journal reported on Japan's use of BW in China. After listing all the plans for the coming annual meeting of the Wyoming State Medical Society, including the fact that "The Laramie County Women's Auxiliary will entertain visiting doctors' wives and will see that no guest may lack social diversion," the August 1942 *Rocky Mountain Medical Journal* printed a lengthy story on BW under the heading, "Japanese Use the Chinese as 'Guinea Pigs' to Test Germ Warfare."[13] Datelined "New York, N.Y.," the account summarized a thirteen-page report on Japan's BW efforts in China by Dr P. Z. King, China's National Health Administration Director.

King cited five separate Japanese BW attacks in China in 1940 and 1941. All five strikes were fully documented and corroborated by several foreign experts who were working in China at the time. The *Journal* quoted Dr King's conclusion that, "The enumeration of facts thus far collected leads to the conclusion that the Japanese Army has attempted bacterial warfare in China." It offered no editorial comment on the report. Nor did it or any other reputable medical publication pursue the issue further. Still, those doctors who read the *Rocky Mountain Medical Journal* were alerted to the fact that the United States was fighting an enemy who possessed some type of BW capability.

In far-off Lima, Peru, Dr Marshall Hertig read reports of Japanese BW attacks in China in *Time* magazine and elsewhere. Recognizing the possible dangers to the United States if these reports were true, Dr Hertig wrote in haste to his friend Dr Charles V. Akin, Assistant Surgeon General in the US Public Health Service. Hertig urged Akin to investigate these reports carefully, since he believed BW to be a potentially important weapon of war. He grasped the fact that the Japanese were field testing BW in China, and warned:

> If the Japanese use of plague in China was a serious attempt at bacterial warfare it means that the matter is being explored, and we may be sure there will be no reluctance to use anything of the sort which offers any hope of success.[14]

IV

Nineteen forty-three was a pivotal year in the war in the Pacific. After a succession of ferociously fought naval campaigns, the tide of battle turned against Japan and in favor of the United States. American forces then began the arduous and bloody task of fighting to liberate islands in the Pacific that were seized by Japan in the early and heady days of the war. The battles on the various islands (Guadalcanal, New Guinea, Tarawa, Iwo Jima, Saipan, Guam, etc.) in 1943 and 1944 were fought fiercely by both sides. Casualties were very high in many of the encounters. Newspapers and magazines in the United States described the ferocity of the struggle, emphasizing the fanatical resistance of the Japanese defenders, including their desire to fight until the last man died in honor of the Emperor and the homeland.

Many of Japan's soldiers did fight and die heroically. Others fought on until it became evident that there was no stopping the American onslaught. These soldiers preferred surrender to death. Among the many thousands of prisoners gathered up in the island-hopping campaigns directed by General Douglas MacArthur, Americans discovered a significant number of medically trained personnel. There were doctors, medical corpsmen, nurses, pharmacists, and veterinarians scattered among the half-starved, fearful captives now in American hands.

These scientifically trained people represented an unexpected plus for the American liberators. They were an intellectual treasure trove that could be mined for information concerning Japan's wartime technological achievements. Interrogators were instructed to obtain from them information on

> Biological Warfare Research, Experimental and Development centers, munitions being developed and manufactured, manufacturing centers, storage centers, actual diseases under investigation, methods of use and units likely to use BW, BW tactics, reason for anthrax immunization, and personnel connected with BW in any manner.[15]

Prisoners were to be questioned closely as to "the number and type of any recent vaccinations they have received," in the hope that this information would reveal something concerning the pathogens Japan planned to use in BW.[16]

Intelligence was so anxious to gain Japanese BW information that it prepared a document containing seventy-five BW-related questions to be asked of the prisoners.[17] A memorandum of 15 August 1944 stated flatly that, since Japan was capable of using BW, it was essential that every American soldier in the Pacific area be "impressed with the importance of capturing and securing any medical documents and supplies." The memorandum concluded with the injunction, "Any evidence of enemy use of bacteriological warfare, no matter to what extent, will be reported immediately" to Intelligence headquarters.[18]

Interrogators from several intelligence agencies questioned the special prisoners closely. It was from these captives that the United States obtained first-hand, reliable confirmation that Japan was engaged in significant BW research. Virtually all the previous Chinese charges of germ and gas warfare were now corroborated.[19] Other information obtained suggested that Japan's BW efforts were on a far larger scale than previously suspected.

Naturally, many of those questioned offered as little information to their interrogators as they believed possible in order to protect Japan's secrets. One medic captured on Saipan in August 1944, for example, showed a surprising knowledge of many of the diseases associated with BW research. He was described as "slightly above intelligence," and "fairly cooperative," yet his information was classified as "*only fairly reliable*." Although he had served for a time in Manchuria, the prisoner claimed to know of no BW research being carried out there, in Japan, or in China proper. This medic did acknowledge, however, that "Five or six years ago a prisoner read in the newspaper of an army doctor (rank unknown), Ishii, Shiro, in connection with the award of decorations. Ishii was then in Tokyo. He is not known to have been in Manchuria."[20]

Other prisoners unwittingly were more cooperative. Most denied participating in BW experiments. Many disavowed knowledge of BW research; some feigned shock and dismay at the very suggestion that Japan would engage in something as unethical as BW. Intensive questioning of these individuals, however, garnered a considerable body of BW data.

The interrogation of two medical officers captured on Iwo Jima on 16 March 1945 illustrates well the techniques of evasiveness on the part of the captives, and the effectiveness of the American questioners in obtaining important BW information. Under questioning, the two officers denied receiving specific instruction in BW. Both refused to "believe that Japan would ever resort to such warfare." Despite their declared lack of knowledge, they admitted knowing of the Water Purification Units headquartered in Harbin. They knew of "biological experimental centers in Tokyo," where research on pathogens useful to BW took place. They were familiar also with leading military personalities associated with BW work.[21]

Another captive, a lieutenant swept up in the fighting on Peleliu in November 1944, emphasized that the Japanese "had absolutely no dealings with BW." The Lieutenant then admitted he had once served as a laboratory assistant in a medical center in Changchun where he worked on glanders research. His work, no doubt, was associated with the studies being done by Unit 100, but the Lieutenant never disclosed knowledge of Wakamatsu's operation there. Under close questioning, he did reveal that glanders "is the only organism being experimented with as a possibility of Japanese using it for bombing purposes," but his interrogator realized that other BW work was underway in Manchuria since he noted parenthetically, "(this is contradicted later)." The contradiction did surface when the prisoner confessed that he understood that BW research was being done at the "Kwantung Army's laboratories and serum-producing plant in Dairen," a facility that fell under Unit 731s jurisdiction.[22]

Other prisoners disclosed startling information concerning a BW factory in Nanking. The disclosures were extremely accurate and detailed. One POW was able to provide his captors with a reasonably accurate sketch of the Nanking BW complex. Another furnished his captors with extensive data as to what types of BW research were undertaken by Japanese scientists at the facility. There was even the suggestion that the Nanking facility might be engaged in human experiments.[23]

Occasionally, even dead soldiers provided American intelligence with useful information. A bound mimeographed file belonging to a second lieutenant was located at Morotai on 24 September 1944. The file contained details concerning diversionary raids on the enemy, including the comment that, "Great results can be obtained by contaminating their food and drink in kitchen by bacterial strategy."[24] A notebook torn from the body of a flying enlisted trainee listed an assortment of bombs available to the Japanese Air Force that included one designated as a "Special Bomb," a "(Bacillus Bomb)." Another notebook discovered on a dead engineering officer killed at Kwajalein also contained a list of bombs, one of which caught the attention of US Intelligence. This was one with the notation, "Special Bombs (TOKUSHUBAKUDAN): Mark 7 – cities, water reservoirs, animals, personnel (bacillus) Example: Air Arsenal (KUSHU) Type 13 Experimental 1 kg Mark 7."[25]

Local freedom fighters were a useful source of information for American BW intelligence seekers. News of Japanese BW activity in Burma, for example, filtered into Intelligence headquarters in December 1944. Three months earlier, Burmese fighters discovered some "20 cubic cm ampoules (yellow and half clear)" that, upon analysis, was disclosed to contain cholera bacilli. The Burmese claimed that the ampules were dropped from Japanese airplanes. In Thailand, a plague epidemic erupted in September 1944. There had been no evidence of plague in that area in recent times. It was assumed by the Thais, and the Americans, that this was an epidemic artificially induced by the Japanese as part of their "bacterial fifth column activities."[26]

On one occasion, American cupidity led to a mistaken belief that Japan had engaged in BW. Shortly after recapturing Guam and Saipan, several marines and naval personnel died from what rumors called "poisoned sake" or "poisoned beer." It was assumed the retreating Japanese left the "poisoned" alcohol for Americans to consume, and to be killed from its effects. Instead of a subtle form of BW, later autopsies provided a more prosaic solution to the sudden eruption of alcohol-based deaths. Drums of methyl alcohol (wood alcohol) left by the Japanese were brewed into drinks by American personnel and native Chammorros. The inevitable result was death due to methyl alcohol poisoning, and not to BW. As the Chief Medical Examiner in the region drily observed, "In every case in which details were obtainable both on Guam and on Saipan, it appeared that the poisoning was due to the common mistake of assuming that anything which was labelled alcohol or which smelled like alcohol was drinkable."[27]

One of the most important prizes for American BW researchers came from an unlikely source: the rubble of Berlin. On 20 June 1945 the United States armed forces in Berlin seized Japan's Science Attaché to Germany, Colonel Hojo Enyro. Hojo, then about fifty-one years old, was a bacteriologist who had worked closely with Ishii in the early Manchurian days as well as at Ping Fan. He knew most of the intimate secrets of Japan's BW program. Colonel Hojo had been in Hitler's capital since February 1941 as a scientific attaché, but he had spent most of his time traveling throughout the country and in Axis countries as well as occupied territories, seeking intelligence on German BW research.[28]

The former Ishii confidant confounded his German colleagues in May 1941 when he delivered a lengthy lecture on BW before the Berlin Medical Academy. Using carefully guarded references, Hojo outlined to his incredulous audience Japan's BW agenda. He urged the Germans to increase their BW research and to cooperate with their Japanese colleagues.[29] His effort to develop BW joint ventures failed, but he greatly impressed those Germans who promoted BW research.[30]

Hojo was considered to be such an important resource that he was transported to Washington for interrogation shortly after his capture. He was given VIP treatment there, and was questioned for five days, 20–24 August 1945, at the Pentagon by a captain in the Medical Corps. Hojo underwent further questioning at the Pentagon in September. His captors described him as "intelligent and cooperative." The information he furnished them was checked against data already at hand, and was regarded as "Generally reliable." Hojo was careful to skirt the human experiments issue,[31] but was otherwise reasonably candid in his discussions.[32] The Pentagon was delighted with the extensive and detailed information gleaned from the former attaché, and repatriated him to Japan shortly after his debriefing.[33]

Gradually, Military Intelligence began to piece together bits and pieces of prisoner-of-war information into a coherent pattern. One POW captured at sea, a Lt. Colonel, turned out to be a knowledgeable pharmacist. His disclosures "confirms the statement made by prisoner of war (JA 147935)" concerning "experiments carried out by Major-General Ishii, Shiro at *Harbin* on a bacillus bomb."[34] Another prisoner, a captain in the Medical Corps, captured at Peleliu on 18 October 1944, disclosed that he knew of the Water Purification Unit in Harbin and its leader Ishii Shiro. He noted that Ishii was also an instructor in the Army Medical Academy, that he was a bacteriologist, "famous for his development of water purification machinery," and that Ishii's unit "is the only unit in the Japanese Army responsible for the bacteriological warfare."[35] A civilian employee captured at Depapre on 12 May 1944 revealed that "While working in Bacteriology Dept of *Chuzan* university at *Canton*, Jun 41, PW heard that Maj-Gen Ishii, Shiro was conducting experiments with *bacillus bombs* at branch of Army Med College in Manchuria."[36]

It was no later than autumn 1944 when American Intelligence sources could confidently draw a reasonably accurate outline of Japanese BW developments.[37] By that date, they knew research laboratories existed in Tokyo, Canton, Nanking, Dairen, Changchun, and Harbin. They were confident that other BW centers existed as well.[38] The Harbin facility was known to be a major research center. It was cited as the headquarters for a Water Purification Unit deeply involved in BW work.

Intelligence concluded that research on potential BW use of glanders, plague, anthrax, cholera, dysentery, tuberculosis, typhoid, and perhaps other diseases had been conducted for several years. Japan was now known to be developing several BW delivery systems, including a bacillus bomb as well as a device designated as "Mark 7." It also was experimenting with the use of paper balloons as BW carriers, which some analysts feared would represent "an immediate threat to the N. A. [North American] continent of possible biological warfare against man, animals and plants."[39]

Although many of the principals in BW development were still undiscovered, Ishii Shiro, inventor of a water filtration device, was perceived to be a major figure in Japan's BW enterprise.[40] This high-ranking military microbiologist repeatedly was identified as being active in BW research in Tokyo as well as in Harbin.[41] The Unit he commanded was also recognized as one intimately associated with BW activities.[42]

On 28 November 1944, Secretary of War Stimson and Federal Security Agency Administrator McNutt forwarded to President Roosevelt a summary of progress on American BW research developments, as well as what was then known of BW work in other countries. The report noted little substantive information on Germany. On Japan, however, it was observed that "There is more positive evidence that Japan is interested in biological warfare and has developed the means of employing it." Captured enemy documents listed "various bacillus bombs, attempts have been made to spread plague in China, and ampules of 'anthrax K vaccine' were captured on New Guinea." The commentary on Japan concluded that "There appears to be little doubt that Japan is preparing defensively and offensively for biological warfare."[43]

On 4 June 1945, the Military Intelligence Service in Washington circulated a remarkable memorandum that summarized the knowledge Intelligence gathered on Japanese BW. It was based on data compiled from many sources, "captured notebooks of Navy Personnel, documents, and Ps/W on the Japanese Bacterial Bomb." The report was comprehensive and chilling in its implications. Its summary stated:

> On the basis of information available, there is no doubt that the Japanese have conducted research on BW and that they have a BW munition in at least the experimental stage of development. . . . It is impossible to state at this time whether the Japanese intend to make tactical use of this weapon.[44]

Less than two months later, on 26 July 1945, Military Intelligence prepared an even more comprehensive analysis of Japanese BW preparations. In thirty-two typewritten pages, this report reviewed all available information on Japanese BW, and came to some sobering conclusions. Among the fifteen findings, Military Intelligence declared, that (1) "No agreements prohibiting the use of BW agents would deter the use of such agents by the Japanese Army and Navy if it were believed military advantage was to be gained therefrom." A second judgment was that "Accusation of Allied use of BW may be for the purpose of justifying Japanese use of such agents, either past, present, or future." The report's final conclusion did little to allay American fears of Japan's BW prowess. After determining that Japanese BW research, as of 26 July 1945, did not represent a serious threat to the American war effort, the report observed, "It is believed the Japanese do not *intend* to initiate the use of BW by mass attack, but they may initiate its use on a small scale where there will be little or no possibility of its detection."[45]

V

American officials were shocked and alarmed by the findings that Japan was engaged in what appeared to be an extensive BW research effort. They concluded that it was essential this intelligence be kept a closely guarded secret. If word of apparent Japanese success with BW were revealed, it could have a crippling effect on morale on the American home front. In addition, it would be telling the enemy of Allied knowledge, thus enabling them to prepare possible counter-measures to protect their BW installations.

Above all else, the secret American BW program could not become public knowledge. The Army Surgeon General's Office, an assortment of military intelligence agencies, and the FBI were frightened of the prospect that, should word leak out concerning either the Japanese or the American BW programs, there would be an inevitable Congressional investigation. The research endeavors at Fort Detrick and elsewhere would be compromised during such an investigation. The war effort would surely suffer from the possible revelations during unpredictable hearings.[46]

It was with these fears in mind that, on 1 June 1944, a certain Captain Saul Jarcho of Medical Intelligence, while in New York on a special assignment, stumbled upon a startling development. He noticed an advertisement in the *New York Times* of the coming publication of a book titled *Japan's Secret Weapon*, a work that its enthusiastic publisher declared would expose Japan's BW menace to the United States. Jarcho charged into a major bookseller's store to purchase a copy, but the sales people there were unaware of the publication. Captain Jarcho ultimately found the publisher, Current Press, operating out of a back room on lower Fifth Avenue. The Current Press owners evidently were also in another business, since Jarcho found the office "cluttered up with a wide variety of objects which suggested that among other things they were engaged in the toy business."

Captain Jarcho's discovery alarmed intelligence and counter-propaganda circles in New York and in Washington. From New York City, Walter Winchell, the radio personality and popular gossip columnist, wrote to his friend J. Edgar Hoover to inform him that *Japan's Secret Weapon* "has startling disclosures and 'inside information'."[47] Responding to Winchell's disclosure, the FBI ordered a copy of the book to be purchased and sent to its laboratory for review.[48]

In Washington, hasty meetings were arranged in which the book's possible damage to the war effort was considered. Five colonels representing the Medical Corps and G-2 discussed the possible consequence of the release of the book. One colonel suggested that the book be suppressed. Another colonel pointed out, however, "that there was considerable question as to whether or not such a thing could be legally suppressed."[49]

The Executive Officer to George W. Merck, Lt. Commander William B. Sarles, was given the assignment to read the book. His report was sent to the top officials in the various Surgeon Generals' Offices as well as to Secretary of War Stimson's principal assistant. Sarles concluded that the book was "an emotional and inflammatory piece of writing." He did agree with the decision not to suppress the work since such action "would only serve to attract attention to it." All he hoped for was that the book would prove to be a "dud," and he suggested that propaganda people use their influence to "prevent reviews and all references to the book eliminated from newspapers and magazines."[50]

Reviews of *Japan's Secret Weapon* were published, despite the efforts of Sarles and others. A few reviews were favorable. Others were highly critical, including one in the important Book Review Section of the *New York Times*.[51] The Book of the Month Club Newsletter reviewer recommended that the book be purchased, but that the reader be cautious in accepting the author's charges, since the book "depends largely on innuendo and suggestion." Nevertheless, "there is a disturbing side to this book, that it is not entirely spun out of whole cloth."[52]

The reviews were so unsettling to Washington that at least three generals, one admiral, two colonels, and a leading civilian BW authority wrote extensive comments on the merits of disclosing some information concerning American "defensive" BW work as a counter to Japan's BW offensive capabilities. These views were then discussed with Elmer Davis, Head of the Office of War Information. Davis and his deputy suggested that nothing be disclosed to the American public at that time. They wanted to continue with the official policy of silence that cloaked American BW work from its inception. Davis noted that there currently was no public apprehension about the subject. He also pointed out that it was unwise to make a statement, because the United States was "handicapped by: (a) our unpreparedness to retaliate (even lack of official decision to do so); and (b) inability to meet most of the forms of attack which might be made by our enemies."[53]

The subject of all the hand-wringing and hasty meetings was a book concocted from the little information that had surfaced publicly about Japan's employment of BW in China. Using these details, and an extremely fertile imagination, the author of *Japan's Secret Weapon* charged that the Japanese had an enormous BW program. He also claimed that the Japanese were so well along in their research that they could disseminate cancer at will throughout the United States. He indicated, further, that the enemy, in its invasion of the Philippines, had spread malaria pathogens in order to reduce the strength and resolve of the defenders of Bataan. His most damaging accusation, however, was that the American authorities were familiar with Japan's plans, and were doing little to counter them.

Japan's Secret Weapon was written by one Barclay Moon Newman, the author of several earlier sensational tomes on topics likely to arouse public fear. Newman had been a science and medical editor for the defunct *Literary Digest*, and possessed some scientific background. He once did malaria research for the US Public Health Service, and served briefly with the Navy as a Lieutenant, J.G. His current effort was described by one reviewer as being "sensational to the point of being frantic."[54] The reviewer concluded that, "The book has great nuisance value, and will scare almost anyone who reads it, unless the reader has a proper background of experience." He conceded that, unfortunately, "there are few such readers."[55]

Newman's book proved to be a "dud." It failed to sell many copies, to the relief of those who were concerned with its potential harm to the war effort. The failure may have been due to poor timing in the release date (summer 1944), its obscure publisher's poor distribution network, or its relatively high retail price of $2.50, or to the concerted effort of the Office of War Information and others either to promote negative reviews, or to encourage the media to shun the book. The end result was that *Japan's Secret Weapon* soon appeared in bookstores on the remainder table. Japan's secret BW work remained known to only a comparative handful of intelligence officers and scientific researchers. The United States BW program continued to be a closely held secret, privy to even fewer Americans.

13 Investigations

The story of Japanese biological warfare implicates more than half the persons tried by the International Military Tribunal for the Far East, and more than 5,000 others who worked on the BW program in some capacity. It involved a genuine conspiracy of silence. . . . Allied prosecutors from half a dozen countries affected by the issue remained silent at the Tokyo War Crimes Trial about what they knew. . . . The Chinese . . . must have lived in hope of gaining some kind of quid pro quo for their silence. . . . The Russian authorities, who sought to raise the matter . . . allowed themselves to be silenced. . . . What seems quite incredible is that the cover-up conspiracy – for it is by no means a demonological exaggeration to speak of it as a conspiracy – was maintained throughout the three years which elapsed between the Japanese defeat and the conclusion of the Tokyo trial . . . and that . . . this conspiracy was sustained for so long afterwards.

(Calvacoressi, Peter, Wint, Guy, and Pritchard, John, *Total War, The Causes and Courses of the Second World War* (revised second edition, New York: Pantheon Books, 1989), pp. 1201–1206)

I

Japan's unconditional surrender to the United Nations[1] in 1945 did not prevent it from enduring an invasion and an occupation of the Home Islands by its enemies, albeit that the incursion was peaceful. General Douglas MacArthur arrived in Japan in early September with an advanced force that ultimately would reach several hundred thousand men and women. Most of the members of this army of occupation consisted of ordinary personnel, garrison troops, interpreters, medics, supply and ordnance people, etc.

Some others, however, normally would not be found among the routine military personnel typical of an occupying army. Anxious to punish Japanese "war criminals," the United Nations furnished the occupation authorities with people who in civilian life were policemen, criminal investigators, lawyers (both criminal and civil), and judges. Social scientists roamed throughout the country investigating and classifying Japanese lifestyles and traditions in order to best assist General MacArthur's staff in devising a new democratic system for the Japanese people. American scientists rushed to Japan to make a thorough investigation of that country's wartime scientific achievements. The Fort Detrick complement of investigators who were sent to Tokyo were most concerned with the reported Japanese advances in CW and BW, and were eager to ascertain the true status of enemy research.

Inevitably, there would be overlap, tensions, and, on occasion, conflict between the various competing parties in their efforts to achieve their respective goals. So many non-traditional personnel flowed into Japan that competition and confusion over jurisdiction concerning investigation of individual suspects or wartime government-sponsored activities erupted periodically. Military investigators, eager to bring to trial those presumed guilty of war crimes, frequently encountered difficulties from those in power who disliked the notion of war crimes trials. The latter believed in Civil War General William Tecumseh Sherman's dictum that "war is hell," and that, consequently, anything done in wartime to try to obtain victory was acceptable.

Others frustrated the war crimes probers because they wished to exploit those under suspicion for their own purposes. This was especially notable among the CW and BW scientists in Washington and in the field in Tokyo. The CW and BW investigators would brook no interference in their quest for what they deemed to be vital knowledge in these fields. They would not permit the issue of war criminal responsibilities to interfere with their research. They were assisted, wittingly or not, in their work by the highest military authorities, and possibly by civilian leaders in Washington, London, and Ottawa. Their posture would be of great importance in determining the fate of Ishii, Kitano, Wakamatsu, Masuda, and the other leading BW personalities.

II

There were few problems during the first months of the occupation. The criminal investigators went about their business of searching Japanese archives for leads, and interrogating suspects. In September and October 1945, Murray Sanders conducted his BW investigation with the wholehearted support of those in command in Tokyo. He returned home in November full of praise for the assistance he had received from the military while in Japan.[2] Tensions between the competing groups began to have an effect in the New Year, but as late as spring 1946 Arvo Thompson still was able to direct his BW inquiries without significantly disturbing the war crimes investigators.[3]

The Tokyo headquarters of both Military Intelligence and the war crimes investigators were flooded with correspondence from disaffected Japanese nationals during the period that Sanders and the others conducted their investigations. Allegations of alleged war crimes committed by literally thousands of Japanese threatened to overwhelm those responsible for determining the validity of the accusations. Each allegation had to be checked carefully, a time-consuming, costly process, which taxed the resources of the large staff engaged in tracking down offenders.

The charges originated from a variety of sources. They came from long-suppressed groups who were now resurgent in the newly democratic Japan. Communists, leftists, moderates, and, occasionally, conservatives, appalled by the wartime depredations of their compatriots, now stepped forth to vent their anger, anguish, or contrition. Still others had old scores to settle with their enemies. These people hoped to utilize the alien invaders to achieve vengeance for their earlier sufferings.

Among the many telegrams, letters, memoranda, and photographs that buttressed the war crimes accusations were at least several dozen items that referred to BW experiments in Manchuria as well as in the Home Islands. Some of these latter allegations could be dismissed out of hand, because they appeared to the investigators to be fantasies conjured up by persons ignorant of the basics pertaining to BW. Others, however, seemed to be based on solid first-hand knowledge, and could not be ignored. The latter named individuals, pinpointed locations of BW bases, and cited specific occasions when BW field trials in Manchuria and China took place. Some accusers raised the specter of human experiments, including the possible use of United Nations prisoners.[4] The allegations poured into Intelligence offices within days of their finding a suitable site for their work. Accusations continued to flood the investigators' chambers until the final weeks of the Tokyo War Crimes Trials in 1948, and beyond.

The charges leveled specifically against Ishii, Wakamatsu, and the entire BW medical establishment were notably accurate. Investigators initially greeted the more extreme allegations skeptically, since many of the sources for the accusations were anonymous. Still others came from the Communist Party of Japan and individuals affiliated with the organization, causing conservative-oriented American agents to be wary of the basis for the charges. Nevertheless, the information received was on the whole so reliable that the people lodging complaints must at one time have been intimately involved in BW work. Some of the allegations were so comprehensive that it is possible Ishii's operation could have been penetrated by either a Soviet or a Chinese communist-controlled cell.

The Japanese Communist Party, for example, forwarded a memorandum to one of the Intelligence agencies on 14 December 1945 that, according to officials who read the document, "reveals the activities of the Ishii B.K.A." It noted that in 1944 researchers in Harbin "succeeded in cultivating pests which were applied to Manchurian and several American citizens captured during the war." The memorandum alleged also that "research work was conducted in cooperation with Tokyo and Kyoto Imperial Universities' medical laboratories." Most damaging, perhaps, were the charges that

the leading personnel engaged in the research were Rinnosuke Shoji and Hisato Yoshimura from the laboratory and Ogata Norio of the Chiba Medical University. Medical Universities and Institutes mobilized for the purpose, were: Densenbyo Kenkyusho, Tokyo; Kyoto University; Medical Bureau of War Ministry; and the Chiba Medical University.[5]

On the following day, one Imaji Setsu forwarded a communication to Intelligence claiming that Ishii was secretly engaged in BW research. Imaji revealed Ishii's earlier alias of Togo Hajime, and alleged that the BW researchers had committed "atrocious acts" against humans. He insisted that Ishii and others had employed humans "instead of animals for their research on bacteria." Imaji claimed:

> although the majority of the victims were convicted criminals, there were also innocent farmers, officers of the Communist Army, women and children and over a thousand victims of the experiments conducted on horse glanders bacteria, pestilence bacteria and other strong poisons.

Imaji was so familiar with Ishii's background that he knew Ishii's wife was the daughter of University President Araki Torasaburo. He reported that early in his career Ishii had been helped greatly by the then War Minister Araki Sadao. He knew of Ishii's embezzlements, and noted that his famous water filter was manufactured by a corporation, the Japan Special Factory, which was given a monopoly privilege by the government. Although the factory was run by one Kuritsu Mitsuichi, the company was eventually incorporated, and "Ishii and his cohorts reaped huge profits by receiving dividends under the names of dummy stockholders."[6]

Still another informant told investigators that Ishii "was in charge of experiments conducted on human subjects in Manchuria during the war . . . in connection with bacterial warfare." This informant also "expressed surprise that this officer, now in hiding in some mountain residence, has not been apprehended as a war criminal." He charged, as did many others, that "this officer took possession of a large sum of money, about ¥ 1,000,000, when he left."[7]

The Japanese Communist Party and individual leftists forwarded so many allegations against Ishii and the BW work he and others had performed that word leaked to the American press. On 6 January 1946, the *Pacific Stars and Stripes*[8] and the *New York Times*[9] carried United Press dispatches from Tokyo citing the Communist Party's claim that "members of the Japanese medical corps had inoculated American and Chinese prisoners with bubonic plague virus [sic – the correct usage should be 'infectious agent'] in experiments in Harbin and Mukden, Manchuria." Under the heading, "Virus Used on Captives," the *New York Times* story quoted other communists as indicting Ishii for having directed the tests. The *Pacific Stars and Stripes* report was more extensive than the *Times*'s, giving details of Ishii's life as well as a War Department assessment which cast doubt on the efficacy of Ishii's BW methods.

Six days later, the *New York Times*[10] printed a one-paragraph, single-sentence United Press story from Tokyo: "Maj Gen Shiro Ishii, said to have directed "human guinea pig" tests on American and Chinese prisoners of war in Manchuria, was ordered arrested for questioning today by American Counter-Intelligence authorities." As noted earlier, however, Ishii was permitted to live in style at his Tokyo residence and was considered under house arrest. He was not transported to the prison where the principal war crimes figures were housed.

These news stories so alarmed the American authorities that intense efforts were initiated immediately after the first stories appeared to suppress further media discussion of Ishii or of Japanese BW. US Counter-Intelligence agents interviewed Ralph Teatsworth, United Press Association's Tokyo Bureau manager. The agents came to his office in the Radio Tokyo Building on 7 January 1946. Teatsworth readily told the agents that the source for his story on Ishii was Shiga Yoshio, editor of Japan's Communist newspaper, *Red Flag*. Shiga told Teatsworth that he and his associates were tracking Ishii, and that they should locate his hiding place within a few days. The agents then "requested" that Teatsworth not "divulge the fact that this headquarters [Counter-Intelligence] was interested in the present whereabouts of Ishii and requested [him] not to write any stories which would indicate to Ishii that the American Army is desirous of obtaining further information on the experiments." U.P.A.'s Teatsworth assured them that "he would respect the requests."[11]

III

News of Japan's surrender had devastated Ishii. He could not accept at first the notion that his country was defeated by inferior peoples, and became disconsolate for a short period of time.[12] The formerly robust Ishii had experienced a nervous collapse when he heard the Emperor's broadcast on 15 August. A few days later he was in Changchun at the Kwantung Army headquarters, preparing some of his forces for evacuation from Manchuria to Korea. He was still in shock. The despairing Ishii met an acquaintance in the headquarters latrine, who recalled sometime later that he found Ishii standing in the middle of the latrine in a slack, immobile position. He was "utterly crestfallen." Sensing the presence of another in the room, Ishii groaned, " 'Oh, it was you,' and groggily left the premises."[13]

Spurred by the instinct for survival, Ishii soon recovered from the initial shock of learning of Japan's surrender. He quickly regained his old self-assurance, and resumed his role of absolute ruler of his BW forces. His first priority was to destroy Ping Fan to keep its secrets out of enemy hands. He then made certain that Unit 731's principal scientists escaped back to Japan ahead of the advancing Soviet and Chinese forces. Once assured that Ping Fan was destroyed, and that his key aides were safe, Ishii flew home from Dairen by military aircraft. The other members of his family, many of his followers, their personal belongings, and a large cache of salvaged BW data and equipment were sent by railroad from Ping Fan to Pusan in Korea in late August 1945. Most of the people and their possessions were evacuated by ship to Japan. Some twenty or so Ishii intimates, including elder brothers Mitsuo and Takeo (and possibly a third brother), along with what was described as "bulky cargo," took a military transport to Port Maizuru in Japan.

For more than one month, 19 August to 22 September, the men used a shrine in Kanazawa as their base. Some of the bulky crates offloaded from the transport may have been buried at the shrine. Other crates were secreted to Ishii's home in Chiba prefecture and to the homes of several of his most dedicated subordinates. The crates were then apparently concealed in Ishii's garden and in other secure places.[14] It is probable that Ishii buried 731's most important documents in the garden of his Tokyo home, since he was able later to produce significant data for his American interrogators almost at will.

Shortly before returning to Japan, the General, his composure recovered, began to think of ways to protect himself from war criminal charges. His initial effort was to go underground, hiding out until he could determine what information the enemy held against him. Ever flamboyant, even in defeat, Ishii called upon some of his powerful friends for help. Together, they planted a story in a newspaper that he had been shot to death.[15] Adding color to an otherwise commonplace announcement, village elders in Ishii's home base collaborated with the fugitive Lt. General on 10 November 1945, by issuing a proclamation declaring him to be dead. They even staged an elaborate mock-funeral in his behalf, complete with mourners, priests, burnt incense, and prayers for his departed soul.[16]

The elders' cooperation in this intricate scheme of deception was obtained evidently by the expenditure of considerable sums of money on their behalf. It was maintained later that the local authorities helped Ishii because they received some of the proceeds from his alleged embezzlement of more than one million yen from military funds previously entrusted to his care. In early 1947, the Jiyu Seinen Association wrote a letter to General MacArthur asserting that the three Ishii brothers, Shiro, Takeo, and Mitsuo, stole large sums of money from the Army at the end of the war. The Association alleged that the Ishii brothers used this money to purchase "real estate in their relatives' name." Other large sums were "deposited in banks, and [they] made donations [to people who would help them in their deceptions]." Some of the money was employed in securing the help of former 731 associates and longtime Army medical school friends to "transport army uniform[s], coat[s], blankets, shoes, leather goods . . . enough for several 10 thousands of people to their place of domicile." They then "gave away portions of this loot to the villagers as a bribe in order that the Ishii family should not be apprehended as war criminals." In another gesture, they supposedly gave away more than ten Army vehicles to former subordinates.[17]

Kitano also participated in a colorful episode at war's termination before he retreated into the general population. He was arrested at his post in Shanghai shortly after the surrender. Then, possibly with the connivance of the local authorities, he "escaped" from the prison where he was being held. The method by which he made his way home to Japan after the "escape" was never disclosed.[18]

Of the three BW principals, Wakamatsu's journey home was the least eventful. His involvement in BW research at Changchun was not widely known even at the end of the war. His preference for a non-public role was so successful that many believed Ishii had commanded Unit 100 and directed its work. Wakamatsu was repatriated from the mainland to Japan, along with the other several million military and civilian Japanese, in the chaotic immediate postwar period. He was discharged from the military, returned to civilian life, and for a short time faded once more into the background.

IV

Ishii's subterfuges failed to deceive American intelligence operatives for more than several months.[19] However, so many complaints reached the occupation command that eventually he was tracked down after an "intensive search" by the authorities.[20] He was located in his home village in mid-January 1946. Then, for undisclosed reasons, Intelligence shied away from confronting Ishii directly. Instead, it directed Japanese officials to deliver him to SCAP (Supreme Command Allied Powers) headquarters; which they did, on 18 January. In another strange turn of events, Ishii was not arrested. He was only required to reside in his Tokyo home while charges against him were being investigated.

Washington was alerted to this prized find, and Arvo Thompson was sent from Fort Detrick to Tokyo "on a special order" to question Ishii. In a lengthy, well-informed, and surprisingly candid dispatch, United Press correspondent Peter Kalisher reported that "Under the supervision of Lt. Col. D. S. Tait, technical intelligence, and with the help of Lt. E. M. Ellis of the War Dept. Intelligence section and several ATIS interpreters, a 7-week interrogation of Ishii was conducted." Kalisher noted that, during the seven-week period, roughly twenty-five Ishii intimates, including a number of medical officers, were questioned about him.

He also reported Ishii's disclaimer that he conducted experiments on POWs, or that he engaged in "large-scale" efforts to develop offensive BW. According to Kalisher, Ishii did boast to his interrogators that he had invented a porcelain bomb that could be used to disseminate plague, and that he also developed two water filters for field use as well as an anti-dysentery pill. Kalisher's sources described Ishii "as a determined, almost ruthless individual who rose from the rank of Colonel in 1941 to Lt. Gen. in 1945."[21]

What Kalisher's informants failed to disclose was the ease with which Ishii lied to Thompson and the others. Ishii sought to portray his BW research as being a local, small-scale, renegade operation. He claimed that research was confined exclusively to Ping Fan. He used only small animals for his studies. Of course, no humans were exposed to any pathogen tests. There were no field tests undertaken. The Navy did not permit their people to attend Ishii's BW lectures because "Naval officers are too proud. They do not have any brains, but their noses are high." The Tokyo High Command knew nothing of his BW activities. The Emperor, as "a lover of humanity," was not informed of the BW program. Had he known, he would have banned further study. Ishii went so far in his deceptions as to try to protect most of his research associates at Ping Fan. He assumed virtually all responsibility for the work conducted there, allotting only a small liability to his close friend Masuda Tomosada. No one else, he insisted, knew what really was happening at Ping Fan.[22]

Army Intelligence continued to pursue Ishii's BW trail while Arvo Thompson was interrogating the former head of Unit 731. Intelligence knew of at least twenty persons who were familiar with Ishii's work. Since it was obvious that Ishii was not being totally candid with Thompson, Intelligence hoped that at least one of the twenty on its list would "be unfriendly toward Ishii; no one of his personal characteristics could fail to make enemies, especialy since his rise was so rapid, and his extracurricular activities so varied." When one of Ishii's enemies was located, he should be questioned as to:

> a. Who were Ishii's backers in high government circles? b. By what means did Ishii acquire the large funds which were apparently at his disposal? c. What is his reputation in Chiyoda-mura? . . . Is he a large land-owner there? d. How was the manufacture and sale (to the public) of the Ishii Water Filter handled and by whom?[23]

Intelligence had its work cut out for itself. The wily Ishii deceived even the best of Intelligence's interrogators. In a June 1947 biographical sketch of Ishii, the compiler observed that Ishii belonged to no organizations, and that he had no political affiliations. As to his personal characteristics, Ishii was "Studious, sincere, benevolent and kind." And in a final abandonment of reality, it was noted that Ishii's attitude toward the United States was that of someone who "is pro-American and respects mental culture and physical science of the US"[24]

At the same time that Intelligence pursued Ishii's background, Peter Kalisher's report in the *Pacific Stars and Stripes* created a brief stir in other circles within the occupation force in Tokyo. Colonel Thomas H. Morrow, a principal assistant to chief war crimes prosecutor Joseph B. Keenan, read the account and reacted strongly. Morrow took note of the Kalisher story in a 2 March 1946 memorandum to Keenan, which summarized items with war crimes potential, including events which were "dramatic and outrageous acts of the Japanese which should be susceptible of proof."

He reminded Keenan that he had previously written to the Investigation Department of the War Crimes Commission "requesting that arrangements be made if possible to interrogate General Ishii." Ishii's interrogation was now even more urgent in light of Kalisher's disclosures that "he [Ishii] has been conducting experiments in bacteriology, in conjunction with the Japanese Army, since 1941." Morrow then came to the indisputable conclusion that

> This matter, as well as the poison gas episodes, assumes importance because of the obvious impossibility of developing such methods of warfare on the field of battle or through the resources of an army general in the field, and indicates that such prohibited methods of warfare were carried on by the Tokyo Government and not the field commanders.[25]

Six days later, Morrow briefed Keenan once again. He reported that he had met with Fort Detrick investigators Arvo Thompson and D. S. Tait, and discussed with them the role of Ishii and the other BW leaders, but asserted that his "interview was negative in its results."[26] A few days later, Morrow flew to China to gather additional evidence on BW and other alleged war crimes activities. He found significant material there on BW, and reported his findings to Keenan on 23 April.[27]

Keenan's reply to Morrow's memoranda, if any, is unknown. What is certain is that Morrow was reassigned to Washington shortly after writing his findings and recommendations. Without Morrow to prod them, the war crimes investigators failed to pursue his leads, although Ishii's activities, as well as those of Kitano and Wakamatsu, should have branded them as high-level Class "A" war criminals. Consequently, almost nothing concerning BW surfaced at the Far East International Military Tribunal's war crimes trials. The one brief discussion of BW occurred on 29 August 1946, and referred to the role of the Nanking-based Unit Ei 1644. It occupied perhaps less than ten minutes of the court's time, but created an awkward interruption in the proceedings.

David N. Sutton, an American serving in the role of assistant to China's prosecutors, observed:

> The enemy . . . took our countrymen as prisoners and used them for drug experiments. They would inject various types of toxic bacteria into their bodies, and then perform experiments on how they reacted. . . . Dogs and cats are commonly sacrificed in experiments on medical drugs, but by sacrificing our brothers and prisoners, this is treatment which would not even be given to dogs and cats. This was an act of barbarism by our enemy.[28]

Sutton's remarks so stunned the court that a brief recess was taken to restore order in the room. The presiding chief judge, the Australian Sir William F. Webb, then asked Sutton, "Are you trying to tell us about a poison liquid being administered? Are you trying to provide more evidence? This is a new fact that you have presented before we judges." Webb, after a short pause, asked Sutton, "How about letting this item go?" Sutton replied, "Well then, I'll leave it." The issue never surfaced again.[29]

It is uncertain today whether Keenan's indifference to prosecuting alleged BW criminals was a decision he took independently, or whether it was made due to instructions from higher authorities. Keenan was a clever, ambitious New Deal politician who was anxious to dominate the front pages in the United States, especially in Ohio where he hoped to run for the United States Senate. It would appear to have been in his best interests to prosecute Ishii and the others, elicit courtroom testimony about human experiments, hinting that some of the victims were American POWs, and emerge from the trial as a popular folk hero for having convicted despicable people who had tormented and killed innocent Americans.

Yet he did not pursue what appears to have been a golden opportunity for a politician hoping to achieve high office. One clue to Keenan's unusual behavior may be Colonel Morrow's enigmatic comment of 8 March concerning the "negative results" of his meeting with Thompson and Tait. By this date, the two scientists were deeply into their seven-week interrogation of Ishii and his associates. Thompson, as his later report indicates, was impressed with the material his investigation elicited from the Japanese BW experts. He, perhaps acting upon his superiors' instructions, was not enthusiastic about endangering the flow of information from the cooperating Japanese.

It is not unreasonable to speculate that Thompson and Tait informed Morrow they were not eager for him to pursue war crimes charges against Ishii and the others. Keenan may also have been told to drop the issue by either MacArthur or War Department officials in Washington. Whatever the correct interpretation may be, the April 1946 failure of Keenan to initiate criminal proceedings against Ishii and the others should be taken as the beginning of the offical American cover-up of the Japanese BW program.[30]

V

After April 1946, an impervious veil appeared over any public review of the Japanese BW principals, their previous activities, or their possible fate at the hands of the United Nations.[31] For the next two years, the *Pacific Stars and Stripes*, the newspaper with the closest ties to the American occupation forces, was silent on the topic. The *New York Times* and other serious newspapers ignored the subject. Japanese BW would remain dormant as a topic for open discussion in the American press until long after the Tokyo War Crimes Trials were concluded.[32]

Behind the scenes, however, the outpouring of allegations against Ishii, Kitano, Wakamatsu, and others continued. On 10 February 1946, Kino Takeshi sent a letter to SCAP's Legal Section accusing Wakamatsu and three other veterinarians of using Allied POWs as human guinea pigs at the Changchun death factory. Kino was first interviewed a little more than four months after SCAP received his letter. On 23 August 1946, Nishimura Takeshi, a former Unit 100 veterinarian, forwarded a document to SCAP which accused Wakamatsu and two other veterinarians of war crimes. Nishimura stated bluntly that the accused "dissected many war prisoners of the Allied Forces at the outdoor dissecting ground of No. 100 Army Corps" as part of their investigation of cattle plague. He concluded his statement by assuring SCAP that "If you would investigate these criminals, you will find many other persons who have participated to [in] the dissections. There are a number of the [sic] witness of the inspections [dissections]."[33]

In early September, SCAP received an anonymous letter dated 3 September. The writer claimed to have been a member of Unit 731, and now wished to make amends for his deeds. He accused Ishii of being a "well-known militarist and enemy of humanity." Other militarists, he charged, were frightened of the prospect that Ishii might be forced to testify, since "His summoning will provide evidence and data against "A" class war criminal suspects and even one Imperial family member will be affected." He accused the Foreign Ministry, the Army Ministry, the Demobilization Board, and the Liaison Office of engaging in a conspiracy "to make this case lost in oblivion." He offered to help American investigators, since "I know quite well about him and his corps and the atrocities committed by them."

The anonymous writer set a time limit for a reply to his offer, which SCAP investigators were unable to meet. The American investigator in reporting on the incident commented that the time limit "could not have been complied with *even had it been desirable.*"[34] Nevertheless, the investigator included the letter in his report since it was "another indication of the mounting complaints concerning the alleged activities of General Ishii and his associates . . . principals among which are alleged to have been infecting prisoners of war with glanders for experimental purposes."[35]

Two months later, the Central Liaison Office of the Japanese government forwarded to SCAP's Legal Section a biographical "history" of Ishii Shiro. This was in response to Legal Section's request for whatever data the Japanese government held on Ishii. The history was nothing more than a recitation of his name, date of birth, home address, current address, military record, and appointments. This sketchy outline, containing supposedly all the facts that survived concerning one of Japan's leading military scientists was then sent to SCAP's Criminal Registry Division, presumably to be added to the Ishii information already on hand. Although Criminal Registry did not pursue further the relevant details on Ishii, the paper trail suggests that as late as 29 November 1946 some people were interested in the possibility of placing criminal charges against him.[36]

VI

At the beginning of 1947, Naito Ryoichi, Ishii's old comrade and Murray Sanders's busybody manipulator, turned against his longtime friend and sponsor. He was interviewed on 24 January, and proceeded to give the occupation authorities a detailed account of the Harbin–Ping Fan operation, carefully avoiding any personally incriminating information. Naito confessed that Ishii had exploited the water purification program as a "cover-up" for his BW experiments. He volunteered the comment that it "was common knowledge among the microbiologists in Japan, all of whom were connected with Ishii, that humans were used for experimentation at the Harbin installation."[37]

Naito expanded upon his revelations in a second interview that winter. Using carefully chosen words, Naito addressed the question of human experiments. He referred to "rumors" that had "circulated all through Japan" concerning human experiments in the Harbin area. Naito noted that "Ishii was very famous among the professors in Japan and they also heard these rumors." He placed a great deal of credence in the rumors because some of the vaccines developed at Harbin/Ping Fan "could only be called successful after observing the results obtained after inoculating humans with the disease and the vaccine."

Naito made it quite evident that the BW program was not a one-person operation. He told his interrogators that "Most microbiologists in Japan were connected in some way or another with Ishii's work." Universities played their part, too, since Ishii "mobilized most of the universities . . . to help in research for his unit." Naito's interview ended with the following colloquy: "Q. Do you have anything else to add that might be of value to the statement? A. Nothing, but if Ishii was guilty of using human beings for his experiments I think that he should be punished."

In his report of the interview, Naito's questioner made the important observation that "This allegation . . . adds one more complaint to the numerous allegations of Ishii using POWs for his experimental work in Bacterial Warfare. . . . *It can be noted that the allegation by Naito is the first not from an anonymous source.*"[38] This assessment, however, is incorrect. Three of Ishii's former subordinates, as we have seen, earlier alluded in writing to "gruesome work" they had performed under his command in Nanking, and the American authorities were aware of the charge.

VII

SCAP's Legal Section began to investigate Wakamatsu toward the end of summer 1946. The late head of Unit 100 could not avoid his past any longer. Too many of Wakamatsu's former subordinates had leveled serious charges against him for even dubious investigators in Legal Section to ignore them. Some Wakamatsu underlings cited extensive glanders experiments with Chinese prisoners. A former civilian employee in Unit 100, Nishimura Takeshi, charged in a 23 August letter that many POWs were subjected to a series of research trials, and then were carved up at an outdoor dissecting facility in Changchun.[39]

By 4 September, Legal Section received a copy of Wakamatsu's service record from the Japanese government. This in turn led investigators to seek out Wakamatsu in Osaka for intensive interrogation.[40] He was questioned at the Kure police station on 28 October 1946, but the inquiry was anything but intensive. The questioning took place under relaxed circumstances for a person under investigation and suspected of committing a series of human rights violations. Wakamatsu was not required to make a sworn statement. He was never pressed to explain contradictions between his testimony and that of his former subordinates.

Wakamatsu smoothly denied that anything untoward had occurred at Changchun during his entire tenure as commander of Unit 100. To his knowledge, none of his men ever engaged in experiments with humans. He denied that any humans, "POWs, Chinese, nor Japanese," were ever exposed to injections in research programs. He insisted that no humans had been dissected in the course of studying the effects of glanders on man. He did acknowledge that two Japanese researchers contracted glanders and died from the disease, but he was so circumspect that he refused to have the bodies dissected. In respect for their departed souls, they were not even given a post mortem examination.

He conceded that he was familiar with the name Ishii Shiro. However, Wakamatsu knew nothing of the work conducted at Harbin/Ping Fan. He argued that Ishii's unit came under the jurisdiction of the Medical Corps, while his organization was responsible to the Veterinary Corps. There was no lateral sharing of information between the two units. They operated in two different spheres of interest and responsibility.

Wakamatsu's testimony was filled with so many inconsistencies, evasions, and contradictions that the agent in charge of his case noted in his report that "Wakamatsu appeared to be withholding information." The agent speculated that the subject most probably would "yield more information if confronted with specific details of the allegations" against him. This did not occur. Wakamatsu was never pressed to reveal what really took place in the research facilities under his control.[41]

Five months after Wakamatsu's meeting with a representative of SCAP's Legal Section, Kino Takeshi disclosed to the Americans what had actually occurred at Unit 100's facility in Changchun. Kino, who served at the Changchun installation for more than four years, was deposed by a Legal Section officer on 5 March 1947 in Fukuoka. Unlike the gentle treatment accorded Wakamatsu, Kino was questioned extensively, and under oath.

Kino testified that he was initially employed by Wakamatsu's people in a civilian capacity from 1938 until 1940. He served in the military during World War II, and was assigned to Wakamatsu's Unit from 1943 until Japan's surrender. As with others who appeared before Legal Section investigators, Kino denied participating in human experiments, but conceded that he was aware that they took place at Changchun. He heard of "rumors" that humans were infected with glanders and then were either vivisected while still alive, or dissected after the disease ran its course. He did not know whether the victims were Chinese laborers or POWs, but "there was a lot of talk going on in camp about these experiments."

He was familiar with at least one experiment that involved thirteen humans exposed to glanders. When asked the number who died during the experiment, Kino replied, "They all died from the experiment." As to who was responsible for the research, the answer was, "General Wakamatsu, Yujiro." He acknowledged that there were other officers who participated in human experiments, and Kino cited several with whom he was personally familiar. He revealed that Unit 100's "Experiment Section," the section that conducted human tests, consisted of approximately three hundred persons, thirty of whom were officers.

When a Legal Section officer confronted Kino with information that a close friend accused him of participating in human research, Kino could only reply that his friend was "mistaken or probably mistook my name for another."

Skeptical, the agent pressed Kino, who then remembered that "one day . . . [he told his friend] that I saw the body of a human being in a sack passing by my stables," and his friend may have thought that he had played a part in that person's death. His selective memory refreshed periodically during his interview, Kino recalled still another person who was familiar with human research, a civilian named Mitomo. This individual had told Kino that he "took part in dissecting humans but warned me not to say anything about it as it was very secretive."[42]

Kino was interrogated even more intensely six days after giving his original evidence. In this later statement, Kino continued to deny participating in human experiments, but identified six individuals who he knew had conducted such research. Wakamatsu was among the six. A seventh, his civilian friend Mitomo, had given him specific details concerning human research. Mitomo was reluctant to impart such information, but Kino, "through curiosity," had ordered him to tell him what he knew. Mitomo did so because Kino was his superior, and subordinates did as they were instructed. He had once asked Mitomo, "did you kill someone during an experiment and he answered that they had."

He now recalled also an incident which further confirmed that human experiments were conducted in Changchun. One day, he saw some officers working behind a screen near his workplace. There was a photographer in attendance as well. Kino knew they were conducting an experiment. They had previously dug a grave nearby "that was too small for a horse and too large for any other animal and it was my opinion that it was for a human being." He could not identify this victim, but he was of the opinion that many of those killed in the experiments were Soviet prisoners.[43]

He had heard other "rumors" of human tests, and he saw "the persons who performed the exper[iments] carry food to the guard house." Among the "rumors," he remembered one in which "they put something into the prisoners food and they also injected the prisoners with some sort of fluid." Twelve persons were "rumored" to have died as a result of these experiments. He knew of the events because "once I heard of something I liked to listen and find out the results."[44]

Kino's testimony may in part have been evasive. He surely avoided making any statement that could possibly implicate himself. Nevertheless, his account of the activities concerning Wakamatsu and the other officers at Changchun was both incriminating and believable since others confirmed his most damaging revelations. Wakamatsu was never called upon to rebut Kino's comments. He continued to remain in the background throughout the BW investigations.

Kitano's turn for interrogation came at the beginning of 1946 during the early days of the BW investigation. He first was interviewed in Tokyo on 11 January by two colonels, S. E. Whitesides and A. H. Schwichtenberg, who presumably enjoyed a medical background and were somewhat familiar with

BW. The meeting, however, was short and unrevealing. Kitano assumed the role of innocent, and insisted that he knew little of the Ishii operation.

Colonel Whitesides began the interview by telling Kitano he wanted information on both offensive and defensive BW research. Kitano's replies to this, and to subsequent questions, were vague and disingenuous at best. When asked whether he was prepared to use BW as a weapon, for example, Kitano replied, "No." He would not use it because, "In my opinion, it is not good to use BW in warfare and, if used, it is not effective." Whitesides pressed Kitano by asking him whether he would use BW if ordered to do so by higher authorities. He replied that he and his superior, General Kobayashi, "would have dissented." On other questions, Kitano played down his role at Harbin or denied that research that could be considered a human rights violation took place during his watch. According to Kitano, only "Monkeys, rats, squirrels and other small animals" were used when testing ordnance developed at Ping Fan. When Whitesides specifically asked him whether he had ever heard "of any Chinese prisoners being used in these tests," Kitano replied without any hesitation, "No. No humans at all were used in these tests."[45]

One day later, Arvo Thompson met with Kitano, but this interview was equally brief and uninformative. Kitano once again did not hesitate to deceive his interrogator, and, although Thompson was a tougher questioner than Whitesides, Kitano brazenly lied to him at every opportunity. He denied any intimate knowledge of BW, and placed the blame on Ishii for any questionable activities. He claimed to be ignorant of virtually all research undertaken at Ping Fan, and replied to most Thompson questions, "I do not know."

Although he was known to have engaged in BW research while stationed at the Mukden Army Medical College, Kitano told Thompson that the only BW research conducted by the Japanese took place at Ping Fan. This statement shocked Thompson. He knew Kitano was lying, and he pressed him to offer a more forthright response. Thus, Thompson observed, "It is inconceivable that BW research was limited to a single institution . . . when other research in Japan, equally classified, was conducted at many institutions." Kitano replied smoothly, "BW is a restricted subject, prohibited by the Geneva Convention, and thus was not an authorized activity."

Kitano tried to portray BW as a rogue operation that Ishii conducted without authorization by the authorities in Tokyo. The Emperor, of course, was ignorant of Ishii's activities. Had he known, "he would have prohibited such work." The medical profession in Japan gave no support to BW research. The Surgeon General provided BW no backing since "he was opposed to it."[46] Thompson got little information from his interview, and Kitano returned to his home satisfied with his performance.

He did not, however, fade into the obscurity that Unit 731 veterans tried so hard to obtain. Kitano's name continued to surface throughout 1946 as one who possessed important BW data. He was mentioned so frequently that SCAP's Legal Section began to take another look at him. One investigator decided to find him and to "obtain from him a complete and exhaustive statement concerning his knowledge of the atrocities committed at the Harbin experimental station."[47]

Kitano was located in Tokyo once again, and on 1 April 1947 he provided investigators with a lengthy, rambling statement that ran to eleven legal-size pages in translation. Investigators noted that it was a "voluntary statement." And Kitano, who was always cautious, was extremely careful in what information he provided in his account. None the less, those who interviewed him believed that he furnished evidence rich enough for the Criminal Registry Division to review it for possible use in criminal proceedings.[48]

Ishii's rival began his account with an innocuous history of the formation of the Ishii Unit, its multi-purpose responsibilities (including its secret BW research), and the organization of the Water Purification Section of the Kwantung Army. He now confirmed that Ishii operated beyond Ping Fan, and identified the five major BW research sites in Manchuria. Kitano found it difficult to conceal his hostility to Ishii, and denigrated his rival's work. He commented that the results of Ishii's research "were not what . . . Ishii claimed them to be and it seems to me that there were few of scientific value."

Kitano was not modest when it came to discussing his own accomplishments. He noted the positive results he achieved in working on various vaccines, including typhoid, and on serums to combat venereal diseases. Kitano listed other achievements, such as his work on epidemic hemorrhagic fever, forest tick encephalitis, and the treatment of communicable diseases such as bubonic plague and dysentery. He also mentioned that positive results were achieved in the treatment of anthrax.

Nowhere in his lengthy statement did Kitano refer to human experiments, except for his work on the treatment of typhoid fever. The patients studied, he claimed, were carriers who were brought to 731's hospital from "all Army hospitals in Manchuria." The implication was that the human subjects were Japanese nationals who were carriers, and he was quite proud of the results he reached while working on 130 patients. Kitano was so arrogant that he lamented the fact that his transfer to Shanghai in 1945 interrupted his work, and expressed the hope that "this problem be solved by American Medical Science. If research is authorized at some later date I would like to complete the experiments." Overall, however, he sought to convey the impression that all research was conducted on animals in well-regulated laboratories.

He reserved his most audacious comments for a discussion of his view of BW. Kitano told his American audience that he believed Japan should have abandoned research on BW (he previously denied this took place), and worked instead on prevention and treatment of communicable diseases. He adopted a noble posture, and declared that "A bacteriological weapon is a misuse of medical science." Kitano noted also that "Based on my own medical knowledge," i.e. his BW research, "I think the application of bacteriological weapons for military purposes requires a good deal of work with little to be gained." It would be of no help to an army that was already winning a war, and for those who were losing, resort to BW "can only be disgrace." There were other drawbacks to the employment of BW, but its greatest liability was that it is a "misapplication of medical science and would bring about an international problem and problem of humanity."[49]

By the end of 1947, if not earlier, the authorities amassed enormous quantities of data suggesting strongly that a number of Japanese scientists – both military and civilian – had conducted BW experiments that involved the use of human guinea pigs. Much of their work constituted blatant human rights violations as defined by the charters governing both the Nuremberg and the Tokyo war crimes trials. The principals (Ishii, Wakamatsu, Kitano, et al.) tried to wriggle their way out from prosecution for their past conduct by lies, deceptions, evasions, and pleas of ignorance during repeated questioning. Still, some of their responses inadvertently damaged their cause. In addition, testimony by former colleagues convincingly branded them as being war criminals. So much evidence was compiled over a two-year investigation, linking the leaders to violations of international law, that any prosecutor could have taken their cases to the proper authorities and secured indictments and probable convictions. All that was required for such a scenario to take place was the desire of responsible officials to see justice done.

Unfortunately for Ishii's victims, the United States military had other priorities. The dominant American view in Tokyo was that the former commander of Ping Fan was too important a figure to be subjected to the criteria used for determining the issue of prosecuting an individual for war crimes. This attitude perhaps was best expressed by Lt. Colonel Robert McQuail of Army Intelligence (G-2). In a "Summary of Information" that McQuail prepared for his office in early January 1947, he noted that "A Confidential Informant claims that Ishii had his assistants inject bubonic plague bacilli into the bodies of some Americans in Mukden, Manchuria, as an experiment." McQuail, instead of being horrified, commented matter-of-factly that "Naturally, the results of these experiments are of the highest intelligence value."[50] Intelligence value, not war crimes, would be the dominant factor in all discussions concerning the Japanese BW experts.

14 Scientists and the cover-up

Evidence gathered in this investigation has greatly supplemented and amplified previous aspects of this field. It represents data which have been obtained by Japanese scientists at the expenditure of many millions of dollars and years of work. Information has accrued with respect to human susceptibility to those diseases as indicated by specific infectious doses of bacteria. Such information could not be obtained in our own laboratories because of scruples attached to human experimentation. These data were secured with a total outlay of ¥250,000 to date, a mere pittance by comparison with the actual cost of the studies.

(Edwin V. Hill, Chief, Basic Sciences, Camp Detrick, to General Alden C. Waitt, Chief, Chemical Corps, 12 December 1947, The National Archives)

As far as I know, it was true that a deal was made. But it was the US side which approached my father, not the other way around. . . . What I would like to emphatically say . . . is: Isn't it important that not a single man under my father's command was ever tried as a war criminal? I am really sorry for those who had to live in seclusion to evade possible prosecution but were it not for my father's courage in making a deal with the occupation authorities . . . you know what I mean.

(Ishii Harumi in the *Japan Times*, 29 August 1982, p. 12)

I

Ishii's encounters with American investigators in early 1946 were productive for both sides. The Americans were anxious to learn all they could about Japanese BW, and the former head of Unit 731, universally recognized as Japan's premier BW expert, appeared to be the ideal person to help them with their inquiry. Murray Sanders's November 1945 report, although preliminary and incomplete, indicated conclusively that Japan was a major BW power, and that Ishii was a most important figure in its program. Later reports and investigations in 1946 and early 1947 made it quite evident that Japanese BW researchers had conducted inquiries using methods involving human rights violations, and that Ishii had probably participated in these practices. It is now known that American scientists, who were prohibited from engaging in such activities, in their desire to make their country pre-eminent in the BW field, welcomed the opportunity to appropriate the findings from this research.[1]

Dr Karl T. Compton, President of Massachusetts Institute of Technology, went to Japan in October 1945 as part of a mission to discover the extent of Japanese scientific development during the war. The scientists Compton interviewed denied studying offensive BW possibilities, but Dr Compton doubted the disclaimers, concluding that "they might be holding back." He found Japanese scientists in general to be cooperative and eager to discuss their work with him, except in the area of biological warfare. Compton told one of his companions that "Japanese scientists had been overheard in conversations among themselves to make remarks like 'we are not supposed to talk about this.' "[2]

The Sanders, Compton, and Thompson investigations were premised in part on the needs of American BW researchers. The BW scientists at Fort Detrick were frustrated in three areas of their studies that were deemed vital. 1. They had to theorize about man's susceptibility to certain toxic agents based on findings from experiments with animals.[3] In their opinion, it would be far more preferable in perfecting BW agents if scientists could rely on human experiments data. 2. The researchers lacked sufficient information on BW delivery systems. One leader in the field confessed that "We had no first-hand knowledge on how biological warfare agents might be disseminated. . . . [We had] no background other than conjecture."[4] 3. Finally, American BW testing in the field was still quite limited and unsatisfactory, yet "The absolute necessity for adequate field tests of the various possible means of dissemination was recognized from the beginning."[5] If Japanese experts collaborated with them, they might help Americans solve all three problems.

The perceived need to secure Ishii's and the other principal BW experts' cooperation appeared to become more imperative as American investigators pursued their search for BW information. The Soviets occupied Manchuria in the closing days of the war, and restricted foreign access to the region.[6] They would press the Americans shortly to share with them whatever BW intelligence Japanese experts disclosed. However, Harbin, Changchun and the other known BW centers were off limits to Murray Sanders or any other American researcher.[7] The Soviets made it clear to the Americans, that Manchuria would remain a closed area for some time. The chill blasts from the onset of the Cold War were already evident in Tokyo by autumn 1945.[8] The mutual distrust displayed by both the Americans and the Soviets on matters relating to BW made it impossible for either side to obtain the information necessary for a complete understanding of the scope of Japan's BW program. Consequently, for the United States, the key to unraveling Japan's BW secrets seemed to be Ishii Shiro and his colleagues.[9]

Ishii soon became conversant with his worth to the Americans. Through Naito Ryoichi, the supposedly dead Ishii learned of Sanders's promises to members of Japan's military/medical hierarchy, that they were in no danger of being charged with war crimes should they provide him with details of their BW investigations.[10] One half-year later, Arvo Thompson's interviews with Ishii were especially enlightening to the past master of Ping Fan. Ishii now understood how eager the Americans were to learn all they could from him about his work in Manchuria. He soon concluded that his knowledge, and that of his former associates, could be bartered with the Americans. The price for their precious information would be immunity from prosecution for war crimes. Doling out driblets of information over a two year period, and employing guile and arrogance throughout his meetings with American interrogators, Ishii succeeded beyond his most optimistic expectations.

II

BW investigations by the occupation authorities continued for the remainder of 1946 after Arvo Thompson returned to Detrick, but produced inconclusive results. Thomas Morrow completed his report in April; however, war crimes prosecutor Keenan ignored it. The War Crimes Trials began, technically, on 3 May 1946, and for a time diverted attention and investigatory resources away from the BW issue. Ultimately, over 2000 judicial proceedings involving 5700 Japanese nationals and their collaborators were conducted in Japan, China, Australia, the Netherlands, and other Allied countries. Neither Ishii nor any of the other BW experts appeared before these tribunals.[11]

In the meantime, the large number of anonymous complaints concerning the Manchurian BW episode that flooded Intelligence headquarters in Tokyo in late 1945 and throughout 1946 finally had some impact on official thinking. G-2, Far East Command, concluded that there was sufficient creditability to the charges that someone from Detrick should come to Tokyo "in order to evaluate the information that had been collected."[12] Detrick selected Dr Norbert H. Fell, Division Chief of its Planning Pilot-Engineering Section, to survey the data. He was given his orders evidently by the Chief of the Chemical Corps, General Alden Waitt,[13] on 4 April 1947, and arrived in Tokyo two weeks later.[14]

Fell was a big, gruff man whom most people at Detrick liked and respected. He had earned his Ph.D. at the University of Chicago, and though he worked in many areas of microbiology, he was known for his accomplishments in the field of infectious diseases. He had a reputation for being a heavy drinker, but it evidently did not interfere with his performance in the laboratory. Fell was a dedicated scientist who was interested in final results. Ethical considerations played a secondary role in his concern to achieve American leadership in the BW field. He was considered to be one of the most influential figures in the American BW program. He was the first important BW scientist charged with the responsibility for measuring the progress of the Japanese program.[15]

In Tokyo, he reviewed the data G-2 had assembled, and concluded that "the information seemed reliable enough to justify further interrogations of leading members of the former Japanese B.W. organization."[16] Within a few days of his arrival in Japan, Fell, "Through a fortunate series of circumstances," and with the help of Dr Kamei Kan'ichiro, "an influential politician," prominent businessman, and alumnus of Ping Fan, met with nearly two dozen of the "key men" in the former BW program. Kamei, who had assisted Naito earlier in deceiving Murray Sanders, now attempted to play a similar role with Fell.[17]

He was not as fortunate in fooling the newcomer. Fell benefited from the knowledge gained by the earlier investigators, thus making Kamei's task more difficult. The final result was that Kamei was only partially successful in his quest to dupe the American. The flourishing businessman tried his best to control the interviews that Fell conducted with scientists throughout April and May – and the Japanese BW experts were not completely forthcoming – but Fell was able to secure such an abundance of valuable information that the results of his inquiries left him euphoric.

Upon returning to Detrick, Fell initially wrote a brief account of results of his investigation. He concluded his "Brief Summary" of eleven typewritten pages with the observation that he "believed that the Japanese have given us a true story with all the details they could remember." Their accounts made it "evident that we were well ahead of the Japanese in production on a large scale, in . . . practical munitions." Their work with humans, however, was invaluable, since it could be coordinated with "the data we and our Allies have on animals." This combination of human and animal findings

> may help materially in our attempts at developing really effective vaccines. .
> . .It also seems possible that now that we have had a complete admission
> from the Japanese[18] about their B.W. research, we may be able to get useful
> information about their actual work in the field of C.W., death rays, and
> Naval research.[19]

Four days after writing his first report, Fell amplified his findings in a second dispatch from Detrick to Tokyo. His 24 June memorandum was twenty-eight pages in length, and consisted of a summary of his findings. This report revealed how cleverly the Japanese had duped Sanders in 1945. Fell, in his interviews with Dr Kamei, learned that Kamei knew that his colleagues had been evasive with Sanders, "giving incomplete information, and avoiding responsibility because of fear of being designated 'war criminals.' " Kamei now felt confident that these people would be more forthcoming with Fell if they "are assured that their information will not be used for 'war crimes' prosecution."

Kamei tantalized Fell by observing that "There were many more offensive experiments and developments in BW than were admitted. It is probable that BW bombs were actually employed in Central China." He thought that "a group other than General Ishii's carried out the tests and knows the results." Perhaps Masuda Tomosada and Kaneko Jun'ichi could help Fell. Using the old Naito ploy, Kamei promised that "I will confer with them and bring them to you."[20]

Masuda did meet with the American on 22 April 1947. Before the interrogaton however, Kamei revealed to Fell the gist of a conversation he held with Masuda earlier in the day. In reporting on the talk, Kamei attempted to convince Fell once more of the need to promise Japanese BW scientists that they would not be prosecuted as war criminals. He assured Fell that Masuda was eager to cooperate, but "information on offensive developments in BW [i.e. human experiments] is extremely delicate, and Japanese formerly connected with this field are very loath to speak about it." He recalled that

Ishii was so unpopular with many of his subordinates that some of the more disgruntled "sent anonymous letters shortly after the surrender to SCAP, accusing Ishii of directing human experiments in BW and requesting that he be prosecuted as a war criminal."[21]

According to Kamei, these anti-Ishii letters were leaked to the other BW experts, and they became fearful that they, too, might be incriminated and be charged with war crimes. It was essential, therefore, Kamei argued, that the individuals "who actually know the detailed results of the experiments can be convinced that your investigation is from a purely scientific standpoint, I believe that you can get more information." He baited Fell by indicating that "There is no question but that BW trials were made against the Chinese Army in Central China." Two of Masuda's friends, Naito Ryoichi and Kaneko Jun'ichi, "have definite information on these trials. I suggest a meeting with these men."[22]

Kamei suggested further that Fell discuss with an official of the Japanese Demobilization Bureau the purpose of his mission. Once reassured that "you are not investigating 'war crimes,'" he was certain the people in the Demobilization Bureau would inform the fearful that it would be safe to cooperate with the American investigation. To reinforce the fact that it was essential for BW scientists be given immunity from prosecution, Kamei reported that Masuda had confessed to him that "experiments were carried out on humans." However, those who had participated in such experiments took "a vow never to disclose information." Kamei was certain, nevertheless, "that if you handle your investigation from a scientific point of view [i.e. giving assurances that Japanese testimony would not be used in war crimes trials], you can obtain detailed information."[23]

Fell met with Kamei once again on 24 April. Kamei now raised the Soviet threat as a device to entice the Americans into granting the scientists immunity. He told Fell of his meeting with an official of the Demobilization Bureau in order to secure interviews with Naito and Kaneko. According to Kamei, the official was reluctant to command the men to appear before Fell because "they are afraid that cooperating and giving information to the United States will be discovered by the Communists and passed to Russia." Playing upon the known American fears of Communism, and aware of how eager Fell was to get BW data, Kamei told him that "The Japanese have a tendency to feel that continued silence is advisable."[24]

Kamei once again raised the specter of the communist menace. He told Fell that Masuda and the others became involved with BW to counter a perceived Soviet BW danger. Fell noted that the "Japanese insist that they were forced into BW program" after capturing Soviet spies armed with BW agents along the Manchurian frontier. Masuda and the others claimed that their BW program began "as a defensive measure." However, "Study of the defensive aspects led to the discovery of its offensive potential." Now, "The Japanese are afraid that if they reveal the [offensive BW] information, that communists will discover it, write letters to SCAP, tell the Russians, cause publicity, and force the investigation into the open." To obviate such dangers, Kamei boldly proposed to Fell that Masuda, Kaneko, and Naito, who allegedly knew the most about BW, be "transported to US territory, [where] they can reconstruct all records from memory."[25]

The conference concluded with several other interesting observations by Kamei. He told Fell that the Japanese were relieved considerably by Murray Sanders's acceptance of their deceptions. Sanders "did not know enough about the technical side of the subject" to realize the extent of the lies and evasions he had been fed. By war's end, Japanese research with humans had achieved a level where "scientific conclusions" could be reached. Kamei cautioned Fell not to interrogate the scientists in a group. He wanted Fell to segregate Masuda, Kaneko, and Naito from the others, because there were "cliques among former Japanese medical officers." Above all, he urged, "Ishii especially should not be involved." Finally, since all BW personnel were sworn to secrecy, "you will have to overcome that obstacle." Kamei was implying, once more, that Fell would get little information unless he offered immunity.[26]

It is difficult to determine why Kamei played the role he did in the Fell investigation. He obviously sought to secure immunity from prosecution for the scientists. His persistent claim that Masuda, Kaneko, and Naito knew everything there was to know about BW was so blatantly untrue that Fell would not accept the argument. Kamei's insistence that Ishii be kept out of the discussions is perplexing. Every American investigator was aware of Ishii's importance to the BW program. Why try to negate the obvious? Perhaps he was operating under instructions from one of the BW "cliques." Or perhaps he was obeying Ishii's orders. In any event, Ishii could not evade Fell, and he, along with the other principal BW specialists, ultimately was interviewed by Detrick's representative during his two-month investigation in Japan.

III

Norbert Fell met with Masuda, Kaneko, and Naito over four consecutive days, 28, 29, and 30 April and 1 May 1947. The three men at first were evasive in their responses to Fell's questions. They denied participating in offensive BW research (human experiments). Their expertise was in defensive BW studies. They could only give Fell "hearsay" information. They did not know anyone who could provide him with hard evidence "at this late date." When confronted with the news that the Soviets wanted to interrogate several of their colleagues, including two who were prisoners of war in Siberia, the three men denigrated the importance of the men the Soviets planned to interview. They described them as being minor participants in the BW efforts.[27]

Sparring between Fell and the three Japanese continued throughout the first two days of interrogations. At the conclusion of the second day of talks, Masuda stated bluntly that "We want to cooperate and know we owe it to you, but we have a responsibility to our friends." He revealed that "We took an oath never to divulge information on human experiments. We are afraid some of us will be prosecuted as war criminals." However, "If you can give us *documentary immunity*,[28] probably we can get everything. The subordinates, not to mention chiefs, know the details." Masuda gratuitously added the threat that "If we contact someone who is a Communist, he is liable to tell the Russians."[29]

In his desire to gain BW data, Fell accepted Masuda's arguments. Fell's report contains the brief observation: "*The Japanese were assured that war crimes were not involved.*"[30] This casual comment opened the floodgates of information. The three Japanese now indicated that they were prepared to cooperate completely with Fell. The American then instructed them to prepare detailed accounts in areas that he was most interested in receiving intelligence. Masuda, Kaneko, and Naito returned the next day with outlines of the material requested. They also told Fell that the men the Soviets wished to interview did possess significant BW knowledge. The three were now so helpful, they offered to aid Fell in securing information from the Japanese experts. Masuda knew that Fell did not want to contact them personally, and proposed to "write a letter for you to show them. It will tell them to let you know all." Naito suggested to Fell that he could locate experts on plant BW, should Fell desire such data. He also promised to contact for the American ex-BW personnel living in the Kyoto–Osaka area. Kaneko pledged to help Masuda write a comprehensive report on BW.[31]

Word of Fell's immunity promise soon spread to anxious former BW workers who were scheduled to appear before Fell. Some were candid in their interviews with him. Others continued to dissemble. Former Major General Kikuchi Hitoshi, who had headed Unit 731's First Section, for example, remained obdurate or evasive during three days of intense questioning. Fell confronted him with evidence obtained from other sources, "but [he] pleaded ignorance or denied knowledge in answer to all questions." It was apparent to Fell that Kikuchi "was excited and afraid." He had the interpreter tell him explicitly that "Investigation was to obtain scientific and technical data and was not concerned with 'war crimes.' " He was to be reminded that "Other Japanese were cooperating."[32]

Kikuchi continued to be uncooperative, despite the immunity blandishment. He could not remember things. He had only heard "rumors" about human experiments. He had no personal knowledge, etc. Fell abandoned any hope of obtaining useful information from him. Kikuchi was let go with the warning that "he was not to reveal information to the Russians" on human experiments, field tests against the Chinese Army, mass production of fleas, Unit 731's chain of command, and, most important, "Instructions by U[.]S[.] personnel."[33]

Interviews with Ishii were expected to be the capstone of Fell's investigation. To prepare Ishii psychologically for his interrogation, Fell relied on the ever-helpful Dr Kamei and a reputed friend of Ishii's, a certain Mr Miyamoto. Ishii was supposed to have been Miyamoto's benefactor, granting him many wartime contracts for his medical supply business, and, no doubt, receiving the usual kickbacks for his favors. The contracts must have been on such a large scale, and so lucrative, that Miyamoto continued to give Ishii financial help two years after the end of the war. Under Kamei's supposed prodding, Miyamoto visited Ishii to persuade him of the necessity for being forthcoming to the Americans when he was interviewed. Ishii demurred. He wanted a "documentary guarantee of immunity." Kamei then agreed to return with Miyamoto to Ishii's house to induce him to testify fully, with the understanding that his "revealing technical information will help and not damage his position." The reluctant Ishii somehow was induced to cooperate, and he agreed to meet with the Americans.[34]

Fell interviewed Ishii for three days on 8, 9, and 10 May 1947. Their meeting took place at Ishii's Tokyo home because he alleged he was ill. Ishii was able, however, to put on a superb performance over a three-day period of intense discussions, despite his claimed malady. It was vintage Ishii. He treated Fell and the others as if they were paying a visit to a feudal lord at the lord's sufferance. He greeted his visitors sitting upright in bed and clad in his best kimono, and remained in that position throughout all interviews he deigned to grant his American guests.[35]

Ishii intermingled facts with lies for Fell. At one point he knew everything; at another, he knew little or nothing. He was totally responsible for all that took place under the guise of BW. But, on the other hand, he never really knew what went on beyond some general knowledge of the subject.

The interviews began with a formula opening that Fell employed with all the individuals he interrogated. He told Ishii that Detrick was interested in him for his "technical and scientific information[,] and not war crimes." Detrick was aware of his earlier statements to Thompson. Fell knew that Ishii had held back considerable information during the previous interrogations, and the knowledge "he had concealed was of interest now." He also wanted Ishii's "statement on human experiments and trials of BW against [the] Chinese Army."[36]

Ishii talked at length during the three-day meeting. He began by promising to reveal nothing to the Soviets. He claimed to have told Murray Sanders in 1945 "that I wouldn't."[37] He could not provide the Americans with "detailed technical data" because all the records at Ping Fan were destroyed. Besides, he never "did know many details, and I have forgotten what I knew." He would be able to give Fell only "general results."

Japan had inaugurated a defensive BW program, according to Ishii, in response to provocations by Chinese and Russian agents. He "never heard of Anda" until 1945. He "did not visit the location." Yet, in a *mea culpa* oration, Ishii declared, "I am responsible for all that went on at Pingfan." Therefore, he was "willing to shoulder all responsibility." He absolved both his superiors and his subordinates of all blame. They had nothing "to do with issuing instructions for experiments."[38] Then, reverting back to his ignorant–innocence pose, Ishii claimed that he knew nothing about field tests. He had "read about the Nimpo [Ning Bo] incident in the Chinese [news]paper

'Shinko.' " Ishii was in Manchuria at the time, and so "do not know anything about the matter."[39]

Suddenly, Ishii became knowledgeable once more. He was "wholly responsible for Pingfan." He did not want to see his superiors and his subordinates in trouble for what took place at Ping Fan. Therefore, he proposed a deal to Fell. Ishii told Fell, "If you will give documentary immunity for myself, superiors, and subordinates, I can get all the information for you." While Masuda, Kaneko, and Naito "can give you a lot [of data]," Ishii implied that he was a far more valuable resource than the three men combined.

He told Fell that he "would like to be hired by the US as a BW expert."[40] If the Americans employed him, he boasted, "In the preparation for the war with Russia, I can give you the advantage of my 20 years research and experience." He had given a "great deal of thought to tactical problems in the use and defense against BW." He admitted to having undertaken "studies on the best agents to be employed in various regions and in cold climates." Ishii became so engrossed in what degenerated into a tirade that he crowed, "I can write volumes about BW, including the little thought of strategic and tactical employment."[41]

The first day's exchange concluded with a warning to Ishii. Fell's Japanese-American translator was instructed to tell him that he would soon be interviewed by Soviet investigators. Ishii was cautioned that he was not to give the Soviets any information on "human experiments, mass production of fleas, trials against Chinese forces," and "instructions by United States personnel."

Fell plainly did not believe Ishii's denials during the interrogation, and wished to make certain that no vital information fell into the hands of the Soviets. He, along with the other American agents, would have liked to insulate Ishii, and to prevent him from even meeting with Soviet representatives. Fell hoped that Ishii's "sickness" could be used as an excuse to postpone or delay the Soviet meeting. On the following day, 9 May, Fell brought an American physician to the Ishii interview. Ishii was examined, and was pronounced to be in good health. The doctor declared "there was no reason not to interrogate him either singly or in conjunction with USSR."

The physical examination had one positive result for Fell. It made Ishii aware that he would be exposed to Soviet interrogators. The fear of what the Soviets might do to him evidently put him "in such a cooperative mood" that what was supposed to be a brief visit became a two-hour discussion. Fell told Ishii that "no decision on immunity" for himself or his subordinates had as yet been determined by the Americans. Nevertheless, Ishii declared that "I will tell you everything needed." Craftily, he pointed out that BW was such an extensive field that he wanted Fell to tell him in what areas he was interested. Ishii presumably did not wish to disclose any information to the American that he could hold back to use at a later time during negotiations for his immunity.

The interview rambled in an unstructured manner. Fell and Ishii touched on many topics without an attempt to follow any coherent pattern of discussion. Ishii now remembered Anda. He knew "very little about the experiments which went on at Anda after I left [in 1942]." He had no information on Japan's use of paper balloons as a BW weapon.[42] The Germans had tried to obtain Japanese BW data, but the Japanese "always stalled." He explained his unorthodox method for working on a BW problem. Ishii "used to think up a problem, assign experts to follow down on the defensive and offensive aspects, and submit a report. For this reason, I do not know the details of experiments."[43] He felt that the three most important BW agents were anthrax, plague, and epidemic encephalitis. He did not know who was responsible for Ping Fan's destruction. He had found it in flames when he returned there on 9 August 1945. He was "unable to get even my personal documents from my office." The two-hour session was terminated with another admonition to Ishii. He was told what answers to give the Soviets in their forthcoming interview. Fell concluded that "It was evident at this time that more instructions must be given at a later date."[44]

Fell returned to Ishii's home on 10 May for a third interview. He brought along with him an "outline questionnaire" he had prepared for Ishii to complete. Fell reviewed the questions with Ishii, who interrupted occasionally to ask questions and to make some suggestions. He told Fell that he was reluctant to continue to cooperate with the Americans without written assurances he would not be prosecuted. Fell left Ishii with the feeling, however, that he would do some work with the questionnaire while waiting for a definite answer on immunity. He also told Fell, with some asperity, "I prefer to be interrogated at my home instead of the NYK building because of my health, and I am afraid to leave my house."

This last remark was not pretense. G-2's Lt. Colonel Robert P. McQuail, a major player in the Ishii cover-up negotiations,[45] observed shrewdly shortly after Fell's visit that "Ishii is reported to be a difficult person to interview, constantly trying to impress the interviewer of his fund of special knowledge. He is now, however, a thoroughly frightened individual."[46] Ishii received anonymous and ominous-sounding telephone calls once it became known that he was back in Tokyo.[47]

He was under constant threat of blackmail. In one typical blackmail letter sent to him by three former underlings, he was told of the hardships they were enduring, and that they were "about to fall into committing wicked things," but thought that first they would turn to "our thoughtful commanding officer to rescue us." They reminded him that "while at Nanking . . . we were ordered to carry out some gruesome work, and we did perform our duties faithfully. It must have been a difficult task to bury all those materials after the war was over." Now, all they could do was to "beg you, our commanding officer, that you loan us, the unfortunate ones, as our rehabilitation funds a sum of 50,000 yen[,] which will be positively returned to you within two months."[48]

Ishii was now so assured of his worth to the United States that he felt free to reveal to investigators, and to the Japanese police, information concerning the anonymous telephone calls he received. Boldly, he turned over to American Counter-Intelligence copies of the blackmail letters as they arrived. Counter-Intelligence took the threats seriously. Ishii's house was put under surveillance by Japanese plainclothes policemen. The fear was that the blackmail letters and the telephone calls might have been the opening gambit by a foreign power to force Ishii into divulging BW secrets. American investigators, therefore, were ordered to "Try to determine whether this is just an ordinary case of blackmail[,] or whether another foreign power [presumably the Soviet Union] is attempting to obtain results of bacteriological warfare experiments."[49] All findings were to be marked "Attention Special Projects Section."[50]

It was with these threats in the background that Fell and the others conducted their interrogations of Ishii. Fell's final interview with Ishii terminated with a technical discussion of dosages required to provide optimum results with several pathogens. The talk covered cholera, and how artificially induced plague begins as typical bubonic plague, but "three days before death" develops into pneumonic plague. They also discussed the Changchun operation, but Ishii claimed that he was forbidden to visit it, and that Ping Fan in return banned visitors from Changchun. He therefore, "knew nothing of their activities." Fell concluded that "Ishii did not specifically state that his technical discussion pertained to humans, but it was obvious."[51]

Fell interviewed several other BW notables before he returned to Detrick. He began all meetings with the now standard carrot-and-stick litany: 1. He promised that he was interested in the information they could provide him solely for scientific purposes. 2. He was not concerned with prosecuting them for war crimes. 3. The Soviets held two of their colleagues prisoners, and they confessed to having participated in human experiments. 4. Masuda Tomosada was cooperating fully with the Americans. 5. The Soviets would be interviewing them shortly. 6. They were not to disclose to the Soviets any information on human experiments, flea production, field tests, or organizational structure of the BW units, or that they had been briefed and given instructions by the Americans.[52]

This tactic was not a complete success. The Japanese supplied Fell with enough information to give him the impression that they were cooperating with him. This was done in order to convince him of the necessity for granting them written guarantees that they would not be prosecuted as war criminals. However, the BW experts did not advance all the data they possessed. They were still wary of the Americans in 1947. Verbal assurances did not assuage their fears.

Fell's interview of 29 May with Wakamatsu is typical of the many meetings he held with key BW personnel. Wakamatsu was fed the litany. He replied by declaring, "I shall be glad to cooperate." He was handicapped, however, because all his records were destroyed, and he would have to reconstruct data from memory. Besides, "Most of our work was in the defensive line." He assured Fell that "you may be disappointed in the small amount of offensive work we carried out." He would try to write a fairly detailed account of Unit 100 activities if the Americans provided him with the assistance of roughly five of his former associates. He completed his statement by declaring, "I can say truthfully that we did not do any special experiments or work on human beings. We had no connection at all with Ishii's Unit." Fell was so impressed with Wakamatsu's performance that he told him "to begin immediately on an outline of his report and to submit it by 4 June." Wakamatsu was "instructed to indicate the additional personnel he needed to assist him and to tell Lt. Col. McQuail."[53] He "was guaranteed expense money and assistance in obtaining food during the time of writing the report."[54]

The Wakamatsu interview was preceded by an urgent telegram from Washington intended to guide Fell in interrogating personnel engaged in crop BW. The telegram contained sixteen questions prepared by a Dr Norman for Fell's use. Questions ranged from a consideration of the principal crops Japanese BW specialists worked with, to an inquiry on whether field trials were attempted, and, if so, "On a small plot basis or on a large scale?" Dr Norman wished to know whether experiments employing either oil, "war gases," poisons, or weedkillers were attempted with different types of crops. He was curious also on whether those interviewed observed "men working in the plots," and if these experts knew "if grain or vegetables from these plots were fed to animals or men."[55] The sixteen questions, as well as others Fell initiated, were part of Wakamatsu's assignment.

IV

Fell returned to the United States in June 1947 a happy man. He knew that the Japanese had attempted to hoodwink him. They had told so many lies, and engaged in so many deceptions, that he was cognizant he did not receive all the data the Japanese possessed. They did supply him, however, with information that he and others at Detrick found to be most useful. The Japanese experts provided Fell with slides, photomicrographs, and printed documents.

Nineteen "of the key figures in the B.W. program" agreed to write a lengthy report on human experiments. They took almost one month to complete their sixty page report written in English for the Americans. While the report was compiled "largely from memory," the nineteen scientists located "some documents still available that were of assistance to the group."[56]

Ten former Unit 100 members prepared a report on BW chemical and plant herbicide research. The head botanist of the group gave Fell a nineteen-page report written in English that covered research on crop diseases. Fell concluded that most of the Japanese plant studies duplicated research conducted at Detrick, but the Japanese, in addition, had conducted studies in areas neglected by their American counterparts.[57]

Ishii promised to write a detailed account of his twenty years of BW experience. His report would "include his ideas about the strategical and

202 Factories of Death

tactical use of B.W. weapons," as well as how the weapons could be used "in various geographical areas (particularly in cold climates)." Ishii agreed also to furnish Fell "a full description of his 'ABEDO' theory about biological warfare."[58]

The Japanese provided Fell with "an interesting report" on the "theoretical and mathematical considerations involved in particle-size determinations." They submitted a short report on their free balloon project. They gave him a printed document that summarized a series of lectures "given to spies and saboteurs by one of the leading B.W. officials." They furnished him with 600 pages of printed articles "covering the entire field of natural and artificial plague" as well as a 100-page printed bulletin dealing with "some phase of B.W. or C.W. warfare."[59]

Fell concluded reasonably that "The information that has been received so far is proving of great interest here and it certainly will have a great deal of value in the future development of our [BW] program."[60]

He achieved one other objective during his tour of duty in the defeated enemy's domain. Fell prepared the BW experts for testimony they were to offer during interrogation sessions by the Soviets. With the Cold War in full swing, American leaders were frightened of giving the Soviets any supposed military advantage. They did not want the Soviets to learn anything from the Japanese.[61] The records that still exist suggest that Fell succeeded in keeping the Japanese BW secrets safe for American use.

The information Detrick obtained from Japan in 1947 and in 1948 came at a price: immunity for the Japanese from prosecution from war crimes. In his two-month stay in Japan, Norbert Fell interviewed more than two dozen Japanese BW experts. During every one of the meetings between Fell and the experts, he promised them immunity for their deeds. These men, by any definition, participated in war crimes. Ishii, Kitano, Wakamatsu, and the other principals fitted the Tokyo War Crimes Tribunal's classification as "A" level war criminals. Mid-level personnel stationed in Ping Fan, Changchun, Nanking, and the other BW stations fell within the "B" or "C" war crimes category. They all were told by Fell that they were in no danger, so long as they gave him and others from Detrick the fruits of their research.

There is no record available currently as to who authorized Fell to make such a significant decision. It is unclear whether he did it without consulting his superiors, although this is highly unlikely, given the hierarchical structure in the BW program that was in place at the time. Fell was an important scientist at Detrick, but he did not have the power there to make such a vital decision on his own. He admitted to Ishii that he lacked the authority to give him a written statement regarding immunity. He had to secure the approval of others for such an action.

Fell did provide a clue as to how complex the consideration of an immunity grant could be in a dispatch he wrote on 24 June, the same day he presented his report. He sent a copy of his findings and recommendations to Major General Charles Willoughby in Tokyo, and included a briefing memo that covered many different items of interest to the Detrick scientists. One detail in the memorandum is of special concern. Paragraph seven notes that a conference attended by Major General Alden Waitt and representatives from the War, State, and Justice Departments was held the previous day in Washington.[62] The conferees "informally agreed" to accept "the recommendations of the C. in C., FEC [General MacArthur], and the Chief, Chemical Corps [General Waitt], i.e. that all information obtained in this investigation would be held in intelligence channels and not used for 'War Crimes' programs." The SWNCC Subcommittee in Tokyo would be informed about the decision and would hold a meeting shortly, where, it was assumed, they would comply with the recommendation. Then, although unstated in the paragraph, it was expected the Subcommittee endorsement would be forwarded to SWNCC in Washington for authorization and action by the Joint Chiefs of Staff.[63] The immunity decision would come full circle.

V

The final decision did not come as neatly, however, as Fell anticipated. More than twelve months would pass before the issue was resolved finally. Many meetings in Washington and in Tokyo would be called to consider the question. Countless hours would be spent by officials weighing the merits of an immunity grant. A considerable number of minutes and memoranda that still survive testify to the weighty deliberations that occupied the men responsible for a conclusive settlement. However, the 23 June meeting signaled the opening phase in Washington of discussions which ultimately would lead to the resolution of the problem.

Major General Alden Waitt, Chief of the Chemical Corps, bore ultimate responsibility for operations at Detrick, and was apprised continuously of Fell's performance in Japan.[64] But Waitt was a two-star general who headed a technical facility for the American military. He was not in the military's political chain of command. Waitt reported to the Joint Chiefs of Staff. There is the likelihood that the Joint Chiefs, upon Waitt's recommendations and that of General MacArthur and his staff, may have believed that Japanese data were so vital for American defense that they should pay any price to secure the information.[65] The messages that shuttled back and forth between Mac-Arthur's headquarters in Tokyo and the Joint Chiefs of Staff in Washington indicate, however, that it was the Joint Chiefs, not MacArthur, who made the final military decision to meet the BW scientists' terms for cooperation.

The immunity question, nevertheless, concerned both military and political issues, and could only be decided after consultation with the highest civilian authorities. The Joint Chiefs' Commander-in-Chief, Harry S. Truman,[66] or his newly appointed Secretary of Defense, James Forrestal, or General George C. Marshall, Secretary of State in 1947–1948, or one of their close subordinates,[67] were theoretically the only ones in a position qualified to authorize such action. There was always the danger that the immunity issue might become public knowledge, with unknown political pitfalls. Exposure during the height of the War Crimes Trials would, at the least, be embarrassing to the United States. Such exposure, if it occurred, could lead to demands that all those involved in the BW program be tried for war crimes. No one could then predict how many politicians, military officers, scientists, and members of the Royal Family would be dragged into the affair.

Moreover, the American military operate within the framework of a command structure which decrees that irrevocable political judgments must be made by elected leaders or their designees. Any officer violating this tradition soon finds himself in some difficulty. Generals who go off on their own frequently find themselves subject to early retirement. General Douglas MacArthur and his public controversy with President Harry Truman in the Korean War, General John Singlaub and his quarrel with President Jimmy Carter over relations with the Soviet Union and North Korea, and, more recently, General H. Norman Schwarzkopf's open differences with President George Bush over the timing of the end of the war with Iraq offer sufficient testimony to the fact that, in a struggle between military and civilian leaders, the latter prevail. The final decision on war crimes immunity must have been taken, therefore, in civilian offices in Washington, DC, and not in Camp Detrick, in Occupation Headquarters in Tokyo, or at the Pentagon.[68]

15 The military and the cover-up

Herewith extracts of telecon held by G-2 Personnel with the Chief of Chemical Corps. . . . These extracts indicate the extreme value of the intelligence information obtained and the danger of publicity on this subject: . . . It is intention of Mil Int representative on SWNCC Sub Committee to recommend that information re B.W. given to us will not be divulged or used in war crimes trials. . . . I [General Alden Waitt] consider it vital that we get the information and that secrecy (which would be impossible if war crimes trials were held) be maintained. . . . The information so far indicates that investigation is producing most important data. It merits all necessary support, financial and otherwise.
(Intelligence Information on Bacteriological Warfare, 9 June 1947, Record Group 331, Box 1434, 13, The National Archives)

I

Scientists at Detrick spent the summer and fall of 1947 digesting the material submitted by Japanese BW specialists after Fell returned from Tokyo. They were impressed with what they found, and insisted on a follow-up expedition to Japan where they expected to extract additional data. Detrick, in response to the arguments of the scientists, dispatched the facility's Technical Director, Dr Edwin V. Hill, a recognized authority on BW, and its most politically powerful scientist, to the Far East on what was developing rapidly into an extremely delicate and sensitive mission. Dr Hill's formal title was Chief, Basic Sciences at Detrick. He was accompanied on the assignment by Dr Joseph Victor, a Detrick pathologist.[1]

Hill and Victor were ordered to Japan on 15 October, arriving there on 28 October. Once in the capital, they found everything had been prepared for their investigations. Hill and Victor were treated so well by the occupation authorities that they expressed their gratitude to Major General Charles A. Willoughby, Assistant Chief of Staff of G-2, and a close associate of General MacArthur, for expediting their mission. Willoughby made certain that the Japanese to be interviewed were available when needed. He helped Hill and Victor in many other ways as well.

Their mission had three objectives. The first was to secure additional information required to clarify issues that were left unclear in the earlier reports. The second purpose was "To examine human pathological material which had been transferred to Japan from B. W. installations." Their final goal was "To obtain protocols necessary for understanding the significance of the pathological material."[2]

Hill and Victor completed their research in little more than one month. Unlike Fell's earlier experience, the newcomers found the Japanese cooperative from their initial to their concluding interviews. They noted only one meeting in which there was a "slight hesitancy . . . before admitting details of human experiments," but even the men in this interview "were extremely cooperative and gave information freely."[3] Hill commented somewhat naively in his report to General Waitt that "It is noteworthy that information supplied by interviewed persons was submitted voluntarily. No question of immunity guarantee from war crimes prosecution was ever raised during these interviews."[4]

The Detrick visitors conducted interviews with a score or more BW specialists. They received reports on aerosols, anthrax, botulism, brucellosis, cholera, decontamination, dysentery, fugu toxin, gas gangrene, glanders, influenza, meningococcus, mucin, plague, plant diseases, salmonella, songo fever, smallpox, tetanus, tick encephalitis, toutsugamushi, tuberculosis, tularemia, typhoid, and typhus. Hill and Victor were given an index to the slides of pathological material previously submitted to American investigators. The index was important, because the slides were in disarray. All the reports, except for one on songo fever, were written allegedly from memory. The reports, however, were exceptionally detailed for having been written solely from recollections of experiments that took place several years earlier, or longer.

For example, the songo fever account, co-authored by Kasahara Shiro and Kitano Masaji, was extremely candid about the use of humans in their research. The report contained observations such as, "Subsequent cases were produced either by blood or blood from extracts of liver, spleen or kidney derived from individuals sacrificed at various times during the course of the disease. Morphine was employed for this purpose." Kasahara and Kitano noted also:

> Blood from febrile man was injected . . . into horses. After incubation period . . . fever appeared lasting 5 to 7 days in 6 of 15 experiments. Blood of febrile horses was injected into other horses with positive results in one or two cases. Conversely, blood of febrile horses injected into man was positive in 2 of 8 experiments.

They concluded their analysis by noting that "Mortality of the natural disease in Japanese soldiers was 30 percent when the disease was first discovered. . . . However, mortality in experimental cases was 100 percent due to the procedure of sacrificing experimental subjects."[5]

Hill and Victor returned to Detrick pleased with what they had learned. Their report, signed by Hill, declared, "Not only was additional information obtained about subjects previously submitted in the Japanese B. W. report, but much information was gathered about human diseases which were intensively investigated by the Japanese, but not previously reported." Hill was convinced that "Evidence gathered in this investigation has greatly supplemented and amplified previous aspects of this field."

He was especially impressed with the pathological material submitted by the Japanese. The 8000 or so slides have not surfaced in the many archival depositories consulted for this study. However, as indicated earlier, three autopsy reports on glanders, plague, and anthrax have survived.[6] They are astonishingly voluminous and graphic in detail. Two of the autopsy reports cover more than 350 pages each. The other is more than 700 pages in length. Pictures of hundreds of slides dealing with tissue cultures dot the reports. Still other hundreds of pastel drawings depicting changes in body organs ornament the narrative descriptions.[7]

Hill was so grateful for the data that he concluded his report by writing, "It is hoped that individuals who voluntarily contributed this information will be spared embarrassment because of it and that every effort will be taken to prevent this information from falling into other hands."[8]

II

The decision to offer immunity to Ishii and the others was not based solely upon the perceived needs of the scientists working at Detrick. Negotiations with the BW specialists operated on two separate tracks. The first was with Detrick personnel; the second was with American Military Intelligence, colloquially known as G-2. Complicating the discussions, however, was a third group, investigators from the Adjutant General's Office in Tokyo, who continued to track down leads in pursuit of evidence to indict the Japanese and bring them to justice. By early February 1946, the authorities had a list of more than twenty former high-ranking officers and academics who had potentially damning information concerning Ishii.[9] The Adjutant General's investigators continued to find additional damaging evidence, but the civilian and military people concerned with obtaining BW data evidently possessed sufficient influence to be able either to impugn or to ignore the findings.

The American military's dilemma was expressed succinctly in an inter-office memorandum dated 24 July 1947. The memorandum stated in blunt language that "In view of subject's [Ishii] experiments and activities in Manchuria, further investigation at this point may reveal that subject is a war criminal wanted by the Chinese authorities and/or the US War Crimes Investigation Agencies." In order to prevent Ishii from being subjected to the humiliation of a war crimes accusation, it was determined that day by a Colonel Bethune that "*no* information is to be released to any agency as data on subject is classified *top* secret."[10] Nine months later, it was noted for the record that

All Agents intrusted [sic] with the handling of this subject should be cautioned that any information which may be obtained [on Ishii and BW] has international implications. It is of a highly sensitive nature, and that every precaution must be taken to maintain its secrecy. The number of persons dealing with this subject should be kept at a minimum.[11]

To put an end to possible further interference by the Adjutant General's Office, the Joint Chiefs of Staff sent an order to Tokyo in March 1947 that placed the BW war criminal investigations under the control of Intelligence (G-2). The Joint Chiefs made it clear that "Every step, interrogation, or contact must be co-ordinated with this section. The utmost secrecy is essential in order to protect the interests of the United States and to guard against embarrassment."[12] The war crimes investigators were directed to make no effort toward prosecution or "any form of publicity of this case without G-2 concurrence." This "is by direct orders of the C-in-C and CS." Their final instructions were that "all future interrogations will be conducted at the Tokyo Office under control of ATIS Central Interrogation Center and previous undeveloped leads set out for the field offices are canceled."[13]

This decision meant that those BW participants who had escaped the investigators network thus far would be safe from possible prosecution. Those already under investigation could be assured that their freedom would be protected. Two months after the directive was issued, the War Department in Washington received a cable from Tokyo that suggested there was "strong circumstantial evidence . . . of use of bacteria warfare at Chuhsien, Kingwha and Changteh." Ishii was cited in the cable as being responsible for the 1940 Ning Bo field tests, as well as other field tests in 1939 and 1942 expeditions. The investigator was of the "opinion that foregoing information warrants conclusion that Japanese P[sic – B]W Group headed by Ishii did violate rules of land warfare." In light of the Joint Chiefs' directive, the investigator concluded that, "this expression of opinion is not a recommendation that group be charged and tried for such."[14]

III

Detrick personnel conducted one group of interviews in 1945, 1946, and 1947. The American military pursued a second set of exchanges in 1947 and 1948 that also led to immunity discussions with the BW specialists in Tokyo. Both groups worked together at times. They also operated independently of each other when their requirements dictated such action. If the final results of the negotiations are a criterion, then the representatives of the military enjoyed greater authority than did the civilian Detrick scientists.

The military contingent was led by a joint armed forces and State Department group known as the State–War–Navy Coordinating Subcommittee for the Far East, or SWNCC Subcommittee. It reported to its parent body, the State–War–Navy Coordinating Committee, which was responsible, as its name implies, for coordinating occupation policy in Japan. SWNCC was an informal organization of State, War, and Navy Department representatives who wielded great power collectively. It was established in 1944 to prevent conflicting or overlapping jurisdictions from interfering with an orderly management of the coming occupation of Japan. The permanent members were from time to time joined by representatives from the Justice Department, or other appropriate Cabinet agencies, when issues affecting their respective departments were being considered. The State Department representative chaired Committee meetings, and all reports were channeled through the Secretary of State, initially James F. Byrnes, but in 1947 through his successor, General George C. Marshall.[15]

SWNCC's Subcommittee functioned in Tokyo. The policy-making body operated from the Pentagon in Washington. The subcommittee recommended action to be taken. The States-side group conveyed to Japan the decisions made in Washington. The usual transmission organ was the Office of the Joint Chiefs of Staff.

SWNCC was charged with achieving two objectives regarding BW. The Committee was expected to prevent the Soviets from learning anything relating to Japanese BW research. Its second responsibility was to make certain that the Japanese BW experts provided American scientists with all the data they had previously amassed. The fear of the Soviets securing BW information pervaded all exchanges on BW. The Adjutant General's Office in Tokyo was warned by Washington as early as 29 November 1946 that "Reference Russian BW shall be topsec[ret], routine biological warfare information secret."[16] SWNCC's minutes, and those of its Tokyo Sub-committee, contain numerous references to discussions held on ways of preventing the Soviets from meeting with the Japanese BW people. They also refer to reviews of what the BW experts would be permitted to divulge to the Soviets in the event they were forced to permit such meetings. Investigators in the Tokyo Adjutant General's Office routinely referred transcripts of their interviews with Japanese BW personnel to SWNCC, thus keeping SWNCC informed of all developments in that segment of war crimes investigations.[17]

Members of the Subcommittee conferred with the various Detrick visitors. Fell appears to have briefed SWNCC on all his discussions with Ishii and the other BW principals. He must have consulted with them on the war crimes question, since there is a cryptic note in the Fort Detrick files, written shortly after Fell submitted his final report, that refers to discussions of granting "Ishii and his associates" immunity. The deliberations were based on consultations Fell held with some occupation officials.[18] Hill and Victor met with the SWNCC Subcommittee on several occasions during their whirlwind tour in October–November 1947.

The SWNCC-Subcommittee in its discussions as to how to deal with the Soviets was guided by official Pentagon policy laid down in late July 1946. The Joint Chiefs ruled that allies were entitled to all information they requested from occupying authorities, if the request was reasonable. The one exception to this policy was "Intelligence which, in the opinion of the American Commander responsible for action . . . might jeopardize the security of the US . . . or derogate from US advantages in the field of scientific research and development." Such information should not be disclosed without checking with the Joint Chiefs and receiving their "authorization," or, "where appropriate, by the State–War–Navy Coordinating Committee."[19] In order to make certain there was no misunderstanding, the directive stated further that "under present circumstances, intelligence relating to research and development in the field of science and war material should not be disclosed to nations other than the British Commonwealth (omitting Eire) without specific authorization of the Joint Chiefs of Staff."[20]

IV

The Soviets began their open campaign to secure Japanese BW secrets at the beginning of 1947. One of their representatives approached an American member of the International Prosecution Section (IPS) with a request that the occupying authority provide the Soviets with Japanese BW experts for interrogation.[21] The Soviets supported their request by informing the American that they had captured some Japanese BW people who told them of horrible experiments conducted upon humans at the now destroyed Ping Fan installation. The Japanese account at first seemed so preposterous that the Soviets sent in their own BW experts to check the Ping Fan ruins. These experts confirmed the Japanese claims, after a thorough investigation. The Americans stalled on the Soviet request, but, at the same time, they were delighted with the information the inquiry provided them. An intelligence agent commented that "Figures on production are new. Experiments on humans was suspected. Information that Pingfan was completely destroyed with documents confirms previous information."[22]

One month later, they increased their pressure on the Americans. The Soviets insisted on interviewing Ishii, a certain Colonel Kikuchi Hitoshi, and Colonel Ota Kiyoshi. They based their desire to interrogate the Japanese on the assumption that these men, as well as some of their associates, would eventually be tried in supplementary war crimes trials. Soviet prosecutors also admitted candidly that they were interested in gaining information from the group on Japanese BW discoveries.

Initial American reaction to the request was favorable. There was nothing fraternal in this response. Instead, Intelligence in Tokyo operated from a selfish perspective. It knew it would be able to orchestrate any meetings between the Soviets and the Japanese, permitting the latter to disclose only that information Intelligence wished to be disseminated. General MacArthur's people therefore cabled Washington for permission to comply with the Soviet request, since "Opinion here that Russians not likely to obtain information from Japanese not already known to United States and that United States might get some additional information from Russian line of questioning in monitored interrogations."[23] Intelligence submitted, in addition, a background paper that buttressed the argument for permitting Soviet interrogations. This paper recognized War Department policy, "that there shall be no more international trials." Therefore, the Soviet request could not be granted simply on the grounds of a possible future supplementary war crimes trial. However, some intelligence could be gained from giving the Soviets an opportunity to question the men since Ishii did not possess all the Japanese BW technical information, and "there is a remote chance they might have some technical knowledge not possessed" by Ishii. The paper observed that "It appears advantageous to the United States to permit the inter-rogation, but in order to be sure that no surprises occur, we should first interrogate Kikuchi and Ota ourselves."[24]

The SWNCC Subcommittee became involved in the discussions no later than mid-February. On 11 February, it received a message from the Joint Chiefs of Staff in Washington requesting the Subcommittee to formulate a policy recommendation on how to deal with the Soviet plea.[25] The Sub-committee responded by forming a working group to draft policy. This new body submitted a report to the Subcommittee on 26 February that also recommended compliance with the Soviet request. The reasoning was similar to that of the G-2 investigator. The United States could gain information by monitoring such interviews. It was believed that "by permitting this interro-gation, under controlled conditions, the general trend of Soviet questioning might serve as a key to Soviet knowledge and activity in the BW field." Ota and Kikuchi heretofore had not been interrogated by American BW experts. They should be, prior to their meeting with the Soviets. Ishii, Ota, and Kikuchi should be told that during their meetings with the Soviet representatives there should be "no mention of the US interview on this subject." If United States BW people determine in their questioning of the men that their "information is considered of such importance that its divulgence to the Soviets should not be permitted, they should be instructed not to reveal such information to the Soviets."

The Working Group concluded its recommendations with an argument that the United States would adopt throughout the long, torturous, frequently acrimonious discussions with the Soviets concerning the Japanese BW authorities. It contended that the United States should focus on Japanese BW abuse of the Chinese. There should be no reference to possible mistreatment of Soviet citizens. Therefore, "since there is no clear cut war crime interest by the Soviets in acts allegedly committed by the Japanese against the Chinese," permission for any interrogation of Ishii et al. should not be given on a war crimes basis. Instead, it should be granted "as an amiable gesture toward a friendly government." The friendly government should be informed that "the permission granted in this instance does not create a precedent for future requests, which shall be considered on their individual merits."[26]

The SWNCC Subcommittee met two days later to consider the report. Several minor modifications were proposed by the Air Force representative, and were adopted by the Subcommittee. The group was now under increasing pressure from Washington. It received that day a message from the Joint Chiefs of Staff urging a rapid decision, since the "USSR prosecutor making daily request for decision on interrogation." The Soviet prosecutors, in an apparent quid pro quo offer, agreed to share their Japanese-derived BW information with the United States, including whatever "documentary evidence" was available. The prosecutors were so anxious to question Ishii and his colleagues that they were willing to grant the United States unimpeded access to the Soviets' prisoners, and guaranteed "100 per cent interrogation of Japanese by US Army using Soviet documents."[27]

Discussions within the Subcommittee on 28 February were extensive, but it is unknown whether a final recommendation was transmitted to Washington. What is known is that, in the course of debate, the Subcommittee concluded that data Ishii and the others had previously provided proved "to be of great value in confirming, supplementing and complementing several phases of US research in BW, and may suggest new fields for future research." Members of the Subcommittee were impressed with the information gleaned from human experiments "showing the direct effects of BW agents on man." This new knowledge was important because "In the past it has been necessary to evaluate the effects of BW agents on man from data obtained through animal experimentation. Such evaluation is inconclusive and far less complete than results obtained from certain types of human experimentation." Similar wording would be employed in virtually every document subsequently written to support negotiations with the BW specialists.

Japanese data on their experiments with animals and with food crops were also important. The Subcommittee was persuaded that "The voluntary imparting of this BW information may serve as a forerunner for obtaining much additional information in other fields of research." Under these circumstances, the group believed it was desirable to avoid prosecuting the scientists as war criminals. The rationale for this conclusion was that

> Since it is believed that the USSR possesses only a small portion of this technical information, and since any "war crimes" trial would completely reveal such data to all nations, it is felt that such publicity must be avoided in interests of defense and security of the US.

Further, "It is believed also that 'war crimes' prosecution of Ishii and his associates would serve to stop the flow of much additional information of a technical and scientific nature." And, finally, "It is felt that the use of this information as a basis for 'war crimes' evidence would be a grave detriment to Japanese cooperation with the United States occupation forces in Japan."[28] Once more, similar language would be employed in subsequent documents written to support immunity for the Japanese.

Washington was receptive to Tokyo's suggestions. On 5 March, the State–War–Navy Coordinating Committee adopted, "by informal action," an official American policy. The Committee accepted without change the SWNCC Subcommittee recommendations, but two weeks would elapse before the adopted procedure was transmitted to MacArthur's headquarters in Japan.[29] In the meantime, Tokyo continued to delay responding to Soviet requests until a decision from Washington was received. This frequently led the Soviets to become "unpleasant," in what had become "almost daily inquiries." MacArthur's aide, Major General Charles Willoughby, noted for the record:

It is apparent that the Soviets are cloaking their interest in the intelligence aspects of Bacteriological Warfare by simulated concern over alleged use of bacteria against Chinese and Manchurians. The evidence which the Soviets say they possess may be of importance, and for that reason it is considered desirable from an intelligence standpoint to attempt coordinated action with the USSR.[30]

Exasperated by the perceived lag in responding to their pleas to interview the BW experts, the Soviets on 7 March petitioned the Americans to surrender Ishii and Ota to them so that they could be "brought to trial for war crimes against the USSR."[31] The occupying authorities refused this new request, and continued to delay responding to the initial Soviet demand to interrogate Ishii and his men. On 20 March, MacArthur's headquarters received a message from the Joint Chiefs of Staff granting permission for Soviet interrogations, subject to all the qualifications and reservations contained in the SWNCC Subcommittee working group report.[32]

Ishii and the others were not turned over to the Soviets for prosecution. Soviet prosecutors were denied access to the men as late as mid-May.[33] They eventually did meet with Soviet interrogators sometime in late spring or early summer 1947, although the dates are uncertain.[34] Little is known about these Soviet interviews. Ishii's wife confirmed later that the Soviets met with her husband, but evidently was told little of what was discussed.[35] American Counter-Intelligence knew that representatives from the Soviet Embassy conferred with Ishii, and that allegedly they informed him that "approximately 30 Japanese who formerly served in the 731st Unit and who were with other Japanese units . . . were taken prisoners and are working on a bacteriological research project near Moscow."[36]

Ishii's daughter Harumi remembers that there were two meetings with her father. The discussions took place at the Ishii Tokyo home, and in the presence of American officers. One of the Soviets was a female stenographer. All members of the Ishii family had been warned previously not to disclose the fact that they had been briefed by the Americans on how to conduct themselves with the Soviets. The discussions appear to have followed the pattern choreographed by G-2, except for one embarrassing moment when a family pet monkey showed great familiarity with one of the American officers. The Americans present glanced uneasily at the Soviets to discern whether they noticed this unusual performance. They evidently did not.[37] In the end, the Soviets gained little information from the Ishii interviews. His "secret of secrets" remained secure within the tight little group of Ishii confederates, and subject to sale to the Americans, if the purchase price – immunity from war crimes prosecution – could be achieved.

V

While G-2 kept the Soviets at bay, agents of SWNCC's Subcommittee continued to dicker with Ishii for a complete accounting of Japan's BW programs. It is clear from those documents that have been declassified that by April 1947 Ishii had become the spokesman and principal negotiator with the SWNCC Subcommittee for the Japanese BW specialists. He met frequently also with American visiting scientists and with specialists from G-2. The investigators would have to meet with him at his home and on his terms. He always sat up in his bed dressed in an elegant kimono, and treated his visitors as if he, not they, were in charge of the meeting.[38] Ishii cleverly disclosed a few more BW details at each of these meetings. At the same time, he would indicate that he could provide much more information once he and his men were spared the indignity of a war crimes trial.

His tactics eventually would succeed brilliantly, although his negotiations with the American authorities would drag on for more than twelve months. A Top Secret Operational Priority message from Tokyo in early May 1947 reveals clearly the Ishii technique, and the willingness of American negotiators to accommodate his needs. This 6 May dispatch[39] contains also the essential ingredients for the arrangement that Ishii and the Americans would ultimately achieve.

General MacArthur's people reported that Japanese BW personnel interviewed in Tokyo now confirmed many of the statements made by their BW compatriots who were Soviet prisoners. Three Japanese (evidently Masuda, Naito, and Kaneko) confessed that humans were used in BW experiments. This revelation was "confirmed tacitly by Ishii." Masuda chipped in with the astonishing detail that, in the final days of Ping Fan, he helped destroy there 400 kilograms of dried anthrax organisms. Other disclosures by Ishii were that he conducted at least three field tests against Chinese armies, and that he and others engaged in BW research against plant life. He made "reluctant statements" indicating that "he had superiors (possibly General Staff) who knew and authorized the program."

Ishii then took an offensive tack. He told his interrogators that if he, his superiors, and his subordinates were guaranteed "immunity from 'war crimes' in documentary from [sic – form]," he would describe his program in "detail." Ishii asserted that he possessed "extensive theoretical high level knowledge including strategic and tactical use of BW on defense and offense, backed by some research on best BW agents to employ by geographical areas of Far East, and the use of BW in cold climates."

G-2 observed in the 6 May dispatch that the information Ishii and others disclosed thus far came about as the result of "persuasion, exploitation of Japanese fear of USSR, and [the] desire to cooperate with US."[40] Intelligence believed that even more important data, "including most of the valuable technical BW information as to results of human experiments and research in BW for crop destruction," could be obtained by using the tactics of "persuasion" and raising the Soviet specter with "low echelon Japanese personnel not believed liable to 'war crimes' trials." Ishii, on the other hand, had to be dealt with somewhat differently. He would cooperate more fully only if assured that "information will be *retained in intelligence channels and will not be employed as 'war crimes' evidence.*"[41] It was believed that he would not be completely candid with investigators, revealing the "complete story . . . include[ing] plans and theories of Ishii and superiors" without "documentary immunity" for himself and his associates.

The message concluded with an innocent-seeming statement. General MacArthur's headquarters recommended to the Joint Chiefs of Staff the "Adoption of method in Part 3B above recommended by CINCFE." Part 3B included the speculative conclusion that Ishii and others would divulge additional BW findings if their testimony were retained in intelligence archives. It suggested further that such information ultimately placed for safekeeping with Intelligence should not be referred to the War Crimes Tribunals. The recommendation, in effect, if adopted, would assure Ishii and the others immunity from prosecution. Copies of the entire dispatch were sent to General Spaatz, Mr Peterson, General Noce, General Norstad, General Aurand, and General Waitt, for their information. It would appear that none of the individuals informed of this recommendation raised any objection to the proposal.[42]

VI

The State–War–Navy Coordinating Committee in Washington now faced a serious dilemma. The 6 May dispatch stated candidly that BW specialists had engaged in human experiments, and their confessions were tacitly confirmed by Ishii. The Chemical Warfare Service eagerly wanted Ishii's intelligence, but he and his colleagues had "tacitly" confessed to what were war crimes. To clear the air,[43] SWNCC cabled MacArthur's headquarters for additional information. Specifically, the Coordinating Committee wanted to know "what evidence of war crimes is now in possession of US authorities" against the BW experts. Did any of the United States' allies file charges against the men? Were Ishii or any of his subordinates included as potential defendants among "major Japanese War Criminals awaiting trial?"

A typewritten comment found on the bottom of the page of a file copy of the cable noted that the Coordinating Committee could not proceed to consider Ishii's immunity request without further clarification of his war criminal status. In response, the Occupation authorities designated Colonel Alva C. Carpenter in the Adjutant General's Office in Tokyo as the person assigned the task of clearing up Ishii's situation. The note concluded with the observation that "ID [War Department Intelligence Division], Chemical Warfare and Navy working members Committee have been notified of War Crimes Branch's intention to obtain requested information before first conference is called."[44]

Alarmed at the sudden turn of events, Major General Alden Waitt held a telephone conference on 2 June with a member of G-2 (presumably, Major General Charles A. Willoughby) in Tokyo.[45] Extracts of the conversation were typed up for the files, and contained the comment that the discussion emphasized "the extreme value of the intelligence information obtained and the danger of publicity on this subject." Manifestly quoting General Willoughby, the extracts declare that "It is intention of mil[itary] int[elligence] representative on SWNCC subcommittee to recommend that information re B. W. given to us will not be divulged or used in war crimes trials." General Waitt evidently replied, "I consider it vital that we get the information and that secrecy (which would be impossible if war crimes trials were held) be maintained." Waitt apparently concluded the conversation by emphasizing that "The information so far indicates that investigation is producing most important data. It merits all necessary support, financial and otherwise."

Whether Willoughby contacted SCAP's Legal Section is unknown, but the legal staff came into line on the following day, 3 June. Colonel R. M. Levy of the Adjutant General's Office in Tokyo, and Alva C. Carpenter, Chief of SCAP's Legal Section, sent a cable in code to the War Department offering a judicial explanation for not prosecuting the BW scientists. The cable referred to the Japanese BW project as the "Baker William project," and Ishii as "Baker King." The United States was "Uncle Sugar," the War Crimes Tribunal was "Uncle Mike," and Dr Peter Z. King, an American physician who had previously corroborated Chinese charges of Japanese use of BW, was evidently "Easy Zebra."

Cutting through the mumbo-jumbo jargon and code gibberish, the message indicated that Legal Section had developed a working thesis to justify a grant of immunity. The complaints against Ishii and the others in Legal Section's files, Levy and Carpenter argued, were "based on anonymous letters . . . hearsay affidavits and rumors." The interrogations of the many persons involved with "Baker William Project" in Manchuria and China, "do not reveal sufficient evidence to support war crimes charges." The "alleged victims" were of "unknown identity." The charges against "Ishii Baker King," including the claim that the "bacterial war army . . . conducted experiments on captured Americans in Mukden," were dismissed because they came from the Japanese Communist Party. The affidavits of captured Kwantung Army leaders and of Ishii subordinates submitted by the Soviets were discounted because of the source. Legal Section contended, moreover, that even if the statements of BW work were true, the affidavits did "not state that the [Japanese] General Staff intended to resort to bacteria warfare."

The Army lawyers pointed out also that "none of our allies to date have filed war crimes charges against Ishii or any of his associates." Neither he "nor his associates are included among major Japanese war criminals awaiting trial." None of Ishii's men were charged, "or held as war crimes suspects, nor is there sufficient evidence on file against them." Then, in a most revealing comment, Colonels Levy and Carpenter conceded that some of Ishii's superiors were on trial before the "Item Mike Tare Fox Easy (International Military Tribunal for the Far East)," and that a "Peter Sugar" (the International Prosecution Section)[46] in December 1946 pondered the use against them of some of the materials that accompanied the BW accusations.

The prosecutor decided not to proceed because, on the basis of the information then available, "evidence was not sufficient to connect any of these accused with Ishii's detachments secret activities." The message concluded on a note of caution. The War Department should be prepared for the Soviet prosecutor to try to introduce into evidence some of the BW material and accusations submitted to Legal Section, as well as "other evidence which may have resulted from their independent investigation."[47]

During the next two months little if any negotiations took place either in Washington or in Tokyo. There appears to have been slight and unimportant cable traffic between the groups working on the BW problem.[48] In the interim lull, the SWNCC Subcommittee in Tokyo established another working group task force, giving it an assignment to devise a proposal that all concerned parties could accept. In June and July, the task force conferred with individuals responsible for providing advice to the representatives on the Subcommittee, as well as knowledgeable members of the War Department's War Crimes Branch, the department's Intelligence Division, and the Army Chemical Corps. Input was secured from the Office of Naval Intelligence. Personnel in the Air Force Headquarters in Tokyo, and the Air Chemical Office were also consulted.[49] The product of all the conferences and researching appropriate files was a lengthy report, including recommendations for specific action, that was submitted to the Subcommittee on 1 August.[50]

VII

In order to facilitate an understanding of the problem, and consideration of specific remedies, the task force drafted an additional two-page précis or outline that encapsulated the issues and summed up its action proposals. The précis reviewed also previous discussions with Ishii and the others. In a section referred to as "Discussion," the authors stated baldly, "There is evidence that the Jap [sic] BW group did commit war crimes but in commenting on this evidence the International Prosecution Section in Tokyo states that this evidence would need an exhaustive investigation in order to test its trustworthiness." It was emphasized in another "Discussion" paragraph that "The BW information given by the Japanese as well as the information which it is expected they will give is considered of vital importance to the security of this country by both the Chemical Warfare Service and the Intelligence Division."[51]

The working group recommended adopting a proposal that was offered previously in early spring, to place all information the Japanese disclosed in intelligence files. The group confessed that such an action would for all intentions preclude prosecution of the Japanese BW experts. This suggested course of action was proposed, it was conceded, with a full understanding of the dangers involved: "That the Soviets may by independent investigation disclose evidence tending to establish or connect Japanese BW activities with a war crime." It was acknowledged, also, "That there is a remote possibility that the evidence which may be disclosed by the Soviets would include evidence that American prisoners of war were used for experimental purposes by the Japanese BW group."[52] Yet, the working group urged adoption of such proposals because "of the vital importance of the Japanese BW information to the security of this nation."

The report,[53] itself, is a complex and frequently contradictory testament to the difficulty Occupation authorities had in arriving at a resolution of the dilemma posed in dealing with BW experts. The report does not spare the Japanese. It quotes affidavits of participants in human experiments.[54] The authors acknowledge that, based upon the information in the possession of the International Prosecution Section in Tokyo on 27 June, "it is of the opinion . . . Japanese BW group, headed by Ishii, did violate the rules of land warfare."

SWNCC's Subcommittee was cautioned that the Soviets might make public some of the human experiment data in cross examination at the Tokyo trials.[55] Left unsaid, but obvious, was the fact that such revelations would cause acute distress to the American occupation authorities. Most troubling, however, was the recognition by the report's authors that

> Experiments on human beings similar to those conducted by the Ishii BW group have been condemned as war crimes by the International Military Tribunal for the trial of major Nazi war criminals in its decision handed down at Nuremberg on 30 September 1946.

The report notes, without additional comment, that "This Government is at present prosecuting leading German scientists and medical doctors at Nuremberg for offenses which included experiments on human beings which resulted in the suffering and death of those experimented on."[56]

The report, in spite of its own admonishments, urged adoption of an understanding previously negotiated with Ishii and the others. The tentative arrangement was that nineteen BW experts surrender a sixty-page report on their experiments with humans. A twenty-page account of nine years' work on crop destruction was already on hand. Ten Japanese veterinarians were expected to complete a summary of research in the field as their contribution to the deal. A Japanese pathologist would reproduce eight thousand slides "of tissues from autopsies of humans and animals subjected to BW experiments." And, finally, Ishii would prepare a "treatise embracing his 20 years experience in all phases of BW."[57] The American part of the bargain was to retain all this information in intelligence channels, with the further understanding that none of the data would be transmitted to the War Crimes Tribunal.

Arguments to endorse the recommendations were the same as those discussed in earlier exchanges. The working group concluded that the Japanese information was of vital significance for United States BW researchers. The group accepted the thesis that there was insufficient evidence to prosecute Ishii "and/or his associates." Besides, even if such evidence appeared, "The value to the US of Japanese BW data is of such importance to national security as to far outweigh the value accruing from 'war crimes' prosecution." By this time, Ishii and the others had so hoodwinked American investigators that, despite known evidence to the contrary, they truly believed the Japanese data was of great worth to American security needs. The "interests of national security" overrode any consideration of a war crimes trial, because BW intelligence would probably be disclosed in such a forum. Such an action would "not be advisable."[58] The implication, once more, was that public disclosure would assist the Soviet BW program. Consequently, the report urged that the parent SWNCC committee in Washington accept the findings, conclusions, and recommendations.

The SWNCC Subcommittee devoted much time and effort in considering the working group's findings. In early September, the State Department member of the Subcommittee raised serious objections to part of the proposal. He would not approve the suggestion that Ishii and the others be "promised" that the information they disclosed be kept in intelligence channels and not be considered " 'war crimes' evidence." The State Department representative believed that Ishii and his associates could be cajoled into surrendering the information without a written promise. He admonished the other Sub-committee members that such a promise "might later be a source of serious embarrassment to the United States."[59] Still, he conceded, "At the same time, every practicable precaution should be taken" to prevent Ishii's knowledge from being disclosed at a war crimes trial.

State recommended that the occupation authorities, "without making any commitment to Ishii and the other Japanese involved," continue efforts to obtain additional BW information. Such new disclosures should "in fact" be retained in intelligence files, unless evidence revealed at the war crimes trials presented "overwhelming reasons why this procedure can no longer be followed." State's representative concluded his argument with the comment that "even though no commitment is made," the authorities, "for security reasons," should not initiate "war crimes charges against Ishii and his associates."[60] State, in effect, would go along with the Ishii arrangement, so long as nothing potentially embarrassing to the United States (i.e. the revelation that immunity was being accorded war criminals) was documented.

A few weeks later, Colonel R. M. Cheseldine, an alternate member of the SWNCC Subcommittee, presented strenuous objections to the State Department's position. Cheseldine argued that it was evident from the earlier negotiations that "it is the wish of CINCFE [Commander-in-Chief Far East] to make the most expeditious arrangements possible with the Japanese group." In Cheseldine's opinion, the promised intelligence channel arrangement, "is the least possible offer that can be successfully made."

He was aware of the inherent dangers in the proposal. Cheseldine agreed that "this government may at a later date be seriously embarrassed." He and the Army and Air Force members were prepared to take the chance. They

strongly believe that this information, particularly that which will finally be obtained from the Japanese with respect to the effect of BW on humans, is of such importance to the security of this country that the risk of subsequent embarrassment should be taken.[61]

Cheseldine claimed that it was "the considered opinion" of all the officials, "both military and civil," who were concerned with the issue, that Ishii and his colleagues would not disclose all of their information without some firm confirmation that the material would not be used as war crimes evidence. Under these circumstances, he felt no obstacle should be placed in the way of securing the desired data. In a disagreement between those who had some political qualms about the proposed arrangement, and those who believed the Japanese BW human experiments findings to be of great importance, in the final analysis, "the security of the United States is of primary importance." Cheseldine and his Army and Air Force colleagues felt so strongly about the issue that, if the differences within the Subcommittee could not be reconciled, "this paper [should] be sent to the SWNCC as a split report setting forth the conflicting views of the respective departments."[62]

VIII

Further deliberations between Tokyo and Washington appear to have been halted during the rest of the summer and the autumn months. In the interim, Naval Intelligence in early August prepared a report, "Naval Aspects of Biological Warfare,"[63] which offered a detailed analysis of Japanese BW work. The Naval report dealt extensively with human experiments revealed by Ishii and the others. It discussed work on anthrax, including the required "infectious or lethal dose," immunization experiments, and field trials with bombs. The report also considered the host of pathogens tested, the field trials, the extensive work with human subjects, and the causes for the failure of the Japanese BW program over the long term. It concluded its assessment with the warning that "It is believed that, should the surveillance of the Occupation Forces be terminated, Japan could make herself ready for B.W. activity within five years."[64]

In early October, State Department members called for a SWNCC meeting to patch up their disagreement with Colonel Cheseldine and his supporters. It was agreed at this meeting to let Chemical Corps people (the Hill and Victor October inspection tour) investigate the issue. Their task would be to determine "whether CINCFE had made the best possible bargain with the Japanese group." It is known that Hill and Victor returned to Washington pleased with the way negotiations had been conducted in Tokyo, and they may have conveyed their reactions to SWNCC. No written SWNCC record mentions a report by either Hill or Victor. A subsequent 12 March 1948 minute noted that the Chemical Corps people had returned, but that "No further action has been taken by the working group."[65]

By March, the issue was resolving itself naturally. SWNCC sent one of its aides to consult with Chemical Corps members of the working group. He reported that the Chemical Corps people believed the "problem presented by

CINCFE has about solved itself by the passage of time." The Tokyo War Crimes Tribunal was winding up its work by this date. No further evidence would be accepted at the hearings. Thus, the disagreement between State and the others no longer existed. It was true that the trial technically would last an additional six weeks, but the time would be spent in hearing arguments. It could be assumed, therefore, that "for the purpose of the matter at issue, the trial is at an end."[66]

The minute contained two handwritten notations which must be considered for their implications. One reported that the war crimes people on 13 February "have no interest & anything we can devise to resolve matter is acceptable." The other note was that, "I recommend that Cressap [SWNCC's secretary] call mtg of working party to draft cable for MacA – to end that matter was a fait accompli [signed] F."[67] On 11 March 1948, SWNCC recommended that the Joint Chiefs cable MacArthur that the reports of the Chemical Corps experts indicated that "to date necessary information and scientific data have been obtained to your satisfaction." The Committee suggested that Mac-Arthur resubmit his headquarters recommendations concerning placement of BW information in intelligence files and non-prosecution of Ishii and associates, "if and when you consider necessary."[68] Two days later, on 13 March, the Joint Chiefs sent the requested cable to Tokyo.[69]

IX

Ishii, Kitano, Wakamatsu, and the others now were no longer in danger. The Tokyo trials were over. There would be no further prosecutions of war criminals in the Far East, if the Americans could influence such a decision. The Cold War was raging in 1948, and few persons concerned themselves with Japanese war criminals evading justice. Instead, they worried over Soviet expansionism, the Berlin blockade, runaway inflation in the United States and, possibly, the American civil rights revolution.

No one in 1948 was prepared to raise the issue of ethics, or morality, or traditional Western or Judeo-Christian human values in confronting those responsible for the Japanese BW negotiations. The questions of ethics and morality as they affected scientists in Japan and in the United States never once entered into a single discussion that is recorded in any of the minutes, notes, records of meetings, etc., from the initial Murray Sanders Report of November 1945 until the Joint Chiefs of Staff cable to General MacArthur on 13 March 1948. In all the considerable documentation that has survived over the more than four decades from the events described, not one individual is chronicled as having said BW human experiments were an abomination, and that their perpetrators should be prosecuted. The only concern voiced was that of the possibility that exposure would cause the United States some embarrassment, should word of the bargain become public knowledge.

The defense of American conduct was perhaps best expressed in an 1982 document located in the Fort Detrick archives. This Memorandum for the

Record[70] declares that Ishii and the others received immunity from prosecution either because the evidence against them was suspect, or because the Soviet Union would not permit the United States to seek the truth in Manchuria, or because the BW scientists never disclosed any incriminating evidence in the "wealth of material" they supplied the Americans.

Ironically, the memorandum states that "*Scientists in the US program said the information was not of significant value, but it was the first data in which human subjects were described.*"[71] After reviewing all the data provided, American BW experts concluded that "within one year of the establishment of its program (in 1943), the level of US expertise already exceeded that of the team at Unit 731; Japanese weaponry was still crude in 1945." The big problem was that, in order to prosecute Ishii and the others, some exposure of Japanese capability "in addition to US expertise" would have become public knowledge. There would have been little possibility for retaining "such information in US-only hands in such a case." Consequently, "LTG Ishii was thus able to escape prosecution. The Joint Chiefs of Staff and SCAP agreed there would be little gained by such prosecution and deferred, offering LTG Ishii immunity in exchange for detailed information."[72]

X

If the data Ishii and the others provided Detrick scientists were of such little value, some, no doubt, would question the need for granting the Japanese immunity.[73] Why were American scientists so eager to acquire information that even Murray Sanders's 1945 report recognized as representing experiments that were, at least in part, crude and ineffective? Other reports, such as the August 1947 Naval Intelligence paper on BW, came to similar conclusions. The fact is, the Americans were far ahead of the Japanese in BW research and development by the time Japan surrendered in 1945. Still, the Detrick scientists persisted in their determination to obtain the Japanese material.

One hypothesis that appears to be credible is that American scientists hungered after forbidden fruit. They were prohibited by law and a code of ethics that denied researchers access to involuntary human experimentation. Some of the scientists must have believed there was always the possibility that these prohibitions could affect the outcome of their BW research. Japanese scientists did not operate under similar constraints. Drs Fell, Hill, Victor, and many other BW researchers expected that the human experimentation data Japan would provide would supplement or even supplant their own studies. In the end, their expectations were unfulfilled. The data Ishii and the others furnished the United States with were – at best – of minor significance. The cost to the United States in terms of honor and integrity appears to be high in comparison to the worth of the material it purchased from Ishii and the remaining BW specialists.

Military Intelligence must bear some of the responsibility for the ultimate decision to deal with Ishii and the others. G-2's motives are less complex than those of the scientists. Intelligence officers, such as Major General Charles Willoughby, had a simple vision of the outside world. These men were dedicated to the protection and preservation of perceived American interests and security. In the mid- and late 1940s, the gravest threat to the United States appeared to emanate from the Soviet Union. Consequently, Intelligence sought to prevent the Soviet Union from achieving any advantage militarily or in the scientific field over the United States. BW was thought to be of great strategic importance. Therefore, although the Soviets were still formally recognized as an ally, they had to be denied access to enemy BW knowledge, even if such action meant that known war criminals escaped justice.

Germany was occupied by four major powers, and the United States did not enjoy total control of the situation there. In contrast, Japan had become an American satrapy, and United States policy decisions could not be questioned by other countries. Needs perceived by Military Intelligence, or those of American BW scientists, could readily be served in Japan. There was little that America's erstwhile allies could do to frustrate the actions taken by occupation authorities in the island nation.

The prediction that the action taken in 1948 could ultimately cause embarrassment for the United States was later fulfilled. Over the years, countless stories have appeared in the press throughout the world that reported with some accuracy the American bargain with the Japanese.[74] Until recently, official American sources continued to cover up the events or to dissemble the truth. In 1976, Alfred Goldberg, Historian in the Office of the Secretary of Defense, responded to a query by Chinese-Americans that his research indicated "that immunity from 'war crimes' prosecution for Japanese involved in biological warfare was not approved by Washington."[75] Ten years later, the Army's Chief Archivist, Dr John Hatcher, denied that the Army held any files on Japanese BW, or "any files relative to Mukden." Hatcher claimed that "We have no evidence that we ever held any materials from those camps."[76] One half-century after the events, United States intelligence agencies still refuse to release materials that may have some bearing on the issue.[77] The embarrassment persists.

16 Epilogue

From 6 to 10 September 1962, Japan Group I-63 visited Rocky Mountain Arsenal. They were briefed on arsenal activities and were conducted on an orientation tour. The group [included] Colonel Hideo Toyama, Chemical Chief, Chemical Section, Ground Staff Office.
(*Rocky Mountain Arsenal Quarterly Historical Report*, 1 July 1962 through 30 September 1962, p. 2)

After what it called a comprehensive review of environmental risks, the Pentagon has concluded that its research in defenses against biological weapons is virtually free of significant danger to people or the environment . . . . The Pentagon is engaged in a growing program of research into defense against weapons that use biological agents . . . but has forsworn the possession or use of biological weapons. The program, which has grown five-fold under the Reagan Administration, costs more than $90 million a year.
(*New York Times*, 14 May 1988, p. A 9)

Japanese, Chinese, and some Western scholars have over the past forty years studied exhaustively the history of Japan's BW program and the subsequent American cover-up. They have examined the mountains of BW-related documents that still exist in their respective countries. Serious journalists have written extensively on the subject.[1] The British tabloids resurrect Ishii and BW periodically. Television documentaries in Japan and in Great Britain in the 1970s and 1980s popularized the topic. In the mid-1980s, the widely viewed American television programs Sixty Minutes and 20/20 devoted segments of their programs to Japanese BW.[2] And, finally, Japan's NHK Television aired a two-part documentary on Ishii and BW in April 1992.[3]

In spite of the extensive research conducted over nearly one half-century, and the periodic public discussions, nagging questions concerning Japanese BW remain unanswered. Some of the questions cannot be resolved because archival depositories containing sensitive material are still closed to scholars in Japan, the United States, Great Britain, China, and the former Soviet Union.[4] It is safe to assume also that the depositories will remain closed to researchers for some time. Nevertheless, because BW is such a dangerous possibility, certain questions should be raised concerning past and present research in this field, and tentative answers should be considered.

CHINA

Japan's BW program caused greater harm to China and to its people than to any other country. The Chinese first raised the alarm against Japanese BW and

CW attacks in the mid-1930s, and continued to warn the world throughout World War II. In condemning the attacks, the Chinese government promised to exact retribution against those engaging in BW strikes as well as committing other atrocities against its citizens. Chiang Kai Shek's Kuomintang government did conduct a series of war crimes trials in the country's principal cities in the immediate postwar period. In 1945 and 1946, Chinese courts convicted over five hundred Japanese for acts described as war crimes.[5] Those Japanese soldiers and civilians who were convicted of committing inhuman acts against the Chinese were punished severely.

Lt. Colonel Thomas Morrow, the American prosecutor, visited China in April 1946, and returned to Tokyo with information Chinese sources provided him concerning BW atrocities.[6] The Northeast Headquarters of the Nationalist government in Manchuria in January 1947 furnished American intelligence officers with information concerning Unit 100 and the Changchun operations.[7] This new information was added to the growing number of complaints lodged against Japanese scientists who had served in Manchuria, and who were suspected of BW human experiments.

Curiously, the Kuomintang government showed little interest in Ishii or his confederates. They had sufficient data on hand to try some of their prisoners known to have engaged in BW activities. Yet, Kitano "escaped" their clutches in Shanghai. Other leading BW specialists managed to "elude" capture, and returned safely to Japan. There is currently no evidence available that suggests any effort on the part of Chiang Kai Shek's people either to interrogate the BW principals, or to charge them with any crime. The Chinese Kuomintang judge at the Tokyo War Crimes Tribunal never raised the BW issue, even though he was known as a hard-liner[8] when it came to Japanese war crimes.

The Chinese surely were aware of Ping Fan, Changchun, Nanking, and the other camps. Their troops examined the remains of the facilities after Japan's surrender. It should have been obvious to anyone with a minimum of scientific knowledge that terrible atrocities were committed in these camps during the Japanese occupation. In addition, there were many surviving workers who helped construct these death factories. They could have provided sufficient documentation to secure, at the least, an indictment against the leading camp officials. Their evidence was not taken. The camp officials were neither charged nor tried for crimes against humanity.[9]

More striking, perhaps, is the posture of Mao Zedong and the Chinese Communist Party. Hundreds, if not thousands, of communist guerrillas provided Ishii, Wakamatsu, and Kitano with the human material employed in their BW experiments. Many communist sympathizers were also sent to the death factories, where they were subjected to pathogenic experiments and killed subsequently. Mao and his followers were aware of what had taken place in Beiyinhe, Ping Fan, Changchun, Mukden, and the numerous smaller BW satellite camps. They had assisted Soviet troops in liberating these communities in August and September 1945. The local Communist partisans surely informed their superiors of the true purpose of the BW camps. It is likely that the Soviets apprised their Chinese friends of what they discovered during their interrogations of captured Japanese BW experts. Moreover, the Chinese Communist Party recognized that the various epidemics that erupted in and around the death camps in 1946, 1947, and 1948 were connected with activities that took place there earlier.

Neither Mao nor any of his spokespersons raised the issue of prosecuting BW experts. This is somewhat unusual, since Mao and his close associates were known to harbor great resentment against the Japanese. They did not treat Japanese prisoners kindly. They exacted retribution against their enemies whenever the opportunity presented itself. Yet, surprisingly, the indifference to seeking justice for their comrades, the victims of BW experiments, continued even after Mao gained complete control of the country, and proclaimed the birth of the People's Republic of China on 1 October 1949. It was not until December 1950, fourteen months after the PRC officially came to power, that the Chinese Communists called for the prosecution of Emperor Hirohito, "and other high ranking Japanese," for waging germ warfare.[10] And even this obvious propaganda ploy, which was waged during the height of the Korean War, was done in tandem with the Soviet Union and the Mongolian People's Republic.[11]

Current Chinese scholarship is seemingly evasive in dealing with the subject of BW punishment. Most scholars in China familiar with the topic suggest that Chiang's forces were too busy trying to re-establish their authority over the country to make the effort to bring Ishii and the others to justice.[12] They argue, also, that Mao and his followers concentrated on winning victory in China's civil war, and ignored any issue that might divert resources from the struggle.[13] Another equally plausible explanation overlooked by Chinese scholars, however, is one that suggests that the allies of the Kuomintang–Communist warring factions, the United States and the Soviet Union, advised their friends not to raise the issue. Both of these countries had a vested interest in Japan's BW program. Neither country, for their own perceived security needs, wanted Japanese BW expertise subjected to public scrutiny in the late 1940s and early 1950s. As a result, perhaps their Chinese friends accommodated their requirements.

KHABAROVSK

On Christmas Eve 1949, a little more than four years after their capture, the Soviet Union indicted twelve Japanese officers for plotting to employ BW during World War II. The men ranged in rank and importance from the former Commander-in-Chief of the Kwantung Army, General Yamada Otozoo, to a lowly former laboratory orderly of Branch 162 of Unit 731, Kurushima Yuji.[14] A Moscow Radio broadcast announcing the indictment named Ishii Shiro as the chief plotter, describing him as being "well known" in Japan as the ideologist of bacteriological warfare."[15] Ishii, however, was not named as a defendant.[16]

The twelve men were tried in the industrial city of Khabarovsk in eastern Siberia, not too far north from the border with Manchuria. Khabarovsk was an unusual site to conduct a trial which, at least in part, was designed for propaganda purposes. What makes the location even more unusual is the fact that the MVD, the KGB's predecessor, took a keen interest in the trial. It had several subordinates inside the courtroom reporting daily events by telegram to an MVD Colonel General in Moscow. In addition, each day of the trial, four of the trial judges sent by telegram to the MVD Colonel General in Moscow summaries of the day's occurrences. The public was admitted to the trial, and each day's events were witnessed by crowds ranging in size from roughly 1000 to 1600 persons.[17]

The proceedings were held there during a period of extreme tensions between the United States and the Soviet Union over the fate of several hundred thousand Japanese prisoners of war still in Soviet hands. Moscow or Leningrad would seemingly have been a more favorable location to mount a propaganda effort to cloud the issue of Japanese POW repatriation. A show trial in either of these principal cities would have been well attended by the foreign press. Khabarovsk was so remote from the outside world that it would have been extremely difficult for any foreign journalist to cover the story, even if the Soviet government granted permission to visit. As a result, coverage in the West was limited to rewriting Moscow newscasts and reports in the Soviet press.[18]

The trial was conducted over a six day period, 25 December through 31 December. Evidence introduced during the hearings was based on eighteen volumes of interrogations and documentary material gathered in investigations over the previous four years. Some of the volumes included more than four hundred pages of depositions.[19] Each of the defendants testified at the trial, and confessed either to being aware of terrible crimes, to initiating the acts named in the indictments, or to committing the deeds.[20] Their confessions included admissions that they or their confederates killed Soviet citizens, men, women, and children, in large numbers, during the course of BW laboratory experiments and in field trials.[21]

Emperor Hirohito was linked to the BW program. He was accused of having secretly ordered the establishment of the Ping Fan and Changchun installations in 1936. The War Ministry and other Cabinet offices were also tied directly to the Manchurian BW operation. Several brief comments by defendants suggested that Allied war prisoners, including Americans, were subjected to BW experiments. As with Ishii, however, neither Hirohito nor any Tokyo-based high military official was indicted or tried in absentia for their alleged criminal behavior.

In retrospect, the published trial record appears to be a combination of fact and programmed statements elicited from defendants by prosecutors familiar with the techniques made famous in the Moscow purge trials of the mid-1930s. One defendant after another took the stand and "confessed" to whatever they were charged with in the indictment. No one pleaded ignorance, or extenuating circumstances. All accepted guilt, and agreed that they should be punished severely. Defense attorneys admitted to the court that their clients were guilty as charged. All they hoped to do was to secure lenient sentences for the defendants.[22] The court returned a verdict of guilty on all counts shortly after the prosecution and defense concluded their final arguments.[23]

News of the Khabarovsk trial triggered alarm bells within the United States State Department. Lengthy daily dispatches from State to General Mac-Arthur's Tokyo headquarters covered all information available on the proceedings. The dispatches included, as well, "comments" by State Department officers who analyzed the data emanating from Moscow. These comments – once the State-speak jargon was deciphered – were to be used as guidelines in responding to press inquiries about the American position on the trial.

According to State, the initial stories coming from Khabarovsk were a replay of some allegations published by a Colonel Galkin in a 28 July 1948 story in the newspaper *Red Star*. More important, the current charges, and the "terminology" used in the indictments, "suggests opening gun [of a] sensational war crimes trial." The "immediate timing" of the trial, State believed, was a means for offsetting Allied charges, especially those published under General MacArthur's signature, regarding the Japanese prisoners still being held by the Soviets. Although the BW issue did not "remotely" relate to the POW question, the trial could " 'Muddy Waters,' which presumably preferable, from propaganda viewpoint, to total silence this moment re. Jap."[24]

The trial contained long-term implications as well. State assumed Khabarovsk was part of a plan to strengthen the Soviet position when serious peace treaty negotiations with Japan would commence. It appeared obvious, also, to the State Department that the delay until December 1949 in holding the trial was due to Soviet "interest in extracting from Jap tech personnel in their hands all possible info re" BW. State found it "significant" that the Emperor was now coming under Soviet attack, and, although the United States was not involved in the charges at Khabarovsk, "presumably Sov Press will exploit subject in prop[aganda] asserting US now sponsoring same Nation which was capable such inhuman practices."

State anticipated further that the Soviets eventually would "probably" suggest that the United States had acquired BW information "from Jap friends" which would be useful for "employment future war against Sov Bloc." General MacArthur's people were urged to rebut whatever charges were leveled against the United States, by reminding inquisitors that the Soviet Union had maintained diplomatic relations with Japan throughout the period the alleged Japanese anti-Soviet BW experiments and field trials took place, that the nationalities of the victims were in question, and that Soviet jurisdiction was dubious since the alleged crimes occurred in Chinese territory.[25]

The fears State Department officials expressed that the Soviets would enjoy a great propaganda victory from the Khabarovsk trial appear to have been justified. The American Ambassador in Moscow believed that the Soviets had long prepared for a "show trial," and waited to stage it "at opportune moment." The Embassy reported that Soviet citizens were "horrified at brutality Japs in developing such inhuman weapons and was convinced Japs enemy of mankind."[26]

The Soviet press emphasized that not all the BW criminals were on trial at Khabarovsk. It stressed further, according to an Embassy dispatch, that Ishii and the others were "sheltered in Jap by those who dream themselves of loosing on mankind 'load of TNT, Atom Bombs and lethal bacteria.' " The newspapers and Moscow radio broadcasts charged that "US suppressed Sov evidence presented S[T]eokyo trials." They painted a picture of culpability in which there was "Personal implication Hirohito and other members Imperial Family stressed."[27] Most damaging, the Soviet assertions were spread worldwide by both traditional left-wing press supporters and responsible newspapers such as the *New York Times*.[28]

The American response was low key and muted. Officials in Tokyo charged that the trial and its accusations were a smoke screen to confuse people, and to deflect attention from the far more important issue of the missing Japanese servicemen. MacArthur's press people issued a statement that was a simple but ingenious lie. The Associated Press reported that "A spokesman for General Douglas MacArthur's headquarters said today that the chemical section of his headquarters, in a 'complete' search of its files, did not find anything relative to Japanese use of bacteriological warfare."[29]

This statement was technically true, but disingenuous. The Chemical Section was not involved with war crimes investigations, and had little or nothing to do with Ishii and BW. A search of the intelligence files, however, would have disclosed considerable American knowledge of Japanese BW preparations. Several days later, a MacArthur spokesman denied that any American POWs were subjected to BW experiments, as charged at Khabarovsk. He conceded that Japan had done research with animals, "but that there was no evidence they ever had used human beings," and that "no Americans held prisoner by the Japanese at Mukden ever accused their captors of having used them as human guinea pigs."[30] Prosecutor Joseph Keenan chipped in with a denial that his investigators had found any evidence that Americans were ever used in experiments.[31]

The ultimate outcome of the Khabarovsk trial seemingly supported initial American suspicions of the purposes for the proceedings. In 1950, Moscow's Foreign Languages Publishing House issued a one-volume abridged account of the trial's proceedings. The book was translated into several major languages, including English, and has been used ever since as a leading source of information on Japanese BW activities. The eighteen volumes of raw data Soviet prosecutors relied upon in presenting their case, however, are still not available to researchers.[32]

The twelve defendants who were convicted received remarkably lenient sentences, given the serious nature of the crimes they committed. The sentences ranged from a low of two years to a high of twenty-five years of hard labor. No one was sentenced to death, despite their confessions to having killed countless Soviet citizens.[33] All twelve were repatriated to Japan by 1956. The speculation that the twelve divulged to the Soviets all the BW information they possessed in exchange for lenient prison terms cannot be discounted.

BW AND THE KOREAN WAR

North Korea invaded South Korea on 25 June 1950. The United States, under the aegis of the United Nations, responded to the aggression, sending combat troops to the Korean peninsula within days of the invasion. The People's Republic of China eventually entered the fighting as well, but on the side of North Korea. The war soon became stalemated, lasting until 1953, when both sides signed an uneasy armistice that still remains in effect.

Communist China raised the issue that the United States was engaging in CW and BW in Korea as early as 5 March 1951.[34] Similar claims were advanced in May and October 1951.[35] A few months later, North Korea and the People's Republic of China launched a full-blown campaign of BW and CW accusations against the United States in early 1952. The operation was conducted throughout the world, with the assistance of many left wing and pacifist organizations, and lasted until the fighting ceased in 1953. The International Scientific Commission, an agency created by the World Peace Council in March 1952, and manned by leading left wing scientists, conducted an investigation that supported many of the allegations.[36]

In February 1953, the Communist Chinese produced two captured American Marine pilots who alleged they had been given details of American BW operations in the Korean campaigns.[37] A Colonel Frank H. Schwable was reported to have stated that "The basic objective was at that time to test under field conditions various elements of bacteriological warfare and possibly expand field tests at a later date into an element of regular combat operations." Schwable disclosed in his press statement that Flying Fortresses, World War II's famed B-29s, supposedly flew BW missions to Korea from airfields in American-occupied Okinawa. Other captured Americans were prevailed upon by their captors to make similar claims.

Inevitably, the names of Ishii, Kitano, Wakamatsu, and the other BW experts were destined to be connected to the Korean BW charges. They were linked, initially, by a communist news agency, to a freighter that allegedly carried them and all equipment necessary to mount a BW campaign to Korea in 1951. The International Scientific Commission in its 31 August 1952 news conference, and in its lengthy final report that October, placed credence in allegations that Ishii made two visits to South Korea in early 1952, and another one in March.[38] Former Lt. Colonel Murray Sanders, in the mid-1980s, claimed to have heard that Ishii and Naito were flown to the United

States about this time to give lectures on BW at a special camp. The lectures supposedly included detailed information on human testing of infectious diseases.[39] For good measure, the Soviet naval newspaper, *Red Fleet*, claimed that General MacArthur dispatched eighteen Japanese BW specialists to the United States in 1946. They were sent there to "carry out experiments in "numerous laboratories and institutes of America."[40]

The American authorities repudiated all allegations of the use of BW in Korea. They denied, as well, the charges of postwar Japanese–United States cooperation in BW developments. General Matthew Ridgeway, United Nations Commander in Korea, denounced the initial charges as early as May 1951. He accused the Communists of spreading "deliberate lies."[41] A few days later, Vice Admiral Charles Turner Joy repeated the denials.[42] To still the chorus of BW charges, the United States in June 1952 proposed to the United Nations Security Council that the Council request the International Red Cross investigate the allegations. The Soviet Union vetoed the American resolution, and, along with its allies, continued to insist on the veracity of the BW accusations.[43]

In a final effort to quell the charges, in March 1953, the United States, along with fifteen other nations, submitted a resolution to the United Nations General Assembly's Political and Security Committee calling for the establishment of a neutral five-member-nation commission to investigate the allegations. The commission, if established, was to have free access to any persons it wished to interview during its journey to China, Korea, and Japan. The assorted American POWs who confessed to being BW agents were to be transported to a neutral nation for questioning. The purpose of the resolution, as one American stated bluntly, was to make the accusers "put up or shut up." Opposition by the Soviet Union and its allies prevented implementation of the resolution.[44]

The furor over alleged American use of BW in Korea, with or without Japanese BW specialists assistance, abated once the fighting ended there in 1953. The allegations, however, continued to surface periodically over the years. In an 1966 review, the editor of the British publication *Science Journal* indicated that the evidence was inconclusive one way or the other.[45] Five years later, Julian Perry Robinson, Britain's leading BW and CW historian, suggested that "although it cannot be said that the allegations have been conclusively proved true or false by the evidence available," it appeared from other studies that BW had still not yet been used on a battlefield.[46]

A generation later, the charges still stir controversy. In 1989, a British study of Unit 731 supported strongly the theory of United States–Japanese BW culpability in Korea.[47] Chinese experts doggedly insist today that BW weapons created in an American–Ishii-and-coterie collaboration were used in the Korean episode.[48] American experts are equally adamant in denying that BW was used in Korea, or that Ishii and his colleagues assisted the United States' BW program after 1950.[49] Until the Korean War documents currently classified by all parties to the conflict are released publicly, a determination that could end the dispute appears impossible to achieve.[50]

PROJECT 112

Upon taking office in January 1961, President John F. Kennedy's Secretary of Defense, Robert S. McNamara, initiated a survey of Defense Department projects that would give him an understanding of the United States military capability. Approximately 150 studies were undertaken. One, code name, "Project 112," was designed to evaluate CW and BW potential as weapons for "use as strategic weapons and for limited war applications."[51] McNamara directed the Joint Chiefs of Staff to consider CW and BW as a possible "alternative to nuclear weapons." The Joint Chiefs, in turn, established a task force that ultimately recommended a three pronged program of research and development.[52]

One key component of the lengthy report was a Project 112 requirement that the military establish a "Joint Task Force to undertake extra continental testing of chemical and biological agents." The Joint Chiefs accepted the recommendation, and established, under Army responsibility, a new command in spring 1962 to be known as the Deseret Test Center. The Center was located at Fort Douglas in Salt Lake City, Utah, but received administrative support from Dugway Proving Grounds, 83 miles to the west. Since the tests were to be designed to assist all three military branches (Army, Navy, and Air Force), the Deseret Test Center was funded by contributions of the three services. Its basic mission, as outlined by a Chemical Corps directive of 28 May 1962, was to

> prepare and conduct extra continental tests to assess chemical and biological weapons and defense systems, both by providing supporting data for research and development and by establishing a basis for the operational and logistic concepts needed for the employment of these systems.[53]

The test program, which began in fall 1962 and which was funded at least through fiscal year 1963, was considered by the Chemical Corps to be "an ambitious one." The tests were designed to cover "not only trials at sea, but Arctic and tropical environmental tests as well."[54] The tests, presumably, were conducted at what research officers designated, but did not name, "satellite sites."[55] These sites were located both in the continental United States and in foreign countries. The tests conducted there were aimed at both human, animal, and plant reaction to BW. It is known that tests were undertaken in Cairo, Egypt, Liberia, in South Korea, and in Japan's satellite province of Okinawa in 1961, or earlier.[56] This was at least one year prior to the creation of Project 112.

The Okinawa anti-crop research project may lend some insight to the larger projects 112 sponsored. BW experts in Okinawa and "at several sites in the midwest and south" conducted in 1961 "field tests" for wheat rust and rice blast disease. These tests met with "partial success" in the gathering of data, and led, therefore, to a significant increase in research dollars in fiscal year 1962 to conduct additional research in these areas. The money was devoted largely to developing "technical advice on the conduct of defoliation and anti crop activities in Southeast Asia."[57] By the end of fiscal year 1962, the Chemical Corps had let or were negotiating contracts for over one thousand chemical defoliants.[58] The Okinawa tests evidently were fruitful.[59]

THE FINAL IRONY

The near-symbiotic one-half century BW relationship between Japan, China, and the United States produced many ironic twists and turns from the moment Major Ishii Shiro established his first research laboratory in Harbin in 1932. The most recent of these paradoxes concern both Japan and China. It was noted at the beginning of this chapter that Japanese military officers, including an official from Japan's Chemical Corps, were given a four day orientation tour of the top secret Denver, Colorado, BW facility, Rocky Mountain Arsenal, in September 1962. This was at a time when John Love, Governor of Colorado, was denied access to the base on the grounds that research there was too sensitive to be reviewed by unauthorized civilians.[60] The possibilities for speculation as to a new BW relationship between the United States and Japan are infinite.

An even greater paradox is the apparent BW collaboration between the United States and the People's Republic of China. Once deadly enemies who accused the other of engaging in BW in Korea, China permitted the United States, in 1986 or 1987, to conduct a joint testing program in Hubei province, and possibly elsewhere. It is known that Hubei Province Medical University and the American Department of Defense worked with 200 "hospitalized volunteers" suffering from hemorrhagic fever with renal syndrome, and that the initial test results with an antiviral drug labeled "ribavirin" were promising from the military's perspective. And in a final historical irony, Colonel David L. Huxsoll, then the Commander of Fort Detrick, informed a newspaper reporter that Detrick's test program in China began "in response to a Chinese initiative." He stressed also that all research conducted by Detrick was unclassified and was "solely intended to protect people against disease."[61]

Appendices

CHINA[1]

Some Information on Discovered Chemical Weapons Abandoned in China by a Foreign State

One of the most urgent tasks in the negotiations on chemical weapons is to resolve, in a just and thorough way, the issue of chemical weapons abandoned on the territory of one State by another State. In response to requests and proposals by some delegations, the Chinese delegation is now authorized to provide the relevant information in the sections below with a view to promoting mutual understanding and facilitating the work of the Conference and its Ad Hoc Committee on Chemical Weapons.

As is known to all, the Chinese people have in the past been victims of the use of chemical weapons by a foreign State. Even today, the chemical weapons abandoned by that foreign State still cause havoc and constitute a grave threat.

After nearly half a century, such weapons continue to be discovered in China. They have done great harm to the safety of the Chinese people and their properties and ecology. As the foreign State concerned has provided no information on the chemical weapons it abandoned in China, it is impossible to take the necessary precautionary measures when such weapons are discovered, and many injuries have occurred as a result.

Preliminary statistics reveal that direct victims alone have numbered more than 2000. Furthermore, the danger posed by such abandoned chemical weapons to the natural environment and to the safety of human beings is increasing. For example, the lives of more than 2000 students and teachers of Gaocheng High School (Shijiazhuang City, Hebei Province) are now threatened by such abandoned chemical weapons discovered on their campus. The normal teaching activities in that school have since been seriously disturbed. In another instance, large amounts of chemical weapons were discovered in the Dunhua region of Jilin Province. They are situated near the upper reaches of the Haerbaling Reservoir. Most of the weapons, manufactured years ago, are now in a badly rusted and eroded state. Any significant leakage will undoubtedly endanger the lives of the local population and have disastrous consequences for their property and the environment. Such instances have been a source of bitter grievance and serious concern for the Chinese people.

I.   Quantities of chemical munitions and agents abandoned in China by a foreign State

1. *Quantities of chemical munitions*

(1) Discovered but not yet destroyed: approximately 2 million pieces (as most of the munitions are still buried, the exact figure has yet to be verified after excavation).

(2) Destroyed or given preliminary treatment by China: more than 300,000 pieces.

2. *Quantities of toxic chemical agents*

(1) Discovered but not yet completely destroyed: approximately 100 tons.

(2) Destroyed by China: more than 20 tons.

II. Types of discovered chemical munitions and toxic agents abandoned in China by a foreign State

1. *Types of chemical munitions*

(1) 150 mm chemical shells: shells containing a mustard gas–Lewisite mixture and shells containing diphenylcyanoarsine.

(2) 105 mm chemical shells: shells containing a mustard gas–Lewisite mixture and shells containing diphenylcyanoarsine.

(3) 90 mm chemical mortar shells: mortar shells containing a mustard gas–Lewisite mixture and mortar shells containing diphenylcyanoarsine.

(4) 75 mm phosgene shells: phosgene shells and diphenylcyanoarsine.

(5) chemical aerial bombs: 81 mm chemical mortar shells, and chemical munitions of other calibers as well as toxic smoke candles and canisters.

2. *Types of toxic agents*

Main types of toxic agents include: mustard gas, mustard gas–Lewisite mixture, diphenylcyanoarsine, hydrocyanic acid, phosgene, chloro-acetophenone.

III. Geographical distribution of the discovered chemical munitions and agents abandoned in China by a foreign State

1. *Locations where chemical munitions and agents have been destroyed or given preliminary treatment by China*

(1) Fujin County in Heilongjiang Province: more than 100,000 chemical shells (150, 105, 75, 90 mm).

(2) Shangzhi City in Heilongjiang Province: more than 200,000 chemical shells (150, 105, 75, 90 mm) and more than 1,100 kilograms of toxic agents.

(3) Mudanjiang City in Heilongjiang Province: 4 barrels of mustard gas–Lewisite toxic agents (more than 400 kg) destroyed in 1982 by a chemical process. Others are still buried and have yet to be excavated.

(4) Acheng City in Heilongjiang Province: more than 300 chemical shells and 10 tons of toxic agents.

(5) Changchun City in Jilin Province as well as Shenyang City, Fencheng County and other places in Liaoning Province: 10.88 tons of various toxic agents destroyed during 1973–1986.

(6) Cities of Taiyuan and Datong in Shanxi Province. Shijiazhuang in Hebei Province, and Bengbu in Anhui Province: more than 10,000 chemical shells (150, 105, 75 mm) completely destroyed by 1988.

2. *Locations where the relevant information is available but the chemical munitions have yet to be destroyed*

(1) Sunwu County in Heilongjiang Province: 513 chemical shells (150, 105 mm), 4 boxes of toxic smoke canisters, 2 barrels of toxic agents.

(2) Bayan County in Heilongjiang Province: more than 100 chemical shells.

(3) Town of Weijin in the Meihekou region of Jilin Province: 74 tons of mustard gas–Lewisite toxic agents, solidified with lime.

(4) Suburbs of Jilin City in Jilin Province: more than 40 chemical shells (75 mm).

(5) Gaocheng City in Hebei Province: 50 phosgene shells (75 mm).

(6) Hangzhou City in Zhejiang Province: 33 chemical shells (75 mm other types unknown).

(7) Nanjing City in Jiangsu Province: 4 barrels of mustard gas (originally there were 6 barrels but two of them began leaking and were therefore destroyed in 1990 by a chemical process).

(8) Suburbs of Hohhot City in Inner Mongolia Autonomous Region: 3 barrels of mustard gas.

3. *Locations where exact quantities of the buried chemical munitions have yet to be verified*

(1) Dunhua region of Jilin Province. Local historical documents as well as statements of those who helped to bury or transport munitions reveal that

there are more than 1.8 million pieces of chemical munitions in the area. They are mainly chemical shells of 75, 105 and 150 mm and chemical mortar shells of 90 mm, as well as small quantities of chemical aerial bombs and other types of chemical munitions.

(2) Meihekou region of Jilin Province. Chemical munitions abandoned by a foreign state were buried under the railroad tracks near the railway station. They are mainly chemical shells of 75, 105 and 150 mm.

4. *Locations where chemical munitions may have been buried, as revealed by preliminary investigations*

Harbin, Acheng, and Qiuligou regions of Heilongjiang Province: Huichun and Changchun regions as well as Quiligou and Malugou in Dunhua region of Jilin Province.

Appendix B

EXCERPTS FROM THE DIARY OF COLONEL GENERAL YAMADA OTOZOO FOR THE YEAR 1944[2]

1	22 July 1944	Yamada arrived in Changchun and assumed command of the Kwantung Army.
2	26 July	Yamada was briefed by a Major General in the Veterinary Service.
3	28 July	Yamada was briefed by the Commanders of the Veterinary Administration and of the Sanitary Administration of the Kwantung Army. These two men were Wakamatsu's and Kitano's superiors.
4	6 August	Yamada met with Wakamatsu who gave him a report of his activities.
5	7 August	Yamada visited the BW facility in Dalian.
6	16 August	Yamada inspected facilities in Hailar, home of a major BW facility.
7	17 August	Yamada inspected the BW facility in Sunyu.
8	19 August	Yamada visited Ping Fan. He inspected its facilities and was briefed by Kitano over the course of his two and one half hour tour.
9	26 August	Yamada inspected BW facilities at Mudantszian (this is a literal translation of the Russian).
10	29 August	Yamada visited the BW installation at Tsziamus (this is a literal translation of the Russian).
11	9 November	Yamada awarded medals to three medical experts for their research work in BW and in frostbite.

12 13 November Yamada attended a presentation by Kitano in Harbin concerning Unit 731's research with plague and glanders. Kitano later showed a motion picture of his research. After viewing the film, and having a conversation with Kitano, Yamada became ill.

13 7 December Yamada noted that American bombers hit a POW camp in Mukden, wounding or killing fifty prisoners. He commented on the irony of fate.

Appendix C

PENTAGON TO END SECRECY ABOUT POISON GAS TESTS[3]

Responding to pressure from Congress and the White House, the Defense Department did an abrupt about-face today and promised to end the serecy surrounding World War II experiments in which servicemen were subjected to poison gases.

Deputy Defense Secretary William Perry rescinded a secrecy oath imposed on the test participants and said the military would declassify research records in an effort to help those who took part qualify for veteran's benefits.

As many as 60,000 servicemen are believed to have been exposed to varying levels of mustard gas and other chemical agents during the war years to test the effectiveness of protective clothing and treatments as well as the strength of the gas. . . .

After decades of silence, participants have been coming forward in recent years, claiming they suffered chronic health problems because of the tests. . . .

In a memorandum provided the committee, Mr Perry directed Pentagon officials to collect specific information about the experiments by July 31 [1993], including location of the tests, chemicals used, the military units at the sites during the tests, the names and service numbers of participants, and specifics about production of the gas.

The tests were conducted by the Army and Navy in Washington [D.C.] and the states of Alabama, Alaska, California, Florida, Louisiana, Mississippi, Maryland, Utah, and in Panama.

Notes

ACKNOWLEDGEMENTS

1 The custom in China and Japan is to cite the family name and then the given name. I have followed this tradition. Americans of Chinese and Japanese descent accept the European practice of given name preceding the family name. I have respected this method when referring to them in the text.

INTRODUCTION

1 On August 9 or 10, 1945, . . . Commander-in-Chief Yamada took a decision to destroy all the laboratories and valuable equipment. . . . Colonel Kusaji . . .drafted an order concerning the destruction . . . and about the evacuation of the personnel . . . to the city of Seoul (South Korea). . . . The order was the basis on which Lt. General Ishii and Major General Wakamatsu received the assistance of local sapper detachments to blow up and destroy the above-mentioned detachments.

   Materials on the Trial of Former Servicemen of the Japanese Army Charged with Manufacturing and Employing Bacteriological Weapons (Moscow: Foreign Languages Publishing House, 1950), p. 125; hereafter referred to as *Khabarovsk Trial*.

2 Interviews with Mr Feng Tian Min, Mr Zhou Chun-Mei, and Mr Zhao Hua in Hailar, 12 and 13 June 1991; visit by the author to the grave site, 13 June 1991.
3 See Han Xiao, "The Evidence of the Japanese Imperialists' Invasion of China – Brief Introduction to the Ruins of the Japanese Bacterial Factory in Ping Fan," translated by Ms Lu Cheng, *Northern Relics*, vol. 6 (Harbin, 1985).
4 Unit 2646 was housed in Hailar. It was at times called Unit 80. The 26 became an 8, and the 46 became a 0. The segment of Unit 2646 known as Unit 80 engaged in secret biological warfare research; 2646 contented itself with health and sanitary duties. Interviews in Hailar with Mr Feng, Mr Zhou, and Mr Zhao, 12 and 13 June 1991.
5 The preceding account is based upon information provided in interviews by Mr Han Xiao, 5 April 1984, 8 June 1989; Mr Li Mao Jie, 5 June 1989; Professor Li Changshan, 7 June 1989; Professor Sheng Zhan Jie, 7 and 9 June 1989; Professor Yen Pei Ren, 31 May 1989; and *Khabarovsk Trial*, passim.

1 MANCHURIA

1 Ironically, Ming dynasty defenders engaged in a primitive type of BW in a vain effort to halt the Manchu advance into China. A number of towns poisoned water

wells in a futile effort to destroy the invader's armies. See Spence, Jonathan D., *The Search for Modern China* (New York: W. W. Norton, 1990), p. 26.

2 The People's Republic of China frowns on the use of the term today. It refers to the region as Northeast China.

3 Myers, Ramon H., *The Japanese Economic Development of Manchuria, 1932 to 1945* (New York: Garland, 1982), p. 21; Jones, F. C., *Manchuria since 1931* (London: Oxford University Press, 1949), p. 4.

4 Jones, *Manchuria since 1931*, pp. 3–8; Myers, *Japanese Economic Development of Manchuria*, pp. 24–31.

5 Much of this information comes from an interview I conducted with Professor Sheng Zhan Jie of Harbin Normal University in June 1989. Additional information was furnished me by Mrs Helen Bonaparte of San Francisco, California, who conducted oral history interviews with Harbin Russian Jewish refugees over a period of time in the 1970s.

6 Coox, Alvin D., *Nomonhan: Japan against Russia, 1939* (2 vols, Stanford, Calif.: Stanford University Press, 1985), vol. 1, pp. 1–16; Harries, Meiron, and Harries, Susie, *Soldiers of the Sun: The Rise and Fall of the Imperial Japanese Army* (New York: Random House, 1991), pp. 100 (on corruption and the drug trade), 142, 145–146, 149–150, 157 (on bacteriological warfare see: 356, 359–361, 463, 481).

7 Behr, Edward, *Hirohito: Behind the Myth* (New York: Villard Books, 1989), pp. 38–39, 80–81.

8 The preceding account of the Japanese takeover of Manchuria was based on Coox, *Nomonhan*, pp. 1–39, and Hsu, Immanuel C. Y., *The Rise of Modern China* (New York: Oxford University Press, third edition, 1983), pp. 548–553.

9 Coox, *Nomonhan*, pp. 45–49; Hsu, *Modern China*, pp. 550–53.

10 Jones, *Manchuria since 1931*, p. 16.

11 Ibid., pp. 88–89.

12 A considerable number of distinguished German scientists and physicians similarly welcomed the advent of Adolf Hitler to power in 1933 because they believed, correctly, that he would enable them to introduce their theories of genetics into society. They supported the Nazis because they could now expect to rid Germany of socially undesirable and corruptive elements such as Jews, Gypsies, the mentally and physically handicapped, and sexual deviants. See Benno Müller-Hill's brilliant study, *Murderous Science*, (translated by George R. Fraser, Oxford: Oxford University Press, 1988).

13 Tsuneishi Kei-ichi, *The Germ Warfare Unit That Disappeared: Kwantung Army's 731st Unit* (Tokyo Kai-mei-sha Publishers, 1981), p. 8 in the English translation kindly furnished me by Mr Norman Covert. All citations hereafter are from the English translation, and the title will be cited as *The Germ Warfare Unit That Disappeared*.

14 ibid., p. 8

15 ibid.

16 ibid., pp. 33–34.

17 See the discussion in Brackman, Arnold C., *The Other Nuremberg: The Untold Story of the Tokyo War Crimes Trials* (New York: William Morrow, 1987), pp. 192–200, and in Harries and Harries, *Soldiers of the Sun*, pp. 243–246.

2 MAJOR ISHII SHIRO COMES TO MANCHURIA

1 The account of the Beiyinhe facility is based on an interview I conducted with Mr Han Xiao, Deputy Director of the Unit 731 Memorial Museum in Ping Fan, Manchuria, 8 June 1989, and the following publications: Han Xiao and Zhou Deli, "Record of Actual Events of the Bacterial Factory in Ping Fan," *People's China*, vol. 3 (1971), translated by Ms Wang Qing Ling; Han Xiao, "Bacterial Factory in

Beiyinhe, Zhong Ma City," *Harbin Historical Chronicle*, vol. 1 (1984), pp. 80–83, translated by Ms Lu Cheng; Dong Zhen Yu, "Kwantung Army Number 731," *Historical Material on Jilin History*, ed. by Jilin Branch of the Committee on Culture and History (Changchun), 1987, pp. 47–77, translated by Ms Wang Qing Ling.

2 The Chinese authorities are a little hazy on the exact date.

3 Quoted in Dong, "Kwantung Army Number 731."

4 Harris, Robert, and Paxton, Jeremy, *A Higher Form of Killing: The Secret Story of Chemical and Biological Warfare* (New York: Hill and Wang, 1982), p. 82.

5 Williams, Peter, and Wallace, David, *Unit 731: The Japanese Army's Secret of Secrets* (London: Hodder and Stoughton, 1989), p. 5.

6 Han Wei, "Factual Account of Japanese Bacteriological Killing," *Historical Material on Jilin History*, Jilin Branch of the Committee on Culture and History, (Changchun), 1987, pp. 1–11. This article was translated from the Chinese by Ms Qing Ling Wang.

7 Morimura, Seiichi, *The Devil's Gluttony*, (Tokyo: Kadokawa Shoten, Tokyo, 1983), vol. 1, p. 249.

8 See Tsuneishi,Kei-ichi, "C. Koizumi: As a Promoter of the Ministry of Health and Welfare and an Originator of the BCW Research Program," *Historia Scientarium*, No. 26 (Tokyo, 1984), pp. 97–98.

9 Telephone interview with Dr Shuichi Kato, Professor of Medicine, University of California, Davis, 6 March 1989.

10 Thompson, Arvo T., "Report on Japanese Biological Warfare (BW) Activities, 31 May 1946," Army Service Forces, Camp Detrick, Frederick, Md., p. 2, Fort Detrick Library Archives. Hereafter referred to as the Thompson Report.

11 Morimura, *Devil's Gluttony*, vol. 1, pp. 250–254.

12 ibid., p. 254.

13 Williams and Wallace, *Unit 731*, pp. 5–6.

14 Tsuneishi, Kei'ichi, and Asano, Tomizo, *The Bacteriological Warfare Unit and the Suicide of Two Physicians* (Tokyo: Shincho-Sha Publishing Co., 1982), p. 132. All citations are from an English translation kindly furnished me by Mr Norman Covert, Public Affairs Officer, Fort Detrick, Frederick, Md.

15 ibid.

16 Handwritten translator's notes of an unidentified microbiologist's testimony to American interrogators during the post-1945 Occupation. The note does not bear a date nor a specific locale, but, presumably, the microbiologist was questioned in Tokyo. See document entitled "Ishii, Shiro, Lt General (Medical Officer)," Record Group 331, Box 1434, folder 13, National Archives.

17 Kyoto Imperial University in the 1920s and 1930s was in a position analogous to post World War II British "red-brick" universities and American state universities.

18 Tsuneishi and Asano, *Suicide of Two Physicians,* p. 138.

19 ibid., p. 47.

20 BW will be cited in place of biological warfare throughout this study. CW will substitute for chemical warfare.

21 Quoted in Tsuneishi and Asano, *Suicide of Two Physicians*, p. 48.

22 ibid., p. 48.

23 Thompson Report, p. 2.

24 Quoted in Tsuneishi and Asano, *Suicide of Two Physicians*, p. 48.

25 ibid., pp. 48–49; "Naval Aspects of Biological Warfare," 5 August 1947, p. 84, transcript copy, Record Group 330, National Archives.

26 Quoted in Tsuneishi and Asano, *Suicide of Two Physicians*, pp. 16, 49.

27 See Moon, John Ellis van Courtland, "Chemical Weapons and Deterrence: The World War II Experience," *International Security* (spring 1984), vol. 8, No. 4, pp. 25–30; Moon, John Ellis van Courtland, "In the Shadow of Ypres: The Chemical

Warfare Dilemma," *The Harrod Lecture Series* (Fitchburg, Mass.: Fitchburg State College Press, 1988–1989), vol. X, pp. 43–52; Tanaka, Yuki, "Poison Gas: The Story Japan Would Like to Forget," *Bulletin of Atomic Scientists*, October 1988, pp. 10–19.

28 Quoted in Tsuneishi, *The Germ Warfare Unit That Disappeared*, p. 11.
29 Tsuneishi and Asano, *Suicide of Two Physicians*, pp. 2–49; Williams and Wallace, *Unit 731*, pp. 8–9.
30 Quoted in Tsuneishi and Asano, *"Suicide of Two Physicians*, p. 49.
31 Tsuneishi, *The Germ Warfare Unit That Disappeared*, pp. 23–25.
32 Quoted ibid., pp. 50–51.
33 ibid., p. 131.

3 BEIYINHE BACTERIA FACTORY

1 Interrogation of General Umezu Yoshijiro by Lt. Colonel Murray Sanders and a Lt. Young, 9 November 1945, Record Group 331, Allied Operational and Occupation Headquarters, SCAP, AG Section, TSC Files, "385," Record Group 331, National Archives.
2 Edward Behr in *Hirohito*, p. 57, implies that Emperor Hirohito supplied Ishii with start-up funds from a secret account that he personally controlled.
3 Tsuneishi and Asano, *Suicide of Two Physicians*, p. 50; various entries in postwar interrogation of Japanese scientists and staff connected with Ishii's BW efforts, National Archives; interview with John W. Powell, Jr, in San Francisco, Cal., 21 February 1989.
4 Some of these streets still exist today in Harbin's waterfront district, and are depressingly grim in appearance.
5 *The Jewish Life, Harbin: A Jewish People's Weekly Magazine*, 2 August 1940, p. 1.
6 Japanese occupation authorities classified Harbin as a "Special City." In 1934 the city encompassed an area of 934 square kilometers. and a population of 404,797 persons. Officially, only 3356 Japanese nationals resided in Harbin. See *The Manchukuo Year Book, 1934* (Tokyo, 1934), p. 21.
7 Interview with Mr Han Xiao, Deputy Director of the Ping Fan Museum, 8 June 1989; interview with Mr Sheng Zhan Jie, Section Head of English, Department of Foreign Languages, Harbin Normal University, 7, 8, 9, 10 June 1989; interview with Mr Wen Ye, Director of the Museum of the Martyrs, Harbin, 9 June 1989. I am indebted to Mr Sheng for his great help to me. Mr Sheng possesses an extraordinary knowledge of the history of his beloved city, knowledge which he shared generously with me.
8 Han Xiao, "Bacterial Factory in Beiyinhe, Zhong Ma City," passim.
9 Dong Zhen Yu, "Kwantung Army Number 731," passim.
10 Doc. 9306, typescript copy, "Statement of Major Karasawa Tomio," p. 10, Record Group 331, National Archives.
11 Segment 36, in "The Night of Shock: The Last Will and Testament of a General: The Diary of General Endo Saburo," *Mainichi Shimbun* (Tokyo), 21 December 1982, translated by Ms Reicko Rose.
12 ibid.
13 Undated memo published in segment 38, "The Footprints of War," ibid.
14 Han, "Bacterial Factory in Beiyinhe, Zhong Ma City," passim.
15 Quoted in Morimura, *Devil's Gluttony*, vol. 3.
16 Han Xiao originally concluded that the prison riot took place in 1936, but in a letter to the author dated 25 November 1989, he revised his account, and now believes the riot occurred two years earlier.

4 PING FAN: THE FIRST PHASE

1 Thompson Report, p. 2.
2 Behr, *Hirohito* pp. 163–167.
3 Williams and Wallace, *Unit 731*, pp. 10–11; Morimura, *Devil's Gluttony*, vol. 1, passim.
4 Quoted in Tsuneishi, *The Germ Warfare Unit That Disappeared*, pp. 29–30.
5 Behr, *Hirohito*, p. 164; Williams and Wallace, *Unit 731*, p. 11.
6 ibid.
7 One xiang equals 1.2 acres. See Myers, *Japanese Economic Development of Manchuria*, pp. 80, 84.
8 See Han and Zhou, "Record of Actual Events of The Bacteriological Factory in Ping Fan," passim.
9 See ibid.
10 Li Zhi An, "Brief Account of the Taxation System of Kwantung under the Occupation of the Japanese Imperialists," in Harbin Social Science Institute, eds., *Fourteen Year History of the Japanese Occupation* (Harbin, 1988).
11 Han and Zhou, "Record of Actual Events of the Bacteriological Factory in Ping Fan".
12 There were actually more than 150 buildings at Ping Fan once the facility was fully operational. See Han, "Brief Introduction to the Ruins of the Japanese Bacterial Factory."
13 The headquarters building was restored after Japan's surrender, and is currently used as a High School by the local residents. A part of the building is devoted to a museum of BW relics salvaged from the ruins of Ishii's shattered death factory.
14 "Concerning the Establishment of a Special Military Zone in the Region of Ping Fan", 30 June 1938, printed in *Khabarovsk Trial*, pp. 159–60.
15 ibid.
16 "Naval Aspects of Biological Warfare," 5 August 1947, p. 84, typescript copy, Record Group 330, National Archives.
17 Han Xiao and Yin Qing Fang, "The Laborers in the Japanese Invader Troop 731 Camp", *Historical Records of Heilongjiang Province*, vol. 22 (Harbin, 1986).
18 Han and Yin in their account estimate that at least 1000 workers survived Ping Fan and were released by the Soviets when the camp was liberated in 1945. The authors were able to track down 170 survivors and interviewed them for their study of working conditions in Ping Fan.
19 The previous account is based upon the detailed study of Han and Yin, "The Laborers in the Japanese Invader Troop 731 Camp", passim.
20 Interview with John W. Powell, Jr., 28 February 1989.
21 Interview with Mr Hao Yun Feng, Professor of Welding, Harbin Institute of Technology, 24 April 1984. Mr Hao, a native of the Ping Fan area, was a teenager during Ping Fan's peak period of operation. He barely avoided being drafted to work in Ping Fan before the end of the war.
22 Behr, *Hirohito*, p. 163.
23 ibid., p. 125.
24 Doc. 9305 P.O.W. – The Former Chief Medical Officer of the 1st Army Group of the Kwantung Army. Major General (Med.) Kiyoshi Kawashima. At Khabarovsk on September 12th 1946; Doc. 9309 P.O.W. – Kwantung Army Major General Kawashima Kiyoshi. At Khabarovsk on September 12–16, 1946, p. 2. Typescript copies, Record Group 153, Records of the Office of the Judge Advocate General Army, National Archives.
25 *Hsu, Modern China*, pp. 546–553; Spence, *The Search for Modern China*, pp. 390–396.
26 Its one great independent source of revenue was its monopoly control over the opium trade. Brackman, *The Other Nuremberg*, pp. 192–195.

27 *Khabarovsk Trial*, p. 106.
28 ibid., pp. 104–105. It is possible, of course, that Kajitsuka was programmed by his Soviet captors to implicate Hirohito in the BW program.

5 PING FAN'S VERSION OF HELL

1 Memoir excerpts printed in the Sunday *Mainichi* (Tokyo), 27 January 1952. Editorial comment in *Mainichi* suggested Sakaki Ryohei was possibly a pseudonym.
2 See Chapter 4.
3 A second unit was created by Imperial edict at the time Ishii's unit was formed. This ' unit was called the Military Equine Epidemic Prevention Water Supply Section of the Kwantung Army, and was led by a young veterinarian officer, Wakamatsu Yujiro. Wakamatsu's "scientific research" activities will be discussed in Chapter 7.
4 Tsuneishi, *The Germ Warfare Unit That Disappeared*, pp. 14–15.
5 Tsuneishi and Asano, *Suicide of Two Physicians*, p. 108.
6 Hong Kong's blood-and-guts film industry produced a film in 1989 about Ishii's Manchurian odyssey. As Hong Kong films go, *Men Behind The Sun, The Ishii Story*, is superior to the usual Kung Fu sex-and-pornography dramas for which the industry is known. However, the film fails to adequately explain Ishii or his men because it emphasizes unrealistically their evil nature. Some of the men may have been evil intrinsically. Most were guilty of nothing more than what Hannah Arendt called the "banality of evil." Although Ian Baruma is mistaken when he criticizes the film's director, Mou tu-fei, for depicting in between scenes "of his ghastly experiments . . . Ishii in a geisha house, giggling as he pours hot sake over naked girls (Ishii did engage in kinky sex in geisha houses), see his perceptive review of *Men Behind The Sun* in *Far Eastern Review*, 2 February 1989, pp. 34–35.
7 Two decades after the end of the war, Dr Akimoto Sueo, age sixty-eight, ruefully confessed that he served in Unit 731 in 1944 after graduating from Tokyo University.

> 'Within a month I knew everything. I was in a living hell,' he said. In the quiet of his wood framed Yokohama home today, his two grandchildren playing in the next room, he expressed despair. His head was downcast and he paused at one point to brush a tear from his face. 'I went there believing it was preventive medicine and medical research,' he said. 'I protested three times to my superior. He told me you came here of your own free will. You have no right to go away.'
> (*Washington Post*, 19 November 1976, pp. A 1, 19)

8 Quoted in Tsuneishi and Asano, *Suicide of Two Physicians*, p. 137.
9 Doc. 9306, typescript copy of a Statement of Major Karasawa Tomio, n.d. (1946), National Archives.
10 "Stenographic Transcript of Interrogation of Major Yoshisada Masuda in Tokyo Japan by Lieutenant Colonel A. C. Thompson on February 9, 1946," in document entitled "Stenographic Transcript of Lt. General Masaji Kitano in Tokyo by Colonel S. E. Whiteside and Colonel A. H. Schwichtenberg on 11 January 1946," Document 004, Dugway Library.
11 Quoted in Tsuneishi, *The Germ Warfare Unit That Disappeared*, p. 71.
12 "About Bacteriological Warfare," by Lt. Colonel (med.) Enryo Hojo to the Army Medical School, September 1941, p. 9, English translation of a German translation, Record Group 112, Entry 295A, Box 9, National Archives.
13 The dominant population treated the aborigines with total contempt. Postwar Japanese attitudes remained unchanged from those of the prewar generations.
14 The influx into Japan of Korean nationals in the early twentieth century did not affect Japanese conceptions of racial superiority. Many Japanese viewed Koreans

as social outcasts, contemptible people who should be shunned whenever possible. The newcomers were allowed to work in only the most menial jobs. They were denied Japanese citizenship, no matter the length of their residence in Japan. Second-generation Japanese-Koreans were also refused citizenship in the land of their birth, and encountered a pattern of discrimination similar to what their parents had endured. Even today in democratic Japan, Japanese of Korean extraction face daily examples of racial bigotry.

There are innumerable reports of Japanese racial attitudes, especially with reference to the treatment of Koreans. See, as examples, Dower, John W., *War Without Mercy: Race and Power in the Pacific War* (New York: Pantheon Books, 1986), especially, pp. 7, 12, 18, 33–52; *The San Francisco Chronicle*, 5 August 1988, Part A, II, p. 1; *The New York Times*, 11 May 1988, p. 6; 25 December 1988, Section E, p. 12; 8 October 1989, p. 10; 3 January 1990, p. A 8; *The Los Angeles Times*, 1 January 1990, pp. A 1, 20, 22.

15 The Tokyo War Crimes Trial tribunal took note of prewar overt Japanese racism. Paragraph 2 of the overall war crimes indictment charged that, "The mind of the Japanese people was systematically poisoned with harmful ideas of the alleged racial superiority of Japan over other peoples of Asia and even of the whole world." Pritchard, R. John, and Zaide, Sonia Magbanua, eds, *The Tokyo War Crimes Trial* (New York: Garland, 1981), p. 4. As recently as 1989, a Bangladesh businessman living in Japan could observe:

> The Japanese consider themselves a single race, and they think their society will become dirty if foreigners come in. . . .This attitude is deep in their hearts. There is no proof of it, but if you talk to people you're made to understand.

Quoted in a lengthy article about Japanese racism ("Issue of Japanese Racism Grows with Immigration") in the *Los Angeles Times*, 1 January 1990, pp. A 1, A 20, A 22.

16 Anonymous, "The Brocade Banner: The Story of Japanese Nationalism, 23 September 1946," pp. 49–50, 61, Record Group 319, Publication File, 1946–51, Box 1776, National Archives.

17 Quoted in ibid., p. 69. Taiwan (Formosa) was ceded to Japan by China at the conclusion of the 1895 Sino-Japanese War. The island remained a colony of Japan until it was returned to China at the end of World War II.

18 Clyde V. Prestowitz, Jr., in the *New York Times* Sunday Book Review Section, 18 February 1990, p. 24.

19 Quoted in "The Brocade Banner", pp. 74–76.

20 Quoted in Behr, *Hirohito*, p. xix. See also pp. 112–122.

21 Current Japanese leaders use the term "Japanese uniqueness" to explain Japan's remarkable success in the postwar era.

22 Quoted in Tsuneishi and Asano, *Suicide of Two Physicians*, p. 102.

23 Professor Peter Duus of Stanford University first introduced me to the notion of Japanese racism in his stimulating and provocative summer 1980 seminar on Modern Japan. This seminar was part of Stanford's 1980 Faculty Renewal Program. Professor Duus periodically has continued to provide me with guidance in my attempt to understand contemporary Japan. However, he bears no responsibility for the assessment I offer as a rationale for Ishii's behavior or that of his colleagues.

24 Han Xiao, "Record of Actual Events of the Biological Factory in Ping Fan," passim. See also, Cook, H. T. and Cook, T. F., *Japan at War: An Oral History* (New York: The New Press, 1992), p. 164.

25 Statement of Naito Ryoichi, 3 April 1947, Document No. 29510, General Headquarters, Supreme Commander for the Allied Powers, Military Intelligence Section, General Staff, Allied Translator and Interpreter Section, "Report on Cases of War Crimes and Civil Crimes', National Archives.

26 ibid.
27 Tsuneishi, *The Germ Warfare Unit That Disappeared*, p. 48; "Naval Aspects of Biological Warfare", p. 85.
28 Williams and Wallace, *Unit 731*, p. 37.
29 Tsuneishi, *The Germ Warfare Unit That Disappeared*, p. 48.
30 The structural dimensions of Ping Fan's Square Building, and that of the Special Prison, are to be found in Han Xiao, "The Remains of 'the Square Building' and 'The Special Prison' of Unit 731," *Harbin Gazette*, 1988, Special Issue No. 4, translated by Ms Lu Chang.
31 Han and Zhou, "Records of Actual Events of the Bacteriological Factory in Ping Fang", passim; Tsuneishi, *The Germ Warfare Unit That Disappeared*, p. 49.
32 Han Xiao, "Compilation of Camp 731 Savage Fascist Acts," *Unforgettable History* (Harbin, 1985), translated by Ms Lu Cheng.
33 ibid.; Dong Zhen Yu, "Kwantung Army Number 731."
34 *Khabarovsk Trial*, p. 145.
35 ibid., pp. 19–20.
36 "Notice Concerning 'Special Consignments'," 12 March 1943, printed in ibid., pp. 165–166.
37 ibid., pp. 359–365.
38 The Scientific Research Institute today is the Heilongjiang Provincial Gymnasium.
39 The mansion today is Harbin's Museum of the Martyrs, and mounts exhibitions documenting Chinese Communists' resistance to the Japanese occupation. I would like to express my appreciation to Mr Zhou Ru Yi, curator of the museum, for giving me permission to tour the facility in June 1989.
40 Dong Zhen Yu, "Kwantung Army Number 731".
41 Chinese laborers at the camp were also given numerical designations. They, however, were not destined for the BW experimental laboratories.
42 Morimura, *Devil's Gluttony*, vol. 3.
43 Tsuneishi, *The Germ Warfare Unit That Disappeared*, pp. 32–40.
44 ibid.; Han Xiao, "Record of Actual Events of the Bacteriological Factory in Ping Fan"; Dong Zhen Yu, "Kwantung Army Number 731".
45 Tsuneishi, *The Germ Warfare Unit That Disappeared*, pp. 67–68; Cook and Cook, *Japan at War*, p. 165.
46 Quoted in ibid., p. 67.
47 Quoted in ibid., pp. 26, 46.
48 Ping Fan was fully operational, however, as early as 1938.
49 See Chapter 6. Four units, Linkow, Hailar, Hailin, and Sunyu, all located in northern Manchuria, were established in 1941, and were under the direct control of the Unit 731 commander. The fifth unit was located in Dairen in southern Manchuria.
50 Tsuneishi, *The Germ Warfare Unit That Disappeared*, pp. 49–54.
51 The Thompson Report noted that, at the time Japan surrendered, Ping Fan most probably was staffed by about 35 Army Surgeons, 18 pharmacologists, 25 Hygienic Officers, 10 Technical Officers, 5 Fiscal Officers, 30 Engineers, 3 Army Instructors, 1 Interpreter, 100 Non-Commissioned Officers, 150 Assistant Engineers, and roughly 150 Medical soldiers and civilian employees. Branch offices were staffed by approximately 824 technical and military personnel. These figures, however, appear to be in error. Ping Fan always enjoyed a much larger complement of staff and soldiers than did branch offices. There surely were more soldiers than NCO's stationed at Ping Fan. The figures cited in the text above appear to be more reliable than those cited in Thompson's overall excellent analysis. See Thompson Report, Supplement 2a, pp. 1–2.
52 "Group News," number 280, 1 August 1936.

53 "Article on the Air Operation Conducted on the Day of the Army Surgeon School's 50th Anniversary Celebration," *Army Surgeon Group Magazine*, number 283, November 1936.
54 *Japan Times*, 29 August 1982, p. 12.
55 The Ping Fan museum displays a photograph of Ishii posing in front of his extraordinary vehicle.
56 Doc. No. 29510, General Headquarters, Supreme Commander for the Allied Powers, Military Intelligence Section, General Staff, Allied Translator and Interpreter Section, 3 April 1947, p. 3, National Archives.
57 See Williams and Wallace, *Unit 731*, pp. 286–304.
58 Thompson Report, p. 1.
59 *Khabarovsk Trial*, p. 13.
60 ibid.
61 ibid., p. 39.
62 ibid., pp. 14, 56.
63 Quoted in Tsuneishi and Asano, *Suicide of Two Physicians*, p. 56.
64 The discussion of Ping Fan's infrastructure is based on accounts in Morimura, *Devil's Gluttony*, vols. 1 and 2; the Thompson Report, Williams and Wallace, *Unit 731*, passim., Tsuneishi, *The Germ Warfare Unit That Disappeared*, pp. 47–52, and Cook and Cook, *Japan at War*, pp. 158–167.

6 HUMAN EXPERIMENTS: "SECRET OF SECRETS"

1 Ishii playfully referred to Unit 731 BW human experiments as his "secret of secrets" frequently over the course of his rule at Ping Fan. See *Khabarovsk Trial*, p. 102.
2 Imperial Japanese Government Central Liaison Office, "Military and Biographical History of Ishi[i] Shiro," 15 November 1946, Document 775011, Army Adjutant General's Office, National Archives.
3 Williams and Wallace, *Unit 731*, pp. 73–74; Report of Scientific Intelligence Survey in Japan, 1 November 1945 (hereafter cited as Sanders Report), Record Group 165, G-2 "P" File, Appendix 29-A-a-1, Supplement 1-c-1-4, National Archives; McDermott, Jeanne, *The Killing Winds* (New York: Arbor House, 1987), pp. 127–128.
4 Interview with John W. Powell, Jr, 21 February 1989.
5 Sanders Report, p. 29-C-a-2.
6 Tsuneishi, Kei'ichi, "The Research Guarded by Military Secrecy – the Isolation of the E.H.F. Virus in Japanese Biological Warfare Unit," *Historia Scientarium* (History Society of Japan), No. 30 (Tokyo, 1986), p. 82.
7 Thompson Report, pp. 4–6; Deposition of Ryoichi Naito, 24 January 1947, under the title "Motoji Yamaguchi," p. 13, Record Group 153, Records of the Office of the Judge Advocate General (Army), National Archives; see also Morimura, *Devil's Gluttony*, vol. 1.
8 "Naval Aspects of Biological Warfare," p. 85.
9 In early summer 1945 Ishii issued a decree demanding that all units under his command provide him with a combined annual total of 3 million rats.
10 "Naval Aspects of Biological Warfare," p. 87.
11 One of Ishii's surviving oven cultivators is on display at the Ping Fan 731 museum. Although considered state-of-the-art for the time, the oven is primitive compared to the cultivators available currently.
12 Sanders Report, p. 1.
13 A porcelain bomb is on display at the Ping Fan 731 museum. It is quite crude by comparison with modern delivery systems.

14 Deposition of Naito Ryoichi, 24 January 1947, previously cited in earlier chapters, National Archives.
15 "Naval Aspects of Biological Warfare," p. 89.
16 ibid., pp. 88–89.
17 *Khabarovsk Trial*, p. 286. Anthrax is not naturally transmitted in the fashion described at the Khabarovsk trial, and possibly it cannot infect via this route. The defendant testifying may have meant to name another disease that could be distributed in food. However, it should be remembered that Ishii's group was testing all possibilities shotgun style, and may have attempted to spread anthrax in the manor described above.
18 Lt. Colonel Naito would play an important role in the postwar United States interrogation of Japanese BW scientists. He ostensibly collaborated fully with the Americans. Once freed of the threat of war crimes prosecution, Naito would go on to an illustrious career in the "ethical drug" industry in the three decades after 1945.
19 Thompson Report, p. 17.
20 Dong, "Kwantung Army Number 731."
21 *Khabarovsk Trial*, p. 80.
22 ibid.
23 Han, "Compilation of Camp 731 Fascist Savage Acts."
24 See, as representative examples, citations in footnotes 34, 35, 36, 37, 38, Tsuneishi, "Research Guarded by Military Secrecy," pp. 88–90; see also, Tsuneishi, *The Germ Warfare Unit That Disappeared*, pp. 164–165; Morimura, *Devil's Gluttony*, vol. 3, Chapter 4.
25 Tsuneishi, "Research Guarded by Military Secrecy," p. 89.
26 See Thompson Report, pp. 11–12.
27 I want to thank United States Representative Wayne Owens (Dem., Utah) for his help in enabling me to visit Dugway Proving Grounds in November 1989.
28 Typescript copy, "Dugway Proving Grounds History" (1987), provided by the Dugway Proving Grounds Public Information Office.
29 Edwin V. Hill to General Alden C. Waitt, 12 December 1947, Folder 56–5365, Dugway Proving Grounds Technical Library (hereafter cited as Dugway Library).
30 "Tuberculosis," Interview with Dr Hideo Futagi, 15 November 1947, Document 020, AA, Dugway Library. Futagi's data are unusual, since it usually takes a longer period of incubation for tuberculosis to have an impact on a subject.
31 "Typhoid," Interview with Dr Tabei, 24 November 1947, Document 022, AC, Dugway Library.
32 "Tick Encephalitis," Information Furnished by Drs Yukio Kasahara and Masaji Kitano, Document 019, Dugway Library.
33 Edwin V. Hill to General Alden C. Waitt, 12 December 1947, Dugway Library.
34 "Tularemia," Interview with Dr Shiro Ishii, 22 November 1947, Document 021, Dugway Library.
35 I have been unable to locate fifteen, or possibly more, reports allegedly submitted to American authorities. These documents may still be in other military archives, protected under some cloak of secrecy.
36 *Tulsa* (Okla.) *Tribune*, 29 February 1984, p. 13 A.
37 The Hill memo to General Waitt gives the figure as 401, but a tally of the data in his memo indicates that the correct figure is 403.
38 Only the three autopsy reports referred to earlier are in the Dugway Technical Library. Others no doubt exist, but their location at present is unknown.
39 Hill to General Alden C. Waitt, 12 December 1947, Dugway Library.
40 *Khabarovsk Trial*, p. 57. Kawashima committed suicide shortly before he was due to be repatriated to Japan in 1956. See the NHK Television documentary, *Modern History Scoop*, 13, 14 April 1992.

41 See, for representative statements, Tsuneishi, *The Germ Warfare Unit That Disappeared*, passim; Morimura, *Devil's Gluttony*, vol. 1; *Japan Times* (Tokyo), 1 August 1982, p. 1; and Pitter, C. and Yamamoto, R., *Gene Wars; Military Control over the New Genetic Technologies* (New York: Beach Books, William Morrow, 1988), p. 87.

42 At present, little is known of the Canton operation, except for the unit's designation, Unit 8604 (called Bo Zi in Chinese, or "Wave Unit"), and that it was housed until 1944 on a site that is today Sun Yat Sen University. Information provided me by Mr Han Xiao in an interview on 10 June 1991.

43 The North China Army established Unit 1855 in Peking in 1938. The 2000-man unit was housed near the Temple of Heaven in Peking, and was headed by a Colonel Nishimura Yeni [*sic*], who was a surgeon. Unit 1855 reported directly to Ishii. There is currently no published material in China on Unit 1855. However, a key authority estimates that the unit killed at least 1000 persons in experiments from 1938 until 1945. Information provided me by Mr Han Xiao in an interview conducted on 10 June 1991.

44 At present, there is no concrete evidence concerning a purported BW unit in Shanghai. However, Kitano worked there from early 1945 until Japan's surrender. There are other tantalizing bits of information suggesting a Shanghai BW operation, but at the moment no substantial body of data has surfaced. For Singapore, see the Singapore *Straits Times*, 19 September 1991, pp. 1, 3; 25 September 1991, p. 1; 11 November 1991, pp. 1, 3; and Sidhu, H., *The Bamboo Fortress: True Singapore War Stories* (Singapore: Native Publications, 1991), pp. 160–184.

45 See Chapters 7 and 8.

46 It was previously noted that Chinese authorities discovered a mass grave in Hailar containing more than ten thousand bodies. These people were killed in the closing days of the war. Many came from the BW facility in Hailar. Interview with Mr E. Er Dun in Hailar, 14 June 1991.

47 Han, "Compilation of Camp 731 Fascist Savage Acts;" Levine, Stephen I., *Anvil of Victory: The Communist Revolution in Manchuria, 1945–1948* (New York: Columbia University Press, 1987), pp. 148–150.

48 "Some Information on Discovered Chemical Weapons Abandoned in China by a Foreign State," CD/1127, CD/CW/WP.384, 18 February 1992, English translation from the Chinese, submitted to the Geneva Conference on Disarmament. I want to thank Col. (Ret.) Donald R. Reinhard for bringing this document to my attention. See Appendix A below, pp. 235–238.

49 *Khabarovsk Trial*, p. 371.

50 "*Question*: What germs were tested most frequently on the proving ground? *Answer*: Plague germs." *Khabarovsk Trial*, p. 259.

51 See the discussion on pp. 28, 34, 69–71 for frostbite tests.

52 *Khabarovsk Trial*, pp. 57, 259.

53 Tsuneishi, *The Germ Warfare Unit That Disappeared*, p. 133.

54 *Khabarovsk Trial*, p. 67.

55 Tsuneishi, *The Germ Warfare Unit That Disappeared*, pp. 130–133.

56 ibid., pp. 131–132.

57 *Khabarovsk Trial*, p. 289.

58 ibid., pp. 367–368.

59 ibid., p. 62.

60 Takao Matsumura, "731 Butai No Jikken Hokokusho" (A Report of Experiments Conducted by Unit 731), *Rekishi Hyoron*, No. 538 (1985), pp. 56–64. See also Tanaka, "Poison Gas," p. 17.

61 *Khabarovsk Trial*, pp. 432–433.

62 Tsuneishi and Asano, *Suicide of Two Physicians*, p. 37.

63 Morimura, *Devil's Gluttony*, vol. 3, ch. 4.

64 Field dispatch from Zhen Lian, Hebei Province, 16 September 1937, To President Chiang, etc., in Milton Leitenberg Collection. I want to thank Professor Leitenberg for furnishing me with xerox copies of a series of telegrams from the field to Chinese military headquarters that detailed purported Japanese use in combat of either CW or BW. The telegrams were translated for me by Ms Qing Ling Wang.

65 Telegram from Zhuang Shi Jia, Hebei Province, 16 September 1937, to President Chiang, etc., Leitenberg Collection.

66 Liu An, Anhui Province, 25 April 1938, to President Chiang, Leitenberg Collection.

67 Xian Yang, Shaanxi Province, 1 July 1938, to President Chiang, Leitenberg Collection.

68 Alden H. Waitt, soon to be one of the dominant figures in American chemical warfare research, took the reports quite seriously. See Waitt, Alden H., "Poison Gas in This War," *The New Republic*, vol. 106, 27 April 1942, pp. 563–565; an American military attache in Chungking, on the other hand, doubted the veracity of many of the Chinese reports. He noted in June 1942 that "Japanese have repeatedly used most types [of CW and BW] . . . experimentally but never on a large scale . . . . I estimate many reported attacks merely alibis for forced withdrawals." Telegram from Chungking to Milid, No. 205, 14 June 1942, Record Group 218, CCS 385.5, Japan (6–14–42), National Archives.

69 "Condensed Statement of Information Available Concerning Japanese Use of War Gas, Information Received through Official Sources," n.d. (1946 or 1947), n.p. (probably Tokyo), Record Group 331, no box number, National Archives.

70 Fu Zuo Yi, Shaanxi Province, 24 December 1938, to President Chiang, Xian, Leitenberg Collection.

71 Han Degin, Shaanxi Province, 16 November 1939, to President Chiang, Leitenberg Collection.

72 Wei Zi Huang, Henan Province 3 December 1939, to President Chiang, Leitenberg Collection.

73 *New York Times* 15 June 1942, p. 23. It is known that huge quantities of poison gas were shipped from Japan's CW production center to Ishii's command in 1939 and 1942. See Tadashi Hattori, Hiroku: *Okunoshima No Ki* (A Secret Memoir: The Record of Okunoshima) (Tokyo: Nihon Bunkyo Shuppan, 1963), pp. 3, 87.

74 Telegram "From the President's Office" to Minister He and Deputy Minister Lu, 21 November 1941, Leitenberg Collection.

75 Roosevelt is quoted in T. V. Soong to Generalissimo Chiang Kai Shek, Washington, 6 June 1943, Leitenberg Collection. This statement should have alerted the Japanese that by 1943 the United States was deeply involved in CW and BW research. See Part II, pp. 149–159.

76 Japan and the Soviet Union engaged in a brief, bloody, but inconclusive encounter in an isolated part of Manchuria a year earlier. See Coox, Alvin D., *The Anatomy of a Small War: The Soviet–Japanese Struggle for Changkufeng/Khasan, 1938* (Westport, Conn.: Greenwood Press, 1977).

77 The most authoritative account of the Nomonhan encounter is Coox's two volume *Nomonhan: Japan against Russia, 1939*.

78 Zhukov would soon win enduring fame in World War II for his accomplishments in Europe in defeating Nazi Germany.

79 Coox, *Nomonhan*, vol. 2, p. 919.

80 Han Xiao, "The Suicide Squads of the 731 Troop in the Nomonhan Incident," *Harbin Gazette*, No. 2, 1989. Translated by Ms Lu Cheng.

81 ibid.

82 Tsuneishi, *The Germ Warfare Unit That Disappeared*, p. 40.

83 "Reader's Voice," Tokyo *Mainichi Shimbun*, 1982. Ishii reportedly lost forty of his men to the pathogens they worked with at Nomonhan. See Han, "Suicide Squad."

84 Professor Coox, the leading authority on the Nomonhan Incident, dismisses in a short comment, and in a footnote, the possibility that either the Kwantung Army or the Soviets employed BW in the fighting. He appears to believe that the fuss about BW use in the war was based on "pseudonymous leftist sources." See Coox, *Nomonhan*, vol. 2, pp. 1020–21, 1167, fn. 35, 37, 38. However, the evidence presented by Han, "Suicide Squad," Tsuneishi, *The Germ Warfare Unit That Disappeared*, pp. 35–40, *Khabarovsk Trial*, p. 288, and the Tokyo *Mainichi Shimbun* article is convincing.

85 Han estimates that several thousand Soviet soldiers became ill with one or another of the diseases cited above, and that the Japanese suffered at least 1340 epidemic-related casualties. Interview with Han Xiao, 7 June 1989, and Han, "Suicide Squad."

86 It is known that one field test in summer 1942 backfired on the Japanese. One of Unit Ei 1644's scientists confessed in a postwar interrogation that in June or July 1942 his unit conducted a field test in Central China. Pathogens were dispersed in wells and streams. Japanese soldiers unwittingly drank water from these sources and contracted an assortment of ailments. Many died as a result of their illnesses. This scientist estimated that a large number of Chinese living in the area also were affected by the contaminated waters and died. Telegram from Khabarovsk, number 147 (6), To the Minister of Internal Affairs of the Soviet Union, Colonel General Comrade Kruglov, 4/11 [1946]. I was given access to this material on condition that I neither reveal the source nor quote from the document.

87 Hirsch, Col. Dr Walter, "Soviet BW and CW Preparations and Capabilities" (the Hirsch Report), 15 May 1951, typescript copy kindly furnished me by Col. (Ret.) Donald R. Rheinhard. See Section II, – "Bacteriological Warfare – Research, Methods of Employment and Preparation", p. 104, of this massive 671 page document.

88 The complete text is printed in Tsuneishi, *The Germ Warfare Unit That Disappeared*, pp. 36–37; Compilation Branch, CIS, G-2, Subject: Ishii Shiro, 1 June 1947, United States Army Intelligence and Security Command Archives, Fort Meade, Md.

89 Interview with Mrs Ada Pivo of Encino, California, 7 February 1989.

90 See Chapter 7.

91 Han, "Compilation of Camp 731 Fascist Savage Acts." This may again be one of Ishii's shotgun efforts. Cholera is not spread by injection. Normally it is ingested, because it is an intestinal disease.

92 *Khabarovsk Trial*, pp. 66–67.

93 ibid., p. 286. It was noted earlier that anthrax bacteria cannot be effectively distributed by the method described at the Khabarovsk trial. Ishii was too good a scientist to be taken in by this proposed method. He must have used some other pathogen, which his associate's faulty memory identified as anthrax.

94 ibid., pp. 354–355.

95 Quoted in Tsuneishi, *The Germ Warfare Unit That Disappeared*, p. 148.

96 Chiang was born in a village near Ning Bo in 1887. Spence, *The Search for Modern China*, pp. 276–277.

97 Han and Zhou, "Record of Actual Events of the Bacteriological Factory in Ping Fan."

98 ibid.

99 *Khabarovsk Trial*, pp. 63, 263, 287–288.

100 Williams and Wallace, *Unit 731*, pp. 95–97; *Khabarovsk Trial*, p. 260; Han and Zhou, "Record of the Actual Events of the Bacteriological Factory in Ping Fan."

101 Han and Zhou, "Record of Actual Events of the Bacteriological Factory in Ping Fan."

102 SFE 188/2 (1 August 1947), Appendix "C," p. 9; "Naval Aspects of Biological Warfare," 5 August 1947, pp. 90, 98, Record Group 330, National Archives.
103 On 1 March 1941: Thompson Report, p. 2.
104 ibid., pp. 3, 6.
105 ibid., p. 6.
106 Tsuneishi and Asano, *Suicide of Two Physicians*, pp. 53–54; Professor Tsuneishi appears to be in error on the dates he cites for Ishii. He graduated Kyoto Imperial University in December 1920, entered the Army on 20 January 1921, and was appointed a First Lieutenant in the Medical Corps on 9 April 1921. See Thompson Report, p. 2.
107 Tsuneishi, *The Germ Warfare Unit That Disappeared*, p. 80.
108 Morimura, *Devil's Gluttony*, vol. 3.
109 *Khabarovsk Trial*, p. 68.
110 ibid., pp. 98–99, 103, 277–278.

7 UNIT 100's BW DEATH FACTORIES IN CHANGCHUN

1 The Chinese applied the term "Gypsy" generally to itinerant musicians.
2 Interview in Changchun with Associate Professor Tien Zi Hei of Northeast Normal University, 4 June 1989. Professor Tien is a distinguished authority on Changchun local history. See also Liu Hong Yu, "Where Are You, Old Changchun?," and Zou Shi Kui, "The Old City of Changchun," in *Changchun Historical and Cultural Materials*, vol. 4, edited by the Political Consultants of the Jilin Branch of the Committee on Culture and History (Changchun, 1986).
3 The camp was located so close to Changchun that most authorities refer to it as "the Changchun camp."
4 The camp today is the home for the radiator assembly plant of the Changchun Automobile Factory, China's largest automotive works. The factory produces principally trucks under the brand name "Liberation Truck." In 1952, while clearing the site to begin construction of the factory, workers unearthed an enormous quantity of human and animal bones. Unfortunately, the bones were then destroyed because the simple workers believed they were of no intrinsic or historical value. Interview in Changchun, 5 June 1989, with Mr Song Guang, Assistant Director of the Changchun Radiator Factory.
5 The first decree issued that year established the Ishii Unit and the Ping Fan research center.
6 *Khabarovsk Trial*, pp. 41, 50–51.
7 ibid., pp. 52–53.
8 See the riveting testimony of Unit 100 personnel in ibid., pp. 312–333.
9 Zou Shi Kui, "An Investigation into the Remains of Army Unit 100," in *Changchun Cultural and Historical Materials*, vol. 4 (Changchun, 1986), translated by Ms Qing Ling Wang; interview with Song Guang in Changchun, 5 June 1989.
10 Quoted in ibid.
11 Dong, "Kwantung Army Unit 100;" Zou, "An Investigation of the Remains of Army Unit 100."
12 Zou, "An Investigation into the Remains of Army Unit 100."
13 Dong, "Japanese Kwantung Army Unit 100."
14 Han, "Factual Account of Japanese Bacteriological Killing by Unit 100."
15 In reality, it was not so strange for an ambulance from that hospital to be present within Unit 100's boundaries. Hospital personnel worked closely with Wakamatu's men, and engaged in human BW experiments. For example, in the summer of 1942, Zhao Ren Chang, a known radical, was arrested for being anti-Japanese. After intense interrogation by the police, Zhao was sent to the Changchun Infectious Disease Hospital, where he was confined in a secret cellar within the main building.

One week later he was set free. He was told, however, that plague was present (it was not), and that he would be given an injection of anti-plague vaccine. A short time later he began to cough and spit blood. His doctor later told him that one lung was infected with plague, and he died shortly thereafter. See Li, "Visit to the Kwantung Army Unit 100 Camp. "

16 Li, "A Visit to the Kwantung Army Unit 100 Camp."
17 Mr Li's memory here may be faulty. It would be quite unusual for a pathogen to cause such immediate results. His narrative is not truly consistent with the facts of the disease process, and over time he may have combined several experiences into one.
18 *Khabarovsk Trial*, p. 327.
19 Dong, "Japanese Kwantung Army Unit 100."
20 *Khabarovsk Trial*, pp. 20–21
21 Report by Neal R. Smith, 4 April 1947, p. 7, Record Group 331, Box 1434, 20, Case 330, National Archives.
22 Quoted in ibid.
23 Han Wei, "Factual Account of Japanese Bacteriological Killing."
24 Report by Joseph Martiano, 28 January 1947, p. 3, Record Group 331, Box 1434, 20, Case 330, National Archives.
25 Human experiments were performed as early as 1936. However, the witness was testifying to what he, personally, observed. Other evidence suggests that the witness confined his testimony to the bare minimum of what his interrogators would accept as credible evidence. Many more "experimental materials" were subjected to BW experiments than this testimony confirms.
26 *Khabarovsk Trial*, pp. 322–325.
27 "The Report of 'A'," English translation given to Fort Detrick, Md., scientists in 1948, currently located in the Technical Library, Dugway Proving Grounds, Dugway, Utah. The autopsy reports were discussed in a program in Japan broadcast on NHK Television on two consecutive evenings, 13 and 14 April 1992. Photographs of the colored drawings were aired in this documentary, which was part of a weekly series known as *Modern History Scoop*.
28 "The Report of 'G' ", English translation furnished Fort Detrick, Md., scientists in 1948, and currently located in the Technical Library, Dugway Proving Grounds, Dugway, Utah.
29 *Khabarovsk Trial*, pp. 51–52, 77–78.
30 ibid., p. 77.
31 See "The Report Of 'Q' ", originally on deposit at Fort Detrick, Frederick, Md., now housed in the Technical Library, Dugway Proving Grounds, Dugway, Utah.
32 Interview with Associate Professor Tien Zi Hei, 4 June 1989, Northeast Normal University, Changchun.
33 The Nongan episode is reliably documented by Chinese scholars. The most thorough account is that of Li Ji Xin, "The Plague in Nongan County, 1940," *Historical Material on Jilin History*; (Changchun, 1987). I benefited greatly, also, from information given to me by Professor Tien during interviews I conducted with him on 4 and 5 June 1989.
34 Zou Shi Kui, "An Investigation into the Remains of Army Unit 100."
35 Zhao Pu Qian, "What I Heard about the Bacteriological Army" *Historical Material on Jilin History*.
36 *Khabarovsk Trial*, pp. 382–383.

8 NANKING'S BW DEATH FACTORY

1 Bergamini, David, *Japan's Imperial Conspiracy* (New York: William Morrow, 1971), pp. 3–48. Quotation is from p. 45, fn. 8. Spence, *The Search for Modern*

China, p. 448, reports that 20,000 women were raped, many of whom were killed after being violated repeatedly. He cites the figures of 30,000 "fugitive soldiers" and 12,000 civilians as being murdered by Japanese soldiers during the rampage.

2 Tsuneishi and Asano, *Suicide of Two Physicians*, p. 109. I am indebted to Asano Tomizo and his study of the suicide of Iijima Mamoru for much of the information presented in this chapter. Asano's study, however, must be used with caution. He is overly casual in his employment of dates, and his numerous anecdotes, while fascinating, at times are third-hand reports.

3 Hsu, *Rise of Modern China*, pp. 524, 585–586.

4 Quoted in Tsuneishi and Asano, *Suicide of The Two Physicians*, p. 132. Ishii was so close to Masuda that he took a fatherly interest in the latter's children. Fearing that Masuda's son Kenichi would not turn out well, he dropped in on the family in late 1944 and ordered Kenichi to meet with him. He then proceeded to cajole him about his future, saying, "Look kid, your father is doing his best to serve his country. He's worrying about you because all you do is hang around making nothing of yourself." He then ordered Kenichi to take the medical school entrance examinations, and refused to let him go home until the son agreed to Ishii's terms. See Tsuneishi and Asano, *Suicide of Two Physicians* p. 143.

5 Masuda was a survivor. He collaborated so freely with American investigators in the immediate postwar period, that he frequently was cited in their reports as a "responsible" or "reliable" informant. See countless references to Masuda's 1946–1947 informer career in Record Group 331, National Archives.

6 Poor syntax in the following quotations is due to a shoddy translation of Masuda's Japanese by an unknown United States Army translator.

7 "Japanese Interrogations & Reports, 15 Dec. 42," Document 013, Dugway Proving Grounds Library.

8 Tsuneishi and Asano, *Suicide of Two Physicians*, pp. 128–129.

9 Quoted in ibid., p. 121.

10 Testimony at the Khabarovsk trial suggested that Ei 1644 held jurisdiction over twelve branch units. This figure should be regarded with skepticism. There is no evidence that the Nanking facility possessed the resources necessary to support such a large undertaking. *Khabarovsk Trial*, p. 307.

11 ibid., pp. 107–120.

12 ibid., pp. 308–309.

13 ibid., pp. 32–33.

14 Quoted in Tsuneishi and Asano, *Suicide of Two Physicians*, p. 111.

15 The former private remembered that in a four-month period he was permitted to leave base and visit in Nanking on only two occasions.

16 All statements quoted from the ex-private are taken from Tsuneishi and Asano, *Suicide of Two Physicians*, pp. 120–122.

17 Quoted in ibid., p. 123.

18 Statements taken from ibid., p. 124.

19 There are no reliable figures as to how many pieces of "lumber" were sacrificed at Nanking. But, if one takes the low end figure of twenty humans killed each week, then it is reasonable to assume that at least 1200 persons were killed during experiments over the six-year period that the Nanking BW station existed.

20 Tsuneishi and Asano, *Suicide of Two Physicians*, p. 125.

21 Williams and Wallace, *Unit 731*, pp. 68–70.

22 *Khabarovsk Trial*, pp. 309, 353–355; Williams and Wallace, *Unit 731*, pp. 69–76.

23 Ota, as with Masuda, became a "cooperative confidential informant" to American Intelligence in Tokyo immediately after Japan's surrender. See numerous entries concerning Ota in Record Group 331, National Archives.

24 In fairness, it should be noted that several scientists in Unit Ei 1644 were appalled to learn that they were expected to conduct human experiments. Some tried to desert

the Unit, but were captured and executed. Telegram from Khabarovsk, Number 147 (6), To the Minister of Internal Affairs of the Soviet Union, Colonel General Comrade Kruglov, 4/11 [1946]. I was given access to this material on the condition that I neither identify the source nor quote from the document.

9 BW EXPERIMENTS ON PRISONERS OF WAR?

1 9 August 1985, p. 21.
2 11 August 1985, pp. 1, 4.
3 11 August 1985.
4 12 August 1985, p. 3.
5 I wish to thank Ms Jo Cavanagh of TVS (Television South) for permitting me to view a copy of the broadcast in London on 10 June 1988. Peter Williams and David Wallace were the two principals responsible for the program. Williams and Wallace also collaborated on a book, *Unit 731:The Japanese Army's Secret of Secrets* (London: Hodder & Stoughton, 1989), dealing with the topic. It was published later that year in the United States in a somewhat modified version.
6 The role of General MacArthur in the postwar cover-up of BW activities is discussed in Part II.
7 6 January 1946, p. 8.
8 *New York Times*, 12 January 1946, p. 9.
9 The cover-up of BW war crimes was already underway, and neither Army Intelligence nor American BW scientists wanted Ishii involved in war crimes proceedings. Therefore, he was not placed in the prison holding suspected major war criminals. The American cover-up is discussed in detail in Part II.
10 English translation of a newspaper clipping found in the folder dealing with Ishii located in the United States Army Intelligence and Security Command Archive, Fort Meade, Md. The italics are mine. Ishii was a Lt General at this time.
11 Takeshi Nishimura to CI & E, GHQ, SCAP, 23 August 1946, Record Group 331, Box 1772/330, The National Archives.
12 All quotations taken from "Report by: Neal R. Smith, Fst. LT., Inf., 4 April 1947," Record Group 331, Box 1772/330, National Archives.
13 SFE 188/2 (1 August 1947), Appendix "B," p. 8, Record Group 165, Box 628, SWNCC 351, The National Archives.
14 ibid.
15 Quoted by John W. Powell, Jr, "Japan's Biological Weapons: 1930–1945," *Bulletin of Atomic Scientists* (October 1981), p. 48. The FBI, under the Freedom of Information Act, provided this writer with some documents on Japanese BW. Curiously, the document quoted in Bill Powell's important article is not included. It is housed in Powell's personal FBI file.
16 The documentary was shown in Europe, but not in the United States. However, a short excerpt of the Japanese program appeared in a CBS *Sixty Minutes* segment in 1982, in which Yoshinaga claimed that Americans were used in BW tests.
17 19 November 1976, pp. A 1, A 19.
18 The three-volume novel was sold in one volume editions over several years. Volume one sold more than one and one half million copies.
19 *Washington Times*, 22 June 1982, p. 1.
20 Powell, "Japan's Biological Weapons," p. 44.
21 Powell was one of the United States' Cold War victims in the 1950s. In 1955 Powell and his wife Sylvia were indicted, and in 1959 tried, on twelve counts of sedition and one count of conspiracy. The trial judge later declared a mistrial, and the Powells were never retried. Sometime later, they were charged with treason, but they were never brought to trial. Their only real crime was their effort to disseminate to the American people their unpopular view of the Korean War

effort by the United States. See the *San Francisco Chronicle*, 13 March 1977, p. C 1;
the *Manchester Guardian Weekly*, 8 November 1981, p. 8 and 18 April 1982, p. 8;
Williams and Wallace, *Unit 731*, pp. 259–263, 301–303.

22 4 April 1982.

23 11 January 1982, pp. 108–109.

24 August 1982, p. 62.

25 8 April 1982, p. A 1; Cook and Cook, *Japan at War*, pp. 158–159.

26 House of Representatives Veterans' Affairs Subcommittee hearings, 17 September
1986, p. 45. The popular British television detective mystery series *Inspector
Morse* offered a two-part feature in 1988 in which Japanese BW human
experiments were an important part of the story. In *Inspector Morse and the
Settling of the Sun*, the heroine's father had been subjected to BW tests while a
prisoner of war in Manchuria. The program was shown in the United States in
spring 1990 on the Public Television Broadcasting System.

27 1982 Veterans' Affairs Subcommittee Hearings, p. 20.

28 ibid., p. 18.

29 ibid., p. 18.

30 ibid., p. 19.

31 Williams held a joint press conference with Murray Sanders in December 1985 to
air the BW/POW charges. Unfortunately for Williams and Sanders, the
conference was poorly attended. This press conference received little media
attention. *Washington Post*, 4 October 1987, p. A 12.

32 Congressman Applegate reportedly told Gregory Rodriguez, Jr- off the record –
that he would adjourn the hearing should General MacArthur's name be
mentioned. Interview with Gregory Rodriguez, Jr, Washington, D.C., 11 April
1989.

33 1986 House of Representatives Subcommittee on Veterans' Affairs Hearing, p. 2.

34 Unless otherwise noted, all quotations henceforth are from the 1986 hearing.
Solomon's statement is to be found on p. 2.

35 p. 4.

36 p. 5.

37 p. 16.

38 p. 17.

39 p. 20.

40 Sanders made a similar statement on the British television program "Unit 731 –
Did the Emperor Know?."

41 p. 29.

42 pp. 7–8.

43 p. 8.

44 This is an exact reproduction of the Subcommittee's printed text. The correct
word is Kanji, but Hatcher was the first to admit that he was not a linguist.

45 My italics.

46 p. 9.

47 p. 9.

48 p. 10.

49 p. 11.

50 p. 12.

51 p. 12.

52 p. 13.

53 p. 13.

54 p. 13.

55 "A Veiled Question of Japanese War Crimes," *Washington Post*, 4 October 1987,
p. A 12.

56 "Poison Gas: The Story Japan Would Like to Forget," October 1988, p. 17. Professor Tanaka, however, did not support the charge with "evidence" in this article.
57 13 August 1990, pp. 1, 6.
58 8 August 1945.
59 20 August 1945.
60 For some POWs, their alleged BW experiences became a television cottage industry. Frank James, for example, recalled his wartime experiences on British, Japanese, and American television programs at different times in the mid-1980s.
61 The CIA has yet to process a Freedom of Information Act inquiry that I filed with the agency in October 1988. The FBI provided me with sixty-two pages of insubstantial material in August 1989 in response to still another October 1988 Freedom of Information request. In an exchange of letters in 1991 with this writer, the Veterans Administration denied that it possessed any information concerning the Mukden POWs. Japanese archives that may contain useful BW–POW information are currently closed to foreign investigators.
62 Interviews with ex-POWs Leslie Brown of Tulsa, Okla., Sol Frommer of Las Vegas, Nevada, Gregory Rodriguez, Sr (with the assistance of his son Greg, Jr), of Okla., and Sig Schreiner of Norwalk, Conn. Interviews were conducted in Albuquerque, New Mexico, 4–6 November 1989, at the Annual Meeting of The Bataan Death March Veterans.
63 There is a typescript copy of the Robert Peaty diary in the Greg Rodriguez, Jr, Collection. I am grateful to Mr Rodriguez for granting me permission to use the material in his collection. The Robert Peaty diary will hereafter be cited as Peaty Diary.
64 Typescript copy of Sig Schreiner Diary, 6 October 1942, p. 68. Hereafter cited as Schreiner Diary. The journey from the Philippine prison camp to the ship's dock in Manila was horrendous. Schreiner recorded in his diary, p. 67:

> Oct. 4th–5th – We were told to pack our meager belongings. At twelve midnight we left camp and started marching to the town of Cabanatuan which was about ten kilometers . . . . Some men had to be taken in on trucks as the trip was too strenuous. . . . [the captives were then put on a train] The train stopped at intervals to give the men time to relieve themselves but it wasn't frequent enough as men with diarrhea were hanging out of the box cars during the entire trip. It seemed like everyone needed to get to the doors by the time we reached Manila. Human excreta was splattered all over the place. In the Manila Railroad Station the Filipino Red Cross was waiting to help us. They had medicine and stretchers to take care of the sick but the Japs wouldn't let them near us. They begged with the Japanese officials but the answer was still No.

65 Schreiner Diary, Oct. 6th–10th (1942), p. 68.
66 ibid., p. 69.
67 ibid., Oct. 23rd–30th, pp. 70–71.
68 ibid., p. 72.
69 ibid., pp. 73–74.
70 ibid., p. 137.
71 ibid., p. 78.
72 ibid., Dec. 21st, p. 93.
73 ibid., Jan. 5th (1943), p. 98.
74 ibid., Feb. 4th, pp. 106–107.
75 ibid., Oct. 11th, 1943, p. 198.
76 ibid., Feb. 14th and Feb. 15th, pp. 109–110.
77 ibid., Feb. 22nd, pp. 112–113.
78 ibid., p. 149.
79 ibid., pp. 149–150.

80 ibid., Nov. 15th, 1943, p. 213.
81 In a statement recorded after the war, former POW US Navy Commander John Guidos wrote:

> If you were to ask me how the Japanese treated me while a prisoner of war [in Camp Mukden] I would reply – tolerantly; just tolerantly. What would be the use of going into details and explaining the various atrocities, beatings, killings, punishments single and collective that only the sadistic Japanese mind can conceive. One would listen but probably not believe such things.

("US *Sea Dragon* – Statement of Guidos, John C., CMM., US Navy," n.d., n.p., Greg Rodriguez, Jr, Collection)

82 Schreiner Diary, pp. 159, 160.
83 Interviews with POWs Leslie Brown, Sol Frommer, Greg Rodriguez, Sr, and Sig Schreiner, 4–6 November 1989.
84 Peaty Diary, p. 1.
85 ibid., p. 4.
86 ibid., p. 6.
87 ibid., 23.2.43, p. 6.
88 ibid., 31.12.43., p. 18. In an entry recorded as 19.9.43, p. 13, Peaty commented:

> Everyone was subjected to the "Mantoux Test." According to our own doctors, this test is practically obsolete. Each man also had about 40cc of blood drawn off for a sedimentation test. The doctors say the only application of this test that they know of, is to determine pregnancy.

89 Undated memorandum attached to the diary, p. 3 in copy cited.
90 Roland, Charles G., M.D., "Stripping Away the Veneer: P.O.W. Survival in the Far East as an Index of Cultural Atavism," *Journal of Military History*, vol. 53 (January 1989), p. 79.
91 Quoted in ibid., p. 80.
92 See also the *Tulsa* (Okla.) *Tribune*, 29 February 1984, pp. 1 A, 12 A, 1 C, 3 C, for a detailed account of POW allegations of Japanese human experiments.
93 *Khabarovsk Trial*, p. 268.
94 See typescript copy, Prisoner of War Circular No. 1, Regulations Governing Prisoners of War (War Department, Washington, 24 September 1943), Section VI, Paragraph 66, p. 30, Record Group 112, Manual – Prisoners of War Procedures, National Archives.
95 Memorandum for Colonel Bayne-Jones from Mrs Ruth Hunsberger, 17 September 1943, Record Group 112, Entry 295 A, Box 12, 56 Serological, National Archives.
96 Report on the Testing of Prisoner-of-War Against "X," 23 October 1944, Record Group 112, Entry 295 A, Box 8, 33, No. 161–260, National Archives. Unfortunately, only the first page is in the file box. The report's remaining pages have not been located.
97 Four-page report, no title, 1 March 1945, Record Group 112, Office of the Surgeon General, Records of the Preventive Division, Biological Warfare Specialized Files, 1941–1947, 33, No. 161–260, National Archives.
98 Sig Schreiner Diary, p. 304.
99 These are the figures cited by Representative Applegate in 1985. See 1985 Subcommittee on Veterans' Affairs Hearing, p. 7.
100 Schreiner Diary, pp. 300–304.
101 SFE 188/2 (1 August 1947), Record Group 165, Entry 468, Box 628, National Archives.
102 Peaty Diary, p. 18.
103 Schreiner Diary, 27 March 1944, p. 253.

104 *New York Times*, 22 March 1983, interview with Mr Han Xiao, p. A 2.

10 WHO KNEW?

1 Hereafter cited as Sanders Report.
2 pp. 75–91.
3 For a detailed account of Units 731 and 100 personnel's postwar activities, see the useful discussion in Williams and Wallace, *Unit 731*, pp. 286–304.
4 Sanders Report, Summary, p. 1. In addition to the Sanders Report and the Thompson Report cited below, see the extensive typescript report titled "Biological Warfare, Activities & Capabilities of Foreign Nations" 30 March 1946, Military Intelligence Division, War Department, Washington, D.C., Record Group 165, National Archives.
5 Sanders Report, p. 2.
6 Sanders Report, Summary, p. 1.
7 Interview with Norman Covert, Fort Detrick, 3 April 1990.
8 See Murray Sanders Curriculum Vitae in United States Army Center of Military History Archives, Washington, D.C..
9 Japan did not work closely with its wartime ally, Germany, on BW. However, German scientists concluded, on the basis of a 1941 Berlin lecture by Hojo Enryo, that the military endorsed BW research. Oberkriegsarzt Professor Kliewe, Germany's leading BW specialist, wrote in a memo that since Hojo's written text was given to the Germans in the presence of a representative of the Japanese Embassy, "it has to be assumed that the article reflects the opinion of the Japanese armed forces." Kliewe to Army General Staff/Attaché Dept., Berlin, 17 September 1945, Record Group 112, Entry 295A, Box 9, National Archives.
10 British BW authorities expressed considerable skepticism after reading the Sanders Report. Lt. Colonel J. M. Barnes commented that, in spite of Sanders's efforts, "the report has practically no technical information of value." Barnes noted also that "This report throws little light on the policy of the Japanese Supreme Command with regard to BW." "Japanese Biological Warfare Intelligence, 21.12.45," Record Group 112, Entry 295A, Box 6, 17, WBC – General "M," 61–254, National Archives.
11 Sanders Report, p. 3.
12 Sanders Report, Appendix, p. 29-A-a-2.
13 ibid., p. 29-A-b-1.
14 ibid., p. 29-B-a-1. In an apparent contradiction to Niizuma's claim, the 1946 "Biological Warfare Activities & Capabilities of Foreign Nations," Annex E, contains a photograph labeled "Japanese 'Anti-Disease Suit'."
15 Sanders Report, p. 29-C-a-2.
16 Ishii was in hiding in fall 1945, and was not interviewed by Sanders. Sanders later claimed to have met Ishii at this time, but there is no credible evidence to support the notion. See Sanders interview in Williams and Wallace, *Unit 731*, pp. 121–140; the television program *Unit 731 – Did the Emperor Know?*; and the *Miami*, (Fla.) *Herald*, 7 December 1985, pp. 1 A, 24 A.
17 Lt. Colonel Howard I. Cole quoting Sanders in "Preliminary Report on Japanese BW Investigation," 4 October 1945, Record Group 112, Entry 295A, Box 8, National Archives.
18 See Sanders's comments on Naito in *Unit 731 – Did The Emperor Know?* and the *Miami Herald*, 7 December 1985, pp. 1 A, 24 A.
19 Lt. Colonel Howard I. Cole, "Summary of Information from a Report by a Member of the Staff of the Army Medical College", n.d. (mid-October 1945), Record Group 112, Entry 295A, Box 8, 33, No. 1, National Archives.
20 Sanders Report, Summary, p. 1.

21 Sanders Report, Appendix, p. 29-C-b-1.
22 ibid., p. 29-C-b-2.
23 Thompson Report, p. 1.
24 ibid., pp. 11–12.
25 All quotations in this and the preceding paragraph were taken from the Thompson Report, Summary, p. 1.
26 Thompson committed suicide in 1948. It should not be assumed that there was a cause and effect between Thompson's investigation in Japan and his suicide. According to Norman Covert in several interviews in 1989, there was a high incidence of alcoholism and of suicide among the Fort Detrick scientists during the immediate postwar period.
27 "Biological Warfare Activities & Capabilities of Foreign Nations," Annex H, pp. 2, 3, 5, 6.
28 This topic is discussed in detail in Part II.
29 See the 535-page *Khabarovsk Trial* record published in Moscow in 1950 in an English-language translation.
30 Behr, *Hirohito*, p. 125; Bergamini, *Japan's Imperial Conspiracy*, pp. 323–324.
31 Tojo, reportedly, was such a close Nagata collaborator that he enjoyed the privilege of lighting his benefactor's cigarettes during lengthy meetings with fellow ranking officers. Bergamini, *Japan's Imperial Conspiracy*, p. 324.
32 Tsuneishi, *The Germ Warfare Unit That Disappeared*, p. 162.
33 See *Khabarovsk Trial*, pp. 68, 93.
34 See for example Doc. 9305, P.O.W., Doc. 9309, P.O.W., and memo from CINCFE to War Department for WDGID, 6 May 1947, all in Record Group 153, Records of the Office of the Judge Advocate General Army, National Archives.
35 *Khabarovsk Trial*, p. 11.
36 ibid., p. 39.
37 ibid., p. 93.
38 ibid., p. 292.
39 ibid., p. 94.
40 Tsuneishi, *The Germ Warfare Unit That Disappeared*, pp. 105–110.
41 Tsuneishi, "Research Guarded by Military Secrecy," p. 89.
42 After the war, Oshima served in a number of important posts dealing with preventive medicine. In March 1954 he became Director of the National Preventive Hygiene Research Center within the Ministry of Health and Welfare, holding the position for the next four years. Tsuneishi and Asano, *Suicide of Two Physicians*, p. 112.
43 ibid., p. 130.
44 ibid., pp. 136–137.
45 Typescript deposition of Naito Ryoichi, 24 January 1947, Record Group 331, Allied Operational and Occupation Headquarters, Boxes 1772/330, The National Archives.
46 Typescript "Report by: Neal R. Smith, 1st Lt., Inf., 4 April 1947," p. 5, Record Group 331, SCAP, Legal Section, Investigation Division, Investigative Report #1117, National Archives.
47 See, for example, Dower, John W., *Empire and Aftermath: Yoshida Shigeru and the Japanese Experience, 1870–1954* (Cambridge, Mass.: Harvard University Press, 1979), pp. 112–115.
48 The harshest critics of Japanese policy during this period concede that most members of the Diet were unaware of these activities. See Behr, *Hirohito*, p. 163; Montgomery, Michael, *Imperialist Japan* (New York: St. Martin's Press, 1988) pp. 276–277; Bergamini, *Japan's Imperial Conspiracy*, pp. 677–680.
49 Behr, *Hirohito*, p. 163.

50 Lt. Colonel Paul Rasch to Colonel R. G. Duff, subj: Biological Warfare Activities, dtd 27 Ja -47, in a document headed, Subj: Ishii , Shiro. dtd 9 Jan 47, US Army Intelligence and Security Command Archives, Fort Meade, Md.

51 Montgomery, *Imperialist Japan*, pp. 3, 300, 388, 390, 448–449; Dower, *Empire and Aftermath*, pp. 204–205, 231, 239.

52 It is possible that Kido's diaries were laundered before they were submitted to occupation authorities in 1945.

53 Interview with Mr Han Xiao, 7 June 1989.

54 "Address by Surgeon Colonel Ishii," in "Current Events Tidbits," *The Military Surgeon Group Magazine* (Tokyo, April 1939), number 311. Ishii repeated his lecture to an equally large and enthusiastic group on 16 February, but it is unknown whether Prince Chichibu or other members of the Royal Family attended this session. The content of the lectures was classified as secret. Therefore, it is impossible to determine whether BW was discussed. It should be noted, however, that by 1939, Ping Fan, Changchun, and Mukden were operating at near capacity, and that Ishii's "secret" was widely known in military circles in Tokyo.

55 *Khabarovsk Trial*, p. 440.

56 Williams and Wallace, *Unit 731*, p. 78.

57 Mikasa-no-miya, Takahito, *Ancient Orient and I* (Tokyo: Gakusei Sha Publishers, 1984), pp. 16–17.

58 22 April 1964, p. 3; see also *Japan Times*, 2 March 1963, p. 3.

59 Tsuneishi, *The Germ Warfare Unit That Disappeared*, pp. 73–74; *Khabarovsk Trial*, p. 124.

60 Takeda lost his princely title in the democratization of Japan after 1945.

61 Quoted in Behr, *Hirohito*, p. 168.

62 In 1989, a right-wing Emperor-worshipper attempted to assassinate the mayor of Nagasaki for daring to suggest that Hirohito was partly responsible for Japan's entry into World War II, and its subsequent defeat. See an earlier story on Mayor Motoshima Hitoshi in the New York Times, 29 December 1988, pp. A 1, A 6.

63 Behr, *Hirohito*, pp. 167–169.

64 See, for example, Bergamini's *Japan's Imperial Conspiracy*, and Montgomery's *Imperialist Japan*, passim; see also the TV program, *Unit 731 – Did the Emperor Know*?, and Williams and Wallace, *Unit 731*, pp. 79–80.

65 Stephen Large and R. John Pritchard are good examples of pro-Hirohito British historians.

66 See Grew, Joseph C., *Ten Years in Japan* (London: Hammond, 1945); Robert Trumbull's tribute to Hirohito in the *New York Times* International Section, 7 January 1989, p. 6; John Dower's review of Behr's Hirohito biography in the *New York Times* Book Review Section, 8 October 1989, p. 8; conversations with Professor Peter Duus, April 1989.

67 See the discussions in Reischauer, Edwin O., *The Japanese* (Cambridge, Mass.: Harvard University Press, 1977), pp. 244–248, and Dower, *Empire and Aftermath*, pp. 27–28, 34, 50–54, 121–122, 206, 223–224.

68 *Khabarovsk Trial*, pp. 104, 112, 113.

69 Professor Peter Duus in conversations in April 1989, and Williams and Wallace, *Unit 731*, p. 80. However, Behr, *Hirohito*, p. 167, quotes a member of the Imperial Family as telling him that "the Emperor read everything he put his seal to – he would never use his seal like a stamp machine."

70 The same argument applies for the United States and all other powers. Official documents bear their leader's signature, but the head of state rarely reviews more than a tiny percentage of the texts he or she allegedly signs.

71 Behr, *Hirohito*, p. 52.

72 See Chapter 4.

73 Behr, *Hirohito*, pp. 191–192; see also Kido Kōichi, *Kido Kōichi Nikki* (Kido Diary) 2 volumes, (Tokyo: Daigaku Shuppankai [University of Tokyo Press], 1966 passim).

74 ibid., pp. 42, 89, 167.
75 See John Dower's *New York Times* review of Behr's *Hirohito*, as well as Behr, p. 56.
76 Montgomery, *Imperialist Japan*, pp. 276–277.
77 Bergamini, *Japan's Imperial Conspiracy*, p. 351.
78 Montgomery, *Imperialist Japan*, p. 277.
79 Lt. Colonel Howard I. Cole, Summary of Information from a Report by a Member . . . of the Army Medical College, Tokyo, n.d. (probably 22 October 1945), Record Group 112, Entry 295A, Box 8, No. 1, National Archives; see also "Naval Aspects of Biological Warfare," passim, and "Biological Warfare Activities and Capabilities of Foreign Nations," the section on Japan.

11 THE UNITED STATES BW PROGRAM

1 *The Military Surgeon*, vol. 72, No. 3. Fox's article was deemed to be so significant that it was reprinted in *The Military Surgeon* without change in 1942.
2 For example:

> It takes more than the harpings of the minds of yesterday to scotch the wheels of progress. It may startle many to talk of world progress in connection with implements of warfare. However, it is not believed that any fair-minded individual can deny the place in world advancement that is due to the spirit of conquest. The peaceful shepherd, content to watch his flocks, has added little to the world's knowledge. The trader and warrior have discovered and spread knowledge.

ibid., p. 2.
3 It is known that Ishii read Fox's article. Ishii, however, employed Fox's arguments to support his view of BW, and not that of the author.
4 "Activities of the United States in the Field of Biological Warfare," a Report to the Secretary of War by George W. Merck, Special Consultant on Biological Warfare, p. 4, Record Group 165, Entry 488, Box 182, National Archives. Referred to hereafter as the Merck Report.
5 Steed, Wickham, "Aerial Warfare: Secret German Plans," *Nineteenth Century and After*, vol. 116 (July 1934), pp. 1–15; (August 1934), pp. 331–336; (September 1934), pp. 337–339.
6 Merck Report, p. 3.
7 Cochrane, Rexmond C., "History of the Chemical Warfare Service in World War II (1 July 1940–15 August 1945), Biological Warfare Research in the United States," vol. 2 (Historical Section, Plans, Training and Intelligence Division, Office of Chief, Chemical Corps, November 1947), unpublished "draft" typescript, Fort Detrick Archives. Referred to hereafter as "Biological Warfare Research".
    Cochrane's monograph is the official Pentagon history of American wartime BW research. It was not published, evidently, because higher authorities deemed it too controversial (interview with Mr Norman Covert, April 1990). Cochrane's nearly 600-page typescript "draft" is difficult to use since its pages are not numbered, and essential photographs and appendices are missing.
8 Merck Report, p. 4.
9 Williams and Wallace, *Unit 731*, pp. 91–93; Cochrane, "Biological Warfare Research", p. 6; "Japanese Attempts to Secure Virulent Strains of Yellow Fever Virus," G-2 to Office of the Surgeon General, 3 February 1941, Record Group 112, National Archives; "Digest of Information Regarding Axis Activities in the Field of Bacteriological Warfare," Federal Security Agency, 8 January 1941, Record Group 112, National Archives.
10 Cochrane, "Biological Warfare Research", p. 6.

11 Memorandum for file, Subject: Bacterial Warfare, Visit to Dr Silverman. Office of the Chief of Chemical Warfare Service, Washington, DC, 28 August 1939, Record Group 112, Entry 295A, Box 2, National Archives.
12 Quoted in Memorandum for Mr Bundy, the Office of the Secretary of War, Subject: Biological and Bacteriological Warfare, n.d. (12 June 1944), Record Group 112, Entry 295A, Box 2, National Archives.
13 G. C. Dunham to C. C. Hillman, 13 September 1939, Record Group 112, Entry 295A, Box 2, National Archives.
14 All quotations taken from the 12 June 1944 Memorandum for Mr Bundy, the Office of the Secretary of War, Subject: Biological and Bacteriological Warfare, Record Group 112, National Archives.
15 Merck Report, p. 5.
16 Colonel James S. Simmons to H. H. Bundy, 14 August 1941, Record Group 112, Entry 295A, Box 6, 26 WBC, 61–253, National Archives.
17 Minutes of a Conference on Biological Warfare, 2101 Constitution Avenue, N.W., 20 August 1941, Record Group 112, Entry 295A, Box 6, National Archives.
18 All quotations taken from minutes of Conference on Biological Warfare, 20 August 1941.
19 Cited in Merck Report, p. 5.
20 Bernstein, Barton J., "America's Biological Warfare Program in the Second World War," *Journal of Strategic Studies*, vol. 2, No. 3 (September 1988), pp. 292–293.
21 Quotations taken from Merck Report, pp. 6–7.
22 Stimson to Roosevelt, 29 April 1942, President's Secretary File 104, Franklin D. Roosevelt Library.
23 Undated memorandum with a typescript note that states, "The original of the above was handed by Mr Bundy to Miss Mary Switzer of Governor McNutt's office 9/3/42," Stimson "Safe File" Biological Warfare Folder, Record Group 107, Records of the Office of the Secretary of War, Box 2, The National Archives.
24 *US Army Activity in the US Biological Warfare Programs*, vol. 1, 24 February 1977, Unclassified (n.p., presumably US Army Publications, Washington, DC), p. 1–1. I wish to thank Mrs Carol Levitt, Frederick, Md., for providing me with a copy of this two-volume publication.
25 Frank B. Jewett, President, National Academy of Sciences, to George W. Merck, 16 October 1942, Record Group 112, Entry 295A, Box 6, The National Archives.
26 F. B. Jewett and Ross G. Harrison to Colonel James S. Simmons, 19 October 1942, Record Group 112, Entry 295A, Box 6, The National Archives.
27 Stimson observed in September 1942 that Roosevelt agreed to support the proposal with an initial grant of $200,000. Stimson memorandum (9/3/42), Stimson "Safe File," Record Group 107, Box 2, The National Archives.
28 Frederick was founded in colonial times and retains today a charming eighteenth-century character.
29 Cochrane, "Biological Warfare Research," p. 7.
30 ibid., p. 44.
31 ibid., pp. 44–48.
32 Merck Report, Part Two, p. 7.
33 Cochrane, "Biological Warfare Research," passim.
34 Harris and Paxton, *A Higher Form of Killing*, passim; Robinson, Julian Perry (SIPRI), *The Problem of Chemical and Biological Warfare, Vol. 1, The Rise of CB Weapons* (Stockholm: Almqvist & Wiksell, , 1971), passim; Bryden, John, *Deadly Allies: Canada's Secret War, 1937–1947* (Toronto: McClelland and Stewart, 1989), passim; Hansen, Friedrich, "Zur Geschichte Der Deutschen Biologischen Waffen" (Towards a History of German Biological Warfare), *1999* (June 1989). I am grateful to Dr Hansen for providing me with an English translation of his important article.

35 Much of the research conducted at Detrick remained classified after 1945. Nevertheless, the military permitted Detrick scientists to publish 156 scholarly papers in 1946 and 1947. Scientists were authorized as well to read an additional twenty-eight papers at scientific meetings in the immediate postwar period. Clendinin, Richard M., *Science and Technology at Fort Detrick, 1943–1968* (Fort Detrick, Frederick, Md., April 1968), p. 23.
36 Merck Report, Part One, p. 16.
37 ibid., pp. 16–17.
38 Conversations with Norman Covert in 1989 and 1990.
39 Bernstein, "America's Biological Warfare Program," p. 292.
40 Theodor Rosebury, "Medical Ethics and Biological Warfare," *Perspectives in Biology and Medicine*, 6 (summer 1963), pp. 514–515. See also the news report, "US to Compensate 4,000 Injured by Poison Gases," *New York Times*, 7 January 1993, p. A 11.
41 Bernstein, "America's Biological Warfare Program," pp. 304–305.
42 Leahy, William, *I Was There* (New York: Whittlesey, 1950), pp. 439–40.
43 Undated memorandum on Provisions for Use of Gas in Pacific Theaters, inked notation on page, "1 May 50," Rodriguez, Jr, Collection.
44 Bernstein, "America's Biological Warfare Program," p. 305.
45 The Truman Library is curiously silent on BW issues.

12 DISCOVERY OF THE "SECRET OF SECRETS"

1 In a joint memo to President Roosevelt, Secretary of War Stimson and Federal Security Agency Administrator Paul V. McNutt confessed:

> There is very little positive evidence to indicate what German intentions or capabilities in this field are. No clues were discovered in Belgium or France. It is assumed that security has been very tight but that Germany has made considerable advances in this field.

Stimson and McNutt to Roosevelt, Summary Status of Biological Warfare, 24 November 1944, Stimson "Safe File," Biological Warfare Folder, Record Group 107, Records of the Office of the Secretary of War, Box 2, The National Archives.
2 Digest of Information Regarding Axis Activities in the Field of Bacteriological Warfare, 8 January 1943, pp. 1–2, enclosure in John P. Marquand to Colonel S. Bayne-Jones, Washington, DC, 11 January 1947, Record Group 112, Entry 295A, Box 6, 26 WBC, 61–253, National Archives.
3 Hansen, "Towards a History of German Biological Warfare" (Zur Geschichte der Deutschen Biologischen Waffen), passim.
4 Bryden, *Deadly Allies*, pp. 83, 98, 122–124, 125, 254; Harris and Paxton, *A Higher Form of Killing*, pp. 55, 90, 91–95, 111.
5 H. T. O'Connor, Special Agent in Charge, to Director, Federal Bureau of Investigation, Milwaukee, 14 January 1942; John Edgar Hoover to Director of Naval Intelligence, and John Edgar Hoover to Honorable Paul V. McNutt, Washington, DC, 30 January 1942. All FBI citations are from the first four volumes of FBIHQ main file 100–93216, provided this writer under the Freedom of Information Act. Hereafter this file will be cited as FBI Docs. John P. Marquand was sufficiently impressed with this report that he included it in his 8 January 1943 "Digest of Information Regarding Axis Activities in the Field of Bacteriological Warfare," Record Group 112, Entry 295 A, Box 6, National Archives.
6 San Francisco, Calif., 2/24/42, Possibility of Bacterial Warfare Sale of Typhoid Vaccine to Japanese. FBI Docs.
7 ibid., p. 5.

8 ibid., p. 4.
9 Report from Ecuador, Maldonado, 11/18/42, "Japanese Activities – Ecuador." FBI Docs.
10 By this date, many Japanese nationals as well as Japanese-Americans were being housed in relocation camps throughout the American southwest.
11 Possibility of Bacterial Warfare Sale of Typhoid Vaccine to Japanese, San Francisco, 11-27-42, FBI Docs.
12 J. Edgar Hoover to George Merck, 5 August 1943, enclosing a six-page memorandum, Re: Bacterial Warfare, written 12 June 1942, FBI Docs.
13 vol. 39, pp. 571–572.
14 Marshall Hertig to Charles V. Akin, Lima, Peru, 20 September 1942, enclosing a four-page memorandum concerning BW, Record Group 112, Entry 295A, Box 6, 26 WBC 61–253, National Archives.
15 Undated memo (1944?), "Japanese Biological Warfare," Record Group 319, Records of the Army Staff, Army – Intelligence Document File, ID 919284, Targets – BW – Japan, National Archives.
16 Memo of Colonel O. N. Thompson, Subject: Change in Standing Operating Procedure, United States Army Forces, Pacific Ocean Areas, 3 March 1945, p. 1, Record Group 112, Entry 295A, Box 11, Current Japanese Intelligence, National Archives.
17 Undated (1944?) questionnaire, "Biological Warfare", Record Group 319, Records of the Army Staff, Army – Intelligence Document File, ID 919284, Targets – BW – Japan, National Archives.
18 Memorandum of Brigadier General Clark L. Ruffner (signed by Colonel O. N. Thompson), Subject: Bacteriological Warfare, 15 August 1944, Record Group 112, Entry 295A, Box 11, Current Intelligence – Japanese, The National Archives.
19 For some unknown reason, American intelligence had tended to ignore or play down earlier reports of Japanese BW activities in China, despite independent confirmation by American missionary doctors on the scene. For example, the report of Dr R. Pollitzer, epidemiologist of the National Health Administration, who happened to be in Changteh at the time of Ishii's plague field test there, was ignored, even though he stated that "Circumstantial evidence strongly suggests that plague outbreak in Changteh was caused by enemy action." See also E. Torvaldson to Colonel William Mayer, Changteh, 19 December 1941; W. W. Pettus, M.D., to Colonel William Mayer, Changsha, 20 December 1941; Epidemiological Report No. 1, Presented to the American Bureau for Medical Aid to China, Received 6 April 1942. All in Record Group 112, Entry 295A, Box 12, Plague Incident in China, The National Archives.
20 "Military Intelligence Service Captured Personnel and Material Branch," 27 March 1945, Rodriguez, Jr, Collection.
21 "Military Intelligence Service Captured Personnel and Material Branch," 11 April 1945, Rodriguez, Jr, Collection.
22 "Military Intelligence Service Captured Personnel and Material Branch, Supplementary to Report No. 1861 dated 24 July 1945, pp. 2, 3, 4, Rodriguez, Jr, Collection.
23 See SINTIC Items #213, 214, 216, 217, 12 and 13 December 1944, Subject: Japanese Chemical and Bacteriological Warfare in China, and memo from Colonel Joseph K. Dickey, G-2, China Theater Report, Subject: Bacterial Warfare, 4 December 1944, all in Record Group 112, Entry 295A, Box 11, 54 POW – Jap, The National Archives.
24 Lt. Colonel Harold Fair to the Chief of Staff, 5 October 1944, Subject: Bacterial Warfare, ibid.
25 Memorandum for Major General Norman T. Kirk, War Department, Office of the Surgeon General, Washington, 17 June 1944, Rodriguez, Jr, Collection. The

correct spelling of one of the bombs should be "Tokushu Bakudan;" however, the text uses the spelling employed in the memorandum quoted. Similarly, "Kusho" should be "Kushu," but the memorandum's author used the word as quoted in the text.

26 Extract from ATIS SWPA Bulletin Preliminary Examination of Doc. No. 1638, 20 December 1944. Rodriguez, Jr, Collection.

27 Headquarters United States Army Forces, Pacific Ocean Areas, Office of the Commanding General, 29 September 1944, Subject: Absence of evidence of Japanese B.W. activity on Saipan and Guam, Record Group 112, Entry 295 A, Box 11, 47, Current Intelligence – Japanese, The National Archives.

28 There evidently was little cooperation between German BW researchers and their Japanese counterparts. German BW scientists, such as Professor H. Kliewe, nominal head of Germany's BW program, expressed genuine astonishment in 1945 and 1946 concerning the extent of Japan's BW activities, when they were interrogated by their American captors. See the Kliewe file in National Archives.

29 Hojo's thirty-seven page lecture was translated into German and circulated widely throughout the German scientific community. In 1945, American BW investigators were equally impressed with Hojo's work, and translated a copy of the German text into English. I want to thank Dr Friedreich Hansen for furnishing me with a copy of the German translation. The English translation, "About Bacteriological Warfare," is to be found in the Suitland, Maryland, branch of the National Archives, Record Group 112, Entry 295 A, Box 9, ALSOS, in a folder devoted to Professor H. Kliewe and German BW. See also Hansen's article, "Towards a History of German Biological Warfare."

30 Professor H. Kliewe, head of Germany's BW program, was so impressed with Hojo's essay that he submitted a list of sixteen questions about BW for Hojo's consideration. Hojo, according to Kliewe, failed to respond. Headquarters European Theatre of Operations, United States Army ALSOS Mission, Subject: Translation of Japanese Documents on BW, no date (summer 1945), Record Group 112, Entry 295A, Box 9, ALSOS, The National Archives.

31 Hojo was quite familiar with the human experiments. He had joined the original Ishii organization when it was disguised as the "Togo Butai" Unit, and, in a 1947 interview in Japan, admitted that in the early BW days he used the alias Minami Seijin. Deposition of Hojo Enryo, Tokyo, 10 April 1947, Record Group 331, Box 1434, 13, The National Archives.

32 Military Intelligence Service, Captured Personnel and Material Branch, Extract 1923 – A Preliminary Report of Interrogation of P/W Hojo, Enyro, 25 August 1945, Record Group 112, Entry 295A, Box 11, Current Intelligence – Japanese, The National Archives.

33 Hojo continued with his military career in the new, democratic Japanese Army, rising, eventually, to become its Surgeon General.

34 Lt. Colonel Harold Fair to the Chief of Staff, Washington, DC, 6 October 1944, Rodriguez, Jr, Collection.

35 A Preliminary Report of Interrogation of P/W Kobayashi, Kenzo, Captured 18 October 1944 Peleliu, Rodriguez, Jr Papers; another copy is located in Record Group 112, Entry 295 A, Box 8, 33, No. 1, The National Archives.

36 Extracts from: Allied Translator and Interpreter Section South West Pacific Area, Serial No. 600, 16 Sept 44, Record Group 319, Records of the Army Staff, Army Intelligence Document File, ID 919284, Targets – BW – Japan, The National Archives.

37 Less than nine months later, so much information flowed into Intelligence centers that one scientist observed, "The volume of evidence emanating from Far Eastern sources and implying Japanese interest and preparedness in biological warfare is very much greater and more specific than that involving Germany." J. F. S. Stone,

Biology Section, Porton, 27 April 1945, "Japan and Biological Warfare", p. 1, Record Group 112, Entry 295A, Box 11, Current Intelligence – Japan, The National Archives.

38 This was confirmed by Hojo Enryo in summer 1945.

39 Handwritten document titled "Extracted from Special Projects Periodic Intelligence Report No. 7," CWS, 7 February 1945, Record Group 112, Entry 295A, Box 11, Current Intelligence – Japanese, The National Archives.

40 See Hojo Enryo interrogation report, 25 August 1945.

41 One Intelligence document pointed out that "Maj. Gen. Ishii, Shiro is often mentioned in connection with BW." "Japanese Biological Warfare", Background for list #100, n.d. (late 1944 or early 1945), Record Group 319, Records of the Army Staff, Army – Intellience Document File ID 919284, Targets – BW – Japan, The National Archives.

42 At least one British analyst could not believe that Ishii, as a medical practitioner, would be involved with BW. The analyst scoffed at such reports, declaring that it was impossible to evaluate statements by POWs of Ishii's BW efforts, "but in general it would seem improbable that an officer in charge of normal hygiene precautions would be concerned to any important degree with offensive B.W. activities." J. F. Stone, "Japan and Biological Warfare," 27 April 1945, "Appendix, Japan and B.W.," p. 9, Record Group 112, Entry 295A, Box 11, Current Intelligence – Japan, The National Archives.

43 Stimson and McNutt to Roosevelt, 24 November 1944, Summary Status of Biological Warfare, p. 3, Record Group 107, Stimson "Safe File," Biological Warfare Folder, Box 2, The National Archives.

44 War Department Military Intelligence Service, Washington, 4 June 1945, BW Information – Summary of Reports on Bacterial Bomb, Record Group 112, Entry 295, Box 11, 50 Jap Pamphlets, The National Archives. See also Military intelligence Service Captured Personnel and Material Branch, 27 March 1945, A Composite Report Based on Interrogation of Four Japanese Medical Officers, re Special Questions on Japanese Biological Warfare, Dated 9 March 1945, Record Group 112, Entry 295 A, Box 11, 54 POW – JAP, The National Archives. See also Gaylord W. Anderson, memorandum for Brig. General James S. Simmons, 24 May 1945, Record Group 112, Entry 295A, Box 11, Current Intelligence – Japanese, The National Archives.

45 Project no. 2263, Intelligence Research Project, Japanese Biological Warfare, 26 July 1945, Record Group 226, Records of the Office of Strategic Services, Entry 146, Box 253, Folder 3502, The National Archives.

46 Memorandum to Mr Harvey H. Bundy, 22 July 1944, from George W. Merck, by William B. Sarles, Record Group 112, Entry 295, Box 11, 51, Book on Japan, The National Archives.

47 Memo from J. F. Buckley to Mr D. M. Lamb, 6-30-44, FBI Docs.

48 ibid.

49 Memo from Lt. Colonel Gaylord W. Anderson to Chief, Preventive Medicine Service, 2 June 1944, Record Group 112, Entry 295, Box 11, Book on Japan, The National Archives.

50 Memo from George W. Merck to Harvey H. Bundy, 3 June 1944, Record Group 112, Entry 295, Box 11, Book on Japan, The National Archives.

51 17 July 1944.

52 A copy of the Book of the Month Club August 1944 Newsletter is part of the FBI Docs. BW file.

53 Memo by George W. Merck to Harvey H. Bundy (written by William B. Sarles), 22 July 1944, Record Group 112, Entry 295, Box 11, Book on Japan, The National Archives.

54 Unsigned, undated review in Record Group 112, Entry 295, Box 11, Book on Japan, The National Archives.

55 In confirmation of the reviewer's fear, one citizen sent a handwritten note to FBI Director Hoover urging him to read the book, in order to

> get some idea of what these Jap baboons might be carrying. If they are going to fight a germ warefar [sic]. We should be prepared & do likewise and not wait until next summer when the snow melts & our water supply is in danger. Bye [sic] that time half of our civilian population would be ill and the other half busy caring for them. Then where would our Home Front effort be.

Censored name, place of origin, and date of letter found in FBI Docs. BW file.

13 INVESTIGATIONS

Some of the material presented in this chapter was published as an article, "Japanese Biological Warfare Experiments and Other Atrocities in Manchuria, 1932–1945, and the Subsequent United States Cover-Up: A Preliminary Assessment," in *Crime, Law and Social Change,* March 1991. This chapter offers additional data, as well as a refinement of the interpretation presented in the earlier article.

1 Japan was occupied by a consortium of countries operating under the rubric of the United Nations. In reality, the occupation force was essentially American, complemented by token numbers of personnel from other interested countries. To all intents and purposes, during the critical period of occupation (1945–1948), Japan fell under the American sphere of influence and control. See the discussion in *Reports of General MacArthur, MacArthur in Japan: The Occupation: Military Phase,* vol. I, Supplement, Prepared by His Staff (Washington, D.C., 1966), p. 69.
2 See Sanders's previously cited "Scientific Intelligence Survey in Japan," vol. V, 1 November 1945, and his lengthy memorandum: Supplementary Biological Warfare Information, 9 November 1945, Record Group 407, Records of the Adjutant General's Office, 1917 – AG (TS) 1940–45, AG 729.2 (Nov. 9, 1945), The National Archives.
3 See the previously cited Thompson Report.
4 The *New York Times* ran a front-page banner headline on 2 September 1945 that read, "ENEMY TORTURED DYING AMERICANS WITH SADIST MEDICAL EXPERIMENT." *Times* reporter Robert Trumbull reported that two American doctors charged Japanese doctors in Shinagawa POW camp near Tokyo with using seriously ill American captives as "guinea pigs" for BW experiments. The story indicated that Japanese doctors confirmed the American physicians' allegations. A certain Captain Tokuda Hisikichi allegedly injected various pathogens into his American patients as part of BW experiments.
5 Unless noted otherwise, all quotations dealing with allegations on BW research are taken from a summary document, 4 April 1947, Case # 330, Report by: Neal R. Smith, Record Group 331, Box 1434, 20, Case 330, The National Archives.
6 ibid., p. 2.
7 Lt. General Ishii (Japanese Army Medical Corps), 28 December 1945, signature unreadable, Document 84, US Army Intelligence and Security Command Archive, Fort Meade, Md. See also Document 82 (in the same archive), Lt General Shiro Ishii, OCCIO (OPS), Legal Section, 5 January 1946, for additional accusations against Ishii.
8 p. 2.
9 p. 8.
10 12 January 1946, p. 8.
11 Memorandum for the Officer in Charge, Subject: Ishii, Lt. General Shiro, Advance Echelon APO 500, 7 January 1946, Document 80, US Army Intelligence and Security Command Archive, Fort Meade, Md.

12 Tsuneishi and Asano, *Suicide of Two Physicians*, p. 56.
13 Tsuneishi, *The Germ Warfare Unit That Disappeared*, pp. 151, 155.
14 *Japan Times*, 5 September 1982, p. 10. Morimura Seiichi speculates in this article that the crates may have contained gold and platinum ingots as well as scientific data. Ishii's daughter rebutted Morimura by declaring that the family was forced to sell heirlooms in order to survive during the first terrible postwar year. See also, *Japan Times*, 29 August 1982, p. 12.
15 Anonymous letter, 3 September 1946, Contribution concerning Surgeon Lt. General Shiro Ishii, Record Group 331, Box 1772, Case # 330, The National Archives.
16 Case # 330, Report by: Neal R. Smith, Record Group 331, Box 1434, 20, Case 330, The National Archives.
17 Doc. No. 29510, To: General MacArthur, From: Jiyu Seinen Assn., Chiba Ken, Sambu Gun, Chiyoda Mura, 10 February 47, Case # 330, The National Archives.
18 George Two (G-2) China Theater Radiogram, 25 November 1945, GHQ, AGO Records, 385 T.S., The National Archives.
19 The Communists dogged Ishii's trail, knowing his whereabouts from the moment he returned to Japan. In early January 1946 they sent word to an American reporter that Ishii was "alive and free today." They were aware of his sham funeral, charging that it was performed with "the connivance of a village mayor." *Pacific Stars and Stripes*, 6 January 1946, p. 2.
20 The search really intensified once Intelligence digested information gleaned from twenty Ishii associates "who were directly connected with the actual [BW] experiments." Summary of Information, Subject: Ishii , Shiro, Document 41, US Army Intelligence and Security Command Archive, Fort Meade, Md.
21 "SCAP Locates and Questions General Ishii," *Pacific Stars and Stripes*, 27 February 1946, p. 1.
22 Two transcripts of Thompson's interrogation of Ishii survive, those of 5 and 6 February 1946. See Document 004, Stenographic Transcript of Interrogation of Lt. General Shiro Ishii in Tokyo, by Lt. Colonel A. T. Thompson, on 5 February 1946 and 6 February 1946, Dugway Proving Grounds Library.
23 From G-2 (WDIT) to CIS 15 Feb 46 (Attn: Lt. Col. Paul Rusch) Document 56, US Army Intelligence and Security Command Archive, Fort Meade, Md.
24 Ishii Shiro Vita, n.d. (June 1947), Document 121, US Army Intelligence and Security Command Archive, Fort Meade, Md.
25 Morrow to Keenan, 2 March 1946, Subject: Sino-Japanese War, Rodriguez, Jr, Collection. Morrow's memo consisted of twelve pages, but only the first and twelfth page appear to have survived.
26 Morrow to Keenan, 8 March 1946, Report Assignment B, GHQ, SCAP, IPS, The National Archives.
27 Williams and Wallace, *Unit 731*, pp. 174–176.
28 There are several different versions of Sutton's statement. All agree on the basic thrust of his comments.
29 All quotations from Tsuneishi and Asano, *Suicide of Two Physicians*, p. 114.
30 It could be argued that the cover-up began earlier with Counter-Intelligence's request to U.P.A.'s Tokyo Bureau Manager Ralph Teatsworth to suppress information on Ishii and BW experiments. See the previously cited memorandum for the Officer in Charge, 7 January 1946.
31 The War Department policy as late as 1947 was that "public discussion of biological warfare is contrary to the best interests of national defense." The reference was to American BW, but the attitude applied to any mention of BW, foreign or domestic. H. I. Stubblefield to Dr B. R. Baldwin, Comments on Chemical Corps History, 3 March 1947, Rodriguez, Jr, Collection.
32 The topic would be reopened during the Korean War, when the People's Republic of China and North Korea both accused the United States of engaging in BW with

the assistance of some of the Japanese scientists. The allegations are discussed in Chapter 16.

33 Case # 330, Report by Neal R. Smith, 4 April 1947, Record Group 331, Box 1434, 20, Case 330, pp. 2–3, The National Archives.

34 My italics.

35 Case # 330, Report by Neal R. Smith.

36 Case # 330, Report by: L. H. Bernard, 29 November 1946, Record Group 331, SCAP, Legal Section, Investigation Division, Investigative Report 1117, The National Archives.

37 Case # 330, pp. 5–6.

38 My italics. Doc. No. 29510, SCAP Military Section, General Staff, Allied Translator and Interpreter Section, 3 April 1947, Record Group 331, SCAP Legal Section, Investigation Division, Report #1117, The National Archives.

39 Report by John G. Donnell, 3 December 1946, Record Group 331, Box 1434, 20, Case 330, The National Archives.

40 There are many documents relating to Wakamatsu in a Legal Section file titled "Motoji Yamaguchi, Inv. Div. No. 330, Record Group 331, Box 1434, 20, Case 330," The National Archives. Unless otherwise noted, citations from this file will read "Motoji Yamaguchi."

41 "Motoji Yamaguchi," report by John G. Donnell, 3 December 1946.

42 "Motoji Yamaguchi," deposition of Kino Takeshi, 5 March 1947.

43 Kino and his interrogator refer to them as "Russians," but many of the prisoners were from other Soviet republics.

44 Deposition of Kino Takeshi, Tokyo, 11 March 1947, Record Group 331, Box 1772, 330, The National Archives.

45 Stenographic transcript of interrogation of Lt. General Masaji Kitano in Tokyo by Colonel S. E. Whitesides and Colonel A. H. Schwichtenberg on 11 January 1946, Document 004, Dugway Proving Grounds Library.

46 Transcript of interrogation of Lt. General Masaji Kitano in Tokyo, Japan, by Lt. Colonel A. T. Thompson on 6 February 1946, Document 004, Dugway Proving Grounds Library.

47 "Motoji Yamaguchi," report by Captain Joseph F. Sartiano, March 1947.

48 Two versions of the Kitano statement survive. One of the statements, a six-page rendering, contains the Criminal Registry comment, and is found in Record Group 331, Records of the Allied Operational and Occupation Headquarters WWII, Legal Section, Investigation Division, Investigative Report # 330, The National Archives.

49 All quotations are taken from Doc. No. 29581, the eleven-page version of Kitano's statement.

50 Summary of Information, Subject Ishii , Shiro, 10 Jan 47, Document 41, US Army Intelligence and Security Command Archive, Fort Meade, Md.

14 SCIENTISTS AND THE COVER-UP

1 See note citations throughout this chapter.

2 Memorandum from Hartwick Kuhlenbeck to Lt. Colonel G.W. Anderson, Washington, D.C., 12 October 1945, Record Group 112, Entry 295A, Box 8, 33, No. 1, The National Archives.

3 Merck Report, p. 7.

4 ibid., p. 9.

5 ibid., pp. 9–10.

6 See Norman M. Covert, memorandum for the Record, 5 May 1982, Subject: Response to Inquiries on Japanese BW Program, p. 2, Fort Detrick Archives.

7 Sanders to Colonel Harlan Worthley, Tokyo, 27 September 1945; Sanders to Worthley, Tokyo, 5 October 1945, Record Group 112, Entry 295A, Box 18, No. 1, The National Archives.

8 On 15 November 1945, G-2 in Washington sent General MacArthur a cable requesting information on Ping Fan, including, "Was institute left intact, destroyed by Japs, by Russians, any equipment removed to Russia, did they interrogate or remove Jap technicians to Russia, what is extent Soviet knowledge Jap offensive developments?" Five days later, G-2 sent Tokyo another cable requesting intelligence on Ping Fan, the fate of BW equipment there, and whether "any technicians either questioned on the site or transported to Russia." These cables are typical of many that were exchanged between Washington and Tokyo from the early days of the occupation until at least 1948. See Washington (WARGTWO) to CINCAFPAC, China Theatre, 15 November 1945, and Colonel Walter A. Buck to CINCAFPAC ADV, Washington, 20 November 1945, Record Group 331, Allied Operational and Occupation Headquarters, SCAP, AG Section, TS Files, 365, The National Archives.

9 Lt. Colonel Robert McQuail of G-2 noted in early 1947 that the United States had interrogated at least twenty Japanese BW experts, "and as a result[,] the United States alone is in full possession of all the details of this work." He observed for the record that "So far as is known, these twenty have been taken care of [,] and no other parties have attempted to contact them." Moreover, "It is well known that the Soviet Union is greatly interested in obtaining as much data as possible concerning all phases of this work. To date, however, it is . . . unlikely that they have received anything of value from Japanese sources." However, given the rising tensions between the United States and the Soviet Union, "It is natural, therefore, that Ishii, and his former medical secretary, should become intelligence targets for interested parties." Summary of Information, Subject: Ishii, Shiro, 10 Jan 47, Document 41, US Army Intelligence and Security Command Archive, Fort Meade, Md.

10 See Sanders Report, and Sanders's memorandum of 9 November 1945 titled "Supplementary Biological Warfare Information," as well as the discussion in Chapter 13 on the role played by Naito Ryoichi in deceiving Sanders on BW developments in Manchuria. Sanders's memorandum is in Record Group 407, Records of the Adjutant General's Office, 1917, AG (TS) 1940–45, AG 729.2 (Nov. 9, 1945), The National Archives.

11 See Piccipallo, Philip R., *The Japanese on Trial: Allied War Crimes Operations in the East, 1945–1951* (Austin, Texas: University of Texas Press, 1979), passim.

12 Norbert H. Fell to Chief, Chemical Corps, "Brief Summary of New Information about Japanese B.W. Activities" (cited hereafter as "Brief Summary"), n.p. (Camp Detrick?), 20 June 1947, p. 1, Document 005, Dugway Library.

13 It is unclear who actually ordered Fell to Japan. No documents containing Fell's orders surfaced in the course of preparing this study. Fell directed his two principal reports to the Chief of the Chemical Corps, and it is reasonable to assume, therefore, that the Chief was responsible for his trip to Tokyo. The official Fort Detrick historian, Norman Covert, believes that the Joint Chiefs of Staff were aware of Fell's mission from the beginning. See Norman Covert, memorandum for Record, 2 April 1982, p. 1, and Subject: Information on Japanese BW Program in World War II, 5 May 1982, Fort Detrick Archives.

14 "Brief Summary," p. 1.

15 Interview with Norman Covert, 24 March 1989. It should be noted that Murray Sanders was a low-level Section Chief at Detrick who faded from the scene no later than December 1945, and that Arvo Thompson was a respected veterinarian.

16 "Brief Summary," p. 1. Fell's 28 June 1947 Summary is especially noteworthy for its revelation that both G-2 and Detrick put credence in the anonymous allegations against Ishii and the others. As the BW cover-up unfolded, these same accusations

would later be dismissed as untrustworthy, in part, because of their anonymous origins.

17 All quotations taken from "Brief Summary."

18 This is an overly optimistic assessment. The Japanese did not disclose everything they knew. Later discussions during the cover-up negotiations led to the Americans receiving additional information. It is debatable whether even the later material combined with the earlier data revealed the complete scope of the Japanese BW program.

19 "Brief Summary," p. 11.

20 Fell to Assistant Chief of Staff, G-2, GHQ, Far East Command, n.p. (Camp Detrick?), 24 June 1947, pp. 1–2, Document 006, Dugway Library. This report is not paginated consecutively. Further citations from the report will indicate the name of the person interrogated, and the typed page number(s) employed for the responses of the individual questioned.

21 Interrogation of Masuda, Tomosada, 22 April 1947, p. 1, in Fell Report, 24 June 1947. This statement confirms the validity of the anonymous charges against Ishii that were later dismissed allegedly because of their anonymity.

22 ibid.

23 ibid., pp. 1–2.

24 Conference with Kamei, Kanichiro, 24 April 1947, p. 1, in Fell Report, 24 June 1947.

25 ibid., p. 2.

26 ibid.

27 Interrogations of Masuda, Kaneko and Naito, 28, 29, 30 April, 1 May 1947, in Fell Report, p. 1, 24 June 1947.

28 My italics.

29 ibid., p. 2.

30 ibid., p. 2. My italics.

31 ibid., p. 4.

32 Interrogations of Kikuchi Hitoshi, 1, 2, 5 May 1947, p. 2, in Fell Report, 24 June 1947.

33 Interrogations of Kikuchi, Hitoshi, 1, 2, 5 May 1947, second set of notes, p. 2, in Fell Report, 24 June 1947.

34 Conversations with Kamei, Kan'ichiro, 7 May 1947, in Fell Report, 24 June 1947.

35 The Japanese-American sergeant who served as interpreter for all sessions between Ishii and the American investigators in 1946 and 1947 remembers quite clearly how Ishii treated his interrogators as if they were his social inferiors. Ishii's bedroom antics remain vivid images in his mind. The interpreter shared his impressions with interviewers from Japan's NHK Television in early February 1992. His name cannot be used under the ground rules he established for the interview. I was permitted access to a transcript of the interview, but, because of the agreement between NHK and the interpreter, I was denied permission to quote from the document. I want to thank Mr Eddie Shuji Noguchi of NHK Television for his help in this matter.

36 Interrogations of Ishii, Shiro, 8 and 9 May 1947, p. 1, in Fell Report, 24 June 1947.

37 This is the only statement available that acknowledges a meeting took place between Sanders and Ishii. Ishii must have confused Sanders for someone else, since he was in hiding in the provinces at the time Sanders pursued his investigations. Sanders made no mention of such a meeting either in his report or in supplementary data submitted to Detrick. Late in life, at the age of seventy-five and in poor health, Sanders claimed to have been "The smoking gun" in arranging a deal between Ishii and the Americans in 1945. He asserted that he acted as the agent for General Douglas MacArthur in consummating an arrangement where the Japanese would disclose BW secrets in exchange for immunity from war crimes

prosecutions. This allegation has received wide currency from 1985 until the present. It is, however, patently false. If the so-called "deal" took place in 1945, why did Thompson, Fell, and others in 1946, 1947, and 1948 pursue BW information in Japan? Why did negotiations for an arrangement for a new "deal" drag on from 1946 until it was concluded in 1948? See The Miami (Fl.) *Herald*, 7 December 1985, pp. 1 A, 24 A, for Sanders's "Smoking Gun" assertion; see also Williams and Wallace, *Unit 731*, ch. 10 and asterisk note on the bottom of p. 195.

38 Allied Intelligence knew as early as 23 November 1945 that Ping Fan "was administered directly from Tokyo." Incoming Message, To: CINCAFPAC ADV:INFO WARG2, From: CONGEN China, 23 November 1945, GHQ AGO Records, 27 Nov 1945, The National Archives.

39 Fell Report, 24 June 1947. All quotations taken from pp. 1, 2.

40 Ever the opportunist, Ishii was apparently seeking a deal with Chinese Intelligence, to be hired as an agent, at the same time that he was conducting negotiations with Fell. He supposedly thought he could help solve Japan's postwar overpopulation problems by sending Japanese emigrants to China disguised as Chinese, if he could influence his former enemy that he could be helpful to them. 607th Counter-Intelligence Corps Memorandum, Summary of Information, 19 June 1947, and Summary of Information, 1 July 1947, GHQ, SCAP, SA, BR, CIS, Documents 33 and 34, US Army Intelligence and Security Command Archive, Fort Meade, Md.

41 Fell Report, 24 June 1947, p. 2.

42 The Japanese launched a barrage of huge paper balloons against the United States mainland in the closing days of the war. Several were discovered as far east as Montana. No BW agents were found to be inside the balloons. See, for example, Colonel W. A. Copthorne, CWS Intell Summary No. 15, Estimate of Japanese Biological Warfare Capabilities and Intentions, 8 March 1945, 6th A Records, 381 BW, Aberdeen Proving Grounds Archives, Aberdeen, Md.

43 Fell Report, p. 3.

44 ibid., p. 3.

45 McQuail refused to be interviewed for this study. In a telephone conversation on 11 May 1992, Mr McQuail indicated that he had "consulted with the Pentagon several months ago," and was "advised not to discuss" the cover-up with anyone.

46 Summary of Information, 10 Jan 47, Document 41, US Army Intelligence and Security Command Archive, Fort Meade, Md.

47 Summary of Information, July 1 1947, S/A Branch, CIS, Document 32, US Army Intelligence and Security Command Archive, Fort Meade, Md.

48 Matsunosuke Hasegawa, Masao Morii, and Tamio Yoshida to Your Excellency Shiro Ishii, Tokyo, 3 June (1946 or 1947), Document 101, US Army Intelligence and Security Command, Fort Meade, Md.

49 General Headquarters Supreme Commander for the Allied Powers, Subject: Ishii, Shiro, 1 July 1947, Document 32, and 441st Counter Intelligence Corps, Subject: Rumors of Bacteriological Warfare, 16 Jun 47, Document 36, both in the US Army Intelligence and Security Command Archive, Fort Meade, Md.

50 ibid.

51 ibid., pp. 3, 4.

52 See, for example, Interrogation of Murakami, Takeshi, 10 May 1947, and Interrogation of Ota, Kiyoshi, 10 May 1947, in Fell Report, 24 June 1947.

53 Lt. Colonel Robert McQuail was the G-2 officer assigned to assist Fell in his survey.

54 Interrogation of Wakamatsu, Yujiro, 29 May 1947, p. 2, in Fell Report, 24 June 1947.

55 Incoming Message From: War (Chemical Corps) To: CINCFE (G-2) (Chief Chemical Officer for Fell), 15 (penciled change to 14) May 47 Record Group 153, Entry 145, Box 73, 000.5, The National Archives.

56 A second rendering of Fell's 20 June 1947 "Brief Summary" surfaced in June 1962. This version was only eight typewritten pages, but it contains information that the

longer eleven-page account omits. The eight-page sketch is from Fell to CCmlC THRU: Tech Dir. Camp Detrick, 20 June 1947, "Brief Summary of New Information about Japanese B.W. Activities." The typescript I quote is dated 8 June 1962 and is located in the Aberdeen Proving Grounds Archives, Aberdeen, Md. Hereafter cited as "Brief Summary," version 2.

57 "Brief Summary," version 2, p. 1.
58 ibid., p. 2. Fell unfortunately did not define Ishii's ABEDO theory.
59 ibid. Unfortunately, with the exception of the three autopsy reports cited previously, none of the other reports or printed documents have been located in any of the archival depositories researched.
60 Fell Report, 24 June 1947, p. 1.
61 Nor did the Soviets cooperate with the Americans, except when they hoped to turn such cooperation to their advantage. They did provide transcripts to the Americans of their interrogation of two captured Japanese BW personnel, but this information was given in the expectation the Americans would permit them access to the large group of BW personnel under American control. Manchuria, however, remained closed to American investigators.
62 This is a reference to a powerful inter-agency group known by the acronym "SWNCC," for State–War–Navy Coordinating Committee. SWNCC's role in the BW immunity negotiations is discussed in Chapter 15.
63 Typescript copy of a memorandum from Norbert E. Fell to the Assistant Chief of Staff G-2, HQ, Far East Command, 24 June 1947, Fort Detrick Archives.
64 Fell's "Brief Summary" of 20 June 1947 was addressed to Waitt; his 24 June report was cc. to Waitt.
65 Fort Detrick's Norman Covert believes that the Joint Chiefs of Staff made the final decision to grant immunity. Norman Covert, memorandum for the record, 5 May 1982, p. 2, and Norman Covert, Subject: Information on Japanese BW Program in World War II, 5 May 1982, p. 2, Fort Detrick Archives.
66 It should be noted that President Truman withdrew the 1925 Geneva Protocol outlawing CW and BW from Senate consideration in 1947. Truman's rationale for his action was that the treaty, as well as several others being withdrawn, was "obsolete." The timing may be coincidental, but it came at a moment when American occupation authorities were engaged in intensive negotiations over the war crimes immunity issue with the Japanese BW experts. Robinson (ed.), *The Problem of Chemical and Biological Warfare* vol. 2, *CB Weapons Today*, p. 194.
67 I refer to the State–War–Navy Coordinating Committee, whose role in the BW cover-up is discussed in Chapter 15.
68 Harry S. Truman is noted for his deep and abiding feeling that the President, as Commander-in-Chief of the armed forces, bears the ultimate responsibility for major politico-military decisions. He is remembered still for dismissing popular "Old Soldier" General MacArthur during the height of the Korean War.

15 THE MILITARY AND THE COVER-UP

1 Biographical information supplied by Mr Norman Covert in a telephone conversation, 8 April 1991.
2 Hill to General Alden C. Waitt, "Summary Report on B. W. Investigations," 12 December 1947 (cited hereafter as "Summary Report), p. 1, Document 008, Dugway Library.
3 Interview with Shiro Kasahara and Masaji Kitano, 13 November, 1947, Document 017, Dugway Library.
4 "Summary Report," p. 1. Hill's observation was made on 12 December 1947, when negotiations for immunity were in the final stages of development.

5 "Songo Epidemic Hemorrhagic Fever," 13 November 1947, Document 017, Dugway Library.
6 There are, no doubt, other autopsy reports. However, they have not been located, possibly because certain agencies in government still consider their findings too sensitive to release to the general public.
7 As noted earlier, the three autopsy reports are housed in the Dugway Proving Grounds Library.
8 "Summary Report," pp. 2, 3. It was in this report that Hill made the observation quoted at the beginning of Chapter 14 concerning how cheaply the Americans acquired the Japanese data.
9 From G-2 (WDIT) To CIS (Attn: Lt. Colonel Paul Rusch), 15 Feb 46, Documents 56 and 57, US Army Intelligence and Security Command Archive, Fort Meade, Md.
10 From: CIS to G-2 Historical, Subject: Ishii, Shiro, 24 Jul 47, Document 28, US Army Intelligence and Security Command Archive, Fort Meade, Md. Italics are in the original document.
11 CIS 441st CIC Det, No. 731 Ishii Unit, Lt. Colonel Aurell, 15 April 1948, Document 13, US Army Intelligence and Security Command Archive, Fort Detrick, Md.
12 Report by Neal R. Smith, Report of Investigation Division, Legal Section, GHQ, SCAP, 18 April 1947, p. 1. The Joint Chiefs' instructions were referred to in this report as SWNCC 351/1, 5 March 1947. Record Group 331, Box 1434. 20, Case 330, The National Archives.
13 ibid., p. 2.
14 Incoming Classified Message, CINCFE Tokyo Japan (Carpenter Legal Section) to War (WDSCA WC), 27 June 1947, pp. 1–3, Record Group 153, Entry 145, Box 73, 107-0, The National Archives.
15 SWNCC was disbanded in 1949. Information on SWNCC and its operations was furnished in a 25 April 1991 telephone interview by Ms Kathy NiCastro, Archivist in Charge of State Department records at the National Archives.
16 Washington (WARGTWO) to CG China Info CINCAFPAC Adv, 29 November 1946, Adjutant General's File, The National Archives.
17 As late as 16 June 1947, the Adjutant General's Office in Tokyo engaged in intensive pursuit of evidence to prosecute BW personnel for war crimes. In a memo of that date, investigators indicated that they were concentrating on Unit 100's activities, "with special reference to the illegal experiments on human beings . . . and other atrocities." The American agents were still determined that Wakamatsu and others

> At the appropriate time [would] set out leads as to insure those Japanese are interviewed and investigated, as it is alleged they formed the greater part of Group No. 2, which is alleged to have performed most of the illegal experiments on the human beings at [Changchun].

Unsigned memo, "Forwarding of Information Concerning Possible War Criminals," to Legal Section, GHQ, Chief, Liaison Section, 16 June 1947, Record Group 165, Entry 468, Box 628, CAD-CCAC, SWNCC, 351, The National Archives.
18 Typewritten notes "written by wetter and stubblefield after meeting of the working group 26 June 47," Fort Detrick Archives.
19 Washington (Joint Chiefs of Staff) To CINCAFPAC (For MacArthur), 24 July 46, p. 2, Record Group 153, Entry 145, Box 73, 000.5, The National Archives.
20 ibid., p. 3. See also Major General Paul J. Mueller's General Orders No. 26, 2 June 1946, in which he orders that no Japanese or other enemy personnel could be subject to interrogation in Japan by officials of a foreign country – allied or otherwise – except with prior permission, and under the direct observation of the

Assistant Chief of Staff, G-2, of the American occupation authority. I was given access to this document with the understanding that I would neither identify the source nor quote from the material.

21 Major General Vasilev to Major General Willoughby, through Investigation Division of the IPS, n.d. (early January 1947), Record Group 153, Entry 145, 000.5, The National Archives.

22 Lt. Colonel Robert P. McQuail to Assistant Chief of Staff, G-2, Far East Command, 17 January 1947, Record Group 153, Entry 145, Box 73, 000.5, The National Archives.

23 Enclosure From: CINCFE Tokyo Japan To: War Department for WDCSA, 10 February 1947, Record Group 153, 000.5, The National Archives. See also "Outline of Main Subjects for the Interrogation of Witnesses Concerning the Activities of Anti-Epidemic Detachment No. 731 of the Kwantung Army (Manchu)." I was given access to this document on condition that I neither identify the source nor quote from the material.

24 SFE 188, "Request of Russian Prosecutor for Permission to Interrogate Certain Japanese," n.d., (late January 1947), n.p. (Tokyo), Record Group 153, Entry 145, Box 73, 000.5, The National Archives.

25 SWNCC 351/D, 11 February 1947, "Directive, Request of Russian Prosecutor for Permission to Interrogate Certain Japanese," Record Group 165, Box 628, SWNCC 351/D, The National Archives.

26 All quotations from the Working Group report were taken from SFE 188, Appendix, "State–War–Navy Coordinating Subcommittee for the Far East, *Request of Russian Prosecutor for Permission to Interrogate Certain Japanese*," 26 February 1947, Record Group 165, Box 628, SWNCC 351, The National Archives.

27 SFE 188/1, 28 February 1947, "Note by the Secretary," Record Group 165, Box 628, SWNCC 351, The National Archives.

28 All quotations taken from a second copy of SFE 188/1, "Note by the Secretary," 28 February 1947, p. 1, and attachment designated "Appendix 'B,' Discussion," SFE 188/2, p. 7, Record Group 165, Box 628, SWNCC 351, The National Archives.

29 Decision on SWNCC 351/1, Note by the Secretaries, 6 March 1947, SWNCC 351/1, Record Group 165, Box 628, SWNCC 351, The National Archives.

30 Memorandum for the Record, Subject: USSR Request to Interrogate and Arrest Japanese Bacteriological Warfare Experts, 27 March 1947, initialed C.(harles) A. W.(illoughby), Record Group 153, Entry 145, Box 73, 000.5, The National Archives.

31 Lt General K. Derevyanko to Chief of Staff Major General Mueller, Tokyo, 7 March 1947, Record Group 153, Box 73, Entry 145, 000.5, The National Archives.

32 War Department Outgoing Classified Message, Topsec, to MacArthur from the Joint Chiefs of Staff, 20 March 1947, Record Group 153, Entry 145, Box 73, 000.5, The National Archives. The following officials received copies of the cable: General Carl Spaatz, Admiral William Leahy, a Mr Petersen, General Noce, General Chamberlin, Admiral Chester A. Nimitz, General Norstad, and a General Aurand, CSA. See Memorandum for the Russian Division Attention: Major Basenko, From Douglas L. Waldorf, Chief, Investigation Division, 4 February 1947, as an indication of the type of delaying tactics Americans used with the Soviets. I was given access to this document on condition that I neither identify the source nor quote from the material.

33 SWNCC 351/2/D, 13 May 1947, p. 8, Record Group 165, Entry 468, Box 628, SWNCC 351, The National Archives.

34 The only document currently available that covers this point is one that indicates Ishii was interrogated by Soviet officials in the presence of G-2 officers on 17 and 19 May and 13 June 1947. No transcripts of the interrogations are presently available. Memorandum For: Colonel Smirnov, Russian Division, IPS, From: Edward P.

Monaghan, Chief, Investigative Division, IPS. Subject: Copies of Interrogations, 1 July and 7 July 1947. I was given access to these documents on condition that I neither identify the source nor quote from the material.
35 "Surgeon General Named in Soviet Germ Warfare Charge Missing," Kyodo News Service clipping, dated 1950, Document 20, US Army Intelligence and Security Command Archive, Fort Meade, Md.
36 441st Counter Intelligence Corps Detachment, Subject: Russian Bacteriological Warfare Research, 19 April 1948, Document 14, US Army Intelligence and Security Command Archive, Fort Meade, Md.
37 A thorough search of the unclassified files in the National Archives failed to reveal any data concerning the Ishii–Soviet exchanges. There is always the possibility that such information exists, but that it is still classified and housed in some closed American archive. Efforts to examine Soviet archives have been met with silence from the appropriate authorities. Consequently, the only information known currently to exist is the comments of Ishii Harumi in the (Tokyo) *Japan Times*, 29 August 1982, p. 12, and the two documents from the Fort Meade archives cited in note 35. See also, Williams and Wallace, *Unit 731*, pp. 198–199, for a somewhat confusing account of the discussions.
38 Comments to NHK interviewer by the Japanese-American Army interpreter who participated in all Ishii interrogations by both American and Soviet investigators. Interview was conducted in February 1992.
39 CINCFE Tokyo Japan to War Department for WGID (pass to CCMLC) MID pass to Major General Alden Waitt, 6 May 1947, Record Group 153, Entry 145, Box 73, 107-0, The National Archives. Unless otherwise cited, all quotations in the discussion of Ishii's negotiating tactics are taken from the 6 May 1947 message.
40 It should be recalled that Ishii previously expressed his ardent pro-American feelings to his interrogators. His protestations of admiration for the United States should be taken with some caution since, as discussed earlier, he was simultaneously trying to work out an understanding with Kuomintang China. See the discussion in Chapter 14 and in Chapter 16, the Epilogue.
41 My italics.
42 No objection was located in any of the declassified files examined in The National Archives.
43 See SWNCC 351/2/D Directive, 13 May 1947, pp. 7, 8, Record Group 153, File 107-0, the National Archives.
44 War Crimes Br.[Branch], R. F. Lyons, Jr., To SCAP Tokyo Japan, 2 June 1947, Record Group 153, Entry 145, Box 73, 107-0, The National Archives.
45 Fragmentary document, "Intelligence Information on Bacteriological Warfare, G-2, 9 June 1947," typed initials C.A.W. (Charles A. Willoughby), Record Group 153, Entry 145, Box 73, 000.5, The National Archives.
46 The specific IPS person referred to as "Peter Sugar" may have been Frank Tavenner, a lawyer from Virginia, who was a prosecutor in IPS, and acted most probably as a liaison between IPS and Carpenter's office.
47 All quotations are taken from CINCFE (Carpenter, Legal Section, SCAP) to War (WDSCA WC), 6 June 1947, Record Group 153, 000.5, GHQ AGO Records, The National Archives. Carpenter sent an intelligible translation of the cable to the War Department on 7 June 1947. CINCFE Tokyo Japan (Carpenter, Legal Section, SCAP), to War (WDSCA WC), 7 June 1947, Incoming Classified Message, Top Secret To Priority, CAD TS Message File, 42-49, The National Archives.
48 There is virtually no documentation in the appropriate Record Groups in the National Archives during June and July 1947.
49 SFE 188/2, 1 August 1947, Cover Sheet, Record Group 153, Entry 145, Box 73, 107-0, The National Archives.
50 ibid. Unless stated otherwise, all quotations used in the discussion of the 1 August report are taken from SFE 188/2, 1 August 1947, The National Archives.

51 Interrogation of Certain Japanese by Russian Prosecutor, Purpose of Paper, p. 1, n.d., attached to SFE/2 document, Record Group 153, Entry 145, Box 73, 000.5, The National Archives.
52 ibid., p. 2.
53 All quotations are taken from SFE 188/2, 1 August 1947.
54 Appendix "A," pp. 4–5.
55 Appendix "A," p. 5.
56 ibid., p. 6.
57 ibid., p. 3.
58 SFE 188/2, p. 1.
59 SFE/3, 8 September 1947, "Enclosure," p. 1, Record Group 153, 107-0, The National Archives.
60 ibid.
61 R. M. Cheseldine, Memorandum for the Secretary, SFE, 26 September 1947, p. 1, Record Group 165, SWNCC 351, The National Archives.
62 ibid., p. 2.
63 Office of the Chief of Naval Operations, "Naval Aspects of Biological Warfare," 5 August 1947, Record Group 330, The National Archives.
64 ibid., p. 9.
65 "Decision on SFE 188/5, 12 March 1948," p. 1, Record Group 165, Box 628, SWNCC 351, The National Archives.
66 ibid.
67 ibid. F is not Norbert Fell. Subsequent notations in the document are initialed "FNE."
68 SFE 188/5, "Note by the Secretary," 11 March 1948, p. 1, Record Group 165, Entry 468, Box 628, SWNCC 351, The National Archives.
69 Joint Chiefs of Staff to MacArthur, 13 March 1948, Outgoing Classified Message, Record Group 153, Entry 145, BOX 73, 107-0, The National Archives.
70 Norman N. Covert, Response to Inquiries on Japanese BW Program, 5 May 1982, p. 3, Fort Detrick Archives.
71 My italics.
72 Covert memorandum, 5 May 1982, p. 3. In addition, American scientists may have engaged in some human experiments with "volunteer" GIs. It is now known that more than 60,000 American soldiers had been exposed to experiments with mustard agents and Lewisite during World War II. These secret experiments could have been exposed in a war crimes trial. *New York Times*, 7 January 1993, p. A 11.
73 A 20 October 1981 handwritten note at the bottom of the page of a 16 October Memorandum for the Record concludes that Japanese supplied information helped American BW researchers develop a BW bomblet. In fact, "Information indicates the bomblets were designed after 1947 and tested at several locations including Dugway Proving Ground, Utah." The note adds that 'Extensive photographic studies were carried out." The memorandum was located in the Fort Detrick Archives.
74 See, for example, the *New York Times*, 27 December 1949, p. 9; 13 April 1951, p. 6; 1 November 1981, p. 45; the *Washington Post*, 19 November 1976, pp. 1, 9. See also John W. Powell, Jr's, "A Hidden Chapter in History," in the *Bulletin of Atomic Scientists* October 1981 issue.
75 Alfred Goldberg, Memorandum for Mr B. G. Oldaker, 14 April, 1977, in folder marked "Biological Warfare," Modern Military History Section, Record Group 319, The National Archives, Washington, DC office.
76 Treatment of American Prisoners of War in Manchuria, pp. 10, 20.
77 The author to the Central Intelligence Agency, 13 October 1988, 13 February 1989, and John H. Wright, Information and Privacy Coordinator, Central Intelligence Agency, to the author, 24 March 1989.

16 EPILOGUE

1 The most important of these articles is John W. Powell, Jr's, "A Hidden Chapter in History"; see also the *New York Times*, 1 November 1981, p. 45.

2 See, as representative examples, memo from Yoshinaga Haruko, Chief Director, Tokyo Broadcasting System, n.d., 1986, Rodriguez, Jr, Collection; Tokyo *Japan Times*, 1 August 1982, p. 1; ITV South, August 1986 television broadcast, *Unit 731 – Did the Emperor Know?*; *Tulsa* (Okla.) *Tribune*, 29 February 1984, p. 13 A; *Miami* (Fla.) *Herald*, 7 December 1985, pp. 1 A, 24 A; *Chicago Tribune*, 19 July 1982, p. 3; *Washington Post*, 19 November 1976, pp. 1 A, 9 A.

3 "Tokyo TV Tells How WWII Germ War Unit Escaped Prosecution, *Los Angeles Times*, 16 April 1992, p. A 9.

4 There are several examples one could cite. The US Army Intelligence and Security Command in Fort Meade, Md., denied to this writer over a period of several years that its archive held any material relevant to either Ishii or Japanese BW. Then, in February 1992, the Archive, under the Freedom of Information Act (FOIA), released more than one hundred pages of documents that are of significance to this study. In mid-April 1992, the National Archives discovered a transcript of an interrogation of Ishii that took place in 1947 (Ishii Interrogation Report 1947, Record Group 175). The transcript was located in a folder marked "Chemical Warfare Service 1954 'Confidential' file, decimal 385." It was still stamped Top Secret. The Pentagon, as of this date, is still "reviewing" the document's classification.

5 Brackman, *The Other Nuremberg*, p. 52.

6 See discussion in Chapter 13.

7 Daily Intelligence Summary #1759, 25 March 1947, p. 12, General Douglas MacArthur Memorial Archives and Library, Norfolk, Virginia; Intelligence Report from: Assistant Military Attaché, Manchuria, Subject: Japanese Bacteriological Research Institute, Changchun, 4 February 1947, Record Group 112, Entry 295 A, Box 6, The National Archives.

8 Brackman, *The Other Nuremberg*, pp. 52–60.

9 Compounding the problem is the fact that American Counter-Intelligence received several reports in the summer of 1947 suggesting that Ishii was negotiating with the Kuomintang to become an intelligence agent for them. The first suggestion surfaced on 19 June. Another report was received on 24 July. Two days later, Counter-Intelligence reported that Ishii wanted to go back to China with a large number of Japanese disguised as Chinese, in order to help relieve Japan of its perceived overpopulation.

It was believed that China was asking Ishii, in return, to cooperate with its agents, and to "collect information about the US and submit it to the Chinese Mission in Tokyo." And, finally, in early September, the authorities recorded for the record that Counter-Intelligence wished to alert the Chinese authorities of Ishii's record, but that

> Action was not completed, on instructions from Colonel Bethune, who advised that information concerning the activities and whereabouts of Ishii, Shiro was a Top Secret matter, and no information re his whereabouts or activities was to be reported to any outside agency. . . . On 31 July a draft of an KKI was made and forwarded through channels . . . concerning the newly reported activities of Ishii. . . . Col Brown advised that Col Bethune desires no further action be taken in this case. No further action was taken.

See Documents 33 (Summary of Information, 19 June 1947), 28 (File Note, Subject: Ishii, Shiro, 24 Jul 47), 26 (Summary of Information, 26 July 1947), 22 (File Note, Subject: Ishii, Shiro, 31 Jul 47), and 20 (Memo for Record, Subject:

Ishii, Shiro, 6 September 1947), all in US Army Intelligence and Security Command Archive, Fort Meade, Md.

10 *New York Times*, 16 December 1950, p. 2.

11 The Soviet Union apprised the United States formally of its charges of Emperor Hirohito's and the principal BW experts' war crimes complicity on 1 February 1950. In a dispatch from Soviet Under Ambassador A. Paniushkin to Secretary of State Dean G. Acheson, the Soviets recited a litany of BW activities involving Hirohito and the BW scientists. The dispatch requested that the United States cooperate with the Soviet Union to establish an international tribunal to try the accused. The United States government did not reply. Ten months later, Paniushkin approached the State Department once more. Paniushkin referred specifically to the activities of Units 100 and 731 and their leaders. He once more called for an international tribunal to try Ishii, Wakamatsu, Kitano, et al., and Hirohito. As far as is known, the State Department did not respond to this request.

A. Paniushkin to Dean G. Acheson, Washington, DC, 1 February 1950 and 15 December 1950. I was given access to this correspondence with the understanding that I would neither identify the source nor quote directly from the documents.

12 This argument evades the fact that countless other Japanese war criminals were tried in Chinese courts.

13 Interviews in June 1989 with Professors He Zhongyi and Yen Peiren of Beijing Institute of Technology, Mr Han Xiao, Deputy Director of "731" Research Society, Professor Sheng Zhan Jie, Harbin Normal University, and Mr Li Mao Jie, Curator of Emperor Pu Yi's Palace, Changchun.

14 *Khabarovsk Trial*, p. 5.

15 *New York Times*, 24 December 1949, p. 4.

16 Word of the indictment reached Ishii on 27 December. He left home that day – whether at the urging of the occupation authorities is unknown – and disappeared for some time. In early February 1950, Ishii's wife was reported to have told the press that he abandoned Tokyo "to gather information in order to speak out when the time comes." She felt that her husband was "probably now leading a life like a Buddhist priest somewhere since he has been deeply interested in Zen, a religious meditation." "Surgeon General Named in Soviet Germ Warfare Charge Missing," Kyodo News Service dispatch, 4 February 1950. Document 90, US Army Intelligence and Security Command Archive, Fort Meade, Md.

17 Telegrams dated 24, 26, 28, 30, 31 (two telegrams were sent on 31 December) December 1949 from Comrades Artemov, Karlin, and Boicharnikov, Khabarovsk, to Colonel General Kobulov. I was given access to this material on condition that I neither identify the source nor quote from the documents.

18 All Tass dispatches from Khabarovsk were submitted first for MVD approval before publication. Telegrams from Khabarovsk, 24, 27 December 1949, Comrades Artemov, Karlin, and Boicharnikov to Colonel General Kobulov.

19 State Department to SCAP, Incoming Message, 26 December 1949, MacArthur Archives.

20 Secretary of State Dean Acheson to CINCFE, 26 December 1949, and State Department to SCAP, 27 December 1949, Incoming Messages, MacArthur Archives.

21 *Khabarovsk Trial*, passim.

22 State Department to SCAP, Incoming Message, 29 December 1949, MacArthur Archives.

23 For a sympathetic account of the Khabarovsk trial, see Williams and Wallace, *Unit 731*, ch. 16.

24 State Department to SCAP, Incoming Message, 26 December 1949, MacArthur Archives.

25 State Department to SCAP, Incoming Message, 26 December 1949, MacArthur Archives.

26 State Department to SCAP, Incoming Message, 27 December 1949, MacArthur Archives.
27 State Department to SCAP, Incoming Message, 2 January 1950, MacArthur Archives.
28 See *New York Times*, 24 December 1949, p. 4.
29 See AP dispatches from London and Tokyo printed in ibid., p. 4.
30 *New York Times*, 27 December 1949, p. 16.
31 United Press dispatch from Washington, ibid.
32 Letters addressed to Soviet authorities in 1990 requesting permission by the author to review the Khabarovsk archive remain unanswered. The authors of *Unit 731* (p. 295) were denied similar privileges.
33 *Khabarovsk Trial*, pp. 523–535. Fortuitously for the defendants, the death sentence in the Soviet Union was outlawed for a short time just before the trial began. However, there were always exceptions made in cases where state security was involved. Moreover, under Stalin, laws were made to be broken at the whim of the dictator.
34 *New York Times*, 5 March 1951, p. 3.
35 ibid., 13 May 1951, p. 1; 3 October 1951, p. 3.
36 See the English edition of Williams and Wallace, *Unit 731*, ch. 17, "Korean War," pp. 235–285, for a sympathetic reading of the Communists' charges. The Korean War chapter is omitted from the American edition published by the Free Press in June 1989.
37 *New York Times*, 23 February 1953, p. 3.
38 Williams and Wallace, *Unit 731* (English edition), p. 271.
39 ibid., p. 272.
40 *New York Times*, 13 April 1951, p. 6.
41 ibid., 11 May 1951, p. 1.
42 ibid., 15 May 1952, p. 2.
43 ibid., 4 July 1952, p. 4.
44 ibid., 28 March 1953, p. 3.
45 Hersh, *Chemical and Biological Warfare*, p. 19.
46 Robinson (SIPRI), *The Rise of CB Weapons*, vol. 1, p. 225.
47 Williams and Wallace, *Unit 731*, ch. 17, passim.
48 Interviews in Beijing and Ping Fan with Professor Yen Peiren and Mr Han Xiao, May and June 1989.
49 Periodic telephone and personal interviews with Fort Detrick's Norman Covert 1988–91; John Ellis van Courtland Moon, "Biological Warfare Allegations: The Korean War Case," a paper read on 4 April 1991, at a conference on The Microbiologist and Biological Defense Research: Ethics, Politics and International Security, sponsored by the Center for Public Issues in Biotechnology, University of Maryland, Baltimore County Campus.
50 See also Robinson (ed.), (SIPRI), *The Problem of Chemical and Biological Warfare*, vol. 5, *The Prevention of CB Weapons*, pp. 238–258; Cookson, J., and Nottingham, J., *A Survey of Chemical and Biological Warfare* (London, 1969), pp. 57–63, 293–308; Clarke, Robin, *The Silent Weapons* (New York: David McKay, 1971 printing), pp. 20–26.
51 *Summary of Major Events and Problems, United States Army Chemical Corps. (U), Fiscal Years 1961–1962* (US Army Chemical Corps Historical Office, Army Chemical Center, Maryland, 1962), p. 9.
52 ibid., pp. 9–12.
53 ibid., p. 15.
54 ibid., p. 16.
55 *US Army Rocky Mountain Arsenal Semi-Annual Historical Report*, 1 July 1963 through 31 December 1963, (Denver, Colorado), p. 6.

56 *New York Times*, 6 February 1989, II, p. 9.
57 *Summary of Major Events*, pp. 131–132.
58 ibid.
59 For a thoughtful discussion of the risks in conducting defensive BW research, see Cole, Leonard A., "Risk and Biological Defense Research," *Physicians for Social Responsibility*, March 1992, vol. 2, No. 1, pp. 40–50.
60 Mr John Fosholt, Channel 9 KUSA Public Affairs Producer, to the author, 13 November 1990.
61 *New York Times*, 6 February 1989, II, p. 9.

APPENDICES

1 CD/1127,/CD/CW/WP.384, 18 February 1992, document submitted by the People's Republic of China to the Geneva Conference on Disarmament. The original is in Chinese.
2 I was given access to Yamada's 1944 date book on condition that I neither identify the source nor quote directly from the document. What follows is paraphrases from the date book.
3 *New York Times*, 11 March 1993, p. A 12.

Select bibliography

1 ARCHIVAL DEPOSITORIES AND PRIVATE COLLECTIONS

Anonymous: Russian documents that relate to the interrogation of captured Japanese scientific personnel and to Kwantung Army leaders. This source contains also dispatches from Khabarovsk describing the trial's proceedings.

Archives of the Federal Bureau of Investigation: Under the Freedom of Information Act, and a two-plus-year campaign by the author, the FBI provided me with a heavily censored file of BW-related documents.

Center of Military History Archives, Washington, D.C.

Fort Detrick Archives, Frederick, Maryland: This archive is an invaluable source even though its vast original holdings eventually were broken up and scattered among numerous governmental research agencies. Today, the Fort Detrick archive still holds a collection of BW documents that is essential for any study of United States or Japanese BW activities from 1942 until the mid-1950s.

Milton Leitenberg Collection of Field Dispatches in China, 1937–1941, University of Maryland, College Park, Maryland.

General Douglas MacArthur Memorial Archives and Library, Norfolk, Virginia: The archive is especially useful for the period of the Khabarovsk trial in 1949 and its aftermath in 1950.

National Archives: The National Archives holdings in Washington, D.C., and Suitland, Maryland, on Japanese BW and the subsequent American cover-up is so extensive that it is fruitless to cite in a bibliography every document used for this study. Footnotes in the text do refer to specific box numbers or document numbers in each record group utilized. Therefore, I indicate here only the record groups that I used in my research. Record Groups 107, 112, 153, 165, 218, 226, 319, 331, 407, Document 29510 (no Record Group number), Document 775011 (Army Adjutant General's Office).

Gregory Rodriguez, Jr., Collection of Japanese BW Documents, Washington, D.C.

Franklin D. Roosevelt Library, Hyde Park, New York: President's Secretary File Number 104.

Technical Library, Fort Dugway Proving Grounds, Utah: This facility houses more than twenty typescript copies of interviews conducted by American scientists with Japanese BW specialists in the postwar era. It also holds three massive autopsy reports compiled by Japanese BW specialists. The Technical Library has several important published secondary sources. It may have other material relating to American and Japanese BW research, but I was told that I was being furnished with all the declassified material currently available.

United States Army Intelligence and Security Commend Archives, Fort Meade, Maryland: This archive is the repository for G-2 reports and comments regarding its postwar investigations of suspected Japanese BW specialists.

2 MANUSCRIPT DIARIES

Robert Peaty Diary, in the Gregory Rodriguez, Jr., Collection.
Sigmund (Sig) Schreiner Diary, Norwalk, Connecticut.

3 INTERVIEWS

Leslie Brown, Tulsa, Oklahoma; Sol Frommer, Las Vegas, Nevada; Gregory
  Rodriguez, Sr., Tulsa, Oklahoma, Sig Schreiner, Norwalk, Connecticut. Interviews
  were conducted in Albuquerque, New Mexico, 4–6 November 1989.
Gregory Rodriguez, Jr., 11 April 1989, 1–2 April 1990, Washington, D.C.
Song Guang, Assistant Director of the Changchun Radiator Factory, 5 June 1989,
  People's Republic of China.
Associate Professor of History Tien Zi Hei, Northeast Normal University, Chang-
  chun, 5 June 1989, 30, 31 May 1991.
Mrs. Ada Pivo, 7 February 1989, Encino, California.
E Er dun, 14 June 1991, Hailar, Inner Mongolia.
Robert McQuail, (telephone interview) 11 May 1992.
Kathy Nicastro, Archivist in Charge of State Department Records, National Archives,
  (telephone interview) 25 April 1991.
Han Xiao, Deputy Director of the Ping Fan Museum, 8 June 1989, 6–7 June 1991, Ping
  Fan.
Dr Shuichi Kato, Professor of Medicine, University of California, Davis, (telephone
  interview) 6 March 1989.
John W. Powell, Jr., 21 February 1989, 19 February 1990, San Francisco, California.
Professor of Welding Hao Yun Feng, Harbin Institute of Technology, 24 April 1984,
  Harbin.
Professor of History Ding Zemin, Northeast Normal University, various times in
  1984, 1989, 1991.
Vice President (retired) Yen Peiren, Beijing Institute of Technology, various times in
  1984, 1985, 1989, 1991.
Associate Professor of English He Zhongyi, Beijing Institute of Technology, various
  times in 1984, 1985, 1989, 1991. ·
Sheng Zhan Jie, Section Head of English, Department of Foreign Languages, Harbin
  Teachers University, 7, 8, 9, 10 June 1989, 2, 3, 4 June 1991.
Wen Ye, Director of the Harbin Museum of the Martyrs, 9 June 1989, 4 June 1991.
Norman Covert, Chief, Public Information Office, Fort Detrick, Frederick, Maryland,
  various times, 1988–1992.

4 JOURNALS

Army Surgeon Group Magazine (Tokyo), August and November 1936.
Bernstein, Barton J., "America's Biological Warfare Program in the Second World
  War," *Journal of Strategic Studies*, vol. 2, no. 3, September 1988.
Cole, Leonard A., "Risk and Biological Defense Research," *Physicians for Social
  Responsibility*, vol. 2, no. 1, March 1992.
Dong Zhen Yu, "Kwantung Army Number 100," *Historical Material on Jilin
  History* (Changchun), 1987.
Fox, Major Leon A., "Bacterial Warfare: the Use of Biologic Agents in Warfare," *The
  Military Surgeon*, vol. 72, no. 3, March 1933.
Han Wei, "Factual Account of Japanese Bacteriological Killing by Unit 100,"
  Historical Material on Jilin History (Changchun), 1987.

Han Xiao, "The Remains of the 'Square Building' and 'the Special Prison' of Unit 731," *Harbin Gazette*, 1988, Special Issue no. 4.

Han Xiao, "The Suicide Squads of the 731 Troop in the Nomonhan Incident," *Harbin Gazette*, no. 2, 1989.

Han Xiao, "Bacterial Factory in BeiYinHe, Zhong Ma City," *Harbin Historical Chronicle*, vol. 1, 1984.

Han Xiao and Yin Qing Fang, "The Laborers in the Japanese Invader Troop 731 Camp," *Historical Records of Heilongjiang Province*, vol. 22 (Harbin), 1986.

Han Xiao and Zhou Deli, "Record of Actual Events of the Bacterial Factory in Ping Fan," *People's China*, vol. 3, 1971.

Hansen, Friedrich, "Zur Geschichte der Deutschen Biologischen Waffen" (Towards a History of German Biological Warfare), *1999*, June 1989.

Li Ji Xin, "The Plague in Nongan County, 1940," *Historical Material on Jilin History*, (Changchun), 1987.

Liu Hong Yu, "Where Are You, Old Changchun?" *Changchun Historical and Cultural Materials*, vol. 4 (Changchun), 1986.

Matsumura, Takao, "731 Butai No Jikken Hokokusho" (A Report of Experiments Conducted by Unit 731), *Rekishi Hyoron* (Tokyo), No. 538, 1985.

The Military Surgeon Group Magazine (Tokyo), No. 311, April 1939.

Moon, John Ellis van Courtland, "Chemical Weapons and Deterrence: The World War II Experience," *International Security*, spring 1989, vol. 8, No. 4.

Moon, John Ellis van Courtland, "In the Shadow of Ypres: The Chemical Warfare Dilemma," *The Harrod Lecture Series* (Fitchburg, Mass.), 1988–1989, vol. X.

The New Japan Medicine Report (Tokyo), No. 607, 1934.

People Magazine, 11 January 1982.

Powell, Jr., John W., "Japan's Biological Weapons: 1930–1945," *Bulletin of Atomic Scientists*, October 1981.

Rocky Mountain Arsenal Quarterly Historical Report, 1 July 1962 through 30 September 1962, Rocky Mountain Flats Proving Grounds, Colorado.

Rocky Mountain Medical Journal, August 1942, vol. 39.

Roland, Charles G., "Stripping Away the Veneer: P.O.W. Survival in the Far East as an Index of Cultural Atavism," *Journal of Military History*, vol. 53, January 1989.

Rosebury, Theodor, "Medical Ethics and Biological Warfare," *Perspectives in Biology and Medicine*, 6, summer 1963.

Steed, Wickham, "Aerial Warfare: Secret German Plans," *Nineteenth Century and After*, vol. 116, July 1934.

Tanaka, Yuki, "Poison Gas: The Story Japan Would Like to Forget," *Bulletin of Atomic Scientists*, October 1988.

Tsuneishi, Kei'ichi, "C. Koizumi: As a Promoter of the Ministry of Health and Welfare and an Originator of the BCW Research Program," *Historia Scientarium*, No. 26 (Tokyo), 1984.

Tsuneishi, Kei'ichi, "The Research Guarded by Military Secrecy – The Isolation of the E.H.F. Virus in Japanese Biological Warfare Unit," *Historia Scientarium*, No. 30 (Tokyo), 1986.

US Army Rocky Mountain Arsenal Semi-Annual Historical Report, 1 July 1963 through 31 December 1963, Denver, Colorado.

Waitt, Alden H., "Poison Gas in This War," *The New Republic*, vol. 106, 27 April 1942.

Zhen Yu, "Kwantung Army Number 731," *Historical Material on Jilin History* (Changchun), 1987.

Zhou Shi Kui, "An Investigation into the Remains of Army Unit 100," *Changchun Historical and Cultural Materials*, vol. 4 (Changchun), 1986.

Zhou Shi Kui, "The Old City of Changchun," *Changchun Historical And Cultural Materials*, vol. 4 (Changchun), 1986.

5 PERIODICALS

Chicago Tribune, July 1982.
The Jewish Life: Harbin a Jewish People's Weekly Magazine, August 1940.
Japan Times, 1962, 1963, 1983.
Kyodo News Service, February 1950.
London *Guardian*, August 1985.
London *Sunday Mail*, August 1985.
London *Sunday Mirror*, August 1985.
London *Standard*, August 1985.
Los Angeles Times, various dates, 1982–1992.
Manchester Guardian Weekly, November 1981, April 1982.
Miami (Florida) *Herald*, December 1985.
New York Times, various dates, 1930–1992.
New York Times Sunday Book Review Section, February 1990.
Pacific Stars and Stripes, 1946, 1947.
San Francisco Chronicle, March 1977, various times 1988, 1989.
Singapore Straits Times, September, November 1991.
Tokyo *Mainichi Shimbun*, December 1982.
Tulsa (Oklahoma) *Tribune*, February 1984.
Washington Post, various dates, 1945–1992.
Washington Times, June 1982.

6 CONFERENCE PAPERS

Harris, Sheldon H., "Japanese Biological Warfare Experiments and Other Atrocities in Manchuria, 1932–1945, and the Subsequent United States Cover-Up, a Preliminary Assessment," a paper presented at the University of Cologne Forum on: "Medicine without Compassion – Past and Present, 29 September 1988.
—— "Japanese Biological Warfare Experimental Research on Humans: A Case Study of Microbiology and Ethics," a paper presented at a Conference on "The Microbiologist and Biological Defense Research: Ethics, Politics and International Security," University of Maryland, Baltimore County Campus, 4 April 1991.
Moon, John Ellis van Courtland, "Biological Warfare Allegations: The Korean Case," a paper presented at a conference on "The Microbiologist and Biological Defense Research: Ethics, Politics and International Security," University of Maryland, Baltimore County Campus, 4 April 1991.

7 CONGRESSIONAL REPORTS

House of Representatives Veterans' Affairs Subcommittee Hearings in Helena, Montana, 1982, Ninety-Seventh Congress, Second Session, 1982.
Subcommittee on Compensation, Pension and Insurance of the Committee on Veterans' Affairs, House of Representatives, Ninety-Ninth Congress, Second Session, 17 September 1986, serial No. 99–61.

8 TELEVISION DOCUMENTARIES AND GENERAL ENTERTAINMENTS

A Bruise – Terror of the 731 Corps, television Documentary Broadcast in Japan, 2 November 1976.
Inspector Morse and the Settling of the Sun, two-part British television mystery program broadcast in the United States by the Public Broadcasting System, spring 1990.

Modern History Scoop, NHK Television documentary broadcast in Japan, 13, 14 April 1992.
Sixty Minutes, interview with John W. Powell, Jr., broadcast on the Columbia Broadcasting System, 4 April 1982.
Twenty/Twenty, (*20/20*) segment dealing with US POW charges of Japanese BW human experiments, broadcast on the American Broadcasting System, December 1985.
Unit 731 – Did The Emperor Know?, television documentary broadcast on British Independent Television, 13 August 1985.

9 BOOKS AND PAMPHLETS

Anonymous, typescript copy, "Dugway Proving Grounds History" (Dugway, Utah: Dugway Proving Grounds Public Information Office, 1987).
Anonymous, *The Manchukuo Yearbook*, 1934 (Tokyo, 1934).
Anonymous, *Reports of General MacArthur: MacArthur in Japan: The Occupation: Military Phase*, vol. I, Supplement, Prepared by his Staff (Washington, DC, 1966).
Anonymous, *Summary of Major Events and Problems, United States Army Chemical Corps (U), Fiscal Years 1961–1962* (US Army Chemical Corps Historical Office, Army Chemical Center, Maryland, 1962).
Anonymous, *US Army Activity in the US Biological Warfare Programs*, 2 volumes (n.p., presumably US Army Publications, Washington, DC, 1977).
Behr, Edward, *Hirohito: Behind the Myth* (New York: Villard Books, 1989).
Bergamini, David, *Japan's Imperial Conspiracy* (New York: William Morrow, 1971).
Brackman, Arnold C., *The Other Nuremberg: The Untold Story of the Tokyo War Crimes Trials* (New York: William Morrow, 1987).
Bryden, John, *Deadly Allies: Canada's Secret War, 1937–1947* (Toronto: McClelland and Stewart, 1989).
Clarke, Robin, *The Silent Weapons* (New York: David McKay, 1971).
Clendinin, Richard M., *Science and Technology at Fort Detrick, 1943–1968* (Fort Detrick, Frederick, Md., April 1968).
Cochrane, Ronald C., "History of the Chemical Warfare Service in World War II (1 July 1940–15 August 1945), Biological Warfare Research in the United States," 2 volumes (Historical Section, Plans, Training and Intelligence Division, Office of Chief, Chemical Corps, November 1947, unpublished "draft" typescript, Fort Detrick Archives).
Cole, Leonard A., *Clouds of Secrecy: The Army's Germ Warfare Tests over Populated Areas* (Totowa, New Jersey: Rowman and Littlefield, 1988).
Cook, Haruko Taya, and Cook, Theodore F., *Japan at War: an Oral History* (New York: the New Press, 1992).
Cookson, J., and Nottingham, J., *A Survey of Chemical and Biological Warfare* (London, 1969).
Coox, Alvin D., *The Anatomy of a Small War: The Soviet–Japanese Struggle for Changkufeng/Khasan, 1938* (Westport, Connecticut: Greenwood Press, 1977).
—— *Nomonhan: Japan against Russia, 1939*, 2 volumes (Stanford, California: Stanford University Press, 1985).
Covert, Norman M., *Cutting Edge: A History of Fort Detrick, Maryland, 1943–1993* (Fort Detrick: Public Affairs Office, 1993).
Dower, John W., *War Without Mercy: Race and Power in the Pacific War* (New York: Pantheon Books, 1986).
—— *Empire and Aftermath: Yoshida Shigeru and the Japanese Experience, 1870–1954* (Cambridge, Massachusetts: Harvard University Press, 1979).
Grew, Joseph C., *Ten Years in Japan* (London: Hammond, 1945).
Han Xiao (translated by Ms Lu Cheng), *Unforgettable History* (Harbin, 1985).

Harries, Meiron, and Harries Susie, *Soldiers of the Sun: The Rise and Fall of the Imperial Japanese Army* (New York: Random House, 1991).

Harris, Robert, and Paxton, Jeremy, *A Higher Form of Killing: The Secret Story of Chemical and Biological Warfare* (New York: Hill and Wang, 1982).

Hersh, Seymour M., *Chemical and Biological Warfare: America's Hidden Arsenal* (Indianapolis, Indiana: Bobbs–Merrill, 1968).

Hsu, Immanuel C. Y., *The Rise of Modern China* (New York: Oxford University Press, 1983).

Jones, F. C., *Manchuria since 1931* (London: Oxford University Press, 1949).

Kido, Kōichi, *Kido Kōichi Nikki* (Kido Diaries), 2 volumes, (Tokyo: Daigaku Shuppankai [University of Tokyo Press], 1966).

Leahy, William, *I Was There* (New York: Whittlesey, 1950).

Levine, Stephen T., *Anvil of Victory: The Communist Revolution in Manchuria, 1945–1948* (New York: Columbia University Press, 1987).

McDermott, Jeanne, *The Killing Winds* (New York: Arbor House, 1987).

Materials on the Trial of Former Servicemen of the Japanese Army Charged with Manufacturing and Employing Bacteriological Weapons (Moscow: Foreign Languages Publishing House, 1950).

Mikasa-no-miya, Takahito, *Ancient Orient and I* (Tokyo: Gakusei Sha Publishers, 1984).

Montgomery, Michael, *Imperialist Japan* (New York: St. Martin's Press, 1988).

Morimura Seiichi, *The Devil's Gluttony*, 3 volumes (Tokyo: Kadokawa Shoten, 1983–85).

Müller-Hill, Benno, *Murderous Science: Elimination by Scientific Selection of Jews, Gypsies, and Others, Germany 1933–1945* (Oxford: Oxford University Press, 1988).

Myers, Ramon H., *The Japanese Economic Development of Manchuria, 1932 to 1945* (New York: Garland, 1982).

Piccipallo, Philip R., *The Japanese on Trial: Allied War Crimes Operations in the East, 1945–1951* (Austin, Texas: University of Texas Press, 1979).

Pitter, C., and Yamamoto, R., *Gene Wars: Military Control over the New Genetic Technologies* (New York: Beach Books/William Morrow, 1988).

Pritchard, John R., and Zaide, Sonia Magbanua, eds., *The Tokyo War Crimes Trial: The Complete Transcripts of the Proceedings of the International Military Tribunal for the Far East* (New York: Garland, 1981).

Reischauer, Edwin O., *The Japanese* (Cambridge, Mass.: Harvard University Press, 1977).

Robinson, Julian Perry (Sipri), *The Problem of Chemical and Biological Warfare: The Rise of CB Weapons* (Stockholm: Almqvist & Wiksell, 1971).

Sidhu, H., *The Bamboo Fortress: True Singapore War Stories* (Singapore: Native Publications, 1991).

Spence, Jonathan D., *The Search for Modern China* (New York: W. W. Norton, 1990).

Tadashi Hattori, Hiroku: Okunoshima No Ki (A Secret Memoir: The Record of Okunoshima), (Tokyo: Nihon Bunkyo Shuppan, 1963).

Tsuneishi, Kei'ichi, *The Germ Warfare Unit That Disappeared* (Kieta Saikinsen Butai) (Tokyo: Kai-mei-sha Publishers, 1981).

Tsuneishi, Kei'ichi, and Asano, Tomizo, *The Bacteriological Warfare Unit and the Suicide of Two Physicians* (Tokyo: Shincho-Sha Publishing Co., 1982).

Williams, Peter, and Wallace, David, *Unit 731: The Japanese Army's Secret of Secrets* (London: Hodder and Stoughton, 1989).

Index